MW01529075

CONFLICTS OF INTEREST

Conflicts
of Interest

Canada
and the
Third World

EDITED BY
Jamie Swift and Brian Tomlinson

between the lines

Copyright © 1991 Between The Lines

Published by Between The Lines
        394 Euclid Avenue,
        Toronto, Ontario
        M6G 2S9 Canada

Cover design by Brian Gee
Typeset by Coach House Printing
Printed in Canada

Between The Lines receives financial assistance from
the Canada Council, the Ontario Arts Council,
and the Department of Communications.

CANADIAN CATALOGUING IN PUBLICATION DATA

Main entry under title:

Conflicts of interest: Canada and the third world

Includes bibliographical references and index.

ISBN 0-921284-40-3 (bound)   ISBN 0-921284-41-1 (pbk.)

1. Canada — Relations — Developing countries.
2. Developing countries — Relations — Canada.
3. Economic assistance, Canadian.
4. Developing countries — Economic conditions.
5. Economic assistance.
I. Swift, Jamie, 1951-
II. Tomlinson, Brian.

HC60.C65 1991   338.9'17101724   C91-094030-4

Contents

Acknowledgements

THIS BOOK emerged from discussions among people at Between The Lines who felt the need for a follow-up to a book the press had published in 1982.

Ties That Bind: Canada and the Third World appeared in the middle of a deep recession, as the hopes of the New International Economic Order of the 1970s gave way to the "crisis decade" of the 1980s. The debt crisis of the past ten years and the increasing transfer of wealth from the Third World to the advanced capitalist countries stimulated both interest and concern among Canadians. *Ties That Bind* was well-received by educators, activists, and the public at large.

Conflicts of Interest owes its existence to the efforts of several of the same people whose names appeared in the table of contents nine years ago. Brian Tomlinson was one of them, and his keen analytical hand helped to shape the present volume. *Ties That Bind* was co-edited by Robert Clarke and the book you are now holding owes its existence to his perseverance and attention to details of both form and content. His unshakeable modesty led to his insistence on not taking his rightful place on the title page of this book. Rob's name should be there.

Acknowledgement should also be made to all the contributors. They gave freely of their time and insights. I want to thank them for their commitment and patience. Other people who offered their time and talents to help with specific parts of the book include Jean Christie, John Dillon, Peter Gillespie, Bob Jeffcott, Richard Marquardt, Errol Sharpe, and Bob Thomson. We are especially grateful to Ken Epps of Project Ploughshares for his contribution to the chapter "Missiles and Malnutrition". Liisa North, John S. Saul, and Peter Saunders also gave much-needed support to the project. And Joyce Nelson came up with the book's title.

This project has also been supported by the Canadian Studies Directorate of the Department of the Secretary of State.

Finally, I'd like to add a note of appreciation to the volunteers whose efforts keep Between The Lines going and to the staff of the press: Pat Desjardins, Raul Gonzalez, Marg Anne Morrison, and Ian Rashid. Their essential contributions are too often overlooked.

J.S.

October 1990

A Note on Terminology

"EUROPE undertook the leadership of the world with ardour, cynicism and violence," wrote Frantz Fanon. "Let us decide not to imitate Europe; let us combine our muscles and our brains in a new direction."

The year was 1961 and the book was *The Wretched of the Earth*. Fanon, a psychiatrist from the French colony of Martinique, had just finished working in a hospital in Algeria where he had found himself in sympathy with the revolutionaries attempting to put an end to French colonialism in their country.

Fanon died of cancer at the age of 36 and did not live long enough to see Algerian independence. But the angry, optimistic tone of his book captured the mood of the day, the hopes of a generation of people living in the lands that had been colonized by the great powers of Europe. Fanon used the expression "Third World" to describe these lands. Today this remains the term most commonly used to denote the countries where the majority of the planet's people, the wretched of the earth, still live. We have used it in the title of this book.

The expression "Third World" was probably first used in France in the 1950s. The French, characteristically, were drawing a comparison between their own history and that of the rest of the world. So their "tiers monde" was a reflection of the "Third Estate" of the French Revolution.

As Raymond Williams put it in his book *Keywords: A Vocabulary of Culture and Society*, "In modern political terms," the description Third World "depends on an assumption of First and Second 'worlds', presumably capitalist and socialist, though this is not often spelled out. The expression is often generous in intention, but in its frequent overlap with *underdeveloped* it can both indicate a generalized area in which First and Second 'worlds' operate and compete, and bring together very diverse lands in an essentially undifferentiated condition."

The term Third World is derived from a distinctly Euro-North American world view that uses Cold War divisions of the globe as its point of departure. Such divisions become more blurred and problematic in light of the erosion of state socialism and the changes in Eastern Europe and the Soviet Union.

In the past ten years or so people writing about the realities of a world fractured by unshared wealth have also been using a horizontal "North-South" paradigm to describe the way things work. The nations of the South tend to be the former colonies and those of the North the former colonizers, with the grim inequalities not much changed since Fanon's day. But "North-South" is unwieldy. Like other terms used, it obscures the internal complexities of class and the external international division of labour characterized by the terms "poor countries" and "rich countries." North-South also introduces a neutral-sounding geographical element into a dynamic that is fundamentally economic (underdeveloped) and political (Third World). Besides, how does Australia, itself a former colony that today plays what might be called a sub-imperial role in parts of the Asia-Pacific region, fit into the North-South axis?

This leaves the other common expressions: "underdeveloped" and "developed" or "developing." Debates around these terms are not new. Their historic and continued use reveals a depressingly familiar mind-set shared by many of the world's most powerful men: They see development as a linear process that begins with traditional (or "backward") non-industrial societies having to pull up their socks and start making their way towards a natural, inevitable, and desirable goal called modernization. This goal is most often shorthand for externally generated economic growth. Former U.S. State Department nabob Walt Rostow even spelled out this goal as a "high, mass consumption" economy.

The late Guyanese historian Walter Rodney once said, "A word such as development can often be used to cover up the reality, because it is used so casually it implies that even if all is not well the direction of change is acceptable."

According to yet another approach, that of the Marxist dependency school, the ideas of development and underdevelopment ignore the fact that the affluence of Northern nations is dependent on the poverty of the South, that the Third World has been systematically pillaged since the dawn of the colonial era. At some point we also have to face the indisputable fact that the "high, mass consumption" society is unsustainable in environmental terms as the North gobbles up the planet's resources to the benefit of a fraction of its inhabitants.

Like "Third World," all the other terms that have attempted to define the relations between "rich" and "poor" countries in some way do illustrate the issue. But they also create false dynamics. All of them obscure historical realities, and all of them are unsatisfactory. But they also seem to be unavoidable, and admittedly most if not all of them are used in the pages that follow.

"If we want to turn Africa into a new Europe," Fanon said, "then let us leave the destiny of our countries to Europeans.... But if we want humanity to advance a step further, if we want to bring it up to a different level than that which Europe has shown it, then we must invent and we must make discoveries."

Perhaps – as the following pages certainly show – we still need to discover a language, a terminology that captures the complexities of the world and offers people a sense of identity rather than, as Raymond Williams put it, a "practice of cancellation."

J.S.

Introduction

Jamie Swift

As the decade closes – with the market approach to economic growth in spectacular triumph over the planned economies of Eastern Europe, and their centralized allocation of resources – structural adjustment looks more relevant with each day that passes.

– Marcel Massé, President, Canadian International Development Agency,
November 1989

IN THE HARDBOILED school of detective fiction, it is not uncommon for someone like Philip Marlowe – Raymond Chandler's famous sleuth – to be knocked unconscious by a lurking villain. The result is predictable: Marlowe wakes up in a pitiful state of disorientation, horrific images dancing in his throbbing head. He is weakened, off balance, temporarily unable to cope.

The instrument of this setback has often been a blackjack, that nasty little hunk of leather-covered lead known to Chandler's readers as a "sap." To lay someone out with a sap is to club them into submission.

Over 50 years after Chandler's work began to appear in pulp magazines like *Black Mask*, the noun "sap" has taken on a different meaning. The word now appears regularly in the pages of official-looking reports commissioned by international agencies. Such reports are usually concerned with the fate of the poor in the world's poorest countries. The word is spelled in capital letters – SAP – and on the surface its meaning is different. But it is really the same. The victims of this new SAP are weakened, off balance, unable to cope.

Today's SAP – an acronym for "Structural Adjustment Program" – has an ideological underpinning: a faith in free-market capitalism. It involves a set of measures prescribed by institutions under the control of the governments of the richest nations, including Canada.

The ostensible purpose of those measures is to help poor countries of the Third World grow their way out of debt. But a report of a conference on the impact of such measures on the people of Africa concluded that the first priority of the programs "is the creation and maintenance of a world capitalist system in which multinational corporations can trade, invest and move capital without restrictions from national governments."[1]

A typical SAP involves adjustments in a nation's policies to encourage foreign investment, cash-crop production, and the privatization of government enterprises. Structural adjustment also involves an end to public subsidies for basic needs: things like food.

If a country wants to qualify for foreign aid, chances are it will have to agree to the terms of a SAP. Not surprisingly, poor people in the Third World often take to the streets, rioting when the effects of a SAP become apparent. Such outbursts are "IMF riots," named after the International Monetary Fund. They are not pleasant.

THE SAP IN ZAMBIA

Zambia is one among many countries that have been hard hit by IMF austerity programs. In December 1986, responding to IMF demands to cut subsidies, the Zambian government removed a major subsidy on maize meal or "mealie-meal" – the staple food of most Zambians. Ordinary people went into shops to buy meal and all they could find on the shelves was the more expensive "breakfast meal," a refined grain preferred by affluent Zambians. Private millers had reprocessed mealie meal into breakfast meal in the hopes of making a quick return.

The result was what has come to be known as the "Christmas riots." Thousands of young, unemployed Zambians (after five years of IMF adjustment programs, 10,000 people had lost their jobs) took to the streets. Over 30 people were killed and $2 billion worth of property was destroyed.

At a 1988 hearing into the international monetary system, sponsored by the World Council of Churches, Zambian economist Cosmas Musumali recounted the horrors: "This is brutal killing where, for example, a policeman is stoned by a group of about ten kids, maybe 10-15 year olds, whose hardships have made them so hardened that despite seeing blood they just keep on stoning the policeman until he dies."[2]

Zambia is like many Third World countries. As its economy slowed down in the 1980s, the business of security and the protection of property boomed. To the outsider, this means high walls studded with broken glass and armed guards. For the wary Zambian like Cosmas Musumali, it means never stopping for anyone on the road. It means getting home and, rather than driving in, driving around the block a few times to make sure no one is following. For poor Zambians, it means allowing their teenage daughters to become prostitutes. It means not being able to do anything about the fact that two out of every three pregnant women in Zambia are anemic. It means health-care spending cuts so drastic that doctors in public hospitals sometimes cannot perform even emergency operations because they have no rubber gloves.

Private clinics in Zambia blossomed, charging high fees out of reach of average citizens who saw their incomes fall from U.S.$600 per year in 1980 to $170 in 1986. By the mid-1980s inflation in Zambia was running at 60 per cent and the kwacha was devalued by 700 per cent. Corruption was rampant. Many civil servants were spending much of their time off the job looking for other means of making ends meet.

In Zambia now, many parents no longer send their children to school simply because free schooling is a thing of the past. Textbooks, if available, are expensive. A nation of illiterates is developing. Growing numbers of young people have nothing better to do than roam the streets.

"Today if you walk the streets of Zambia, you must hold your bag very tightly because young boys will be running behind you trying to help themselves to your pocket," Musumali testified. "People will be pointing knives at you whenever no one is looking so that they can take your watch or even your shoes.... All this shows just one thing: the economic situation that the country is facing has eroded not only its economic substance but the moral fabric upon which a future country could have been built."

Perhaps the most tragic thing here is the verb tense Musumali uses: *could have*. It indicates a sense of hopelessness, of opportunities lost. This is a country whose optimistic independence celebrations in 1964 were based on its rich deposits of copper. Zambians hoped the red metal would be the building block for its post-colonial future. The 1974 crash of copper prices put Zambia in the same boat as many other commodity-dependent countries: increased poverty and debt have been the order of the day in the Third World ever since.

Rocked by the Christmas riots, the Zambian government took a step back to rethink its relations with the IMF. It opted out of the structural adjustment program and reduced payments to service its debt to 10 per cent of its export earnings. To service the debt completely would have eaten up 90 to 100 per cent of its export earnings.[3] Most aid and investment credits quickly dried up and the country's decline continued. All the Northern countries, including Canada – with the exception of the Nordic nations – have made their foreign aid for Zambia contingent on the country coming to terms with the IMF. Canada pushed this agenda to the extent that it secured an agreement under which a vice-president of the Bank of Canada would be seconded as the *Governor* of the Bank of Zambia – the body that determines Zambia's internal and external economic policies and its responses to the IMF.

The 1980s started out with some hope for the Third World – despite the fact that the two previous "decades of development" had failed to stop the flow of money from the poor to the rich. The Brandt Commission, set up at the urging of Robert McNamara, president of the World Bank, bravely proclaimed the 1980s as "a new development decade." Brandt recommended a transfer of resources *to* the Third World.

What actually came to pass was exactly the opposite. Per capita output for the Third World as a whole declined by nearly 1 per cent per year during the 1980s.[4] Between 1980 and 1987 there was a net transfer of U.S.$287 billion from Third World countries to their Northern creditors.

The Third World was attacked and weakened during the 1980s. It was sapped.

CHANGES: NORTH–SOUTH AND EAST–WEST

In 1982 Between The Lines published a book called *Ties That Bind* that explored Canada's relations with the Third World. At that time the Brandt Commission had just delivered its report and the term "North / South" had come into vogue. The term described the tensions between the Third World nations of the South and the industrial capitalist countries of the North. The Brandt Commission and a Canadian parliamentary Task Force on North-South Relations both held out hopes that international trade could be reformed to give those countries engaged in primary commodity production (the South) a better comparative advantage in their dealings with their principal trading partners (the North).

Brian Tomlinson warned in *Ties That Bind* that the Brandt Commission proposals "consistently ignore the need for change in political structures in both North and South and the fundamental influence of transnational corporations on those structures." He argued for a change in development priorities that are "now organized for the profits of corporations and local elites, which have continued to worsen social inequalities globally and locally."[5] Tomlinson's new chapter in the pages that follow updates his earlier contribution. His analysis of the broader development picture is buttressed by Charles Lane's examination of the Tanzania-Canada Wheat Program, wherein it is revealed that Canadian manufacturers of agricultural implements have benefited at the expense of African pastoralists.

In 1982 the wave of debt that had been building for several years crested when Mexico announced it could not meet its payments. The debt crisis, which I examine here in a chapter co-written with the Ecumenical Coalition for Economic Justice, dashed the hopes for a more just North-South division of the world's wealth. The burden of debt bondage was to define the debates over development in the 1980s. By 1987 the nations of the South, with *four-fifths* of the world's population (83.8 per cent) were sharing less than *one-fifth* (19.8 per cent) of the world income.[6] The debt crisis had simply siphoned more wealth from the poor to the rich.

Yet if things were uncertain on the North-South front in 1982, they seemed to be unfolding predictably on the other axis. East-West relations were cooling rapidly. The Reagan administration had begun an unprecedented peacetime arms buildup, expanding conventional forces and deploying new weapons systems in Western Europe. Confronting the vision of a "Communist conspiracy" throughout the world, the Reagan Doctrine exported terrorist interventions to the Third World, from Nicaragua to Angola.[7] The leaders of the Soviet bloc, the state socialist countries of the East, gave the hawks on the other side ample opportunity to vilify their opponents in the peace movement as naive appeasers. The Soviet Union invaded Afghanistan; the Polish government declared martial law and tossed members of the Solidarity opposition into jail.

By 1990 East-West relations had been profoundly transformed. In the final few months of 1989 the people of the "Second World" took to the streets in a massive challenge to two generations of authoritarian rule in Eastern Europe. All the old certainties evaporated with remarkable quickness as Gorbachev's *glasnost* reforms shook Soviet society. Various Soviet republics seemed poised to declare independence and unprecedented freedoms of expression and dissent abounded. Elsewhere a Solidarity leader became President of Poland. Romania's Nicolae Ceausescu was deposed and executed as his people took to the streets. (Ironically, the Romanian dictator had been doing the right thing according to conventional IMF wisdom: starving the people to pay off the foreign debt.) The Hungarian Communist Party redefined itself as a social democratic party and proclaimed the need for the market to guide the economy. The Berlin Wall came down as East Germany's young citizens voted with their feet and headed West. On October 3, 1990, German unification within the Western alliance became official, "with cheers and fireworks and pealing bells and a few sobs."[8]

These momentous changes created new challenges for the nations of the South. As the world economy headed into a new polarized structure characterized by distinct blocs – North America, Japan, East Asia, and an economically unified Europe – the Third World seemed likely to become even more lost on the margins. New investment, new trade opportunities, and Northern priorities for aid to Eastern Europe were being focused on existing and emerging consumer markets. The majority of the world's population, facing increasing poverty, had become increasingly irrelevant to the profit centres of global capitalism.

The events in Eastern Europe and the Soviet Union and the decline in East-West tension gave new hope to those who had long opposed the insanity of the global arms race. For the first time it seemed possible that a new era had dawned in which money for guns could be channelled into prenatal care and clean water. Yet as Esther Epp-Tiessen reveals in her chapter on militarism and the arms race in the Third World, the effects of decades of Northern-backed militarization in the South cannot be so easily undone.

Those decades came quickly back to haunt us. Tragically, the first year of the new decade was not over before the United States chose to escalate a regional conflict between Saddam Hussein's vicious regime in Iraq and a U.S. client, the Emir of Kuwait, into a major war. With Iraq's August 2, 1990, invasion of Kuwait and the massive military response by the U.S.-led coalition, hopes for a so-called "peace dividend" seemed to evaporate.

The real losers in the conflict – aside from the innocent civilians who died during the war and the oil barons of Kuwait who had some of their property destroyed or stolen by Iraq – would be the people of the Third World. Most directly affected were the estimated two million Third World workers who toiled in the Middle East at everything from construction to cleaning floors. Workers from countries such as Sri Lanka, the Philippines, and Bangladesh fled the war zone, cutting out the $3 billion they had been sending home every year and adding to the mass of unemployed in their own countries.

The indirect effects have been no less dramatic. For instance, the Zambian economy, already devastated by debt, was hammered by a rise in oil prices, and the government's meagre spending on its own people was further curtailed. The poor in dozens of other have-not nations suffered similar setbacks, and would suffer more in the future.

Most dramatic were the comparisons: on one side, the amounts spent by each government on killing people; on the other side, the constructive development that could have been accomplished using the same sums. Canada, playing the role of U.S. acolyte in the gulf, was spending $3 million a day on its military efforts there by February 1991. By then the Canadian government had spent enough on its adventure to easily make up for the cuts it had made to its development assistance program the year before. In general, the amount spent on a single hour and a half of the war by all participants would have paid for bringing safe water to the whole of Central America.

But what of the wider political agendas of the warring countries? Iraq's was clear enough: annex and loot a rich neighbour. U.S. president George Bush talked before and during the war of "a new world order" that he was struggling to achieve in the aftermath of the decline of Soviet power. This was simply shorthand for a renewed Pax Americana. The United States and its allies were basically reasserting Western hegemony in a traditional – and strategic – Third World area of influence. More than anything else, the Gulf War was aimed at maintaining a region's effective colonization while providing a renewed gloss of legitimation for the use of military force in solving conflict.

IDEOLOGY AND THE STANDARDIZATION OF CULTURE

The changes in Eastern Europe also offered opinion-makers in Canada and other industrial nations a chance to trumpet one of the great I-told-you-sos of recent history. The old notion of "the end of ideology" took on new life. A CBC-Radio journalist reported breathlessly from Hanoi that the Vietnamese had forsaken "Marxism for the marketplace." A *Globe and Mail* editorialist wrote of "the victory of the liberal idea (including freedom of markets) over Marxist determinism."

"Coca-Cola is great," cried a young East German who had sneaked over from Hungary a few days before the border was opened. "McDonald's is great. Playboy magazine is great. There is nothing like this in the East. The West is great!"[9]

A typical cartoon showed a hammer and sickle prostrate on a bed in an intensive care unit. The old Soviet symbol was hooked up to an assortment of wires as nearby machines uttered a series of fading beeps. Articles and books began to appear, all centring around the theme that the very idea of socialism was dead. It all comes down to how you see the world, and two chapters in this book, one by Eleanor O'Donnell and the other by Anton Allahar, examine this question. They discuss how the media help to mould our ideologies and consider the natur of the prevailing ideologies.

The commentators who clucked with self-satisfaction assumed that free-market capitalism had been vindicated, finally winning the day. Such logic will no doubt be puzzling to the mother in Porto Alegre, Brazil, who makes little cakes out of discarded newspapers to feed her children so that their stomachs will feel full. It will also be curious to the Penan people of Sarawak, Malaysia, who have watched their ancestral forest home being rapidly stripped to feed the appetite of Japanese business. The contributors to this book challenge these ideological blinkers by showing how it is unrestrained growth, driven by the needs of Northern markets, that has perpetuated the poverty of the Third World in the name of "development" and "progress."

By the late 1980s capitalism had succeeded in penetrating almost every corner of the globe. There had been a significant decline in the rate of foreign direct investment in the Third World and the United States had moved from being the largest source of such investment to the largest recipient. New technologies had dramatically altered the economics of production, with control over service industries and information technologies emerging as important factors in an interdependent world economy.

Corporate control of technology is not, however, simply confined to computerization and machine-managed production processes. With the internationalization of the economy, there has been a steady drift towards homogenization, a levelling brought on by the standardization of products – and even culture.

"The plastic pail has replaced the gourd, the earthen pot and the banana leaf," Raymond Vernon wrote in a 1977 book about the effects of international business in the Third World. "Tin roofs are replacing the local varieties of thatch."[10]

Go to any Third World market. Footwear produced locally out of indigenous material has been replaced by plastic shoes. The manufacturer may well be Bata, a Canadian firm. If the market is in a town of any size, there is likely to be a crush of imported private automobiles pushing their way through the crowded streets. Images created by advertisers abound. Luridly painted posters of Sylvester Stallone or Clint Eastwood will be staring down from the sides of movie houses. For a North American tourist, things have a familiar feel.

The standardization of culture is more and more direct – from North to South. Throughout Central America and the Caribbean, North American television is beamed directly by satellite and cable into the homes of the middle and upper classes. The schedules of many Third World television outlets look like those of a network affiliate in Atlanta. If you watch the news in Bogota or Colombo, the reporter describing events in Seoul will likely be a U.S. correspondent employed by the Cable News Network. Inuit people in Nain, Labrador, are most likely able to pull in the same program.

The young East German emigré spouting the virtues of consumer culture may not have heard it, but over 20 years ago the social theorist Ivan Illich summed up the implications of global cultural homogenization. He told of watching while a 60-foot Coca-Cola advertisement was being erected in the Mexican highlands that had just been hit by a wave of drought and famine. Illich recalled his anger when a poor Indian, his host in Ixmiquilpan, offered his European guest a tiny glass of the expensive sugar-water.

We live in a paradoxical world. An investment banker alert to shifting international interest rates can relax at his poolside in the Bahamas, transferring huge sums from country to country, his laptop computer linked to a satellite. At the same time that hundreds of millions of people are suffering from lack of food, hundreds of millions of dollars and marks and yen are wasted on advertising campaigns promoting useless and sometimes harmful products.

What Illich pointed out in 1969 is ever more true today. The majority of people in the world have less food than they did in 1945, less care in illness, less useful work. "Mass needs are converted into the demand for new brands of packaged solutions which are forever beyond the needs of the majority," Illich wrote. "Thirst [is converted] into the need for a Coke. This kind of reification occurs in the manipulation of primary human needs by vast bureaucratic organizations which have succeeded in dominating the imaginations of potential consumers."[11]

It is these "vast bureaucratic organizations" that are the intended beneficiaries of the structural adjustment programs imposed on Zambia and other countries in recent years. Countries no longer produce for local needs. Decisions are entrusted to the managers of global enterprises, men accountable to no one in the "host country."

In spite of the transnational corporation's astonishing success in expanding into every possible market, cornering every possible source of raw material, the simple fact is that this growth has failed to improve the lot of the poor.

THE 1990S: BEYOND PARADOX

As the 1980s ended, another landmark commission by another former European head of state was the subject of debate even more intense than that generated by the Brandt Commission. The Brundtland Commission (after Gro Harlem Brundtland of Norway) forced us to consider the compelling evidence that the world faces an ecological catastrophe. The commission called for "sustainable development" – ostensibly a new approach to economic growth and world development.

In his chapter, Richard Swift examines the environmental crisis as it affects the Third World and the assumptions behind the notion of "sustainable development." Despite a pessimistic prognosis for the global ecosystem, he concludes that the new concern for the environment – and the rise of citizen-based environment movements in the North and South – offer reason for optimism. The grounds for hope could well be expanded by paying new attention to alternative ways of both viewing the resources of land, sea, and air and dealing with human relations, as Pam Colorado suggests in her chapter, "A Native View of Development." In a similar vein, Betty Plewes and Reiky Stuart look at the role of the women's movement in shaping debates around gender and development, especially as those debates influence the activities of Non-Governmental Organizations (NGOs). Plewes and Stuart challenge both development workers and feminists to seek alternatives that take into account women's positions and strategic interests, as well as the power relationships within the development process. Their critique of the dominant Women in Development (WID) approach suggests that Third World feminists offer a more holistic and radical approach to NGOs.

In a chapter dealing comprehensively with NGOs, Brian Murphy examines the history and politics of these organizations in Canada. He situates their work in the political landscape of popular movements in the Third World that are working for fundamental changes in relationships between the poor and the rich. The choices of Canadian agencies are shaped by their vision and commitment to social change. Some of them, drawing on experiences of partnership with Southern NGOs, have developed a strategic agenda and an alternative development model. This approach involves people in the decisions that affect their lives: It is nothing short of revolutionary because it assumes that Canadians actively assist the poor in the Third World in attempting to transform the structures of injustice; and it does so on their own terms. Needless to say, this agenda is far removed from that outlined by Marcel Massé of CIDA, who talks of "realistic economic policies" (read, SAPs) as opposed to the "naive ideas and simplistic theories" (read, collective self-reliance) of previous decades.

Massé quit his job as executive director of the International Monetary Fund in 1989, moving back to Canada and the job as head of CIDA. From this $130,000-up position, he redoubled his efforts to lecture poor people on the need to tighten their belts. He did not spare Canadians the hard-faced advice that IMF bureaucrats regularly dole out to the Third World: "It isn't just the Third World that needs structural adjustment ... we *all* do, in one form or another."[12]

The need to bow to the discipline of the free market will be familiar to Canadians who opposed the Free Trade Agreement before the 1988 election. They were told to wake up to the facts of life in the *real world:* It's tough out there and we have to compete or wither away. Again, this is simply shorthand for opening up national economies to the transnational corporations that span many countries and erode the control people have over their own economies – and over the decisions that have an impact on their lives.

Canada is conventionally seen as a "rich" country, a member of the G-7 group of leading industrial nations, a major aid donor. The country's business class itself controls a number of powerful corporations with operations spanning the globe. Canadians themselves support a vast array of non-governmental organizations that maintain development projects in the Third World.

But the nation's economic policies in the 1980s were a striking reflection of the conventional structural adjustment policies imposed on the Third World. We saw the privatization of public enterprises such as Air Canada, the dismantling of VIA Rail, proposals to privatize Petro-Canada and the Post Office; cutbacks in unemployment insurance, regional development funds, child care, women's support services, and Native organizations. Trade policy became increasingly export-oriented. The high-interest policies that continue into the 1990s are aimed at preventing capital from fleeing the country – something the state can do through exchange controls – but also have the effect of creating unemployment.[13]

During a 1989 debate on unemployment insurance cuts, employment minister Barbara McDougall explained to the House of Commons that "privatization, deregulation, tax reform and free trade are all part of the same agenda" as the U.I. cuts."[14] Clearly, Canada has a SAP all of its own.

This brings up the always-puzzling question of just where Canada fits into the international scheme of things. We are a major aid-giver. Most Canadians enjoy a standard of living incomparably higher than people in Third World countries. As the chapters in this book illustrate, Canada has a particular role to play vis-à-vis those countries.

It is also a peculiar role, as was illustrated by a story that unfolded in 1990 concerning Canada's relations with Guyana.[15]

In 1989 Canada had agreed – at the specific request of the United States – to take the lead role in formulating a tough austerity plan that would accompany new credits for the nearly bankrupt Caribbean nation. It was the usual package of free-market reforms that resulted in the usual drop in living standards for the Guyanese. Guyana replaced Haiti as the poorest nation in the hemisphere. Canada soldiered on, its image in the region tarnished by ugly demonstrations outside its High Commission office in Georgetown, Guyana, and the widespread recognition that Canada was the architect of the new austerity. Ottawa apparently believed that the new credits that were to accompany the "reforms" would help the Guyanese pull themselves up by their bootstraps.

Then, at an IMF meeting in Washington in the spring of 1990, the United States announced that it would not be coming up with the dollars it had promised to Guyana. The reason was that Washington was suddenly faced by competing demands that were driven by its need to maintain its imperial hegemony in the region. It had just invaded Panama and its new client government there was crying out for assistance. Then Nicaragua had surprised everyone by electing a U.S.-funded coalition that would also be desperate for money to salvage its war-ravaged economy.

Canadian officials were livid that the United States had reneged on its promise. But they could only swallow their pride and go begging to other potential donors in the hopes of making up the shortfall. The alternative would be the complete collapse of the "Canadian" SAP and a major loss of face in the Commonwealth Caribbean, a region long considered Canada's sphere of influence.

So Canada's special ties with the Third World – through aid and trade as well as through its membership in the Commonwealth and *la francophonie* – remain ambiguous. Yet Canada is also a member of Northern alliances like the prestigious Group of Seven and NATO. In many ways it experiences its own post-colonial problems in its dependent relationship with the United States. Undoubtedly, Canada's "most special" ties are with its neighbour to the south, and the effects of U.S. hegemony tend to play no small part in Canada's relations with the outside world, sometimes to our embarrassment.

Certainly, Canada's role – the middle power, the helpful fixer, the second-tier nation – is fraught with paradox … with conflicts of interest.

Notes

1. Institute for African Alternatives, *The IMF, World Bank and Africa* (London: IFAA Publications, 1987), p.7.

2. *Testimony of Cosmas M. Musumali to the Ecumenical Hearing on the International Monetary System and the Churches' Responsibility,* West Berlin, August 1988.

3. Marcia Burdette, *"Living on the Edge of the Precipice: Zambia Under Structural Adjustment": Testimony to the House of Commons Standing Committee on External Affairs and International Trade, December 7, 1989* (Ottawa: North-South Institute, 1990).

4. UN Centre on Transnational Corporations, *Transnational Corporations in World Development: Trends and Prospects* (New York: United Nations, 1988), p.19.

5. Brian Tomlinson, "Reaching an Impasse: The North-South Debate," in *Ties That Bind:*

Canada and the Third World, ed. Robert Clarke and Richard Swift (Toronto: Between The Lines, 1982), p.82.

6. World Bank data, cited by Roy Culpeper of the North-South Institute in the forum, "Effective Use of Development Aid," Toronto, September 1989.

7. Noam Chomsky, *The Culture of Terrorism* (Montreal: Black Rose Books, 1988).

8. John Gray, "New Germany Born," *The Globe and Mail,* October 3, 1990, p.A1.

9. *Toronto Star,* September 12, 1989.

10. Raymond Vernon, *Storm over the Multinationals: The Real Issues* (London: Macmillan, 1977), p.4.

11. Ivan Illich, "Outwitting the 'Developed' Countries," in *The Political Economy of Development and Underdevelopment,* ed. C.K. Wilber (New York: Random House, 1973), p.404-405.

12. Marcel Massé, "Adjustment in Perspective: Notes for Remarks to an International Colloquium on Structural Adjustment and Social Realities in Africa," Institute for International Development and Co-operation, University of Ottawa, November 17, 1989, p.5.

13. For an excellent analysis of the way structural adjustment is being applied to both Canada and the Third World, see Ecumenical Coalition for Economic Justice, *Recolonization or Liberation: The Bonds of Structural Adjustment and Struggles for Emancipation* (Toronto: ECEJ, 1990).

14. House of Commons, *Debates,* Ottawa, June 6, 1989.

15. For more on this Guyana story see the chapter here, "The Debt Crisis: A Case of Global Usury."

ONE

Development in the 1990s: Critical Reflections on Canada's Economic Relations with the Third World

Brian Tomlinson

IN 1980 THE Brandt Commission called upon the rich industrial nations to meet what it termed the "greatest social challenge of our times" – the massive transfer of economic resources from the North to the South.

For the Brandt Commission, an independent collection of world notables established in 1977 at the urging of Robert McNamara, then president of the World Bank, this transfer was critical to the survival of some 800 million people living in absolute destitution in the Third World. If the transfer was not forthcoming, if the North did not act to break the deadlock of North-South negotiations around a New International Economic Order, the commission foresaw a catastropic "crisis decade." Accordingly, the commission proposed that the industrial countries support a set of emergency plans for global reform leading to economic and social justice, based not on altruism but on their own self-interest.[1]

The Brandt commission generated an initial hope that the industrial countries would take up its proposed agenda and begin to bridge the widening gap between North and South. In Canada, in the same year, a parliamentary task force on North-South relations focused widespread public support on a leadership role for the Canadian government. Given Canada's strong commitment to international development as well as our role as a "middle power" trading nation, Prime Minister Pierre Trudeau did in fact promote North-South economic and political discussion at Cancun in October 1981.

In 1982 Brandt and his commission reiterated the urgency of programs for the alleviation of poverty, stressing the reform of the global framework for trade and development. Yet the appeal brought little response from the international community, which was only beginning to recognize the threat of economic collapse posed by the failure of Mexico to meet its debt obligations.

Viewed from the vantage point of the 1990s, the Brandt proposals seem hopelessly utopian. The early years of the 1980s saw the worst economic recession since the 1930s, largely brought on by the co-ordinated policies of the central banks of Europe and North America. The global debt of Third World countries expanded exponentially during this recession and stood at U.S.$1.3 trillion by 1990. While Brandt called for economic transfers to the South of $50 to $60 billion annually, the total aid budgets of the developed countries stood at $48.5 billion in 1988, compared to $27.3 billion in 1980.[2]

At the same time, the transfer of resources by private sources (banks and transnational corporations) collapsed from U.S.$40.4 billion in 1980 to $18.8 billion in 1987. More astounding, the developing countries received a total of $458.1 billion in net development assistance between 1980 and 1988; during the same period these same countries paid out a total of $1.167 trillion to the industrial countries to cover amortization and services on debt owed to largely private sources.[3]

Between 1984 and 1988 the International Monetary Fund (IMF), one of the financial institutions to which Brandt issued the challenge of reform, became a net *recipient* (due to payments on current loans) of $4.2 billion from the developing countries, including the poorest countries of Sub-Saharan Africa. In 1987 these same African countries, the scene of ecological and human devastation shown on television screens throughout the North, were able to purchase 50 per cent less with their raw material exports to Europe and North America than in 1980, as a result of severely declining commodity prices. Per capita incomes in Africa declined by 20 per cent after 1981. Economic growth through exports to Northern markets, a practice long promoted by the IMF and the industrial countries, did not provide the foreign currency urgently needed to reduce mounting debts. Raw-material exports, upon which many highly indebted countries were still dependent, returned 30 per cent less to the developing countries in 1987 than in 1980.[4]

There is now widespread recognition that the poor in all but a few Asian countries have suffered dramatic declines in living standards. For the first time in the post-war period there has also been a marked decline in the living conditions of the shrinking urban middle classes in many developing countries. Throughout the Andean region of Latin America, health and nutrition expenditures were reduced by 61 per cent and education by 59 per cent in the 1980s. The International Labour Organization reported a 40 per cent increase in unemployment in Latin America between 1980 and 1984, with a 67 per cent growth in the number of unemployed. At the same time, as Susan George calculated, "In 1980, a Peruvian earning the minumum wage had to work seventeen minutes for a kilo of rice, in 1984 two hours and five minutes – over seven times as long."[5] Inflation and currency devaluations brought escalating food prices for those who could least afford to pay – as well as deteriorating housing, education, and health facilities.

There is no doubt that the decade's "development crisis" surpassed even the most dire predictions of the Brandt Commission in 1980. Global economic instability, resulting from the recession of 1982–83, and the failure of earlier development strategies in Africa and Latin America brought out a new and urgent interest in Canada and other Northern countries for a reassessment of development programs and economic policies with developing countries.[6] The publication of *Sharing Our Future* in 1987 provided a summation of these deliberations by the Canadian International Development Agency (CIDA), Canada's official aid agency. As the first statement of a policy framework since 1975, *Sharing Our Future* set out a bold new strategy and action plan, which would define Canada's Official Development Assistance (ODA) policies for the next decade.[7]

CIDA's new strategy stressed the important development issues for the 1990s:

1. the alleviation of poverty through partnership programs with Third World peoples;
2. support for economic structural adjustment in the debt-ridden Third World nations;
3. increased involvement of women in development;
4. environmentally sustainable development; and
5. a concern for human rights abuses and their impact on the delivery of development programs.

The focus on these issues is indeed essential, but the key question is how CIDA's activities, based on these stated objectives and priorities, relate to the realities facing the poor Third World majorities in the 1990s. How effectively can this strategy promote ecologically sustainable development and poverty alleviation given the broader movements in the world economic order in the past decade and Canada's economic relations with the South? Fundamental to the aid strategy is the notion that "sound development is in Canada's own long-term economic interest"; Canada is seeking "complementarity between the objectives of the development cooperation program and other foreign policy objectives ... within the development context."[8]

While Canada's aid program is significant, it is not the only – or even the major – aspect of Canada's economic and political relationships with the Third World. Canadian trade and private investment with developing countries is relatively small when compared with that of Europe or the United States; nevertheless official aid is dwarfed by the flows of trade and capital investment. Therefore the potential impact of aid policies in realizing their primary purpose "to help the poorest countries and people" must be assessed from a wider perspective of economic and political relationships.

Some Statistics

- [ ] Official Development Assistance (1989) $2.7 billion
- [ ] Canadian exports to the Third World (1989) $11.5 billion
- [ ] Canadian imports from the Third World (1989) $16.2 billion
- [ ] Official exports credits for the Third World (1987) $0.9 billion
- [ ] Outstanding loans owed to Canadian banks (1990) $16.0 billion
- [ ] Reserves set aside by Canadian banks against Third World loan losses (1990) $9.8 billion
- [ ] Value of Canadian private investment in the Third World (1985) $6.3 billion

Beginning with the Colombo Plan of 1950, the structure and impact of Canadian aid programs have been defined by economic and political relationships and their origins and motivations in Canadian business, trade, and foreign-policy interests.[9] More profoundly, the promotion of Canadian private investment and trade with the Third World has been accompanied by a particular interpretation and definition of "development" – as rooted in "economic growth" and industrial "progress" – which is reflected in the strategy and practice of Canada's aid programs.

Canadian aid strategy, then, must be assessed from two inter-related perspectives. The first looks at the concept of "development" and North-South relations, with its deep historical patterns of dependency and social, economic, and political inequality. Rooted in a colonial past, the Third World has been integrated into a global economy now organized by and for transnational corporations (TNCs). An equitable and just development strategy should respond to this context and address the political and economic realities facing the vast majority of the world's poor and their own struggles for survival and self-improvement. The second perspective analyses Canada's relation to these global socio-economic and political structures.

DEVELOPMENT FOR WHOM?

From the standpoint of the poor, the development strategies of the last three decades have failed dramatically. The Organization for Economic Cooperation and Development (OECD) estimates roughly that one billion people still live in poverty. With few exceptions Third World countries are economically and politically bankrupt and deeply dependent on shrinking commodity trade and economic assistance from the North. Yet growth and development are among the oldest and most powerful ideas in Western political and economic thought. Since the nineteenth century, the evolution of industrial capitalism out of agricultural societies has been seen to be an inevitable "natural development" supported by advances in science and technology and leading to improved standards of living.

After the Second World War, theories of development and modernization for newly emerging Third World nations drew heavily on the experience of Europe and North America to predict a similar road.

The optimism of the early development theories was tempered by the persistence of poverty; nevertheless, more sophisticated approaches retained the underlying assumptions about "progress" and "growth." The Brandt Report did not question the proposition that "The successive industrial revolutions of the past two hundred years in Europe and North America are now being followed by industrialization in Latin America, Asia, and Africa, a natural and indeed inevitable development which is already beginning to change the pattern of comparative advantage in the world economy." [10] More recently, CIDA praised "an approach to development which combines growth promotion with programs specifically designed to alleviate poverty." While the alleviation of poverty is always the objective of development assistance, there is an over-riding assumption: "Development takes place through economic growth, social change and the appropriate use of resources." Consequently, "Poverty alleviation is part of growth promotion." [11] Both the World Bank and the IMF provide development financing to Third World countries based on the viability of domestic plans to foster economic growth and the expansion of exports. [12]

The development crisis facing the poor cannot be separated from either its roots in the social structures or the political and economic relationships that have been part of the actual process of development over the past two hundred years. More important still, an alternative vision of development, one emerging from the conditions and perspective of the poor majorities, necessarily confronts the crises created by the dominant growth model – and therefore the growth model itself. How does one explain the persistence of this model?

In the words of Raymond Williams, "What matters is the origin and impetus of any particular development process." [13] From an historical perspective, "economic growth" and "progress" for the Third World have been one-sided and imposed; they have been characterized by the the brutal and dependent relationships of colonialism, by the exploitation of Third World resources and raw materials for the industrial development of Europe and North America, and by the integration of Third World economies into a global market for goods produced largely in the North or for the North. [14]

The emergence of this global "interdependence" of nations from the seventeenth century onward has been at the expense of the majority of people living in Asia, Africa, the Caribbean, and Latin America (as well as the indigenous peoples of North America). These historic North-South economic and political links, from the African slave trade to plantation economies to present-day transnational corporations, have been secured by local political and economic elites. These elites have shared economic and political interests with their counterparts in the North, in manufacturing, trade, banking, and the arms trade; in turn they secured their own wealth (and control of land) through political, social, cultural, and ultimately military means of domination over the social classes of the poor in their societies.

In the late twentieth century "economic growth" throughout the world has been largely controlled and determined by transnational corporations. These are global private empires that traverse the world seeking profits in manufactures, raw materials, and services, adapting local conditions to their corporate priorities of profit and growth. The Brandt Commission estimated that these corporations, most of them with headquarters in the United States, Europe, or Japan, controlled between a quarter and a third of all world production. [15] By 1985 a United Nations study calculated that the 600 largest corporations employed only 3 per cent of the world's workforce and accounted for 80 to 90 per cent of exports in the developed countries. [16] These same companies have set the terms and the pace for resource development and post-war industrialization in the Third World. In doing so, their operations have skewed development priorities and have drained off income and development capital to their shareholders in the North through massive profit and interest repatriation, management fees, unequal terms of trade and internal artificial pricing, and control over shipping.

In the modern era, the corporate requirements for open economic policies and political stability are widely accepted and seldom questioned; they are mirrored in modern development models. The pressure on Third World countries to adapt to the interests of external corporate development is immense. The use of sophisticated technology controlled by transnationals establishes a seemingly irreversible bias, world-wide, for a high-growth and industrial model of development. To be cost effective, advanced technology requires large-scale plants, global marketing, and management structures. Transnationals have effectively tied domestic elites and capital in the Third World to corporate goals through their control over access to the new technology and the inputs and capital required to put that technology to use for local profit.

A leading example is the new farming technology largely controlled by agribusiness and oil corporations, which offer a complete technological package of genetic plant material, chemical inputs essential for plant growth, and harvesting and processing equipment for large-scale production. Once accepted, the new technology has profoundly transformed land ownership patterns and social relations in rural societies. Social change in rural areas becomes geared not to the expressed needs of the rural poor but to the maximization of returns to the corporate suppliers of technology and to the domestic elites involved in the new productive processes. As researcher Michael Redclift noted, "The essential point is that, increasingly, technological control of the production process replaces the physical coercion associated with colonization and the North's control of trading relations.... The social relations of production are modified in line with technological change." [17]

These processes of development and social change are quite visible in the agricultural sector throughout the Third World. Examples from Latin America, Africa, and Asia point to the particular ways in which the rural crisis manifests itself. The production of export crops for global food corporations and ecological and population pressures have accentuated inequality in the ownership of land and the growing poverty and urban migration of the rural poor.

Throughout Latin America, from the nineteenth century to the modern era there was a dramatic expansion of production for export – cash crops of coffee, sugar, bananas, cotton, or beef – on the most arable land. A rural elite most often expanded their production by forcibly removing Indian communities and small farmers from the best land. As ownership became increasingly skewed, peasants were left to work on resource-poor land where they produced food for subsistence and depended on small cash incomes to pay mounting debts. Often pressed into labour by private armies, many peasants also migrated to rural estates for seasonal employment at minimum wages. This development of an agro-export industry, closely tied to transnational corporations such as United Fruit in Central America, was highly profitable and accounted for high economic growth rates from 1950 to 1976. The mechanization of the export-oriented estates during the 1970s and the ecological deterioration of the less productive but now overcrowded lands forced thousands of peasant producers off the land and into urban slums where they formed a massive unemployed labour pool for a failing process of industrialization. Given the highly unequal income distribution and rising unemployment, there was no internal market for the industrial production of consumer goods. As food production declined through neglect, many of these countries began to rely on imports of basic food supplies to meet urban needs.[18] A social and economic crisis for the daily survival of the poor became a political crisis for ruling elites. They continued to benefit from the agro-export growth model despite declining world prices for their exports and began to rely on the military and massive human-rights violations to hold an increasingly desperate population in check.

Similar economic forces brought social and economic changes to many parts of Africa. Indeed, it is now widely accepted that the extreme vulnerability of the rural people of the African Sahel has not only been the consequence of natural forces of drought and desertification but was also the result of changing economic and social conditions in the region over the past century, and particularly since 1945. The production and promotion of cash crops, taxation policies, and other incentives for food production have profoundly changed the ability of people in these societies to market and purchase food. These changes have been brought to dramatic focus in the repeated droughts and food crises of the past 15 years. Michael Redclift concluded:

It is thus impossible to separate the ecological processes that determined the strategies of the nomads and poor farmers of the Sahel from the political and economic conditions of the region. Deforestation, intensive agriculture and over-grazing were all responses to reduced

31

environmental flexibility. The growth of commercial farming, especially cash-cropping, had reduced the mutual benefits to both pastoralists and peasant farmers. New crops such as cotton were harvested later than traditional crops and dictated a different seasonal rhythm. Before the 'push' towards commercial farming much of the dry Sahel had resembled 'open-field' agriculture in rural England, the animals grazing on the post-harvest stubble and fertilizing the fields by providing dung. Commercial farming not only displaced the pastoralists from their land; it undermined their symbiotic relationship with food-producing peasant farmers. [19]

Throughout Africa there was a dramatic expansion in the use of agricultural land for cash crops. From 1960 to the 1980s the production of coffee in Africa quadrupled; the output of tea increased six-fold and sugar three-fold; cotton and cocoa production doubled. Over 70 per cent of Gambia's arable land and 50 per cent of Senegal's became used for growing groundnuts. In fact, during a period of drought and starvation between 1965 and 1972 the areas planted with peanuts and cotton in Mali were expanded by almost 50 per cent and 100 per cent respectively, to meet the export needs of Europe and North America. The marketing, processing, and production of these export crops came under tight control by a few transnationals. Only eight companies controlled about 90 per cent of the tea marketed in Europe and North America; Tate & Lyle controlled 95 per cent of the sugarcane imported into the European Economic Community; and four companies accounted for 60 to 80 per cent of the world's cocoa sales. Most often these companies reduced their risks and maximized profits by allowing small producers to grow crops under contract, and they exercised their control through technology and market access. [20]

As increasing numbers of peasants came to grow peanuts and other crops for cash income, they were forced to expand the amount of land under cultivation due to declining prices for their crop and increased input costs for fertilizer. The result was pressure on fallow land, which previously had been normally reserved as insurance against periods of crop failure; decline in the soil fertility; and pressure on the cattle of pastoral people who were also encouraged to expand herds for an export market. The roots of the crisis rest in the global economic system whereby peasants and pastoralists have few alternatives but to participate in economic growth through commercial export crops; as a result they are working along a path towards ecological and social catastrophe, all for the sake of helping transnational businesses and the commercial African elites make profits. [21]

Population pressures and resource scarcity are often cited as the sources of extreme poverty in Bangladesh. Here again the adoption of new agricultural technologies by wealthier landowners (who could afford the costs of the new seeds and required inputs) expanded productivity; but in doing so, they also pushed other more marginal farmers off the land to join a growing class of extremely vulnerable rural workers or urban slum dwellers. Access to food in times of crisis has been closely linked to socio-economic status. In 1974, 81 per cent of those seeking food relief owned no land at all or less than half an acre. [22]

Throughout the Indian subcontinent the development of agricultural and natural resources has been widely equated with growth of an urban market economy; at the same time, these developments have dramatically increased economic polarization. The natural resource base – the agricultural land, the water reservoirs, and the forests, all essential for the survival of the economically poor and powerless, and particularly the millions of tribal peoples – has been severely damaged over the past three decades by the economic demands of industrialization in an urban market economy. Two Indian ecologists, Jayanta Bandyopadhyay and Vandana Shiva, challenged this dominant development paradigm:

The impoverishment of the peripheries and the erosion of the resources and rights of marginal communities actually pay for the material basis of the prosperity of the enclaves. This prosperity can neither be reproduced for regions and peoples whose impoverishment and deprivation are rooted materially and ecologically in the same process of growth nor can the enclavisation process be sustained.... The simplistic dichotomy between the modern and traditional sectors ... needs to be replaced by the more complex contradiction between sectors of society making conflicting and unequal demands on limited resources; between demands for profits and requirements of survival; between sustainable and non-sustainable patterns of resource use, and between socially just and unjust use of natural resources. [23]

While the president of the World Bank can assert that the interests of the poor and a better environment "more often than not" depend on "continued economic growth," there is growing recognition that such development removes control over resources, the forests, the land, water, and their uses, out of the hands of local communities, and even away from nation states, and places them at the service of a market. Throughout India, tribal peoples, forest dwellers, poor farmers, and agricultural workers have organized themselves to protect their resource base from encroachment by the domestic and transnational corporations that view these same resources simply as factors in a global production system. [24]

TOWARDS A NEW MODEL

An alternative development model challenges the prescriptions for economic growth of the World Bank and transnational corporations. A model emerging out of the survival needs of the poor on the land and in their urban communities focuses on attaining sustainable security and livelihoods for the majority. This model challenges the unequal social and economic relationships that perpetuate poverty.

The most important goal of development is not economic growth per se, but

33

rather the strengthening of the capacities and power of the majority poor to improve their lives through access to land, credit, appropriate technology and jobs, and training. The poor must become the *agents* of change in their societies to bring about a redistribution of essential health, education, and other services to meet needs that have been defined through their representative associations and communities. Development is therefore not merely a cluster of social and economic benefits allocated to people in need at the discretion of outside agencies and governments. These social, economic, cultural, and political needs arise in response to unjust structures of society and therefore development must ultimately contribute to the restructuring of social, economic, and political relationships. With powerful elites and governments in the North and South defending their privileges in the present socio-economic order, the issue of control over the development process, of how needs and solutions are articulated at the local and national levels, becomes critical to a development model sustainable for the poor.

For more than a century the distribution of wealth and social power has been the subject of powerful political struggles in countries around the world. Equally important, the desire for national self-determination, for political freedoms and security of person, and for democratic participation in the widest sense has been the foundation for movements that aim to improve working and living conditions. It should come as no surprise, then, that in the Third World the establishment of autonomous, local-based organizations is essential if the poor are to have the political capacity to direct the course of development in their own communities and to influence national and regional development policies that affect their lives.

Finally, development is not only concerned with national economic and social advancement and with building strong political structures to represent the interests of the majority against the interests of a transnational elite. It must also be rooted in an ongoing community praxis of empowerment. This process – empowerment for development – would draw the poor, through their own actions and analysis, into what Suzanne Kindervatter refers to as "an understanding of and control over social, economic and / or political forces in order to improve their standing in society."[25]

To formulate an alternative development strategy it is also crucial to confront the denial of civil, political, and human rights. Throughout the history of Latin America, for example, private armies, the military, and the economic elites have organized political repression to prevent the poor from organizing to challenge the distribution of economic resources. More broadly speaking, as Canadian political scientist Liisa North points out, "The movement towards development and respect for human rights forms part and parcel of the establishment of democracy. Democratic pluralism, opposition organization and critical thought per se cannot be sustained without respect for human rights. Formal political rights, in turn, are

34

of limited value to the individual if his / her basic social and economic needs are not being satisfied."[26]

Since the 1930s the pressures for democratization in Latin America have come mainly from the middle classes, from people seeking to expand their participation in an economic model promoting growth through modernization and industrialization. Yet the achievement of democracy in many countries after 1945 did little to challenge the entrenched structures of power and distribution of economic benefits. By the mid-1970s in almost all Latin American countries this growth model had exhausted itself because it had failed to create a market among the three-quarters of the people who were too poor to purchase common consumer goods. Formal democratic institutions and rights tended to be suspended and replaced by military regimes combining military might with severe political repression against "emerging reformist movements and popular organizations which questioned the social consequences of the economic model and demanded structural redistributive reforms," as North puts it.[27]

The militarization of many Latin American societies was related to the prevailing development model and its economic, political, and cultural manifestations. In ruling circles there was widespread acceptance of a laissez-faire ideology, the belief that growth through private enterprise was the base for economic and social advancement. The military's control over the state did not change the original structure of social domination – that is, the growing partnership between the national private sector, the state, and transnational corporations. Thus, as Brazilian writer Fernando Cardoso states, "Between 1965 and 1975, multinational corporations invested massively in some of the region's countries, particularly Brazil. Willing or not, the military in this case guaranteed that the economy would be internationalized and, through their use of repression, helped contain redistributionist tendencies, thus facilitating capital accumulation and economic growth."[28]

"Post-authoritarian" politics were only able to emerge in the 1980s as trade unions and other popular organizations began to press demands for democratization. These movements for change grew out of years of carefully nurturing "apolitical demands" for survival needs among women in urban slums or among industrial workers hurt by spiralling inflation.[29] Through their actions the region's trade unions, peasant leagues, rural co-operative movements, barrio associations of the urban poor, women's action and education centres, and human rights associations played an essential role in articulating an alternative development model. These movements suggest a model that will ultimately link socially just development with deeply rooted democratization and respect for the broadest range of human rights.[30]

In summary, an effective development strategy requires an analysis of societal and global obstacles to a new redistributive order, starting from the necessity to achieve sustained and secure livelihoods for the poor. Such a strategy will be, therefore, fundamentally rooted in challenges to existing economic and political structures. More often than not the assumption that economic growth and private capital will transform and create a better world for the poor fails to ask "what kind of growth?" and "for whom?". There is a fundamental deception at play. Quoting Rudolf Bahro, Michael Redclift concludes, "We are deceived into believing 'that the commodity world we find around is a *necessary* condition of human existence'" and adds, "But even more objectionable is the deception we are practising on the South. Through complicity with capitalist industrial society we are following a model of development which the South cannot emulate." Redclift points out that the "expanded reproduction of capital" in the North requires the South's resources; but that this system does not have the capacity to "develop" the South in the South's own interests. [31]

Consequently, an alternative development strategy, and a critique of CIDA's policies for the next decade, must take into account the recent dramatic changes in the global economic environment for developing countries. The failure to bring about the New International Economic Order first articulated at the United Nations in 1973 set the stage for economic warfare against many of the debt-ridden developing nations in the 1980s. [32] How has Canada responded to this new environment, and what role has this country played in securing a more favourable economic and political climate for the developing nations? How do the key issues of trade, investment, and debt influence the goals of an aid strategy "to help the poorest countries and people"?

THE GLOBAL ECONOMIC ENVIRONMENT – OR "WHATEVER HAPPENED TO THE NIEO?"

The 1970s were a time of confidence and optimism for Third World nations. Many of them were convinced that they could duplicate the experience of the Organization of Petroleum Exporting Countries (OPEC) and thereby lay the groundwork for an indigenous development process, sustained through local control of resource development. Yet, in what now seems a favourable economic and political climate – rising commodity prices, the formation of producer associations, growing nationalist political movements, and political consciousness of the need to limit and direct the activities of TNCs – the developing countries failed in their resolve to alter the international economic patterns of trade and investment, widely recognized to be the block to a more self-reliant strategy. [33] International "negotiations" were "concluded" (or more often abandoned) in the early years of the 1980s, as the world slipped into a deep economic recession.

While the first years of the 1980s brought deep recession, the later ones saw economic growth and expansion for all the industrial nations. For the less developed countries (LDCs), there was no such economic recovery; rather, declining terms of trade, the drying up of new sources of investment and development capital, and mounting debt obligations plunged most of them into deeper economic and social depression. The consequence was a development crisis unprecedented in the post-war period – which has shown all signs of continuing well into the 1990s.

TRADING WITH THE THIRD WORLD

The economic dimensions of the crisis are evident in the trade data for the decade. Between 1980 and 1986 the less developed countries' share of world trade dropped from 28 per cent to 19 per cent. By 1983 petroleum, exported by only a few Third World nations, accounted for more than half the value of all Third World exports. In 1980 the industrial countries bought 66 per cent of their imports from each other and 29 per cent from developing countries. By 1986, their mutual trading had increased to 77 per cent and the share of developing countries in their imports had been reduced to 19 per cent. [34]

Many of the poorest countries, particularly those in Sub-Saharan Africa, remained heavily dependent on primary commodities as their only source of export earnings. The prices for these commodities (excluding petroleum), since 1980, had lost 30 per cent in real terms and were close to their 50-year lows by 1987. [35] Increased volumes of export crops and minerals provided only small net increases in export revenues.

Trade also became more diversified in the 1980s. The share of primary commodities in the total export earnings of all Third World countries declined from 75 per cent in 1970 to 45 per cent in 1987. But diversification was not the experience of most Third World nations. The growth in manufacturing exports was isolated in a handful of so-called "Newly Industrialized Countries" (NICs), several of which became deeply immersed in debt. [36] By the late 1980s more than 50 Third World countries still relied on primary commodities, such as coffee or copper, for more than half their export earnings. The World Bank reported in 1986 that 14 Asian, 19 Latin American and Caribbean, and 37 African nations depended on only one commodity for more than one-fifth of their yearly export earnings. [37] These economies remained extremely vulnerable to fluctuations in commodity prices.

The real value of non-fuel commodities (when deflated by a measure of the price of manufactures exported by industrial countries) declined sharply from the early 1970s to the late 1980s. In their 1988 reports both the IMF and the World Bank calculated a decline of more than 30 per cent in purchasing power of these raw material exports since 1980 – a year when these prices were already 25 per cent lower than their peak in 1973. [38] Even for those few exporters of manufactures, the rate of growth had slowed considerably, from an average rate of 25 per cent in the 1970s to 9 per cent in the 1980s. In Sub-Saharan Africa and Latin America, the declines in the growth of manufactured exports were even more pronounced. In its 1988 World Development Report the World Bank noted that differences in the structure of trade had marked divergent effects on the major country groups: "The purchasing power of East Asia's exports rose by 45% from 1980 to 1987, after doubling during the preceding five years. In South Asia purchasing power of exports improved moderately, while in Latin America it fell by 26%. Sub-Saharan Africa fared worst. The purchasing power of its exports were cut by more than 50% between 1980 and 1987; this fully reversed the gains of the 1970s."[39] In 1986 alone, falling commodity prices for the low-income nations of Africa resulted in a 32 per cent reduction in their terms of trade with the industrial countries. This meant a $19 billion loss in export earnings in a year when these same countries received a total of $11 billion in net development assistance.[40]

These relatively short-term economic trends must be understood within more global and long-term changes in the world economy. While there is considerable debate as to the root causes, there is widespread agreement that the industrial nations, and particularly the United States, have seen their share of global production reduced, and that since the late 1960s major corporations based in these countries have seen their profits reduced. Corporate attacks against the rights of trade unions, protectionist legislation, and trade restrictions against Third World exports have all been more pronounced in recent years, as the elites in industrial countries blamed their slowing growth rates on lower productivity and the expansion of manufacturing production in the Newly Industrializing Third World Countries.

Recent economic analysis tells a different story. Long-range economic data demonstrate that the overall share of Third World countries in global production was no higher in 1984 than it was in 1948. The industrial production of the NICs, itself showing a long-term trend of slower growth since the late 1960s, "simply recouped the losses in production share which [less developed countries] suffered from 1948 to 1966."[41]

The changing structure of Canadian trade with the Third World became the subject of similar debates around protectionism and resource dependency. Some analysts have argued that Canada should have common cause with Third World economies that are equally dependent on resource extraction and trade.[42] But Canada has always maintained a more privileged position within the global economy than Third World nations and there is strong evidence that we have aligned ourselves with the interests of the industrial countries on key North-South trade issues. Nevertheless, Canada's trading relations with the Third World have changed significantly over the past 15 years.

Trade has always been the most significant economic aspect of Canada's link with Third World societies. Canada's exports of $11.5 billion in 1989 and its imports of $16.2 billion were greater by four times and six times, respectively, than

Commodity Price Index, 1970-1987
(as % of 1979-81 average)

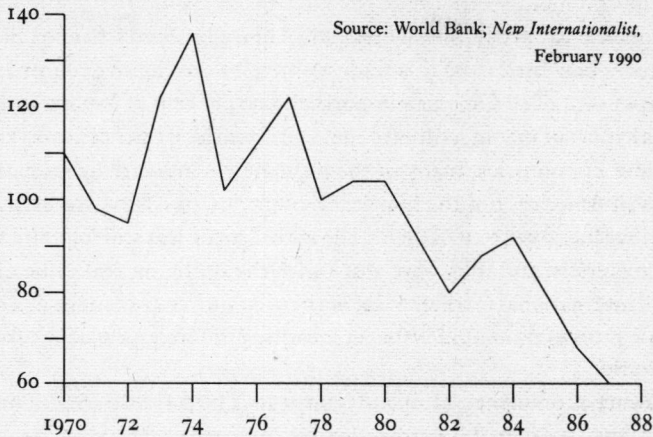

Source: World Bank; *New Internationalist,*
February 1990

the country's total Official Development Assistance (ODA) for the same year. Even when the oil exporting nations and the Newly Industrialized Countries are removed from the Canadian figures, the value of exports and imports still exceeded development assistance.

The preponderance of the United States in Canadian trade is reflected in the share of the Third World in Canada's trading profile. In 1989, imports from the Third World made up only 12 per cent of our world imports, while exports to developing countries accounted for 8.6 per cent. But when the United States is removed from the trade data, the share of the Third World in Canadian imports and exports climbs to 34.5 per cent and 32.3 per cent respectively. Canada also shared in the global decline in Third World trade in the 1980s – from a high in 1980 when Canadian imports from the Third World represented 14.3 per cent of our global trade and exports to the Third World represented 19.3 per cent. As a consequence, the positive trade balance of $4.7 billion in favour of the Third World in 1989 does not make up for the greater loss in value due to the Third World's declining volume of exports to Canada.

Unlike the trading patterns of other industrial countries, only 55 per cent of the total Canadian exports in 1987 were composed of processed goods and finished manufactures. Canadian exports of food, which stood at 26.6 per cent of our trade with the Third World in 1987, continued to play a significant role in our trade relations with many developing countries.

The pattern for imports changed dramatically after 1975. By 1987 finished manufactured products accounted for 53.4 per cent of Canadian imports from the

39

Third World, compared to 12.5 per cent in 1975. Food and unprocessed raw materials declined from 70 per cent of total imports as late as 1980 to 26.7 per cent in 1987, a significant departure from the commonly held image of a Third World dependent on commodity exports.

A closer look at the geographical breakdown of trade reveals that not all developing countries benefited from this trade. A mere 11 developing countries commanded 72 per cent of all Canadian imports and 60 per cent of exports in 1989.[43] Of Canada's export of manufactures to the Third World, 91 per cent was concentrated in these 11 countries, many of them the newly industrializing nations of Asia and Latin America. For the remaining countries, of Africa, Latin America, and the Caribbean, 48 per cent of their trade with Canada was still food and unprocessed raw materials, and they were stuck with the declining real value of those items on the international market. Most of these countries are caught in a dependency on one or two commodities for their earning of foreign exchange from the industrial world.

The growing prominence of manufactures in Third World production and trade has occurred in a climate of protectionism and increased barriers to this trade in Canada, particularly pressed by those sectors (such as clothing and footware) most harmed by the competition. While this impact is real in certain instances, Canadian manufacturing is not about to disappear under a flood of Third World

Geographical Distribution of Canada-Third World Trade Balance (Can$billion)

	1975	1980	1989
Africa (with South Africa)	-0.1	0.6	-0.1
Sub-Saharan Africa (not South Africa)	–	0.2	-0.5
Asia	0.4	0.9	-2.7
Latin America and the Caribbean	-0.3	-0.3	-2.6
Middle East	-1.6	3.2	0.5
Total Third World	-1.9	4.4	-4.7
Newly Industrialized Countries	-0.2	-0.1	-3.5
Selected Eleven Countries	-0.6	-0.4	-4.8

SOURCE: OECD, *Development Cooperation*, Annual Reports, various years.

imports. A study by Canadian economist Gerald Helleiner demonstrated that developing countries' market share of Canadian consumption of manufactured goods only increased from 1.2 per cent in 1970 to 2 per cent in 1980, a level below that of most other industrial countries.[44] Nevertheless, in the mid-1970s the average tariff facing developing countries for their manufactured imports was more than twice that encountered by developed countries, and in the following decade non-tariff "restraint agreements" increased substantially. As Helleiner put it to the Macdonald Commission in 1984: "The view of the developing countries that they are being 'scapegoated' for particular industries' problems and that other industrial countries are being systematically favoured in emerging trade policy at their expense is understandably turned even more bitter by the fact that they have not yet even begun to make a serious mark in the Canadian market [with the possible exception of clothing]."[45]

As an exporter of primary commodities Canada would appear to share common interests with developing countries in trade negotiations and commodity agreements to maintain price levels and increase domestic processing before export. This has not been the case. Instead, Canada has maintained that commodity agreements distort trade by restricting market forces.[46] Trade negotiators have focused their attention on reducing tariffs for processed commodities of export interest to Canada and have been very slow to support changes to similar Canadian tariffs when they affect Third World imports to Canada. Tariff and non-tariff barriers to Third World producers remained the subject of continued discussions at the round of GATT negotiations that began in Uruguay in late 1986 and were scheduled to finish in December 1990. By early 1990 there was every indication that those negotiations had failed to address Third World trade concerns (a pessimism supported by the results of previous rounds). In the 1990s, developing countries will be increasingly shunted to the side in a multipolar global economy.

Global trading patterns in the 1990s are moving towards three regions of relatively equal and autonomous economic strength: Japan and the Western Pacific (including China, New Zealand, Australia, and nine Asian NICs), North America (including Canada and Mexico), and Europe (including the integration of Eastern Europe within the European Economic Community). The political and economic upheavals in Eastern Europe and the reunification of Germany will augment the long-term strength of a new Europe, with its potential market of 750 million people, following the economic union of the European community in 1992. But as the political and economic priorities of Britain, France, and Germany turn to the East, all Third World nations except for a few Asian NICs will suffer. Commodity-exporting Third World countries, dependent on long-standing colonial relationships, will be unable to adapt their economic base to compete against those few countries with more favoured access to the markets of North America and Europe (such as Mexico and the Southern European countries respectively).

INVESTING IN THE THIRD WORLD

Despite economic recession in the North and depression throughout most of the Third World in the 1980s, transnational corporations (TNCs) continued to expand their activities. Ironically, this expansion was accompanied by a dramatic decline in new foreign investment in the Third World in all but the export-oriented industries of the newly industrialized countries. Invested capital was not the means for expansion. Increased control by TNCs was assured through joint production ventures, licencing arrangements, and subcontracts. Corporate integration with long-term suppliers and collaborative arrangements between TNCs based in different countries were similarly important for expansion. As a UN report put it, such institutional arrangements allowed "firms to maintain an economic presence without the risks associated with direct investment."[47] Consequently, the levels of foreign stock of TNCs do not indicate the degree of control exercised by global corporations in host countries.

There has been a significant shift away from corporations based in the United States. Thus, as David Gordon states, "The U.S. and U.K. share of foreign investment flows to the LDCs [less developed countries] declined from 60.4% in 1970 to 53.1% in 1981, while the combined German, Japanese, Swiss, Swedish and Canadian shares increased from 19.9% in 1970 to 33.9% in 1981."[48] Most significant was the rise of Japanese corporations as leading exporters of capital in the 1980s. Japanese global foreign investment increased from U.S.$36.5 billion in 1980 to U.S.$186 billion in 1988; Japanese direct investment in developing countries (mostly those nations centred in the Pacific and East Asian regions) increased more than 700 per cent between 1985 and 1988.[49]

TNCs expanded into services (such as telecommunications, transport, financial, trading, mass media, and public utilities) that by the mid-1980s represented 40 per cent of the world's TNC stock. As the UN report points out, "There appears to be substantial potential for increased transnationalization in the service sector if policies are adjusted to allow for the expansion of service TNC's."[50] National governments, including those in the Third World, have historically protected this sector because of its profound implications for national and cultural development. It is not accidental, then, that the industrialized countries promoted reduced protection in the service sector at the Uruguay round of GATT negotiations.

While never large when measured against other industrial countries, the proportion of Canadian foreign investment flowing to the Third World declined after 1975, from 23.3 per cent of total Canadian investment stock abroad to 16.5 per cent in 1980 and 12.6 per cent in 1985. At the same time total investment by Canadian companies abroad grew by more than 100 per cent between 1980 and 1985; in the same period Canadian investment in the Third World grew by only 44 per cent. Asian countries accounted for almost all of this growth. Investment in Indonesia, for example, increased from $570 million to $1.05 billion from 1980 to 1985.

From the late 1970s, investments of Canadian capital were consistent with the patterns of other industrial countries. Reflecting the global trends, private direct investment of capital from Canada increased dramatically from 1979 to 1982 and then dropped off precipitously as the economic crisis in developing countries became more apparent. [51] In 1987 the flow of private investment capital was in fact reversed. The flow of profits and investments repatriated to Canada exceeded new funds: There was a net capital flow into Canada from direct investments of U.S.$82 million from developing countries. Because of dramatic declines in net private financial flows to the Third World after 1984, total Canadian financial

Net Canadian Financial Flows to the Third World,
1975-1987 (Balance of Flows from and to Canada)
(Real US$million*)

	1975	1980	1982	1985	1986	1987
Official development assistance (including food aid)	1,376.7	1,267.2	1,223.1	1,601.2	1,695.0	1,717.8
Food aid	268.5	89.6	103.2	147.3	152.0	162.2
Official export credits	237.4	747.5	550.8	-150.0	-198.0	194.1
Grants by private voluntary agencies	104.1	120.2	125.7	168.8	176.0	99.3
Direct private investment	469.5	471.5	126.7	86.0	104.0	-74.7
Private portfolio investment (bank loans)	981.2	1,511.1	–	-244.8	-234.0	154.0
Private export credits	-6.4	-45.6	-151.2	-12.8	17.0	90.2
Total public and private flows**	3,194.7	4,104.8	1,903.6	1,666.3	1,557.0	2,185.3
ODA as % of total financial flows	43.1	30.9	64.3	96.1	108.9	78.6
Total private flows including Office Export Credits	1,681.7	2,684.5	526.2	-321.7	-311.0	363.6

* 1986 = 100
** Not the sum of the above.
SOURCE: OECD, *Development Cooperation*, Annual Reports, various years.

contributions (public and private) dropped by an average of a billion U.S. dollars each year up to 1987 – an amount equal to two-thirds of the value of official development assistance in those years.

The high level of foreign investment and control of the Canadian economy (especially by U.S. corporations) has limited the external strategies of the Canadian-based subsidiaries for both investment and trade. Close to 50 per cent of Canada's manufacturing sector is foreign-controlled. As Linda Freeman notes, "Decisions about which part of a transnational corporation will pursue a project in a Third World country are made by the parent corporation in terms of the interests of the transnational as a whole, and not of the Canadian branch plant or of the Canadian government."[52] Only 20 per cent of branch plants use their facilities to manufacture products for export anywhere in the world. Freeman quotes a government study that concludes: "Because of corporate policy, many firms were either unwilling or unable to pursue projects abroad unless financing was available from CIDA or the EDC [Export Development Corporation], and even then, subsidiaries would not pursue follow-up business."[53]

As with that of the United States, Canadian corporate investment in the Third World has historically been concentrated in Latin America and the Caribbean. Almost all of this investment has been in the manufacturing and banking services sector, aimed at production for the local market. The firms include Hiram Walker in Argentina, Crush International and Massey-Ferguson in Brazil, and Stelco in Argentina, Brazil, and Venezuela. A recent North-South Institute review of Latin America suggested that Massey-Ferguson is often dominant in the local market serving agribusiness and large-scale farming technology: "In 1983 its sales of tractors supplied 29 percent of the Argentinian market, while in neighbouring Brazil the company's subsidiary is the largest tractor producer and met 41 per cent of total demand in 1982."[54]

Canadian corporations are the prime sources of advanced-technology transfer – particularly in areas of power generation, telecommunications, mining, and transportation. Their direct investments are therefore tied directly to the growth strategies for economic and social development promoted by foreign and domestic elites. But, as the North-South study concluded, "As long as the notion prevails that inventions and technological advances are strictly private property, and as long as what has been patented and put in the public domain represents only absolute or even discarded stages of technology, it is not going to be easy for Latin America to acquire the modern technology which they urgently need to achieve unprecedented gains in productivity, unless they find the money to pay for it."[55] In the 1980s, the debt crisis, in part the result of inappropriate earlier investment programs, replaced the concern expressed in previous decades by national elites over control of technology and investment.

44

BANKING ON THE THIRD WORLD

In the 1980s the most important issue for the Third World was the mounting debt crisis, the most profound crisis for the world economy since the 1930s. By 1989, debt owed by the Third World totalled U.S.$1.3 trillion and was increasing daily. To fully understand the meaning of the debt for the poor majorities and for development strategies, one cannot ignore its origins – or its beneficiaries. Much of the debt was contracted when international banks assumed global operations by following their clients, the transnational corporations, into the Third World as the companies dramatically expanded corporate investments from the mid-1970s into the early 1980s.

The major Canadian banks aggressively joined the "debt game," seeking out investment opportunities with transnational corporations and governments to finance large-scale investment and development projects, mainly in Latin America. New loans to developing countries from Canadian sources peaked in 1981 when total private bank exposure in the Third World, including oil exporters, reached $34 billion. Of this amount about $24 billion had been committed to countries with critical debt problems. The public sector, through CIDA, the Export Development Corporation, and the Wheat Board, had an additional $5 billion in outstanding loans to 32 "problem" Third World debtor countries.[56]

With the threat of financial collapse in Mexico in 1982, Canadian and other international banks put on hold any new "voluntary" loans. Nevertheless, Canadian bank loans to countries with critical debt problems had increased by an additional $1 billion (to more than $25 billion) by 1986. Banks were "forced" to lend further funds to enable debtors to meet prior debt payment obligations. It was not until 1987 that several of the major Canadian banks were able to reduce their risk by selling off some of their "problem loans" and gradually increasing their reserves against default. By the end of 1989 Canadian banks were still owed a total of $16 billion in outstanding Third World loans, against which they had set aside close to $10 billion in loan loss reserves.[57]

Clearly, the banks had overestimated the strength of the "growth-oriented" capital development model, supported by the TNCs and the economic and Third World political elites. For example, Brazil's debt totalled some U.S.$50 billion in 1980 and grew to more than $121 billion by 1988. When the Brazilian Congress of Trade Unions looked into this spectacular growth in debt, it discovered that $16.6 billion had been loaned to TNCs, guaranteed by the state, for various large-scale industrial and infrastructural "development projects," many still uncompleted and non-productive. Despite some difficulties of exact accounting, the congress concluded that $18 billion to $20 billion had never entered the country, but was deposited in Swiss bank accounts by a local, wealthy elite concerned about the economic and political stability of the country; $41 billion was required for increased import costs due to the devaluation of the Brazilian currency (imposed by the IMF

45

as a condition for further bank loans); and $34 billion had resulted from arbitrary and dramatic increases in interest rates by the central banks of the industrial countries during the early part of the decade. The same study points out that estimated tax evasion by these same TNCs had cost Brazil $6 to $7 billion *annually* since 1973 or about $65 billion in just a decade. [58]

Capital flight – both legal and illegal – was another significant source of the growing debt obligations of developing countries. For instance, Mexico, with a total debt of U.S.$100 billion, lost $36 billion to capital flight between 1976 and 1982 and a further $17 billion in 1982-85. In reviewing the accounts of several Third World countries, Morgan Guaranty Trust Company concluded that Mexico's debt would have been only $12 billion without this capital flight. There are similar dramatic impacts on the debt of other highly indebted countries. [59]

In its 1988 annual report the IMF calculated that the gross capital flight for indebted developing countries ranged from highs of U.S.$31 billion in 1981 and $36 billion in 1982 to a low of $10 billion in 1987. Another review found that capital flight from Latin America alone in 1988 stood at $27 billion. [60]

Militarism throughout the Third World was an equally significant source of debt accumulation. The industrial countries promoted arms sales to one military infrastructure after another, all committed to defending their political and economic interests in the Third World. The resulting political roles assumed by the military hierarchy in turn most often maintained grossly unequal social orders. The Stockholm International Peace Research Institute estimated that 20 per cent of Third World debt could be directly attributed to arms purchases. [61]

Finally, the economic crisis in the industrial countries from 1981 to 1983 was a critical factor in what amounted to an artificial accumulation of debt. At the root of this crisis was the large deficit run by the U.S. government during the 1980s, primarily to sustain its military-industrial complex. This deficit resulted in high interest rates to attract foreign capital to finance U.S. military and government expenditures and a lower U.S. dollar to promote exports and reduce imports. Almost all the increase in debt after 1985 was due to the falling value of the U.S. dollar against other currencies. [62]

It is next to impossible to comprehend what it means to owe financial institutions a total of $1.3 trillion. Yet the significance of this debt lies not so much in the absolute number as in the more fundamental question of "democratic control over investment, the question of the purposes and objectives of our economic life." [63] In seeking a solution, what is at stake is not so much the amount of debt relief offered by the international banks and industrial countries, but rather the quality of the proposals to enhance the position and power of the poor. [64] For it is the majority poor, who in the past reaped few benefits from the original loans, who are now forced to pay – and pay they do, through a constantly declining economic welfare and often with their lives.

There are powerful interests in the heavily indebted countries that have a direct interest in meeting debt repayments, no matter what the burden on the poor. Government bureaucrats and local business elites have been closely associated with TNC investments and the development of large-scale infrastructure projects, all supported with loans from the international banks. Ironically, since the late 1970s this elite has also been responsible for the massive capital flight of their private incomes to the same international banks, as they sought to protect their own incomes from domestic inflation and political risks by investing U.S. dollars in safe and profitable investments in the industrial countries. Meanwhile the populations as a whole must repay the debt incurred, often by the same elites, for the expansion of TNC and other economic projects. [65]

The threat of international bank insolvencies through the inability of the Mexican government to meet its debt payments in 1982 began to concentrate the minds of the industrial and financial elites on the extent of their debt problem. The essential premise of all the solutions proposed by the creditors to the debt crisis has been the non-repudiation of debts by the indebted countries. One U.S. banker was quoted as saying, "If any Latin American country repudiates its debts with us, we have the legal machinery all ready to go. It would be lightning-fast: we would seize all the country's assets on land, on sea and in the air." The deputy secretary of the U.S. Treasury stated rhetorically, "Have you ever contemplated what would happen to the president of a country if the government couldn't get insulin for its diabetics?" [66]

The "solutions" negotiated by Northern governments and the international banks, and enforced by the IMF and World Bank, made even more paramount the role of "free enterprise" in the development process. All new funds loaned to the indebted countries since 1982, largely from the IMF or the World Bank – U.S.$12 billion for Mexico in 1986 alone – have been *returned* to the private banks to pay overdue interest owed, while at the same time generating new debt and compound interest. In turn, the IMF has insisted that developing countries adopt severe "adjustment programs" designed by the industrial countries that control the fund. The most common features of these programs have been:

- ❏ the devaluation of the currency (to promote exports and reduce imports);
- ❏ drastic cuts in government expenditures, particularly social spending, food subsidies, and other price controls;
- ❏ privatization of government enterprises; and
- ❏ cuts in the public service, drastic controls on wage increases, and higher taxes to reduce inflation.

All major national and international development institutions stressed "the key importance of structural adjustment" as "the only way in which most developing countries can make real headway in the struggle to develop."[67] Yet structural adjustment has failed profoundly to encourage development or even realize its own stated objectives. Programs assume that domestic economic growth will only occur with a greater role for private enterprise, both domestic and international, and that economic policy must be devoted to maximizing government revenue to pay foreign holders of debt. Nevertheless *The Economist* reported that the highly indebted developing countries were no better off in 1987 than they were in 1983. During that period they slashed imports by U.S.$2 billion and increased the volume of exports by 4 per cent per year. All of these adjustments were offset by the declining prices for their commodity exports.[68] Declining prices were a direct result of adjustment policies that encouraged developing countries to increase their exports of raw materials; but increased volume from all producers resulted in significantly reduced prices.[69] Thailand, for example, following the advice of the IMF, increased the volume of rubber exported by 31 per cent between 1984 and 1985, and at the same time took in 8 per cent less revenue because of declining prices. The industrial countries, consuming the largest share of the earth's resources, have been the main beneficiaries of these misguided policies.

The impact of these practices on the poorest sectors of Third World populations has been unseen and largely left out of the calculations of the IMF or its masters in the developed world. In April 1988 the IMF reaffirmed its policy of making its loans to less developed countries conditional on the adoption of strict economic controls. It sought to "improve program design so as to protect the poorest segments of the population during the period in which adjustment policies are being implemented."[70] Conditionality is still the main requirement to get new loans, largely granted to prevent default on old debt. In the words of the director of the IMF, "In adapting our financial instruments, we are seeking to promote adjustment, not postpone it; to strengthen it, not dilute it; and to sustain it, not short-circuit it."[71] But there is overwhelming evidence that it is the adjustment policies themselves, and their objectives, that have determined the harsh impact on the poor.

Canadian banks have been fully supportive of IMF and World Bank adjustment policies that orient domestic economic activities to assure that banks will receive maximum recoveries on their loan portfolio. The Canadian banks have recognized that "a balance has to be struck between economic hardship and the maintenance of a country's obligation to repay its debt."[72] They have encouraged moderation in austerity policies so that some economic growth can occur. But they have also been adamant that any new private loans for development to encourage such growth are out of the question. The private banks are clear that they have no moral obligations to consider the situation of the poor and they continue to reject debt forgiveness as a solution to the crisis.[73]

A Brazilian trade union leader described the impact of the debt as a war against the people of the Third World: "Instead of soldiers dying there are children, instead of millions of wounded there are millions of unemployed; instead of destruction of bridges there is the tearing down of factories, schools, hospitals, and entire economies."[74] In Bolivia malnutrition in the Cochabamba Valley, one of the country's most agriculturally productive regions, increased from 11 per cent to 56 per cent from 1983 to 1986. After food subsidies for the poor were withdrawn, food prices rose by ten times in the 12 months up to 1984. Brought to the edge of bankruptcy by the low price of tin on the world market, Bolivia stopped making payments on its debt.

Throughout the Third World poor women, already on the margin of societies, are hurt most by the IMF conditions:

Direct cutbacks in health care, childcare, old people care, mean that women are implicitly expected to take up the additional burden of providing these services. With rising inflation, mounting unemployment, falling wages, and cuts in subsidies on basic goods and public services, poor women face the daily survival crisis of their families. When educational services are cut, again it is women who suffer the most personally as adult education classes in literacy for women are the first to be axed. In most cultures, it is women, the food providers, whose spending power is reduced by falling wages and rising prices.[75]

In Africa the expansion of cash crops to increase export earnings has been at the expense of growing food for local consumption and again women are the most dramatically affected as they are pushed on to less fertile land for food production.

There is no doubt that a significant increase in financial resources to meet development objectives for the poor is essential if the world is to avoid further catastrophe and increased hardship. Those who propose increased *new* investment in the Third World often ignore the nature of governments and elite interests in both the developed and less developed countries – interests that have determined the direction of these investments in the past.

For the IMF and the large industrial countries, "External financing is crucial for the debt strategy" – not least because it "helps authorities in debtor countries to mobilize the social consensus needed for a steady implementation of adjustment and structural reform policies." Yet at the same time during the 1980s there have been significant shifts in the sources of financing for the Third World away from private sources, as well as the large net capital losses from debtor countries draining potential resources for development to the developed countries.

Lending to developing countries from private banks fell from a high of U.S.$75 billion in 1980 to $3 billion in 1986 and $8 billion in 1987, and almost all of the recent loans were "forced lending" to prevent default on existing loans. The lending has not been replaced by the growth of official development assistance, nor has private corporate investment increased to supplement the fall in private lending.

49

Net Transfer of Resources to All
Developing Countries, Fiscal Years 1980-1987
(US$billions)

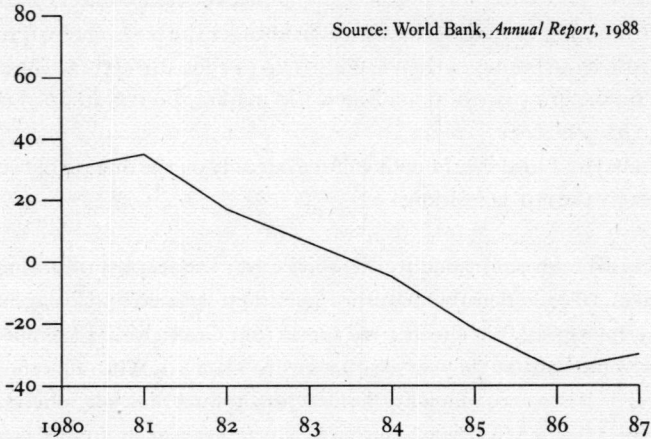

Source: World Bank, *Annual Report*, 1988

The highly indebted countries also suffered a severe net loss of billions of dollars after 1982 – in the order of U.S.$180 billion for Latin America, equal to about 45 per cent of the total stock of debt owed by these nations. Canadian banks alone took in an estimated $4 billion more than they invested in Latin America in 1988.[76]

The economic health of the international financial system based in the industrial countries has been the overriding concern. The six major Canadian banks increased their reserves against loan losses from less than 20 per cent of risky loans in 1985 to more than 60 per cent at the end of 1989. Such provisions provided no relief for the Third World. The potential losses to Canadian banks that loaned the funds in the first place were still covered. Loss of income to the banks because of these reserves (up to 45 per cent of outstanding loans), some $7 billion, was absorbed by the Canadian public through income tax relief for the banks. By 1990 some Canadian banks (for example, the Toronto Dominion and the Royal) had sold off almost all of their Third World loan portfolios on the secondary market at a significant discount. Having done so, they were able to reap further tax credits on the actual loan loss *above* the 45 per cent allowed for reserves.[77] Third World debtors received no such relief, even for debt held by the public sector. They continued to be responsible for the full repayment of their loans with interest.

Having created large reserves against loan losses, some banks, such as the Canadian Imperial Bank of Commerce, suggested that it might be possible to write down "unpayable" portions of current loans (that is, the portion they have pro-

tected with reserves). They nevertheless link such "debt forgiveness" to a continuation of a Third World "development model" that has provided maximum
extraction of "surplus" capital from the debtor countries to service their loans in
the past. One Canadian banker reported that any "new funds" from Canadian
banks through agreements for debt reduction would only be for "trade related
credits." He strongly supported a "case-by-case market-based strategy" for debt
reduction, where the IMF and World Bank would guarantee payment of servicing
on the balance with severe penalties if there were any further defaults. [78]

Faced with the threat of default, "Most commercial lenders shared an interest
in concerted lending to protect the financial system and gain time to reduce their
individual exposures to developing countries."[79] Development of adequate food
supplies at affordable prices for the poor and of housing, health, and education
programs has all been subsumed to these interests. Indeed, by 1988 lending to
indebted countries by government sources and the multilateral banks had "left the
banks with stronger balance sheets than at any time since 1982." According to a
report in *The Economist,* there was "no longer the risk of a domino-like collapse of
the banking system" as a result of any future default on Third World loans. [80]

The poor in the Third World have not been nearly so fortunate. The hopes for
global economic justice and a New International Economic Order have been
replaced with deepening dependent relationships and concomitant poverty
unprecedented in the post-war period. Through trade and investment relations in
the post-war period, and debt policies in the 1980s, Canadian business interests
participated directly in sustaining the orthodox growth model for development in
the Third World. In the 1980s these economic factors more openly and directly
structured our aid relations with the Third World than in previous decades.

A NEW STRATEGY FOR
CANADIAN DEVELOPMENT ASSISTANCE?

The failure of earlier development strategies and the global crisis for the poor
throughout the Third World set the stage in 1987 and 1988 for a review of Canada's
aid programs and the presentation of a new strategy for Canadian development
assistance. The CIDA strategic review, *Sharing Our Future,* seemed to recognize the
limitations of earlier aid strategies and set out a new course for aid policies in the
1990s.

International humanitarianism has been a longstanding and explicit goal for
Canada's aid program. The primary objective therefore has been to reach and
improve the lives of the poor in Asia, Africa, the Caribbean, and Latin America.
Emergency relief work quickly gave way to projects for long-term development
assistance in health, housing, education, or for improved agricultural methods. At
the same time, international humanitarianism, rooted in public support for the
social justice ideals of the post-war industrial welfare state, lived in tension with

notions of Canadian economic and political self-interest in the global economy. Unfortunately, these motivations of self-interest began to dominate the debate on development policy in the 1980s as the Third World entered into a period of economic collapse without parallel since the Great Depression of the 1930s.

The appropriateness of development policies for the 1990s must take account of their ideological origins in this tension between two ideological paradigms so evident in the 1980s. In Canada, as in other industrial donor countries, free global movements of capital according to international corporate interests in profit and the "free market" regulation of the economy became politically dominant over the post-war welfare policies of state intervention aimed at solving national social and economic problems. Correspondingly, in the plans for an appropriate development model for the 1990s, the humanitarian aspects of development assistance have been increasingly reduced, replaced by a greater reliance on market forces and corporate economic and political interests, which are both national and international in scope.

CIDA president Marcel Massé, returning in 1989 to manage Canada's aid program after four years as the Canadian director at the IMF, clearly articulated policy goals using the framework of the neo-liberal growth and development model. He repeatedly pointed to the central importance of structural adjustment programs as the basis for effective Canadian aid. In doing so, he also revealed the ideological option which these policies imply: "With the market approach to economic growth in spectacular triumph over the planned economies of Eastern Europe, and their centralised allocation of resources, structural adjustment looks more relevant with each day that passes."[81] Although he recognized that "the difficulty with [the world market] is that those who already have an advantage in that market have considerable amounts of power in determining its structure," Massé accepted that this structure must be taken as given by the poor countries.[82]

These strategic directions for aid policy are not new: Canadian foreign policy and economic self-interest have always been implicit within CIDA's priorities. By 1989, however, the response to the development crisis of the past decade by the elites of the industrial countries, co-ordinated by international financial institutions, had tied Canadian aid programs more closely than ever before to the same economic policy objectives that had dramatically reduced social and economic conditions for the poor in the Third World.

AN OVERVIEW OF
CANADIAN DEVELOPMENT PROGRAMS, 1975-88

In recent time the official aid program (ODA) appeared to become a vital component of Canadian foreign policy, growing from $760 million in 1975 to $1.24 billion in 1980 to $2.52 billion in 1986 – an absolute increase of more than 200 per cent in ten years. But when measured against Gross National Product, the increases in aid from 1984 to 1988 merely regained what was a substantial decline in the years from 1979 to 1983. Moreover, assistance fell sharply as CIDA budget cuts in 1989 reduced aid as a percentage of GNP to approximately 0.43 per cent, far short of the OECD and UN target of 0.7 per cent of GNP. When measured in constant (1987) U.S. dollars, there was an 8 per cent decrease from 1975 to 1980 and only a 25 per cent increase between 1975 and 1987. The 24 per cent increase between 1987 and 1988 was eliminated with negative growth in 1989, a marginal increase in 1990, and the impact of inflation and increased administration costs.

The geographic shifts in the allocation of ODA from 1975 to 1987 demonstrate the relevance of aid to Canadian foreign-policy interests. Assistance to South Asian countries declined significantly after the mid-1970s while resources for Latin America (including the Caribbean) and other Asian countries nearly doubled. The aid to these other Asian countries reflects a significant growth of programs for Indonesia and the Philippines in the late 1980s. The shifts also reflect a renewed interest in Latin America and the Pacific Rim countries that exhibited strong economic growth in the 1980s.

Canadian Overseas Development Assistance

	$Can	Real $US*	% of Canadian GNP
1975-76	760.0	1,505.0	.50
1980-81	1,241.1	1,387.0	.43
1982-83	1,670.0	1,341.0	.41
1983-84	1,812.0	1,515.0	.45
1984-85	2,097.0	1,755.0	.50
1985-86	2,174.0	1,810.0	.46
1986-87	2,522.3	1,848.0	.50
1987-88	2,624.1	1,885.0	.48
1988-89	2,930.7	2,339.0	.49
1989-90	2,720.0**		.43***

* 1987 = 100, including effects of exchange rates.
Based on GNP Deflators, 1970-87, OECD, *Development Cooperation in the 1990s,* 1989, Table 55.
** CIDA, 1990-91 estimates, Part III, Expenditure Plan.
*** Estimated.
SOURCE: CIDA *Annual Report,* Ottawa, Supply and Services Canada, various years; OECD, *Development Cooperation Report,* Geneva, various years.

Geographic Distribution of Net Official Development Assistance
1975-87

	1975	1980	1987
Sub-Saharan Africa	35.5	38.6	38.3
Americas	9.4	12.8	16.6
South Asia	41.8	34.8	24.9
Other Asia & Oceania	6.5	5.8	12.9
Middle East & North Africa	6.8	8.0	7.3

Source: OECD, *Development Corporation: 1989 Report,* Paris, December 1989, p. 212.

Surprisingly, despite the human and ecological crises so visible in Africa during the 1980s, Sub-Saharan Africa's share of ODA did not change over this 12-year period. In a 1988 study the United Nations concluded that Africa required a *minimum* of U.S.$9.1 billion in *additional* funding a year to meet development needs into the 1990s – on top of $14.6 billion to cover debt servicing. Few people anywhere expect that these additional funds will be forthcoming. Indeed these countries are expected to continue to experience declining real net resources, just as they have over the past decade. Canada's disbursements to Sub-Saharan Africa declined from a high of $856 million in 1984 to $344 million in 1986 and $520 million in 1988.[83]

Despite the overall growth of the program, important changes in Canadian development assistance occurred during the 1980s. Commercial objectives became more apparent in both the sectoral focus for many projects and in their links with other foreign economic policies. The maxim that economic growth is a central goal in the Canadian development strategy for the poor of the Third World has remained constant in the post-war period. Nevertheless, CIDA reacted in the 1970s and early 1980s to the changing development needs of Third World nations with increasingly sophisticated social, cultural, and economic programs for human development and self-reliance. But by the mid-1980s the government was placing new attention on the private sector as the primary and even pivotal agent for the economic and social recovery of the developing countries. Monique Landry, the Minister for External Relations and International Development, stated on two separate occasions:

In many developing countries, the private sector is emerging as the engine of national development. Indeed countries that have experienced the highest levels of economic growth are those in which growth is led and sustained by a thriving private sector. Developing countries know this.... Many governments that used to emphasize a dominant public sector, and strictly regulate all aspects of economic life, are now actively encouraging the private sector to play a greater entrepreneurial role.

If the private sector in developing countries is going to play the key role in their development efforts, Canadian business has to be the key ally in Canada's development program. The private sector offers the biggest reservoir of skills, know-how and capacity that we can draw on. Without the active participation of our business, industry and professions, it would not be possible for Canada to deliver a high quality development program relevant to the needs of the developing countries.[84]

The relationship of aid and trade was reinforced by the integration of Canadian trade policy into the Department of External Affairs in 1982. A policy of "concentrated bilateralism" attempted to focus aid programs on about 40 countries, many of them – for example, Indonesia, China, Colombia – chosen in part for their trade potential for Canada.

CIDA made explicit its concern to involve the private sector in development programming by establishing the Industrial Co-operation Program (ICP) in September 1978 and the Business Co-operation Branch in 1984. The petroleum industry was also to have its own "window" on energy development in the Third World through the Petro-Canada International Assistance Corporation (PCIAC), established in 1981. The proportion of the Canadian bilateral aid budget allocated to sectors of advantage to Canadian business has remained high throughout the history of the aid program.[85] Combined with PCIAC, by 1988 these programs totalled $104 million, an amount almost equal to CIDA's responsive program for the Canadian non-governmental voluntary sector ($106.2 million) in that year.

Concentrating on the manufacturing sector, the Industrial Co-operation Program grew significantly in the 1980s, from $23 million in 1983 to $60.6 million in 1989. Much of its assistance targeted the newly industrializing countries of Asia (Thailand, Malaysia, India, China) and Latin America, as well as projects in Egypt, Cameroon, the Ivory Coast, and Tunisia in Africa. Commenting on Latin America, the North-South Institute pointed to the ICP as an important resource for the Canadian private sector "to penetrate markets in Latin America and support Canadian firms seeking opportunities for investment, joint ventures and transfers of technology to these markets."[86]

Canadian business has also benefited through the tying of the Canadian bilateral and food aid programs to purchases of Canadian goods and services. Tied aid has been a controversial issue for recipient countries since the 1960s. The Canadian economist Gerald Helleiner pointed out that in 1982 Canada had the second highest percentage of bilateral aid tied to Canadian procurement among

Growth in the Industrial Co-operation Program,
Petro-Canada International Assistance Corporation, and
Canadian NGOs*, 1982-87 (Can $million)

	82-83	83-84	84-85	85-86	86-87
ICP	16.3	23.1	38.5	27.8	32.4
PCIAC	18.7	42.7	53.2	22.6	58.1
Subtotal	35.0	65.8	91.7	50.4	90.5
NGOs	53.9	81.0	74.9	93.9	97.4

* Non-governmental organizations receiving matching grants from CIDA's NGO division.
Source: CIDA, Annual Report, Various Years.

the OECD countries (at 64.8 per cent versus an OECD average of 32.5 per cent). By 1987 the tied component of bilateral aid had declined to 58.7 per cent (still significantly higher than some other OECD donors) and the OECD average had increased to 53.6 per cent.[87] CIDA itself estimated in 1990 that between 60 and 65 per cent of ODA returned directly to Canada for procurement of goods and services or for program administration.[88] According to Helleiner, tying aid "not only raises costs to the recipient but it also distorts priorities, biases techniques inappropriately, raises administrative costs, slows disbursements, and renders it difficult to employ it for rural projects or poverty alleviation purposes."[89] It is therefore not surprising that in the 1980s Canada also joined other OECD countries in a trend that saw the explicit combining of development assistance with commercial export credits for developing countries. The Export Development Corporation in Canada is responsible for providing credit to importers of Canadian products. In the period 1985-87, 80 per cent of its export financing was directed to developing countries, for a total value of $1.7 billion.[90] In 1987 official export credits accounted for 22 per cent of total Canadian government funds allocated to Third World countries (compared to only 7 per cent for OECD countries as a whole).[91] One researcher, D.W. Gilles, calculated that in 1986 joint financing had been used 17 times since 1978 for projects with a total value of $1.1 billion, of which CIDA's portion was $300 million. A further 19 projects were under consideration at the time.[92] A review of CIDA lines of credit with developing countries in the summer of 1988 revealed 8 out of 48 lines of credit with EDC participation. But these eight represented more than 30 per cent of the total value of ODA credit facilities.

There is little doubt that linking aid with export credits increases the "tying effectiveness" of the aid program. The use of these credit mixes cannot help but emphasize and encourage large-scale infrastructural projects – hydro power, rail-ways and port facilities, transportation and communications equipment – all geared to Canadian export interests. For example, in May 1988 CIDA announced a grant of $18 million for the extension of Pakistan's Tarbela Dam on the Indus River. The dam would be the world's largest earth-filled dam for hydro power and irrigation, and the EDC was to advance $52 million in export credits at commercial rates for the project.[93] Gilles concluded: "These devices ... may alter the empha-sis of the donor's program since they are largely focused on middle income LDCs of good market potential, and on the newly industrializing countries.... In sum, both poorer nations, which are not likely to be the targets of most export credit projects, and the poorest groups are likely to suffer from the current practice of blending aid into concessional export loans."[94]

In the 1990s, program lending and balance of payments support, related to Canadian official participation in structural adjustment programs, are to become a larger component of bilateral aid agreements with indebted Third World coun-tries (in 1989 these facets already made up 20 per cent of bilateral budgets). Export credits will become an increasingly important component of these agreements.

Through all of these financial mechanisms, CIDA has been assisting the private sector by giving priority to development projects where Canadian corporations have expertise and are in a position to obtain contracts. Such project decisions, made on political and trade grounds, are often inappropriate for an aid strategy directed at the more basic needs of the poor for health, education, or housing. The analysis and approval process for these large-scale and capital-intensive projects has widely accepted these donor self-interests while sometimes making technical improvements based on economic and environmental studies. They very seldom take into full account the broader and significant socio-economic impacts on those most harmed – the rural poor or indigenous peoples displaced from their land and way of life.[95]

NEW DIRECTIONS FOR THE 1990S –
"SHARING OUR FUTURE"

The 1988 Charter of Principles and Priorities for Canada's aid program for the 1990s puts "the alleviation of poverty first" and "aims to strengthen the ability of people and institutions in developing countries to solve their own problems in harmony with the natural environment."[96] *Sharing Our Future* puts forward a progressive vision of development – poverty alleviation, human resource develop-ment, social justice and human rights, gender issues, and sustainable development – which could challenge the traditional infrastructural and resource-oriented CIDA programs of the past.

The report describes a renewed partnership relationship between Canadians and Third World peoples. It elaborates important organizational changes within CIDA itself and the decentralization of operations, including CIDA personnel based directly in the Third World. It describes a more humane approach to the questions of debt and structural adjustment for the poorest nations. Yet the business and trade orientation of the Conservative government's economic and foreign policies towards the Third World (and the increasing influence of U.S. priorities in setting these policies) remains dominant.

A PRIORITY FOR THE POOR

By tackling poverty as a first priority in its aid strategy, CIDA sets out a challenge for itself: "Poverty ... is lack of access – access to education, to jobs, to income, to services, and *to decision-making power.* Poverty is inequity in opportunities, in the distribution of benefits of growth, and in social justice."[97]

But there are powerful forces poised against a more just world for the poor. These are economic and political interests, in both developing and developed countries (including Canada), which require inequality of opportunity and social injustice to maintain their profits, power, and influence. Marcel Massé, as president of CIDA, recognized these structural impediments for more equitable development as a "given" for CIDA.[98] Consequently, in lauding the new directions of *Sharing Our Future* we must also ask what changes will be essential if the Canadian aid program is to meet these important goals.

Making the poor a priority does not only mean bringing more resources for community-based development of agriculture or health or more scholarships and technical training in Canada for Third World people. More essentially, the question of "empowerment" must assume priority in any such development strategy. The organizations of the poor must be able to transcend their unequal status and gain access to economic resources and political power. The poor themselves must be able to participate in defining their needs through these and other community organizations.

The possibility of resources and greater social justice for the poor has been significantly influenced by the structure of the aid relationship. In the words of Robert Chambers, who has analysed the effectiveness of development projects, "There seems to be a general law that the greater amount of money spent and the shorter the period in which money has to be spent on a rural development program, the more likely it is that the rural elite will benefit disproportionately."[99] Decentralization of the Canadian aid program to regional offices may bring the aid bureaucracy "closer to the people we are trying to reach – the poorest" but it may also do little to tackle the question of dependency and accountability to the poor in community-oriented aid programs that CIDA might support.[100]

More often than not, projects are designed, appraised, and evaluated according to institutional structures and guidelines that remove and transfer power and control from intended beneficiaries (particularly rural people and communities) to national and international development institutions. Contrary to large-scale, highly visible, and capital-intensive infrastructural projects, historically a major focus for CIDA, poverty-focused projects are often small and highly dispersed. With a different emphasis on building local institutions controlled by the poor, the agency might seek to integrate the development of *local* technical and organizational skills within these projects. With greater geographic dispersion and an emphasis on qualitative and sensitive social and political relationships, such projects would resist monitoring and evaluation techniques using quantitative socioeconomic indicators. Fixed-project budget allocations, on the other hand, can conflict with slow project implementation, with the major logistic problems of remote areas, and with the pace of the project as determined by the level and nature of local participation. [101]

But CIDA does not share a vision of development focusing on the empowerment of the poor. Despite the rhetoric of sustainable development and support for the poorest, the underlying (and sometimes overt) assumption of *Sharing Our Future* is the growth model of the private sector. *Sharing Our Future* suggests, "Developing countries must be able to earn their living by producing goods and services that meet demand, and selling them on the international market – functions at which the private sector excels." In expanding production for export with the encouragement of Canadian aid to the private sector of developing countries, these countries will "advance toward self-reliant prosperity, so they can become equal partners with industrialized countries in creating global prosperity." [102] This brings to mind the fundamental deception – that the South can duplicate the industrial development model of the North – which depends on the exploitation of the South's human and natural resources.

According to CIDA, the Canadian business community will be an equally "indispensible partner in international development efforts, and the main source of the goods and services needed in development projects." The strategy proposed is to double the budget for the Industrial Co-operation Program over the following five years. Already this program increased from $28 million to $61 million between 1985 and 1988. The plan suggests that business can make substantial contributions to human resource development through participation in technical and vocational training. The report goes so far as to ensure that bilateral "Country-focus project submissions will include an analysis of the private-sector capacity to undertake the project." [103] Implementation of these objectives will certainly solidify the role of the aid program as an instrument for enlarging the market in Third World countries for Canadian technologies and business services, with minimal concern for their relevance to the development needs of the poor. The report therefore sets out a direction for Canadian aid policy in the 1990s that is entirely consistent with the Canadian aid priorities of the past decade.

Many policy analysts have pointed to the easing of tied aid in the new strategy as an important recognition that these restrictions were inappropriate for meeting a poverty-focused development strategy. Indeed, particularly for Africa and the poorest countries, provisions for tied aid have been substantially reduced, from 80 per cent to 50 per cent; but for other countries they remain at just over 66 per cent for the bilateral programs; and all food aid is tied to 95 per cent Canadian purchases. Multilateral food aid is also tied at 80 per cent. If we apply these new tying provisions arbitrarily to the 1986 CIDA bilateral and food aid budgets, the amount of tied aid is reduced by about 15 per cent. Even then the level of Canada's tied aid remains higher than many OECD countries.

For CIDA, the solutions to the debt crisis remain clearly within the purview of the IMF and World Bank and under the political control of the governments of the industrial countries and their private banks. Moreover, "The cornerstone of the international approach is continued internal structural adjustment by the debtor countries. This is a long-term remedy designed to re-establish a climate of growth in developing countries and ensure the effective management of their economies and of the foreign aid they receive." [104] Yet there is clear evidence that such adjustments impinge disproportionately on the urban poor and rural landless. The aid strategy does not cover the broader economic and social issues of debt and structural adjustment in any detail. Nevertheless there is little doubt that CIDA sees its aid program as alleviating the worst impacts of poverty, which may not have been adequately taken into account in earlier structural adjustment programs. For example, "Food aid will be used especially to help the recipient country reform its agricultural policy and / or carry out structural adjustments." [105] As political scientist Cranford Pratt noted, these stated concerns for the poor must be placed against the "marked tendency for government officials in the Departments of External Affairs and Finance to accept as professionally unquestionable the analysis offered by the IMF and the World Bank." [106]

In 1987 and 1988, and again in 1990, Canada took important decisions to forgive the official debt (but not commercial debt owed to the banks or the EDC) of the poorest countries in Sub-Saharan Africa and the Caribbean. Earlier CIDA had decided to convert all outstanding loans to grants for the least developed countries. Thus the proportion of the bilateral aid program in the form of loan disbursements fell significantly, from more than 40 per cent in 1981 to less than 10 per cent in 1987 – to zero in 1988.

There is no doubt that the debt issue is a social justice issue of the first order. Yet in making poverty alleviation the highest priority, *Sharing Our Future* passes over the implications of the debt for the poor. Global reform of North-South economic and *political* relationships is essential if the debt issue is to be resolved in favour of the social and economic well-being of the poor. The current Canadian policy, though, places responsibility solely on the developing countries to reform their economies, albeit with "a human face," so that Northern financial institutions may still extract the maximum return for their loans.

ECOLOGICALLY SUSTAINABLE DEVELOPMENT

The CIDA submission to the World Commission on Environment and Development (the Brundtland Commission) in 1986 recognized that the Third World faces an interlocking environmental and development crisis where environmental destruction goes hand-in-hand with social injustice, "almost like two sides of the same coin."[107] *Sharing Our Future* strongly reiterates the important priority for environmental concerns in development planning. In its words, "The burden [of environmental crises] is being felt most severely by the poorest people in the poorest countries, where resource exploitation combined with a poor understanding of the environment has led to ecological disaster."[108] Sustainable development must break "a vicious circle of poverty and environmental destruction." Yet the report provides few clues as to how CIDA will realize its objectives of environmentally sustainable development. While CIDA recognizes that the poor have been the victims and not the agents of environmental destruction, the agency offers little analysis of the poverty-ecology dynamic.

The political and economic relationships underlying unequal land distribution or urban unemployment receive no attention in the analysis. There is even less concern that the potential for sustainable development will be blocked by Third World debt, unequal trade, and inappropriate investment by market-oriented TNCs. In the Sahel, for instance, sustainable development is not just a matter of "re-establishing the socio-ecological balance" through "stabilization of the plant cover, restoration of the food balance and energy development."[109] The "choice" for peasants to grow more food and improve land use may not be present where debt payments, transnational food corporations, and the IMF push extensive cash-crop production to maximize export earnings.

Large-scale infrastructural projects (hydroelectric dams and massive irrigation), widely criticized for their impact on the environment, remain a priority as essential for a "development" model based on and supporting Northern industrialization. In July 1988, CIDA approved a major project to provide Indonesia with railway equipment to move coal from the Bukit Asam mine in South Sumatra to the coast. Earlier in 1988 CIDA approved a third extension for the Tarbela Dam in Pakistan. These projects are not put against alternative development models that favour the poor, whose very survival may be threatened by the exploitation of the resources (land, water, forests) required for a distant urban industrial plant.[110]

Inevitably, environmental concerns are reduced to a methodology of project assessment and planning rather than an approach to development itself. Even the CIDA submission to the Brundtland Commission admitted that "While the new jargon [eco-development, sustainable development] may represent some advance in thinking, the words are too often devoid of more than good intentions" with little operational content to distinguish the sustainable from the unsustainable. [111] Indian commentators Jayanta Bandyopadhyay and Vandana Shiva go even further:

Under such pressures [from a global environmental movement] the agencies of [the] classical model of development are turning 'environmental' overnight, and a new co-optation attempt has begun.... The new packaging of [the] old development model is characterised by the co-optation of the language of the movements to decorate the contents of old development programmes guided by the market and biased in favour of those who already enjoy economic superiority. [112]

No doubt this is an extreme view; but it clearly situates the rhetoric and the limits for a commitment to incorporate environmental concerns into the planning and implementation of projects by CIDA and the multilateral development banks.

The actual history of environmental sensitivity within CIDA is mixed at best. [113] Planning documents suggested in the early 1980s that an in-depth environmental review would affect only 5 to 10 per cent of CIDA's projects, despite the high concentration of forestry, hydro and petroleum energy, and agricultural assistance among CIDA's programs. CIDA has taken on a growing number of specific environmental projects: wildlife planning, social forestry, training in environmental impact assessment, and the management of natural resources.

Sharing Our Future gives high priority to environmental impact assessment for bilateral and NGO projects likely to involve environmental risks. But impact assessment often takes little account of the more global social costs inherent in development based on the ideology of economic growth. Rather, these planning methodologies are "top-down" and their aim is to ameliorate some of the worst aspects of environmental risks, balancing them against other economic and social benefits.

There are many examples. Deforestation is not only a problem associated with overpopulation and lack of environmental consciousness among the rural poor. Michael Redclift argues, "As increasing quantities of charcoal are required for urban consumption, rural women and children have to spend greater amounts of time gathering firewood. It is in this sense that we must pose the problem not in terms of whether or not there is an energy crisis, but rather, *whose* crisis it is." [114]

International agencies, working with the assumption of a "market ideology" for forestry so common in the industrial countries, attempt to balance the competing claims of timber concession holders, cattle ranchers, and peasant transmigrants on tropical rainforests. But deforestation fundamentally threatens the livelihood of the rural poor while enriching ranchers and lumber companies. Development programs that focus on deforestation in analysing environmental impact cannot avoid confronting the powerful political and economic interests that determine the use of forest resources in the first place. The assassination in December 1988 of Chico Mendes, a leader of the Brazilian rubber tappers' union who led a campaign against cattle ranching and for the protection of the rain forests, points to these political stakes.

Quite often CIDA and Third World governments have chosen large-scale technologically sophisticated projects because they produce quick and visible results largely under the control of the sponsors. Thus the minister responsible for CIDA assured the Canadian business community, "Infrastructural projects will, of course, be undertaken [in the new CIDA strategy], but with a lot more training, follow-up, downstream input and technical assistance needed to ensure that developing countries can manage such projects." [115] Encouraging the private sector to provide such training and advanced technology is not likely to create viable ecological alternatives for the poor. Proper alternatives require a flexible planning process where communities, villagers and the poor themselves analyse their resources, develop long range plans to manage basic resources to sustain their livelihoods, and secure sufficient political and economic control over these resources to carry out the plans. [116]

The pressure for this alternative approach comes not from international aid agencies but from the increasing political sophistication of Third World ecological movements rooted within popular organizations of the poor. In India popular ecological movements have grown among the rural poor as they respond to threats to their survival. These have focused on the impact of large river valley projects, the protection of forest resources held in common, movements against the environomental impact of aluminum production in the Gandhamardon hills, or the anti-drought and desertification movements in the dry areas of Orissa and Maharashtra. [117]

Northern environmentalists have focused their attention on the worst consequences of advanced industrialization. In contrast, in the South it has been impossible to separate "environmental poverty" from the structural conditions that determine the resources available to the poor for their survival. [118] Thus, ecological movements in the Third World are slowly evolving an alternative model for economic development which is based on "the various dimensions of social movements, for survival, for democratic values, for decentralized decision making at the local levels." [119] These movements are increasingly demanding political support for these alternatives from their governments.

More visible has been the international pressure on the multilateral banks to turn down and restrict large infrastructural and industrialization projects that have had profound environmental impacts on the urban and rural poor. Some governments, including Canada, have supported greater environmental awareness at annual meetings of the World Bank. But the real pressure for change has been the result of important alliances between environmental movements in the North and popular ecological movements in the South. [120] Again, the issue is not improved environmental impact assessment by bank staff, as posed by Northern governments. Rather, the international alliances have lobbied against specific and massive hydroelectric projects in the Amazon region of Brazil, for example. There they have demanded the recognition of the rights of indigenous peoples to survival and to self-determination. They have asked for assurances that there will be mandatory consultation with all populations affected by bank loans before approval is considered. [121]

CIDA and the Canadian government have responded in the aid strategy to growing public consciousness in Canada of serious global environmental issues. Nevertheless, the degree to which CIDA works for sustainable development remains to be tested against the practice of bilateral and multilateral programs. The environmental movement in Canada has put forward suggestions for a more open and public assessment process for CIDA projects. Public accountability would ensure discussion around a more holistic approach to the social, economic, and political determinants of an eco-development responsive to the needs of the poor.

GENDER AND DEVELOPMENT

Sharing Our Future also gives high priority to women in its development policy. It does so largely from a perspective that development must involve both men and women to be effective and that women must be included as both agents and beneficiaries of the development process. The policy, however, provides little analysis about why women have been excluded from the current development process and how women's special interests and needs will be assessed within the agency. At best the strategy may ensure some attention to the "practical gender interests" of women, that is, those immediate needs arising out of the difficult living conditions that women in the Third World face on a daily basis. However, CIDA – along with most Canadian NGOs – has not seen the transformation of gender relations as a fundamental goal in achieving development objectives. From the perspective of gender, development strategies must include and incorporate into project planning methodologies and analysis of the roots of women's subordination to men both in productive work and in reproductive work (ensuring human life through activities in the home). Alternative development strategies that recognize the importance of social transformation and political relations in the development process cannot ignore gender relations and the organization and participation of women around gender issues.

HUMAN RIGHTS AND DEVELOPMENT PRIORITIES

One of the most important aspects of the strategy put forward in *Sharing Our Future* is the commitment that "human rights will be fully integrated into Canada's development policies." Concern for human rights is to be a part of the process of determining the channels of assistance and the level of bilateral assistance for each eligible country. Moreover:

In countries where violations of human rights are systematic, gross and continuous, and where it cannot be ensured that Canadian assistance reaches the people for whom it is intended, government-to-government (bilateral) aid will be reduced or denied. Canadian assistance will be channeled through our development partners working at the grassroots level – such as non-governmental and multilateral organizations – who can ensure that the aid goes directly to the poor in areas where it is most needed. [122]

In the Third World, where the systematic violation of the rights of the poor, trade unionists, women, and peasant organizations is all too common, a human rights policy cannot be separated from the humanitarian motivation of development assistance. But like other aspects of the aid strategy, CIDA's concern for human rights should not be separated from the totality of Canada's relations with governments that have brutalized or killed those who are organizing to improve their lives.

Development and human rights are inseparable. Where the development model has given priority to rapid economic growth (as it has in many countries in Southeast and South Asia and Latin America), the resulting gross disparities in the distribution of wealth are defended by military or oligarchic governments in the name of political stability. Oppression of those who resist has been necessary to "promote confidence among private domestic and foreign investors." [123] At the same time it is clear that authentic development for the poor will not occur unless the majority participate and obtain some measure of equality and control through autonomous and representative organizations, either national or local. The systematic violation of human rights by the "national security state" has not only been a humanitarian concern but has also sustained "traditional" development models of economic growth. The targets for systematic repression have not been random: the leaders and members of peasant co-operatives, trade unions, community organizations, literacy and health workers, and human rights organizations themselves continue to be the victims. There is no doubt, as Jan Pronk puts it, that "The link between human rights and development aid is based primarily on the degree to which priority is given to policies fostering structural change benefitting the underprivileged, the poorest and the oppressed." [124]

To what degree do Canada's record over the past decade and CIDA's policy linking human rights and development sustain an active commitment to social justice? The policy has consistently followed a "pragmatic" approach. Its goal has been "to assimilate human rights considerations into the broader matrix of foreign policy and to determine the relative weight of human rights considerations in the light of overall objectives in particular circumstances." [125] The question of human rights and development has been reduced to questions of effective *delivery* of the aid program and does not look at the development model promoting abuses at a societal level. In cases where CIDA determines that effective delivery of the aid program is possible and where concern for human rights collides with other commercial or strategic foreign-policy goals, CIDA argues that cutting off assistance would doubly punish the poor. Thus, the agency was able to rationalize a renewal of bilateral aid to El Salvador in 1986 and in 1990 and seemingly "ignore" the human rights implications of a government waging a massive and destructive war on its people. There is also a range of policy options, short of cutting off aid, that a government could choose to demonstrate its abhorrence of abuses. [126]

The degree to which human rights concerns have been integrated within the larger matrix of Canadian foreign policy has not been encouraging. Canada has taken important initiatives at the United Nations where delegates have been instrumental in various resolutions censoring major human rights violators around the world, including the government of Guatemala and that of Chile under Pinochet. But in the multilateral banks our delegates have repeatedly refused to apply human rights criteria to "development" loans to these same regimes. The concerns have also not influenced government support for trade and private investment in countries practising systematic violation of human rights. These economic relations sustain the very model of economic development that these regimes defend through repression of popular organizations.

The human rights policy has also not limited Canadian arms sales to Third World armed forces. Military sales to Third World countries have increased three fold since the 1970s. Researcher Ernie Regehr of Project Ploughshares calculated, "In the years 1980 to 1984, Canada approved military exports to an estimated forty-five countries. Of these, twenty-eight, or sixty per cent, were cited by Amnesty International as carrying out, on a regular basis, torture, disappearances, brutal treatment of dissidents and other forms of human-rights violations." [127] Increasingly, military production in Canada is justified in terms of its high-technology spin-offs and its contribution to economic growth. Marketing in the Third World becomes essential to attain large production runs of this sophisticated equipment. As the world moves closer to disarmament in the early 1990s, the Third World will become the primary focus for trade in armaments. Already, 60 per cent of the armed forces in the world are in the Third World and these countries account for 80 per cent of all arms imports. [128]

The International Defence Programs Branch of the Department of External Affairs functions to promote Canadian-made defence products abroad. This list of products includes "a full range of crowd control and anti-riot equipment … [with] a special Canadian-made vomiting gas that paralyzes the victim for up to five minutes." [129] Such equipment clearly raises questions about the serious intent of the Canadian government to implement a consistent human rights policy in its aid programs, which are purportedly designed to assist the poor to confront social and economic inequalities and to support Third World NGO partners to protect their human rights.

LINKS AND LIMITATIONS

The Canadian aid strategy *Sharing Our Future* cannot be divorced from the economic and political imperatives of Canadian foreign policy in the 1990s. These imperatives arise from several inter-related factors: the creation of a North American trade bloc through the Free Trade Agreement with the United States, the creation of a multipolar global trading economy that in turn will marginalize almost all Third World nations, and the overwhelming acceptance by the Canadian state of market-based economic and social policies.

The language of sustainable development, human rights, and the priority on the alleviation of poverty is shared by development agencies from CIDA to the World Bank to Oxfam, but the reality of economic interests – the accumulation of wealth by powerful transnational corporations and banks – tells a different story. At the same time there is little doubt about the profound social crisis for the poor of the Third World. In many cases their very survival demands not only a radical restructuring of North-South relationships but also a transformation of domestic social and economic relations. Popular movements in Africa, Asia, and Latin America are seeking alternative development strategies that effectively challenge the dominant economic growth models imposed on their countries by the industrialized world. If Canadian aid policies are to be relevant for these alternatives, they cannot be separated from Canada's global economic policies and from public support within Canada to create more ecologically sustainable and equitable models for economic and social development.

There has been considerable debate among political economists about Canada's role and position in the world economy. Since 1945 this debate has largely focused on the Canada-U.S. relationship, the impact of U.S. corporate investment in and control over major sectors of the Canadian economy, and the overwhelming predominance of the United States in Canadian trade patterns. These links, along with the more recent movement towards continental economic integration, have directly influenced Canada's economic and political relations with the Third World. They will be increasingly important in setting the limits for the future policy options available to a dependent and weakened Canadian state.

In the 1980s the declining position of the United States in the world economy raised widespread fear that U.S. industry was being threatened by "unfair" competition from the large integrated trading bloc of the European Economic Community (EEC) and from Southeast Asia (particularly Japan). The Canada-U.S. Free Trade Agreement responds to a Canadian concern (promoted by Canadian businesses and U.S.-based transnational corporations operating in Canada) that this country might lose its access to the neighbouring market through growing U.S. protectionism. These fears were reinforced by the movement for European economic integration in 1992 and the focus on profound political and economic changes in Eastern Europe towards market-based economies linked to the EEC. Australia and Japan, along with the newly industrializing nations of Southeast Asia, have been actively promoting closer trade and investment ties based on the paramount power of Japanese capital in the region.

Nevertheless, Canada's "privileged access" to the U.S. market has substantial costs. There is little doubt that Canadian "structural adjustments" in the late 1980s – deregulation of foreign corporate investment; privatization of state companies; and major cuts in social programs for the poor, regional economic development funds, and unemployment insurance – drew Canada closer to the U.S. goals for continental integration. Mexico has adopted similar policies to denationalize its economy in the face of great pressure to reach an agreement to reduce its massive debt load. Some analysts conclude that "movement toward U.S.-Mexico free trade has great momentum" under President Carlos Salinas de Gortari, who "has staked his political future on an export-led growth strategy." [130]

After the 1988 election the Progressive Conservative government initiated a clear political agenda for Canada based on this imperative of continental integration and structural adjustment for Canada. The ideological framework is taken for granted by those implementing government policy, including the CIDA bureaucracy. In 1989 Canada took a leading role through the IMF and World Bank to organize a structural adjustment program for Guyana and CIDA officials started to refer more openly to similar requirements as a basis for CIDA development assistance in Africa and Latin America. A 1989 manual for CIDA program officers was clear on this point: "Accordingly, to be considered effective adjustment assistance, Canadian aid should normally be provided within the framework of an agreed IMF / IBRD [World Bank] supported program. In addition, CIDA aid flows in support of adjustment should ideally be conditional upon the existence and achievement of IMF / IBRD conditions." A request to recognize the serious macro-economic implications of these policies for trade and investment priorities was dismissed as "external" and "beyond the purview of Desk Officers at CIDA." [131]

The Macdonald Royal Commission predicted that a free trade agreement with the United States would give rise to "expectations of co-operative Canadian behaviour [in foreign policy] that would be much more deeply rooted in American perceptions than they are now." [132] Once this agreement was in effect, the economic dimensions of this integration for Canada's Third World relationships in terms of trade, investment, continental energy policies, and services (consulting and banking) became more evident. As tariff and non-tariff barriers are removed, goods produced within the North American "common market" will have a potential economic advantage over those same goods produced in Third World countries. The possibilities of Canadian preferential treatment of Third World products will be further reduced. The "harmonization" of Canadian and U.S. non-tariff rules and regulations governing trade will more likely reflect the protectionist mood of the U.S. Congress because U.S. laws will have weight over and above the Free Trade Agreement itself (unlike Canadian laws, which must be brought into line with the agreement).

Bernard Wood, former director of the North-South Institute, warned in 1985 that free trade could affect "Canada's real or perceived freedom to act on trade, investment, technology, finance and monetary policies, and on wider international questions of East-West and North-South relations, support for multilateral institutions, and even military links and involvements."[133] These issues are all central to development policies and to whether Canada can assist the poor in the Third World to achieve greater equality and control over their own economies and societies. The practice of Canadian foreign policy in responding to the challenges of social change movements in Third World societies in the next decade will demonstrate the degree to which Canada has taken on a U.S. agenda – an agenda not only economic but also profoundly political.

Notes

1. Willy Brandt et al., *North-South: A Program for Survival: The Report of the Independent Commission on International Development Issues under the Chairmanship of Willy Brandt* (London: Pan Books, 1980).

2. In real terms, using constant 1987 prices and exchange rates, total official development assistance to developing countries declined from U.S.$49.9 billion in 1980 to $47.9 billion in 1988. For the industrial countries of the North, development assistance in real terms increased from $36.0 billion to $44.8 billion in 1987 U.S. dollars. See Table 13 in Organization for Economic Cooperation and Development (OECD), *Development Cooperation in the 1990s: 1989 Report* (Paris, December 1989).

3. Ibid., Table 20, Table 13; and OECD, *Financing and External Debt of Developing Countries: 1988 Survey,* Tables V.4, V.6, V.8 (Paris, 1989).

4. IMF, *Annual Report 1988* (Washington, 1989), pp.18,32; and OECD, *Development Cooperation,* Table 13; World Bank, *World Development Report 1988* (Washington, 1989), p.27.

5. Susan George, *A Fate Worse Than Debt* (Harmondsworth, Middlesex: Penguin Books, 1988), pp.136,121. For the decline in living standards see also the detailed studies in the various essays in Giovanni Andrea Cornia, Richard Jolly, and Frances Stewart (eds.),

Adjustment with a Human Face, vol.1, Protecting the Vulnerable and Promoting Growth (Clarendon: Oxford University Press, 1987); and *Andean Focus,* July 1987, p.3.

6. This reassessment is reflected in three parliamentary reports: *For Whose Benefit? Report of the Standing Committee on External Affairs and International Trade on Canada's Official Development Assistance Policies and Programs* [Winegard Report] (Ottawa: Supply and Services Canada, May 1987); The Standing Senate Committee on Foreign Affairs, *Canada, the International Financial Institutions and the Debt Problem of Developing Countries* (Ottawa: Supply and Services Canada, April 1987); and *Competitiveness and Security: Directions for Canada's International Relations,* presented by the Right Honourable Joe Clark, Secretary of State for External Affairs (Ottawa: Supply and Services Canada, 1985).

7. CIDA, *Sharing Our Future: Canadian International Development Assistance* (Ottawa: Supply and Services Canada, 1987). The last previous stategy document from CIDA had been *Strategy for International Development Cooperation 1975-1980* (Ottawa, Supply and Services Canada, 1975).

8. CIDA, *Canadian International Development Assistance: To Benefit a Better World: Response of the Government of Canada to the Report by the Standing Committee on External Affairs and International Trade* (Ottawa: Supply and Services Canada, September 1987), p.6.

9. In taking this point of departure I recognize the ongoing debate around the issue of motivation in Canada's aid program. It is beyond the scope of this analysis to review this literature. See, for example, the review by K.R. Nossal, "Mixed Motives Revisited: Canada's Interest in Development Assistance," *Canadian Journal of Political Science,* Vol.XXI, No.1 (March 1988); and Robert Carty and Virginia Smith, *Perpetuating Poverty: The Political Economy of Canadian Foreign Aid* (Toronto: Between The Lines, 1981).

10. Brandt, *North-South,* p. 172. (emphasis added).

11. CIDA, *Canadian International Development Assistance,* pp.13,18-19. At the same time that these are the assumptions of the development strategy, there is also less optimism. In the global environment for development of the 1980s, "This process [of development] is neither automatic nor certain in a world of managed economies, vested interests, volatile prices and interest rates and protectionism." (p.13).

12. World Bank, *World Development Report 1988,* p.32; IMF, *Annual Report 1988,* pp.50-51.

13. Raymond Williams, *The Year 2000* (New York: Pantheon, 1983), p.206.

14. The literature on the "development of underdevelopment" over the past two centuries is vast. See, for example, André Gunder Frank, *Latin America: Underdevelopment or Revolution: Essays on the Development of Underdevelopment and the Immediate Enemy* (New York: Monthly Review Press, 1969); Walter Rodney, *How Europe Underdeveloped Africa* (London: Bogle-L'Ouverture Publications and Dar-es-Salaam: Tanzania Publishing House, 1972); and Eduardo Galeano, *Open Veins of Latin America: Five Centuries of the Pillage of a Continent* (New York: Monthly Review Press, 1973).

15. Brandt, *North-South*, p.187. For an earlier discussion of the role of transnational corporations in development, see Brian Tomlinson, "Reaching an Impasse: The North-South Debate," and D'Arcy Martin, "Facing the Octopus – The Transnational Corporation," in *Ties that Bind: Canada and the Third World*, ed. Robert Clarke and Richard Swift (Toronto: Between The Lines, 1982).

16. Martin Mittelstaedt, "World Learns to Love Multinationals," *The Globe and Mail*, October 20, 1988. Those corporations based in the Third World commanded a 3.2 per cent share of the total market represented by these 600 corporations.

17. Michael Redclift, *Development and the Environmental Crisis: Red or Green Alternatives?* (London: Methuen, 1984), p.120.

18. For a discussion of agro-exports in Central America, see Solon Barraclough and Michael Scott, *The Rich Have Already Eaten: Roots of Catastrophe in Central America* (Amsterdam: Transnational Institute, 1987), pp.39-77,69-72.

19. Redclift, *Development and the Environmental Crisis*, pp.65-66.

20. See B. Dinham and C. Hines, *Agribusiness in Africa: A Study of the Impact of Big Business on Africa's Food and Agricultural Production* (Trenton, N.J.: Africa World Press, 1984), pp.33-35,187; and Frances Moore Lappé and Joseph Collins, *Food First: Beyond The Myth of Scarcity* (Boston: Houghton Mifflin, 1977), p.41.

21. See, for example, R. Franke and B. Chasom, "Peasants, Peanuts, Profits and Pastoralists," *The Ecologist*, Vol.11, No.4 (July-August 1981).

22. Ibid., p.76.

23. Jayanta Bandyopadhyay and Vandana Shiva, "Political Economy of Ecology Movements," *Economic and Political Weekly* (India), Vol.XXII, No.24 (June 11, 1988), p.1226.

24. Ibid., pp.1129-1130,1225-1226.

25. Suzanne Kindervatter, *Nonformal Education as an Empowering Process* (Boston: University of Massachusetts, 1979), p.150.

26. Liisa North, "The Geopolitical Situation in the Americas and the Canadian NGO Response," mimeo, presentation to a CIDA / NGO consultation, Central America Policy Alternatives (CAPA), Toronto, 1988, pp.5-6.

27. Ibid., p.6. North provides an excellent summary of the history of the development model in Latin America and its relation to the forces for democratization (pp.6-13). See also Liisa North (ed.), *Between War and Peace in Central America: Choices for Canada* (Toronto: Between The Lines, 1990).

28. Fernando Henrique Cardoso, "Democracy in Latin America," *Politics and Society*, Vol.15, No.1 (1986-87), p.26.

29. Ibid., pp.35-37.

30. See, for example, North, "Geopolitical Situation," pp.15-17.

31. Redclift, *Development and the Environmental Crisis*, p.54.

32. Susan George suggests this dramatic language in her notion of Financial Low Intensity Conflict, "an ongoing, dialectical ... global struggle, exactly like [Low Intensity Conflict] but played out on another terrain." George, *Fate Worse Than Debt*, p.234.

33. The literature on the NIEO and the international negotiations around trade and investment issues in the 1970s is vast. Tomlinson, "Reaching an Impasse," traces the roots of this failure and the resistance of the developed countries. See also J.A. Finlayson, *Limits on Middle Power Diplomacy: The Case of Commodities* (Ottawa: North-South Institute, 1988), which (like this chapter) sets out Canada's positions within this debate.

34. Figures are from the General Agreement on Tariffs and Trade (GATT), quoted in George, *Fate Worse Than Debt*, p.73.

35. North-South Institute, "Commodity Trade: The Harsh Realities," *Briefing Paper*, Ottawa, May 1988, p.1.

36. Third World NICs include Brazil, India, Mexico, Singapore, South Korea, and Taiwan.

37. North-South Institute, "Commodity Trade," p.2.

38. IMF, *Annual Report 1988*, p.18; World Bank, *World Development Report 1988*, p.25.

39. World Bank, *World Development Report 1988*, p.27.

40. J. Sinclair, "Africa and Structural Adustment: A Personal Perspective," in North-South Institute, *Structural Adustment in Africa* (Ottawa, 1988), p.37.

41. David Gordon, "The Global Economy: New Edifice or Crumbling Foundations," *New Left Review*, No.168 (March-April 1988), pp.34-40 provides a detailed review of the literature. Gordon points out: "The Latin American and Asian NICs accounted for 7.8% of total world exports in 1950; their share dropped to 3.7% in 1966 and had climbed back to 6.3% in 1984." (p.45).

42. See the review of these positions in Glen Williams, "On Determining Canada's Location Within the International Political Economy," *Studies in Political Economy*, No.25 (Spring 1988). From a different perspective, the North-South Institute has a research program focusing around the distinct interests of Canada in global trade and commodity negotiations as a "Middle Power" in alliance with other likeminded states (particularly the United States and European Economic Community). See Finlayson, *Limits on Middle Power Diplomacy*.

43. These countries are: China, India, South Africa, Venezuela, Mexico, Brazil, Taiwan, Singapore, Hong Kong, South Korea, and Indonesia.

44. G.K. Helleiner, "Underutilized Potential: Canada's Economic Relations with Developing Countries," a study prepared for the Royal Commission on the Economic Union and Development Prospects for Canada, Ottawa, February 1984, pp.22-23.

45. Ibid., p.23. For discussion of tariffs, see pp.23-27.

46. For many commodities, such as copper and other metals, these "market forces" really refer to the transnational corporations' intra-firm exchanges linked to a global system of mining and processing plants tied to market shares in the industrial countries.

47. United Nations Centre on Transnational Corporations, *Transnational Corporations in World Development: Trends and Prospects,* New York, 1988.

48. Gordon, "The Global Economy," p.42.

49. See "The Yen Warriors," *South,* No. 111 (January 1990), p. 13; and OECD, *Development Cooperation,* Table 55.

50. UN Centre on Transnational Corporations, *Transnational Corporations,* p.4.

51. Helleiner, "Underutilized Potential," pp.44-45.

52. Linda Freeman, "The Effects of the World Crisis on Canada's Involvement with Africa," *Studies in Political Economy,* No.17 (Summer 1985), pp.132-133.

53. Ibid., pp.133-134.

54. Wilson Ruiz, "A View from the South: Canadian / Latin American Links," North-South Institute *Briefing Paper,* Ottawa, March 1988, p.8.

55. Ibid., pp.9-10.

56. Exact figures are difficult to come by. The amounts here are calculated from Helleiner, "Underutilized Potential," p.49; Roy Culpeper, "Beyond Baker: The Maturing Debt Crisis," North-South Institute *Briefing Paper,* Ottawa, May 1987, pp.4-6; and Ten Days for World Development, "Working Paper of the Canadian Churches on the International Development Crisis," Toronto, August 1988, pp.7-8.

57. See a series of articles in *The Globe and Mail,* October 17, 1989, November 8, 1989, November 10, 1989, and November 20, 1989, for details of increases in loan-loss provisions, which at the time totalled about $10 billion.

58. These estimates have been made by researchers with the Brazilian Congress of Trade Unions (CUT). Quoted in Mennonite Central Committee, "New Study Shows Brazil's Debt Already Paid," *Newsletter on the Americas,* September 1988, p.12.

59. P. Kirby, "Latin America: How Capital Flight Affects Debt," *IDOC Internazionale,* No.2 (April-May 1987), p.19; and J. Petras and H. Brill, "Latin America's Transnational Capitalists and the Debt: A Class Analysis Perspective," *Development and Change,* Vol.19 (1988), p.187.

60. IMF, *Annual Report 1988,* p.31; see the line "Other Foreign Asset Accumulation, net" for Capital Importing Developing Countries in Table 10, Developing Countries: External Financing, 1980-87. *The Financial Times of Canada* (Toronto), April 3, 1989.

61. Cited in George, *Fate Worse Than Debt,* p.22.

62. World Bank, *World Development Report 1988,* p.30.

63. John Foster, "Notes for an Opening Address, Ecumenical Church Consultation on Third World Debt," Inter-Church Taskforce on Corporate Responsibility, Toronto, April 1987, p.2.

64. See Ten Days for World Development, "Working Paper," for a church perspective on a set of criteria for assessing the proposed resolutions of the international debt crisis from the

point of view of meeting the basic needs of the majority. Among other questions, Ten Days asks, "Will the proposal strengthen political structures through which the will of the majority can be expressed and through which the people can participate in shaping the decisions which will affect their lives, giving them a sense of their own worth and capacity?"

65. Petras and Brill, "Latin America's Transnational Capitalists," pp.187-191; this article provides a good summary of the interests of transnational capitalists.

66. Quoted in George, *Fate Worse Than Debt*, p.68; this book offers a useful overview of the various "solutions" proposed for the debt crisis by the political and banking elites of the industrial countries.

67. Marcel Massé, President of CIDA, "Testimony before the Standing Committee on Foreign Affairs and International Trade," House of Commons, Ottawa, October 31, 1989.

68. "Survey of World Economy," *The Economist*, September 24, 1988, p.58.

69. George, *Fate Worse Than Debt*, p.61.

70. IMF, *Annual Report 1988*, p.48.

71. S. Sparks, "Camdessus' Quiet Revolution," *South*, September 1988, p.21.

72. There have been several in-depth meetings between representatives of Canadian churches and bank officials to exchange views on the debt crisis. This quote is taken from a summary of one of these meetings.

73. The multilateral banks borrow money for these loans on the world market from the same private banks using guaranteed contributions from their member governments as collateral.

74. Quoted in George, *Fate Worse Than Debt*, p.238.

75. "The International Debt Crisis," *ISIS Women's World*, No.17 (March 1988), p.4.

76. *The Globe and Mail*, April 1, 1989, p.B2; *The Financial Times of Canada* (Toronto), April 3, 1989.

77. Margaret Philips, "Royal Fattens Cushion on Third World Loans," *The Globe and Mail*, November 8, 1989, p.B1.

78. Ed Neufeld (Vice-President, Royal Bank of Canada), "Testimony before the Standing Committee on External Affairs and International Trade," House of Commons, Ottawa, October 12, 1989.

79. IMF, *Annual Report 1988*, p.34.

80. "Survey of World Economy," p.65. The real interests of the banks were also revealed by Ed Neufeld before the Standing Committee on External Affairs when he said, "Perhaps the most important achievement [of] the case-by-case approach to resolving the debt problem [is that] it bought time for the international financial system to strengthen its balance sheets, and thereby ... contributed to the avoidance, so far, of an international financial crisis." Neufeld, "Testimony."

81. Marcel Massé, "Adjustment in Perspective: Notes for Remarks to an International Colloquium on Structural Adjustment and Social Realities in Africa," Institute for International Development and Cooperation, University of Ottawa, November 17, 1989, p.1.

82. Marcel Massé, "Testimony before the Standing Committee of External Affairs and International Trade," House of Commons, Ottawa, October 31, 1989.

83. OECD, *Development Cooperation*, Table 36, p.243.

84. The first quote is from Monique Landry, "Building Development Partnerships: Speech to the Canadian Exporters Association," Toronto, May 11, 1988, p.2; the second is from Monique Landry, "Private Sector Partnerships," speech on the launching of Building Partnerships for Tomorrow, a research project of the International Business Research Centre of the Conference Board of Canada, Montreal, November 5, 1987, p.4.

85. Aid allocated to economic infrastructure (transportation, communication, energy, industry, mining, and construction) of interest to Canadian business accounted for at least 30 per cent of the bilateral aid budget from 1975 to 1983.

86. Ruiz, "A View from the South," p.10.

87. OECD, *Development Cooperation*, Table 5, p.209.

88. CIDA, *1990-91 Estimates*, Part III Expenditure Plan, Ottawa, March 1990, p.34.

89. Helleiner, "Underutilized Potential," pp.50-51; and OECD, *Development Cooperation*, Table 3, p.193.

90. Calculated from Export Development Corporation, *Annual Report* (Ottawa: Supply and Services Canada, 1985, 1986, 1987).

91. OECD, *Development Corporation*, Tables 53 and 58.

92. D.W. Gilles, "Commerce over Conscience?: Aid-Trade Links in Canada's Foreign Aid Program," Centre for Developing Area Studies, McGill University, discussion paper no.48, Montreal, May 1988, p.8.

93. Monique Landry, "The Third Tarbela Extension," CIDA press release, Ottawa, May 20, 1988.

94. Gilles, "Commerce over Conscience?" p.10.

95. Robert Chambers, "Project Selection for Poverty-Focused Rural Development: Simple is Optimal," *World Development*, Vol.6, No.2 (1978), p.212; see also Bruce Rich, "Funding Deforestation: Conservation Woes at the World Bank," *The Nation*, January 23, 1989.

96. CIDA, *Sharing Our Future*, pp.23,24.

97. Ibid., p.23 (emphasis added).

98. Massé, "Testimony."

99. Chambers, "Project Selection," p.210.

100. The quoted phrase is from CIDA, *Sharing Our Future*, p.35.

101. See Chambers, "Project Selection," for a full discussion of these issues. See also Kari Levitt, "Canadian Policy in the Caribbean," in House of Commons, *Report to the Sub-Committee of the Standing Committee on External Affairs and National Defence on Canada's Relations with Latin America and the Caribbean*, Ottawa, June 1982.

102. CIDA, *Sharing Our Future*, p.59.

103. Ibid., p.77.

104. Ibid., p.57. Canada's political support for the proposals of the U.S. secretary of commerce, Nicholas Brady, to look at debt reduction for the most hard pressed Third World countries is similarly tied to IMF-World Bank structural adjustment policies. It attempts to draw these international institutions, and hence the Canadian public, into guarantees of interest and principle payments to the private banks once loans have been reduced to their secondary market value.

105. Ibid., p.54.

106. Cranford Pratt, "Canadian Policy Towards the International Monetary Fund: An Attempt to Define a Position," *Canadian Journal of Development Studies*, Vol.6, No.1 (1985), p.17.

107. CIDA, "Written Submission to the World Commission on Environment and Development," Ottawa, May 26-27, 1986, p.2.

108. CIDA, *Sharing Our Future*, p.44.

109. CIDA, *Sharing Our Future*, p.45.

110. See the recent analysis of these issues for the World Bank in Rich, "Funding Deforestation."

111. CIDA, "Written Submission," p.30.

112. Bandyopadhyay and Shiva, "Political Economy of Ecology Movements," p.1231.

113. See CIDA, "Written Submission," pp.13-24; and J. Ferretti, P. Muldoon, and M. Valiante, "CIDA's New Environmental Strategy," *Probe Post*, Winter 1987.

114. Redclift, *Development and the Environmental Crisis*, pp.27-28.

115. Monique Landry, "New Development Directions: The Growing Role of the Private Sector," speech to the Canadian Exporters' Association, Ottawa, October 6, 1987, p.5.

116. For an excellent analysis of the lessons from development projects in planning for sustainable development, see R. Chambers, "Sustainable Rural Livelihoods: A Key Strategy for People, Environment and Development," mimeo, paper for the International Institute for Environment and Development, Conference on Sustainable Development, London, April 28-30, 1987.

117. Bandyopadhyay and Shiva, "Political Economy of Ecology Movements," p.1125.

118. See the discussion of various tendencies in the environmental movements, North and South, in Redclift, *Development and the Environmental Crisis*, pp.40-79.

119. Bandyopadhyay and Shiva, "Political Economy of Ecology Movements," p.1231.

120. NGOs from the North have also played a role in pressing reforms onto the agenda of the World Bank; see the "Position Paper of the NGO Working Group on the World Bank," mimeo, New York, October 1989.

121. For an analysis of the impact of this international environmental movement, see P. Aufderheide and B. Rich, "Environmental Reform and the Multilateral Banks," *World Policy Journal*, No.2 (Spring, 1988); see also various statements by Pollution Probe International and Energy Probe in Canada over the past decade.

122. CIDA, *Sharing Our Future*, p.31.

123. Jan Pronk, "Linking Aid and Human Rights," *Development: Seeds of Change*, No.3 (1984). Pronk provides a useful discussion of these issues.

124. Ibid., p.73.

125. CIDA, *Elements of Canada's Official Development Assistance Strategy, 1984* (Ottawa: Supply and Services Canada, 1984), p.34.

126. See Robert Matthews and Cranford Pratt, "Human Rights and Foreign Policy: Principles and Canadian Practice," *Human Rights Quarterly*, Vol.7, No.2 (May 1985), p.185.

127. Ernie Regehr, "Arms for Sale: Canada Targets the Third World," *This Magazine*, Vol.20, No.6 (February 1987), p.22.

128. *South*, No.111 (January 1990), p.8.

129. Wilson Ruiz, "Canadian Munitions Sales to Latin America Taking Off," *The Globe and Mail*, September 9, 1988, p.B18.

130. Common Frontiers Project, "Prospects for Mexico–U.S. Free Trade: Washington Report," mimeo, Toronto, November 1989, p.8.

131. CIDA, "Structural Adjustment: Working Paper for the 4As," mimeo, Area Coordination Group, Ottawa, July 1988, pp.52,12-13.

132. Quoted by Mel Watkins, "Free Trade," *CUPE Facts*, Vol.8, No.2 (March 1986), p.13.

133. Bernard Wood, "Trade and Investment: Meeting the Challenge Honestly," in The Group of 77, *Canada and the World* (Ottawa, 1985), p.42.

TWO

The Debt Crisis:
A Case of Global Usury

Jamie Swift &
The Ecumenical Coalition for Economic Justice

They are content, in the name of formal principles, to find all direct violence inexcusable and then to sanction that diffuse form of violence which takes place on the scale of world history.

– Albert Camus, *The Rebel*

The poverty of the poor
Is the rich man's feast.

– a reggae lament

IN JUNE 1989 Canadian External Affairs minister Joe Clark travelled to Venezuela to attend a meeting of the Group of 77, whose membership includes the nations of the Third World. High on the agenda was the question of the U.S.$1.3 trillion owed by Third World countries to private banks and public agencies in the industrial countries.

The location of the meeting was appropriate. Four months earlier Venezuela – once one of the most prosperous nations in Latin America – had been rocked by riots in which three hundred citizens had died. The protestors had focused their anger on the International Monetary Fund and the austerity program it had imposed on the Venezuelan government of Carlos Andrés Pérez. Such "IMF riots" – which used to be called food riots – had become a regular phenomenon throughout the Third World in the 1980s, as people rebelled against what Allan Taylor, the president of the Royal Bank of Canada, refers to favourably as the IMF's "traditional economic policy supervision."[1] Such supervision usually involves cuts in government spending (including subsidies for food, health care, and public transit), devaluation of the local currency, and an open door to foreign investment.

Joe Clark was interested in more than just observing the Group of 77's deliberations. After a private lunch with Pérez, Clark spoke enthusiastically to reporters about Canada's interest in stepping up its investments in Venezuela's oil industry, mines, hydro system, and transportation and telecommunications. In fact, soon after Clark left Venezuela a Canadian company, Combustion Engineering, announced the completion of a $200 million deal with a Venezuelan group. The Canadian firm had gained access to the Venezuelan petrochemical industry, setting up a plastics plant using technology and marketing expertise from another "Canadian" company, Du Pont Canada.

"Historically, we used to be more active than we are now – that may well change," Clark said. "Certainly, we've been involved in political questions in the region."[2]

Clark referred specifically to the issue of the debt that plagues Venezuela and other countries in the region. For Canadians interested in the nature of their government's political involvement with the vexing problem of Third World debt, it was a simple matter to look to Venezuela's next-door neighbour, Guyana – a country of over 750,000 inhabitants with an external debt of $1.8 billion. Only two months before the Group of 77 meeting, outraged Guyanese had picketed the Canadian High Commissioner's office to protest against remarks he had made endorsing a controversial austerity plan. Canada had undertaken the role of lead nation in organizing a seven-nation "support group" to turn the Guyanese economy around.

According to a report from a fact-finding mission organized by the Canadian Council for International Cooperation, this "structural adjustment" program involved a 230 per cent currency devaluation, a rise in interest rates to 35 per cent, and a wage rise of only 20 per cent. The result was that the new minimum daily wage would purchase one loaf of bread, a half pound of chicken, or three-quarters of a gallon of rice. The CCIC report referred to the austerity scheme as an "economic assault."[3]

The IMF plan prompted widespread strikes and political turmoil, although in a local television interview Canadian high commissioner Frank Jackman reassured the Guyanese people that they should "take heart" because the austerity package would encourage Canadian multinational corporations to look favourably on Guyana in making decisions about where to invest. What most angered the picketers outside Jackman's office was his observation, "There is great admiration within the government of Canada for the steps that are being taken here, and for the budgetary moves, albeit unpopular, that have been introduced." Jackman said that his government saw this kind of strong medicine as "a precedent" for other Third World countries facing debt problems.[4] The bauxite miners, sugarcane cutters, students, and teachers who launched a general strike against the austerity plan no doubt did not share Jackman's optimistic perspective. Some of them could no longer get to work because they could not afford the bus fare.

The Venezuelan and Guyanese events cast considerable light on the issue of exactly where Canada stands in the early 1990s. The poor nations – and the poor people – of the Third World continue to face economic problems of monumental proportions. Meanwhile, through corporate and institutional interventions, more money than ever before is being transferred from less developed regions to the industrialized world. It's no wonder that the 1980s have been described as "a lost decade."[5]

But the debt crisis that has driven so many people deeper into poverty, simultaneously enriching international banks and ruling elites in the Third World, is not simply a phenomenon of the 1980s. Its roots can be traced to the post-war struggle between industrial capitalist powers. The groundwork for the post-war economic system was laid in 1944 at a conference held in a mountain resort hotel far from the pockmarked streets of Georgetown, Guyana.

THE NEW HAMPSHIRE SOLUTION

In July 1944 the soon-to-be-victorious allies gathered at the Mt. Washington Hotel in Bretton Woods, New Hampshire, to discuss proposals for solving post-war international payments problems and, essentially, to work out the details of a new international financial system.

It was clear to all that the sun had set on the British Empire. The previous world war had ended British hegemony over the world trade and payments system. "As a result of the war the locus of world economic power shifted dramatically," Michael Moffitt states in his book on international banking.[6] It remained only to finalize the details of Britain's economic eclipse.

According to Moffitt, Britain had "pulled the legs out from under the old system" during World War I "by effectively suspending the link between the pound sterling and gold." By the time the next war was over, the dominant power would unquestionably be the United States. It would emerge from World War II with its economy strengthened, while Britain would be weaker than ever. The pre-war powerhouses of Japan and Germany would be left surveying the ashes of their industrial economies. It would take them a generation to rebuild and challenge the United States.

But though the United States ultimately gained supremacy after the Bretton Woods negotiations, the conference did feature an interesting contest. The British representative was that giant among economists, John Maynard Keynes. In the middle of the Great Depression of the 1930s Keynes had expressed serious doubts about the notion that greater world trade (or "free trade") would lead to an ideal international division of labour. "Ideas, knowledge, science, hospitality, travel – these are the things which should of their nature be international," Keynes had written in 1933. "But let goods be homespun whenever it is reasonably and conveniently possible, and, *above all, let finance be primarily national.*"[7]

Keynes was looking for an international financial system that would minimize the risks of disorder and put the burden of adjustment on creditor as well as debtor nations. He represented a debtor nation, so this stance is not surprising. But Keynes's view of national self-sufficiency and his desire for a neutral international monetary system based on a unit he called the "bancor" did not prevail. The United States had different ideas. Its representative, H. D. White, wanted a post-war system reflecting the interests of the dominant power, his own country.

A crucial issue at Bretton Woods concerned whether nations would have automatic access to what was to become the International Monetary Fund, as Keynes wanted; or whether conditions would be attached to access, as White wanted. In the end, White won out and the new economic order reflected the U.S. desire for a form of internationalism dominated by America. The U.S. dollar, linked to gold, would be the world's most important reserve currency and the United States effectively became banker to the Western world, with the right to print and spend the principal currency.

The Bretton Woods agreement led to the establishment of the two key post-war financial institutions: the International Monetary Fund (IMF) and the International Bank for Reconstruction and Development (which later became known as the World Bank). Members of the IMF were required to observe an exchange rate, with strict limits on fluctuations, based on the U.S. dollar.

Six months after the conference, White wrote that the newly created International Monetary Fund (IMF) would not simply lend out money to help debtor nations: There would be conditions attached. Some four decades later, even though fixed exchange rates and a U.S. dollar backed by gold are no longer features of the monetary system, the ability of the IMF to impose strict conditions on countries applying for credit has continued and indeed been strengthened.

The immediate post-war years were marked by an unprecedented expansion of international (principally U.S.) business into all parts of what became known as the "free" world. The era of the multinational or transnational corporation had arrived.

Other nations were represented at Bretton Woods, including Canada and the independent nations of Latin America. One of the key players was Louis Rasminsky, a young Canadian economist who had played a major role in the preconference negotiations. Rasminsky had an intellectual preference for the British plan but submitted a draft compromise, labelled "off-White" by the British. In the aftermath of the conference it was widely acknowledged that he had been important in bringing the U.S. and British representatives together – on the basis of U.S. policy goals.

"Rasminsky had chosen to go in White's direction rather than Keynes', and this choice made the British critical and their position more difficult," historian J.L. Granatstein concluded. "It also helped ensure that the major outlines of the American plan were the ones that were followed."[8]

Wynn Plumptre, another member of Canada's delegation at Bretton Woods, agreed:

It is true … that the [post-war] international institutions, largely fashioned in Washington, were designed to serve the international interests of the United States. The charge that they could in many respects be considered as the creatures of American 'capitalist imperialism' can in a sense be accepted. It does not follow, however, that their establishment and operation were contrary to Canadian interests as perceived at the time or subsequently by Canadian governments. [9]

The Bretton Woods conference was something of a watershed for Canada, marking the first time this country had played a key role at an international economic policy conference. Its role reflected the newly found strength Canada had started to enjoy during the war. Its economy was booming; the real GNP had grown by 80 per cent between 1938 and 1944 as the government adopted a set of policies inspired by Keynes himself. Canada's industrial infrastructure did not suffer the ravages of war. On the contrary, the country was greatly strengthened as a result of state planning of the economy and government investment in new plants and equipment. The manufacturing sector boomed, with new factories springing up, particularly in Central Canada, to produce the goods needed by the allied armies. The levers of economic power had been centralized in Ottawa under the leadership of Liberal cabinet minister C.D. Howe, "Minister of Everything."

A few weeks after Bretton Woods, Rasminsky – who was to emerge as one of Ottawa's most important economic planners in the post-war period – reported to a friend that Canada "had been listened to with great attention, not only by the big powers but also by the smaller countries including the Europeans and the Latinos. *If we had wanted to do it,* I am quite sure that we could establish for ourselves a position of natural leader of the smaller countries." [10]

In fact, Canadian policy makers let the opportunity to chart an independent economic course slip away. The Liberal government under William Lyon Mackenzie King and C.D. Howe, together with its civil service advisers, had no intention of leading an independent bloc of smaller countries. Instead, following the war they ushered in what has been called "the American boom in Canada." A deliberate policy of quick deregulation of the war economy was accompanied by a retreat from the government's central role in economic planning. The Liberal policy was continentalist, depending on the U.S. demand for Canadian raw materials to fuel a military-based and consumer-based economy. The Canadian government shared the U.S. approach on economic planning, favouring a new kind of internationalism based on the free-wheeling expansion of (U.S.) business into all parts of the world.

Canada had not just abandoned any potential leadership role as a second-tier nation. By allowing its industrial development policy to be based on imported U.S. capital, the country also became settled into an economy that was more and more foreign-controlled and, as always, dependent on the export of resources. Manufacturing declined in relative terms and came to be dominated by multinational firms aiming at the protected Canadian market in branch plants concentrated in Southern Ontario.[11] One group of economic players continued to exercise an independent existence – the banks.

ALL FALL DOWN

Things seemed to be proceeding nicely, for we remember the 1950s as a time of happy expansion for the economy. But by 1965 readers of the U.S. financial press noticed a strange series of ads placed by their government. "Who beat Goldfinger to Fort Knox?" was the headline. In the 1950s the United States had begun running a balance of payments deficit. By 1960 the amount of gold held by the U.S. Treasury was already smaller than the amount of dollars held abroad and in the next few years U.S. gold supplies dwindled while foreign dollar holdings swelled. The post-war arrangements were starting to become unglued, for the United States could not indefinitely run a balance of payments deficit and at the same time maintain the convertibility of its dollar into gold.

Europe (particularly West Germany) and Japan were starting to re-emerge as strong competitors on world markets. U.S. exports declined and imports rose. Since fewer imports could be paid for with foreign exchange earned from exports, the growing import bill had to be paid in U.S. dollars.

Why did this happen? The U.S. government ads provided a soothing answer. "American industry, dynamically expanding abroad. American military might defending democracy around the world.... These are some of the ways we spend money overseas, all for good purposes. Yet when we spend more from abroad than we receive from abroad, we have a balance of payments deficit."

By the mid-1960s the United States was financing its war in Vietnam and a "War on Poverty" at home by printing more dollars instead of raising taxes. Although the Vietnamese and domestic poverty won these wars, the implications for the international economy were enormous. The link between the dollar and gold was growing tenuous as speculators wondered whether the dollar could sustain its value relative to gold and other currencies. The Bretton Woods system was crumbling and at the same time an international financial market in U.S. dollars was developing. More and more U.S. currency held in foreign banks was promptly lent back to the United States to finance its growing budget deficits and the war in Vietnam. By lending their U.S. dollars back to the Americans, the European, Canadian, and Japanese central banks were not only financing the deficit and the war but also helping to increase inflation within the United States itself.

Bankers had diminishing confidence in the ability of the United States to redeem dollars for gold at the official rate. As European central banks became reluctant to hold dollar reserves, speculators in the currency trading departments of transnational corporations and banks stepped in to take U.S. deposits and lend them out again. This was the beginning of what would come to be known as the "Eurodollar" market.

The competitive position of the United States continued to deteriorate and by 1971 the nation showed a trade deficit for the first time since the beginning of the century. Faced with a decline in its world economic hegemony, the United States did the same thing Britain had done during World War I. It abrogated the system it had set up at Bretton Woods by breaking the link between its currency and gold. In a famous address on August 15, 1971, President Richard Nixon abandoned the gold standard, changing the terms of his country's debt with what amounted to a single stroke of the pen. Almost as an afterthought, the managing director of the IMF was invited to the offices of the Secretary of the Treasury to watch Nixon's announcement on television. Henceforth U.S. debts would be paid in devalued U.S. paper currency no longer backed by gold.

By denying its creditors the option of holding gold rather than dollars, the U.S. government radically altered the nature of the $61 billion debt it owed to foreigners. It did this unilaterally. In the 1990s it is worth remembering this, for the United States continues to be forcefully opposed to the debtor nations of Latin America following its example by acting independently to relieve their own debt burden.

seems quite harsh on US, but...

THE INTERNATIONAL LENDING BOOM

After Nixon arbitrarily ended the Bretton Woods commitment to fixed exchange rates, a system of floating rates arose. The banks also started the practice of making international loans at floating interest rates, adding another uncertainty to an already volatile international financial market. A wave of currency speculation swept financial capitals. Currencies became commodities in themselves and the Eurodollar market developed into a "Eurocurrency" market in which a nation's money is deposited outside its borders. The yen, the Deutschmark, the pound, the Swiss franc, and even the Canadian dollar joined the speculative list. In 1971 the gross value of Eurocurrencies was estimated at $150 billion. With the partial collapse of Bretton Woods, it reached $2.76 trillion by 1984 and had doubled again, to $5.4 trillion, by 1988.[12] Little of this money was connected to any real trade in goods and services.

But this huge pool of capital had to have somewhere to go. It had to be invested. Much of it was lent to the Third World. International banks (including Canadian ones) rushed to lend money to the riskiest borrowers. A 1988 study of the Latin American debt crisis concluded: "The managers of the multinationals' financial departments discarded the careful tailoring of a conservative banker for the snazzy sportswear of adventurous dealers in international money markets.... The era of Casino Capitalism had arrived." [13]

A former Latin American finance minister recalled the determination of the multinational banks: "I remember how the bankers tried to corner me at conferences, to offer me loans. They wouldn't leave me alone. If you're trying to balance your budget it's terribly tempting to borrow money instead of raising taxes." [14]

Because much of this lending took place in the 1970s and early 1980s, it has been argued that the money came from OPEC countries. In fact, OPEC money (so-called "Petro-dollars") never accounted for more than 15 per cent of the total value of Eurocurrencies held at one time. [15] By the end of 1983, when the magnitude of the problem of Third World indebtedness had become apparent, the combined debt in loans to all underdeveloped countries was $800 billion. Much of the money was loaned to countries perceived as having good economic prospects, either as oil exporters or as newly emerging producers of manufactured goods. Mexico, Brazil, Venezuela, South Korea, and Argentina were among the leading debtors. [16]

Canadian banks have always had a high profile in Latin America and the Caribbean. When it appeared that there was money to be made in providing loans to governments in the region, they were quick to step in. By 1983 the big five Canadian banks had $18 billion in outstanding loans to Latin America. [17]

WHERE HAVE ALL THE DOLLARS GONE?

It is impossible to generalize about how different nations spent the dollars the banks were so eager to lend them. In the age of electronic funds-transfer, money can be moved from country to country with a few strokes of the computer keyboard. In 1985 William Mulholland, head of the Bank of Montreal, boasted, "I can hide money in a twinkling of an eye from all of the bloodhounds that could be put on the case, and I would be so far ahead of them that there would never be a hope of unraveling the trail." He added, "Technology today means that sort of thing can be done through electronic means." [18]

What is clear is that the money was for the most part *not* invested in development projects aimed at improving the living conditions of the poor in the Third World. According to the UNICEF book *The State of the World's Children 1990*, "Over the course of the 1980's, average incomes have fallen by 10% in most of Latin America and by over 20% in Sub-Saharan Africa. For many the story has been even worse.... In many urban areas, real minimum wages have declined by as much as 50%." [19] Another UNICEF report, published in December 1988 and looking back on the ten years since the International Year of the Child, said that at least 500,000 children had died in the previous year because development had been stalled or reversed by the immense debt loads and decreased earnings of Third World countries.

"It is hardly too brutal an oversimplification to say that the rich got the loans and the poor got the debts," the agency concluded.

And when the impact becomes visible in rising death rates among children ... then it is essential to strip away the niceties of economic parlance and say that what has happened is simply an outrage against a large section of humanity. The developing world's debt, both in the manner in which it was incurred and the manner in which it is being 'adjusted to,' is an economic stain on the second half of the twentieth century.[20]

For the poor and powerless in many Third World countries the Depression of the 1980s was far more severe than that of the 1930s. Father Tom Burns, a U.S. Maryknoll missionary in Peru, told the U.S. Congress about a 30 per cent increase in the number of "babies who die before they learn to walk."[21]

The uses to which the money was put were of little concern to the lenders, for the borrowers are to a great extent a reflection of the class structure of many economies in the Third World, dominated by civilian and military elites hardly known for their concern for national independence or the welfare of the population. Richard Gott, a veteran reporter for *The Guardian*, described the apparent changes wrought by the upsurge in foreign borrowing in Bolivia, which experienced a 77 per cent cut in spending on health care between 1980 and 1984:

In La Paz today there are many large skyscrapers where once there was only one. They are the fruit of the foreign-funded economic explosion of the 1970s, [when] the foreign debt grew from US$500 million in 1970 to nearly five times that (US$2,400 million) in 1980. The skyscrapers provide flats and offices for bankers. The ruling elite, however defined, has had a wonderful two decades, laughing all the way to the banks in Miami.[22]

Miami is, not coincidentally, the centre of the international trade in drugs and weapons, a city where rich people from poor Latin American countries maintain bank accounts and expensive condominiums. It is not uncommon for wealthy Latin Americans to invest in U.S. Treasury Bills, thus – in an ironic twist – helping to finance the U.S. government debt.

By 1985 the estimated value of the assets owned by Latin American and Caribbean citizens in the United States was $200.3 billion, just slightly less than the $208.4 billion worth of loans extended by U.S. banks to Latin American countries.[23] According to the IMF, about $30 billion worth of flight capital was taken out of Africa between 1974 and 1985. The resulting foreign deposits represent wealth generated by debtor economies – a wealth unavailable for reinvestment in productive domestic projects. Ever since the Third World lending boom started to wind down in the early to mid-1980s, when the banks recognized the mistakes they had been making, these sums have been invested in the economies of creditor

87

countries, financing Ontario's nuclear reactors or Washington's own debt.[24] Third World governments have been forced to borrow equivalent amounts abroad, often just to meet loan payments.

What we see in looking at capital flight is a sort of round trip: private banks lend money to the Third World, where many of the people are so poor that they scarcely participate in the cash economy; the dominant classes in less developed countries participate to such an extent that they have lots of money to deposit in foreign banks. The banks then turn around and lend money back to the Third World, at returns ranging up to 70 per cent on equity.[25]

Some of the capital from the Third World borrowing boom was invested in megaprojects. The Philippines borrowed $1.5 billion to pay Westinghouse for a nuclear power plant that cost twice as much as anticipated and could not be operated safely. The reactor is located five miles from a volcano.[26] President Ferdinand Marcos received some $80 million in bribes and kickbacks from the nuclear plant alone. Another dubious energy project that ate up foreign capital was the Chingaza hydroelectric project in Colombia, which shut down after four months of operation when the main tunnel collapsed.

Corruption among Third World leaders such as Marcos helped drain off some of the borrowed cash. Zaire's president Mobutu Sese Seko, who leads one of the most important U.S. client states in Africa, became a multi-millionaire through gross corruption and abuse of power. A foreign official sent to examine the books when Zaire was put into virtual receivership by the IMF quit in frustration. He discovered a $4 million payment to a Belgian professor who was the guardian of Mobutu's son, as well as a discrepancy of $32.6 million in the government's bank accounts abroad.[27]

Popular movements in the Third World have demanded that their governments selectively repudiate debts incurred by former dictators who either stole money outright or wasted it on weapons which they then used against their own people. An estimated 25 per cent of the total Third World debt was spent on weapons, often by military governments that took power by force.[28]

In 1981-82 the former military government of Argentina, notorious for murdering tens of thousands of its citizens, spent $13.9 billion on arms purchases abroad.[29] In 1988 Argentina ranked third in the debt parade with $69 billion in external debt. Debt service was eating up an astounding 45.3 per cent of its export earnings.[30]

GLOBAL USURY

The size of the debt load is not simply due to the dubious practices of Third World rulers. To get an idea of the underlying causes of the debt crisis we must turn again to the larger world picture, marked by increased competition among the big industrial powers – and particularly the United States and its attempts to bolster its sagging international position.

At the end of the 1970s the United States was still in a trade deficit position, just as it had been when Nixon abandoned the gold standard in 1971. It was also a nation with a net *outflow* of foreign investment. In October 1979 the U.S. Federal Reserve Board adopted a monetarist policy in an attempt to combat inflation. At the same time the Board moved to prop up a weak U.S. dollar. These moves initiated a meteoric rise in domestic – and world – interest rates.

Monetarist thinkers see inflation as the greatest threat to prosperity. Their chief weapon in the fight against inflation is high interest rates, which cut the rate of growth of the money supply. Raising the cost of borrowed money and cooling what is usually described as an "overheated" economy also result in more unemployment, thereby making the labour market a buyers' market. It becomes easier for employers to win wage concessions from workers who realize that, should they try to maintain their real wages, there is a large jobless reserve waiting to take over from them. Since monetarists see "excessive" wages as a cause of inflation in the first place, this is integral to their assault on inflation. Keeping unemployment high and wage increases low is fine by them. So are the increased profits that result. In essence, monetarism is a strategy for assisting corporations and banks to accumulate more capital.

With Ronald Reagan in the White House, the U.S. commitment to monetarism was underscored. U.S. interest rates soared to almost 20 per cent and unemployment rose throughout the capitalist world as economic activity stagnated. Inflation did fall. Corporate profits did rise. But the United States failed to improve its trade balance because its trading partners adopted monetarist policies of their own.

The United States did, however, succeed in bringing in Eurodollars. Investors and speculators were becoming wary of growing Third World debt and liked the high interest rates in the United States. The global banking business has changed from the days when the banks simply made money through loans to businesses in need of capital to fund new ventures. "Some banks still use deposits to lend to non-bank borrowers," Joyce Kolko observed in her book *Restructuring the World Economy,* "but they are normally used for short term gambling in interest rates, exchange rates, swaps, futures and the like. Profits for banks were increasingly from the 'treasury' division specializing in high risk currency exchange rate differentials and other innovative 'products' rather than loans."[31]

Other countries responded to the U.S. move by raising their own interest rates. This created what has been called a "ratchet effect" whereby rates go up but not down as fractional increases entice and excite speculators. Canada has been locked into U.S. interest rates for over 50 years, with rates on its government bonds locked into comparable rates in the United States. This means that Canada has been without an independent interest-rate policy since the 1930s.

Among the high rollers attracted by high U.S. interest rates were those members of the dominant classes of indebted countries who added their money to the U.S.-bound flow. As a result, within five short years, from 1981 to 1986, the United States was transformed from the world's biggest creditor nation to the biggest debtor. Other factors contributed to this remarkable turnaround. One was the declining competitiveness of U.S. industry: U.S. capitalists were concentrating on leveraged buy-outs rather than innovation and competition. Another was the growing U.S. trade deficit. In addition the Reagan administration went on a massive military spending spree without raising the taxes necessary to pay for the guns.

These developments failed to arrest the decline of the U.S. economy. But the impact of the U.S. high-interest-rate policy was devastating for underdeveloped nations. By 1983, 40 per cent of all Third World debt was tied to floating interest rates, compared to only 5 per cent ten years earlier. [32] Debt service is tied to the U.S. prime rate or the London Inter-Bank Offered Rate (LIBOR: the rate at which banks lend to each other), which followed U.S. rates upwards. A 1 per cent rise in the U.S. prime rate added $4 billion to the cost of servicing Third World loans. [33]

Alarm bells began to ring in the head offices of the multinational banks when financiers began to realize that they were dangerously overexposed in the Third World, especially in Latin America. After building up for several years the debt crisis officially arrived in August of 1982 with Mexico's declaration that it was unable to continue payments. Mexico temporarily halted all debt payments and nationalized its banks, accusing them of looting the country by encouraging capital flight.

Mexico was forced into tough negotiations with the United States, along with the private banks and the IMF. It was immediately forced to adopt a stiff austerity program and had to sell oil to its northern neighbour at four dollars below the world price. Then U.S. treasury secretary Donald Regan proudly reported that the president had called him "one hard-hearted SOB" in the wake of the Mexican negotiations. [34]

A senior vice-president of Morgan Guaranty Trust declared, "It was like an atom bomb being dropped on the world financial system." [35] The financial system withstood the shock rather well, in contrast to the Mexican people, who saw their real wages decline by 25 per cent from 1982 to 1983. [36] While the nationalization of Mexico's banks appeared to have been a bold stroke, it was in fact a desperate attempt by the government of José Lopez Portillo to shore up its legitimacy. Mexican bankers were well compensated for their nationalized assets. International bankers actually welcomed the nationalization, believing that it would increase their chances of collecting interest on their loans. [37]

The Mexican government also swallowed the traditional IMF medicine for debtor countries: It privatized state-owned companies, relaxed restrictions on foreign investment, and cut subsidies and raised prices for food and energy. By 1988 there had been 4.5 million unemployed and a 46 per cent drop in the purchasing power of the minimum wage. [38]

WHAT IS TO BE DONE?

The private banks reacted to the debt crisis with attempts to stabilize the situation, establishing large reserves for loan losses and reducing new lending to the Third World while at the same time collecting as much interest from the debtors as possible.

The banking system rests on that elusive quality called confidence. The bankers have above all attempted to project an image of being in control of the situation. The banks do not want people to even begin to think that their money is not safe. The last thing they want is a country to default completely on a loan. So the banks, together with governments of the industrial countries and institutions like the IMF, have done everything possible to deal with each debtor nation separately and to avoid anything faintly resembling a debtors' cartel. This strategy has been quite successful, as negotiations on the debt have been largely bilateral. As the president of the Royal Bank emphasized in 1989, "Each case *must be considered by itself,* using a voluntary and market-based approach." [39]

"We in the Royal Bank have been operating in Latin America for 70 or 80 years," said a vice-president of Canada's largest bank, which had $4.2 billion in loans to Latin America in 1984. "And most governments, whatever their political colour, extreme left or right, tend to be reasonably good managers and recognize their international debt obligations ... not only past, but future [obligations] and will, for lack of a better term, play the game." [40]

The rules of this game have been set by transnational capital, with the IMF acting as the umpire. Its actions reflect the interests of its creators and masters – the ruling elites in the United States and the other countries of the industrialized world.

Another Royal Bank executive admitted, "There certainly is a need for [the IMF] to be in there as a lender and as a disciplinarian and that's the thing all of us like about the IMF.... They, perhaps like no one else, can make conditions on loans – which ensures some tightening of the belt." [41]

The IMF's disciplinary measures are a group of familiar conditions it imposes on countries in need of credits to ward off insolvency. The conditions include cutbacks on government spending (in areas like health care, food subsidies, and education, but not defence), opening the borders to more imports (usually by devaluing the national currency), raising interest rates and lowering or eliminating exchange controls, controlling wages, dismantling state enterprises, and opening the door to foreign investment. All of these policies discourage local consumption and encourage production for export.

When a country becomes swamped with a heavy debt, the IMF and (since 1985) the World Bank move in with emergency credits. The price of this aid is a reorganization of the national economy to make sure sufficient surplus is generated to repay foreign loans. This is done by reorienting local resources from domestic consumption to exports. While Keynes had argued for an inward-looking national economic plan – in effect, national self-reliance – the IMF and the World Bank are looking for precisely the opposite. They want to promote an export-led model of development. This approach is the key to all the so-called "structural adjustment" programs that have been foisted on the Third World by powerful creditors. The approach really means locking local economies more firmly into the global capitalist order. Countries are routinely encouraged to shift their agricultural production from food crops to export crops. This means that it is possible to buy Senegalese string-beans in Manhattan gourmet shops and that the international price of sugar and coffee is kept low. This has been called a recipe for starvation. Senegalese peasants do not include *haricots verts* among their staples. Nor can Kenyan farmers support their families on a diet of coffee.

During the 1980s protectionism rose and commodity prices plummeted to near their lowest levels since the 1930s. All debtor countries cannot simultaneously increase exports of the same products on world markets where demand is stagnant or declining and substitution is occurring (corn sweeteners for cane sugar, fibre optics for copper wire). A flood of exports simply lowers the price, no doubt satisfying the Northern interests that advocate the policy in the first place. The export model is ultimately based on ensuring global competitive "success" through low wages and guaranteeing the transnational corporations and industrial countries access to cheap raw materials from the Third World. The result is competitive impoverishment as countries strive to underbid each other in the low-wage sweepstakes.

The whole menu of Structural Adjustment Programs (SAPs) thus contains striking internal contradictions. They will not, cannot, and indeed are not meant to benefit the poor any more than the original colonization of Asia, Africa, and Latin America was designed to do so. Indeed, the debt crisis and the measures designed by international business to deal with the debt have been called a *recolonization* of the Third World. When the IMF or the World Bank meet to discuss the fate of a group of African debtors, it is not all that different from when the Great Powers gathered in Berlin in 1885 to carve up Africa between them. The goal then was the same as it is today: access to cheap raw materials, cheap labour, and a foreign market.

"Under structural adjustment, these agencies do not merely supervise individual sectors of the economy as in the past," said a report from the Institute for African Alternatives. "*They now manage each country entirely.*"[42]

As in the past, when Britain's district commissioner was the most important official governing African affairs, Europeans have offices in the central banks and the trade and finance ministries of independent nations. Here they supervise monetary, fiscal, and tariff policies.

Structural adjustment is aimed at continuing the siphoning of wealth from the Third World to the banks and corporations that control the economy of the industrial nations. This goal was realized during the 1980s. Between 1980 and 1987 the net transfer of resources (debt payments minus new loans) from less developed countries to their creditors amounted to U.S.$287 billion.[43] Although Latin America and the Caribbean paid U.S.$150 billion more in debt service than they received in new credits between 1982 and 1987, their total debts *still grew* from U.S.$330 to $410 billion.[44] (Debt service in these cases was most of the interest with little of the principal; unpaid interest was added to the stock of existing debt.) The analogy to racketeering loan sharks is only too obvious.

During this period the plight of the poor in the Third World became ever more serious. UNICEF documented the increased hunger, sickness, and poverty that resulted from these perverse capital flows and from adjustment policies forced on debtor nations by their creditors – including Canada.[45] More than a million African children have died as a result of the debt crisis. In Peru child malnutrition grew from 41 per cent to 68 per cent between 1980 and 1983. In the 40 least developed countries, government spending on health care has been cut by 50 per cent per capita. Throughout Africa and in many parts of Latin America, average family incomes have fallen by between 10 and 25 per cent since 1980.

THE BEST-LAID PLANS ...

As the 1980s unfolded and it became obvious that things were getting worse, various bodies hatched various schemes for dealing with the debt crisis. Most notable – at least from the creditor side – was the Baker Plan, unveiled in 1985 by U.S. treasury secretary James Baker (subsequently secretary of state under George Bush).

Announced at a joint IMF-World Bank meeting, the plan was aimed at buying time for the banks who had drastically reduced their lending to the Third World. Baker proposed that an additional U.S.$40 billion be lent to the 15 most undebted Third World countries. Half of the new money would come from private banks, half from multinational institutions like the World Bank and the regional development banks. One interesting adjunct to the plan was the introduction of "cross-conditionality" under which the United States would increase its funding for the World Bank and the regional banks only so long as all these institutions applied the same harsh conditions to their loans. Under this solidarity of the rich, failure to meet the conditions set down by one bank would mean a halt in disbursements by all.

Canada's five main chartered banks took advantage of the respite offered by the

Baker Plan to cut their exposure (outstanding loans as a percentage of shareholders' equity) to between 26 and 100 per cent. [46]

The Baker Plan also expanded the role of the World Bank by establishing structural adjustment as a condition for new Bank financing. To qualify for assistance – to be given on a case by case basis – countries had to "strengthen their private sectors and reduce budget deficits, put in supply-side programs such as tax reductions, liberalize trade and promote foreign investment." [47] In exchange, debtor countries were supposed to receive small amounts of additional financing at commercial rates. As it turned out, in the first year of the plan there was an actual decline in lending from banks and multilateral agencies.

The politics of this scheme soon became obvious. The plan allowed the banks to present a common front to individual debtor nations while forestalling any possible collective action on the part of all the debtors. This bilateral orientation was accompanied by a shift in the role of the World Bank as it added its muscle to that of the IMF as policy policeman of the poor. The Bank had traditionally focused on funding large-scale infrastructure projects such as highways, dams, and agricultural and forestry efforts ostensibly aimed at improving the lot of ordinary citizens.

By the late 1980s senior World Bank officials were beginning to echo those private bankers and academics who were saying the time had come for debt reduction. According to the Canadian Imperial Bank of Commerce (CBIC), "It is time to think the unthinkable in respect to all the heavily indebted LDCs [less developed countries] and that is, by one means or another, to reduce debt quickly to the point where it can be serviced." [48] The Royal Bank called for more conditional lending by governments and international institutions like the IMF and World Bank to strengthen the export sectors of debtor countries. Export earnings could be used to continue to service the debt under such controlled debt-relief strategies, which clearly distinguish between what is collectable from debtors who endure austerity and structural adjustment and what is uncollectable under any conditions and only serviceable through new involuntary loans – loans that the banks do not wish to make. The condition for writing down the uncollectable loans is that the debtors distort their economies in order to keep on paying the interest on loans that are deemed collectable.

Should less developed countries fail to follow externally imposed policies aimed at generating enough surplus to keep the interest flowing to the banks, things will go poorly for them. "If we make such concessions and reduce the debt to what we consider a manageable amount," warned the chairman of the CBIC, "then it should be clearly understood that failure to perform in other than the most extreme circumstances would be accompanied by unpleasant economic sanctions." [49]

Other bankers, such as a senior official of the Toronto Dominion Bank who declared Third World lending a "discontinued business," felt that new credits

94

would have to come from governments and the World Bank. What these bankers are really saying is that they expect the public to bail them out by funding export-led growth aimed at providing them with continued debt payments. Whatever their minor differences of approach, the private bankers agreed with the assessment of Allan Taylor, chairman of the Royal Bank, whose ideal solution to the problems of the Third World was succinct: "Development strategies are export oriented and there is a high reliance on markets to allocate resources."[50] Several months later, in 1989, Taylor added, "Foreign investment in the borrowing countries would have to play a much larger role in resolving the problem."[51]

A glance at the other side of the ledger is revealing. Two voices from the Third World sum up what the advice of Canadian bankers really means for the poor.

In the Philippines, large landlords on the island of Negros have been trying to diversify away from sugar production because of the low price of sugar on the world market. The sugar workers – always a desperately poor class – faced starvation. The solution? "The landlords in that area have converted much of the land they cannot use for sugar any more into prawn fishing," explained Dr. Manuel Montes, a professor of finance at the University of the Philippines' School of Economics. "This is what is known as agribusiness in the Philippines – the growing of prawns for export to Japan."

Montes also explained that prawn fishing results in permanent ecological damage because it requires salt-water ponds. The salt seeps into the land, destroying its agricultural capability. What's more, prawn production uses only half the labour required by sugar production, so the desperate position of rural workers becomes even more acute. Montes concluded: "Of course the more natural way to diversify would have been to start transferring control over the land to the people who can make a livelihood out of it."[52]

In Zambia, African peasants are facing starvation while their government faces a major debt problem. Shimwaayi Muntemba, a Zambian woman who heads the Environment Liasion Centre based in Nairobi, Kenya, and co-ordinates the work of non-governmental organizations, stated that with the government facing great pressure from the debt problem, "Foreign companies have come in and what this has meant is land has to be found for these companies.... Peasants have to be moved."[53]

The foreign investors are interested in cotton cultivation and, while the government claims to be promoting food production by putting land in the hands of small-holders, it is concentrating on the export sector dominated by international capital.

"They are going to grow cotton which is needed for debt clearing," Muntemba said at a Toronto conference in 1988. "At the same time we are doing this, land is being taken away from small-scale farmers. The whole thing is just a mess because of the great burden of debt clearing and the food crisis coming at the same time."[54]

THE BRADY PLAN: SAME WINE, NEW GLASS

As the 1980s drew to a close with a new U.S. administration, a new plan to deal with the debt crisis was floated by a new treasury secretary, Nicholas Brady. It was basically a continuation of the old Baker Plan – aimed at helping out private banks and ensuring continued servitude by debtor nations. Brady boosted market-oriented palliatives such as debt-equity swaps (exchanging debt for ownership in a country's internal assets), sales of debt (a kind of international factoring scam in which debt is purchased at a discount and the buyer then tries to collect), and debt-bond exchanges, which substitute lower yielding bonds but relieve banks of the need to provide new money.[55] This ostensible relief would be offered only to countries toeing the IMF-World Bank market-oriented line, attempting to grow their way out of debt.

As with the Baker Plan, the Brady Plan was an attempt at bank relief rather than debt relief. "Citicorp will love the plan," analyst Shafique Islam observed in reference to the biggest bank in the United States. "Trading in Third World debt will boom and it will make a lot of money for Citicorp."[56]

The first test of the Brady Plan was instructive. In summer 1989 a long-awaited debt reduction plan for Mexico dominated the pages of the financial press. A *Globe and Mail* headline heralded a 35 per cent write-down of the Mexican debt. In fact, the amount of debt relief gained by Mexico was less than the $3 billion increase in debt-service payments that hit the country as interest rates rose between 1988 and 1989. Well before the Mexican deal was finalized, the *Wall Street Journal* reported that "even a substantial reduction in debt or debt relief may only get Mexico back to where it was a year ago."[57]

Under the Brady Plan, the ostensible relief Mexico gained was accompanied by the usual austerity measures and structural adjustment criteria designed to make its economy better serve the needs of foreign investors. It was also jigged to Mexico's domestic political situation, expiring just a year after that country's next presidential election, scheduled for 1994.

"Mexico has at least five million unemployed workers and will add as many as a million job seekers in each of the next five years," noted *Forbes,* a U.S. business magazine. "That's ten million workers willing to work for a dollar an hour, available to add value to U.S.-produced goods and services and to help keep U.S. products world-competitive."

Forbes pointed out that if Mexico's economic situation did not improve before its next election it could end up with "a leftist regime." "Any scaling down of the Mexican debts is no act of sentimental generosity," the magazine concluded. "It is based on a recognition that the fates of the U.S. and Mexico are inextricably intermingled."[58]

The most important point the Mexican deal and any others cut under the

Brady Plan is that they enshrine structural adjustment even more centrally than did the Baker Plan. The World Bank has gained an even greater role in regulating the internal affairs of debtor nations, adding a veneer of respectability because the Bank, unlike the IMF, maintains that one of its principal priorities is the alleviation of poverty.

In fact, structural adjustment supplements the traditional austerity measures demanded by the IMF: reduced government spending, currency devaluation, and a cut in real wages. Structural adjustments mean a country adjusts its economic structures to suit the private sector. Additional credits are extended to countries that privatize public enterprises and reduce the size of the government sector as a whole, adopt export-oriented trade policies, remove trade and exchange controls, and raise interest rates to reward investors.

"First, we should avoid the temptation to let our desires for more justice in the world obscure the view of reality as it is," Marcel Massé, former Canadian executive director of the IMF, explained to an Ottawa seminar on African development. "Structural adjustment usually means to let the market set [interest] rates.... choices such as this one, in structural adjustment, involve a choice of philosophy." [59]

Canadian economist John Loxley of the University of Manitoba has advised several African governments in their dealings with the IMF and the World Bank. He explained the reality of new World Bank programs in Africa differently. "The overall result would be unambiguously a deterioration of the living standards of the poor and growing inequalities in general. Structural adjustment lending as currently conditioned would run directly counter to the [World] Bank's professed concern for alleviating poverty and meeting basic needs." [60]

The experience of another African country bears him out. Zaire is a potentially-rich country, an important U.S. client state. It is often cited as one of the IMF–World Bank success stories. Zaire began following the foreign recipe for economic recovery in 1977. "Export!" said the institutions run by the countries that import copper – Zaire's chief product. By 1986 the price of copper was 45 per cent what it had been in 1974.

Foreign debt in Zaire rose in the early 1980s and between 1983 and 1985 there was a net capital outflow of $550 million annually, increasing to $830 million in 1986. In a five-year period, the total debt-service payments were $4.31 billion. A grand total of $36 million in foreign investment entered the country during the same period. Average Zaireans were no doubt unaware of this larceny. They were aware that by the mid-1980s an "agent second class" (a lower-level civil servant) was taking home $250 Zaire per month. The average budget needed for a family of six to get by for a month stood at $3,037 Zaire. [61]

WHAT'S REALLY TO BE DONE?

Bankers like the Royal Bank's Taylor can be expected to indulge in sober, responsible-sounding rhetoric as they admonish Third World countries. However, the reality of the pinstriped world of international banking has little or nothing to do with the careful assessment of productive investment decisions. The world of global banking, or the "supranational economy" as it has been called, has become one of chaotic speculation where an astounding $150 billion to $200 billion in foreign exchange trading is conducted every day. Banks trade money with each other with the frenzy of gamblers at the roulette table. No longer do they simply take deposits and look cautiously for safe places to lend. Interbank deposits represent as much as two-thirds of the business of many major banks, with some $50 trillion in hot money traded annually. In this world it is far easier to raise a few hundred million for a leveraged buy-out of one conglomerate by another or a shady international arms purchase or drug deal than it is to come up with a few hundred thousand for, say, a well-digging project in a drought-stricken Third World country. [62]

As Canadian economist Tom Naylor puts it, in this world of homeless money the bankers play a game of "peekaboo finance," whisking money around the world in search of a fractional interest-rate spread or exchange-rate change. Naylor concludes that an environment was created "in which hot money, multiplying out of the control of any single actor, public or private, became a major determinant of economic and financial action." [63]

All this is a reminder of Keynes's admonition over 50 years ago to "Let finance be national." The supranational financial system is totally out of control and is increasingly subject to the whims of a tiny group of speculators. But this new globalism, in which Third World countries have been encouraged to open their doors ever wider to foreign investment and export as much as possible, has resulted in nothing but poverty, destitution, and despair for the vast majority of people. Clearly, some new answers are needed to the question "What is to be done?" – answers that go beyond the stale, self-serving prescriptions of bankers and businessmen.

The debt crisis has led to greater flows of money from the South to the North and to the increased dependence of Southern economies. The only way for the majority poor in the Third World to escape the debt trap is to disengage themselves from an international system that is not geared to meeting their needs and is in fact a principal source of their poverty. International trade could be used selectively, as a planned extension of production for the domestic market – a market deliberately ignored by the various SAPs, austerity programs, and reforms advocated by international banks and agencies. This market is now being neglected. It features demand for food, housing, and educational and health-care services needed by poor people – not "demand" by wealthy North Americans who want fresh produce while the ground is frozen outside. Groups representing farmers, workers, and unemployed slum dwellers are frequently demanding that their economies be delinked from the international capitalist economy.

Such a self-reliant path would involve local production of the things people need to live: food, shelter, energy. It would also involve a redistribution of income to shift production away from luxury items for the wealthy to basic needs. A thorough-going land reform would be needed to put control over agriculture into the hands of the needy peasants who in fact do the work on the land. International trade would be a planned extension of the domestic market, not the central motor of the economy as prescribed by IMF orthodoxy. The basic simplicity of this common-sense approach is worth emphasizing. People in the Third World are starving. They need food, shelter, health care, clean water. In most cases their countries have the resources to produce such basic needs. They do not need to be growing snow peas for nouvelle cuisine dieters in the nations of the North.

Such a path would challenge the entrenched interests of the dominant classes in most Third World countries and the wishes of IMF bureaucrats and private bankers whose priorities include a continuation of the present haemorrhage of wealth from the poor to the rich. They would respond with warnings about how the "real world" does not work this way and the folly of "autarky."

A point of *realpolitik* from a Canadian diplomat puts the lie to such self-interested claims. In spring 1989, following the massacre of Beijing students calling for democratic reforms in China, the Canadian government recalled its ambassador in protest. Many Canadians were calling for economic sanctions against China, such was the public outcry at the killings and the executions that followed. The response of Canada's ambassador to China, Earl Drake, was simple: There is no point in applying economic pressure to China for the simple reason that the country has such a self-sufficient economy – strong enough to withstand any outside pressure. China's self-reliant economic path has not only led to its insulation from international pressures. More importantly, it has also given that country's people a standard of living superior to that of most of the Third World. The Chinese take basic needs such as food, housing, and health care for granted.

One does not have to be sympathetic to the outrages of a group of octogenarian Stalinists (or the Canadian businessmen reluctant to abandon profitable investment opportunities in China) to appreciate the strength of their position. Of course, China carries on a growing trade with the world. But it still has the basis of a self-reliant economy laid by the government of Mao Zedong after 1949. It is also worth remembering that one of the first actions of Chairman Mao's new government was to repudiate its pre-1949 debt on the grounds that the government that borrowed the money was illegitimate.

A self-reliant road is both a possible and realistic alternative to the conventional, laissez-faire development model advocated by Canada and the other industrial powers. No country has *ever* developed a strong economy using laissez-faire

99

policies. Britain adopted free trade only after its economy was dominant and even then forced its colonies to deindustrialize, smashing India's textile industry. The United States erected tariff walls and even passed constitutional amendments repudiating its debt until it had gained a dominant position after World War II. Japan used protectionism and state subsidies to develop its formidable industrial economy. The major Latin American countries now beleaguered by debt did well during the 1930s and 1940s when they fell into default and then were isolated from the world economy during the war, giving them the chance to turn their attention to domestic markets.

THE CANADIAN CONUNDRUM

Where does Canada fit into a situation in which decisions made by institutions controlled by the rich have such devastating effects on the lives of the poor? Back in the 1940s, when the post-war economic order was being carved out at Bretton Woods, Canada's top official mused about how — if we had wanted to — we could have seized the opportunity to become a leader of the small countries, including "the Latinos."

This obviously didn't happen. Every summer the leaders of what the media usually call "the seven most powerful industrial nations" gather for a "summit" to discuss the state of the globe. Canada is there, the prime minister puffing himself up, looking proud to be a player in the big leagues. Canadian banks are right up there warning their clients in the Third World to "tighten their belts." And diplomats like the Canadian high commissioner to Guyana have even played a role in lecturing the locals about the need for restraint and tough medicine if they want to attract Canadian companies to their troubled land.

So it seems as if Canada is like the other powerful creditor nations. It certainly behaves like one. In 1989 the government recalled its representative to the IMF and installed him as the head of CIDA, the foreign-aid agency. Marcel Massé is a firm believer in structural adjustment. But Canada's role as junior policeman in the Third World masks a situation in which Canada itself is sliding deeper into debt. In this respect it looks much more like a Third World country, less like a member of the "Group of Seven."

Canada's own *external* debt grew slowly in the immediate post-war period but began to take off in the 1970s and 1980s to the point where it hit $228 billion in 1988. This is smaller than that of the country with the biggest debt, the United States. But on a per capita basis it is three and a half times the U.S. debt – the largest in the world. [64] This debt includes all international money transactions, both loans and "direct investment" – another term for *foreign* investment – held by corporations, governments, and individuals. After more than doubling as a percentage of Gross Domestic Product between 1975 and 1982, this net investment income flowing out of Canada has remained at about 3 per cent since 1983.

To pay off these debts Canada faces a constantly growing need for a steady stream of foreign capital into the country. Lately Ottawa has been falling all over itself to attract rich immigrants from Hong Kong who essentially buy their way into Canada. As recently as 1980 the "Immigrant Funds and Inheritances" column of the balance of payments measured $840 million. By 1988 it had exploded to over $5 billion. [65] Canada also earns money through its surplus trade in merchandise (raw materials and cars and car parts). But exporting cars and importing Hong Kong business people is not enough, so that in 1988 Canada had to attract $21.2 billion in new foreign currency through new debt.

The way to attract new money is to offer its owners high rates of interest, higher than they would get elsewhere. But Canadian rates have long been locked into a position above those in the United States. And the premium paid to attract U.S. money is widening. For the 50 years before 1986 the long-term rate on federal government bonds averaged 0.7 per cent over the U.S. rate. Since 1986 the spread has jumped to 1.7 per cent. [66]

A government's ability to manage interest rates determines to a great extent its ability to manage its own economy. Canada's international indebtedness may well have become the most powerful force in determining interest rates *and* domestic economic policy. In this way we are in a similar position to many Third World countries. The struggle to service our foreign debt has been crucial in shaping Ottawa's economic policies.

And, like Third World countries, Canada is under constant surveillance by the IMF. Just before the 1989 budget, an IMF staff report calling for massive federal spending cuts was the subject of a pre-budget leak by officials in the Department of Finance. The finance minister immediately chimed in with the predictable "Ready, aye, ready." His budget cut spending and raised taxes. This was nothing new, of course. The Mulroney government had been pursuing a neo-liberal agenda for five years. It was becoming clear that Canada had a SAP of its own, albeit self-imposed.

The terms of the plan have included cuts in social spending as well as in regional development and agricultural subsidies. The Free Trade Agreement is very much in line with the policy prescriptions doled out to dependent economies: an export-oriented trade policy and the removal of trade and exchange controls. Privatization (Air Canada, the aircraft industry, and even the Post Office) has been a watchword of the administration, as has been the general reduction in size of the state sector, particularly that designed to help the poor. The other side of the coin is an ever-greater subservience to transnational capital; in fact, that is where Canada's SAP coincides most fundamentally with the SAPs forced on the Third World.

This neo-liberal doctrine (often called neo-conservative but in fact a simple extension of nineteenth-century liberalism into the late twentieth century) was much in vogue during the 1980s in Thatcher's Britain, Reagan's America, and to a lesser extent in Mulroney's Canada. It is of course familiar to the Third World under various names, the most recent of which has been structural adjustment.

The international investment bankers at Morgan Guaranty Trust have referred to such policies as a "liberation of the private sector from distorting price, wage, trade, exchange and credit controls."[67] An equally sanguine appraisal was offered by Eugene Forsey, Canada's perennial constitutional authority, as "just a fancy name for the biggest international romp ever mounted by the rich for skinning the poor."[68]

THE SYSTEM OF APPROPRIATION

Once upon a time free enterprise was commonly called capitalism. The eminent French historian Fernand Braudel tells us that Louis Blanc provided the first truly accurate definition of capitalism in the modern sense of the term. At least 17 years before Karl Marx ever used the word, Blanc wrote about "What I call 'capitalism', that is to say the appropriation of capital by some to the exclusion of others."[69]

In a way, the preservation and extension of this system of appropriation — and its extension to every corner of the globe — is more important to the rich and powerful than the collection of specific debts in specific countries. Creditors have been attempting to use the debt crisis to eliminate all restraints on private capital.

Braudel closed the second volume of his history of the development of capitalism with a comment on "the liberating action of world trade" which was "the only doorway to a superior profit level." The new global economies of the 17th and 18th centuries "expanded as Europe embarked upon her conquest of the world. With these *world-economies*, we shall be moving to a different level of competition, a different scale of domination, one with rules that have been so often repeated that for once we shall be able to follow them without risk of error.... There is an old expression for this — but it is none the worse for that and says what it means: the international division of labour and (of course) the fruits of that labour."[70]

The IMF and the World Bank were born when the post-war world economy was being shaped at the Bretton Woods conference. Things have changed since then; the United States no longer wields the same unchallenged clout it did in 1944. The whole debt crisis was in part the result of competition for supremacy among the economic superpowers. But these great powers still share a common vision of the broad outlines of the global economy. This global vision is one in which both private capital in the form of transnational corporations and banks have as much freedom as possible: freedom from threat of interference by national governments; freedom to move money around the world; freedom to make as much money as possible with as little regulation as possible; and, most recently, freedom to have a direct hand in dictating the internal development policies of many Third World nations.

Notes

1. Allan R. Taylor, "Third World Debt: The Fables and the Facts," speech to the Canadian Club of Montreal, April 24, 1989.

2. *The Globe and Mail,* June 22, 1989.

3. Canadian Council for International Cooperation, *Guyana: Recovery and the Role of Canadian NGOs – A Report on a CCIC Mission to Guyana,* Ottawa, 1989.

4. Fax from Guyana received by Oxfam-Canada, Ottawa, April 17, 1989.

5. Sue Branford and Barnardo Kucinski, *The Debt Squads: The U.S., the Banks and Latin America* (London: Zed Books, 1988), p.1.

6. Michael Moffitt, *The World's Money: International Banking from Bretton Woods to the Brink of Insolvency* (New York: Simon and Schuster, 1983), pp.17-18.

7. J.M. Keynes, "National Self-Sufficiency," *The Yale Review,* 1933, p.758 (emphasis added).

8. J.L. Granatstein, *The Ottawa Men: The Civil Service Mandarins 1935-1957* (Toronto: Oxford University Press, 1982), p.306.

9. A.F.W. Plumptre, *Three Decades of Decision: Canada and the World Monetary System 1944-1975* (Toronto: McClelland and Stewart, 1977), p.31.

10. L. Rasminsky to T.A. Stone, cited in Granatstein, *Ottawa Men,* n.70, p.306.

11. Kari Levitt, *Silent Surrender: The Multinational Corporation in Canada* (Toronto: Macmillan, 1970), chapter.4; see also subsequent work by R.T. Naylor, Wallace Clement, and others.

12. Morgan Guaranty Trust, *World Financial Markets,* New York, various issues.

13. Jackie Roddick, *The Dance of the Millions: Latin America and the Debt Crisis* (London: Latin America Bureau, 1988), p.23.

14. Quoted in Anthony Sampson, *The Money Lenders: Bankers in a Dangerous World* (London: Hodder & Stoughton, 1983).

15. R.T. Naylor, "The Crisis of Debt," *The Canadian Forum,* June / July, 1984.

16. D. Delmaide, *Debt Shock* (Toronto: Lester and Orpen Dennys, 1984), p.54; and Roddick, *Dance of the Millions,* p.28.

17. Bank annual reports, 1983; and Economic Council of Canada, *Twenty-First Annual Review,* Ottawa, 1984, Tables 4-6, p.61.

18. Quoted in R.T. Naylor, *Hot Money and the Politics of Debt,* (Toronto: McClelland and Stewart, 1987), p.12.

19. UNICEF, *The State of the World's Children 1990* (Oxford: Oxford University Press, 1990), p.8.

20. Quoted in *The Globe and Mail*, December 21, 1988.

21. *GATT-Fly Report*, Vol.VIII, No.4 (October 1987).

22. *The Guardian* (U.K.), October 9, 1987.

23. Roddick, *Dance of the Millions*, p.222.

24. In fact, growth rates for new lending were *already* falling in 1982. But just to keep up the fiction that the debt was being paid, "involuntary loans" were continued throughout the 1980s to allow the banks to show on their books that interest was being paid. Thus the total nominal debt continued to rise. But in real terms (allowing for inflation) and – most importantly – in relation to the banks' total assets, the debt as a percentage of the banks' primary capital has fallen ever since 1982. See *GATT-Fly Report*, Vol.VII, No.4 (November 1986).

25. James S. Henry, "Where the Money Went," *The New Republic*, April 14, 1986.

26. *Fortune*, September 1, 1987.

27. *Time*, January 10, 1983.

28. *The Ploughshares Monitor*, June 1987.

29. IBASE, *Brazil Information*, No.13 (June / July 1984).

30. World Bank, cited in *The Globe and Mail*, April 1, 1989.

31. Joyce Kolko, *Restructuring the World Economy* (New York: Pantheon, 1988), p.108.

32. H. Lever et al., *The Debt Crisis and the World Economy: Report by a Commonwealth Group of Experts* (London: Commonwealth Secretariat, 1984), p.15.

33. *Latin America Weekly Report*, March 30, 1984, citing *The Financial Times* (London).

34. Penny Lernoux, "Rescue Missions Impossible," *The Nation*, October 6, 1984. For a discussion of this first Mexican debt crisis see Gatt-Fly, *Debt Bondage or Self-Reliance: A Popular Perspective on the Global Debt Crisis* (Toronto, 1985), pp.34-37.

35. *Time*, January 10, 1983.

36. Morgan Guaranty Trust, *World Financial Markets*, New York, February 1984.

37. For details of the Mexican situation, see Judith A. Teichman, *Policymaking in Mexico: From Boom to Crisis* (Boston: Allen & Unwin, 1988).

38. *GATT-Fly Report*, Vol. X, No.1 (February 1989).

39. Taylor, "Third World Debt" (emphasis added).

40. *The Globe and Mail*, October 5, 1981.

41. *The Globe and Mail*, January 16, 1982.

42. The Institute for African Alternatives (IAFF), *The IMF, the World Bank and Africa*, report of Conference on the Impact of the IMF and World Bank Policies on the People of Africa, London, 1987, p.9 (emphasis in original).

43. Abdul Rahman M. Babu, "The Berlin Trial," *Africa Events*, November 1988.

44. Data compiled by SELA (Sistema Economico Latinamericano) in *Excelsior* (Mexico City), September 7, 1988.

45. UNICEF, *The State of the World's Children 1990*.

46. *The Financial Times of Canada*, November 21, 1988.

47. *Fortune*, December 23, 1985, p.101.

48. *The Financial Post* (Toronto), February 1, 1988.

49. Ibid.

50. *The Globe and Mail*, December 2, 1988.

51. Taylor, "Third World Debt."

52. Dr. Manuel Montes, "Testimony to the Ecumenical Hearing on the International Monetary System and the Churches' Responsibility," West Berlin, August 1988.

53. CBC-Radio, *Ideas*, November 9, 1988.

54. Ibid.

55. For an example of a debt-equity swap: Ford bought $50 million of Mexican debt for U.S.$29 million, exchanging it for pesos worth $43.5 million and then investing the money in a plant it had already decided to build at Hermosillo just south of the border with Texas; see "Mexico's Capital Idea," *Euromoney*, September 1986, p.172.

56. *The New York Times*, March 19, 1989.

57. *The Wall Street Journal*, March 22, 1989.

58. *Forbes*, March 6, 1989.

59. Marcel Massé, "The Role of External Actors in Promoting Development and Change in Africa," in *Structural Adjustment in Africa* (Ottawa: North-South Institute, 1988).

60. John Loxley, *Debt and Disorder: External Financing for Development* (Boulder, Col.: Westview Press, and London: The North-South Institute, 1986), p.146.

61. IAFF, *The IMF, the World Bank and Africa*, p.13.

62. For descriptions of the scale and workings of this supranational economy see Naylor, *Hot Money;* and Kolko, *Restructuring the World Economy*.

63. Naylor, *Hot Money*, p.13.

64. Statistics Canada, *Canada's International Investment Position*, Catalogue 67-202, Ottawa, Annual.

65. Bank of Canada, *Review*, Table J1, Ottawa, June 1989.

66. *GATT-Fly Report*, August 1989.

67. Morgan Guaranty Trust, *World Financial Markets*, September 1986.

68. Quoted in Charles Taylor, *Radical Tories: The Conservative Tradition in Canada* (Toronto: Anansi, 1982), p.113.

69. Quoted in Fernand Braudel, *Civilization and Capitalism 15th-18th Century,* vol.II, *The Wheels of Commerce* (London: Fontana Press, 1985), p.237.

70. Ibid., p.601.

THREE

Women and Development Revisited: The Case for a Gender and Development Approach

Betty Plewes &
Rieky Stuart

And with the beauty of our vision,
  We'll be free.

                                        —song by J. Selby

The almost uniform conclusion of the [International Women's] Decade research is that with a few exceptions, women's relative access to economic resources, incomes, and employment has worsened, their burdens of work have increased, and their relative and even absolute health, nutritional, and educational status has declined.[1]

HOW IS IT possible – in view of all the information, publicity, and pressure surrounding women and development issues over the last 15 years – that the position of women internationally has declined? A poor Third World woman living in a rural area faces an appalling workday of 16 to 18 hours. Her housework is likely to include walking miles to fetch water and firewood to carry home on her head; pounding grain into flour by hand; cooking over a wood fire; washing clothes in the nearest stream. This alone is more than a full day's hard work, but she is also responsible for the other part of her "double day" – growing most of the family's food with little technological assistance beyond a hoe – and also for additional work on cash crops or "income-generating" activities.

The benefits of her labour accrue mainly to her husband and children as she does not often participate in local co-operative or political organizations where decisions that affect her life and work are made.

Although the majority of women in the Third World live in rural areas, an increasing number are moving to towns, with dreams of finding a better life. Once in town they have difficulty finding a place to live, transportation, or child care. The choices for earning a living are limited: domestic service, low paying jobs in export production industries, or small-scale trade in the "informal sector."

The life of poor Third World women has only worsened in the last 30 years of so-called development. In many instances, Third World women's workloads in tasks such as gathering fuel and collecting water have increased with development, as wastelands and commons have been privatized for capital-intensive production, and as traditional tree cover has been removed for commercial purposes.

The introduction of cash crops or irrigated agriculture may have improved the economic position of some men in rural areas, but it has most often worsened the income and work status of the women they live with. Men have increased the area under cultivation with the help of technology, which has increased women's workload of planting, weeding, and harvesting. Women seldom have access to increased revenue from the sale of cash crops. Where women's hand-labour has been replaced by technology – for example where mechanical milling of grain is replacing manual pounding – the newly mechanized jobs have frequently been taken over by paid male labour.

Structural adjustment policies, which drastically cut social services, place an increased burden on poor women to earn money for school fees for their children or medicine for the sick. Research in Zambia shows that after structural adjustment women earned less for their maize, in spite of deregulated prices, because of the higher cost of inputs.

Women-headed households in the Third World comprise the poorest families there – just as they do in Canada – and statistics indicate that in some Third World countries they represent from one-half to two-thirds of all households. Children in these households are more likely to suffer from malnutrition.

Only in the past 20 years have we become aware of the negative impact of development policies and programs on Third World women. A rapidly growing literature documents and analyses this impact. Women working in global, national, and non-governmental development organizations have lobbied, sometimes successfully, for policies and programs to assist women. This increased emphasis on the issues relating to women's role in development has become known as WID, Women in Development, a term coined by the women's committee of the Washington chapter of the Society for International Development, a learned society for development academics and professionals.

However, even as large and small development institutions were paying increased attention to women during the early 1980s, feminists in both the Third World and the West were becoming increasingly critical of the ideologies and values behind the various WID strategies adopted by United Nations agencies, the World Bank, and national development agencies like CIDA (Canadian International Development Agency) or USAID (United States Agency for International Development) as well as non-governmental development organizations.

THE HISTORICAL ROOTS OF THE
"WOMEN IN DEVELOPMENT" APPROACH

Development assistance to Third World countries has gone through a number of phases, including planned economic growth through infrastructure development (an approach associated with W.W. Rostow), meeting basic human needs (associated with Robert McNamara), and, in the 1980s and 1990s, structural adjustment. Each of these development programs, policies, and strategies is based on a notion of development as grounded in economic growth. That notion included predictions that increased productivity and mechanization in agriculture and increased industrialization would lead to increased exports, wealth, and domestic consumption just as it had in the "developed" countries.

The programs based on these development theories have failed, in part because this notion of development does not take into account the increasing disparities resulting from these policies – both between nations and within nations. The rich get richer and insulate themselves from the pollution, environmental degradation, and lack of basic human amenities suffered by the poor. Even more insidiously, this notion of development renders invisible the structures of power, decision-making, and control that are increasingly in the hands of those already privileged. A more complete definition of development takes into account social justice as well as modernization; a capacity for valuing and promoting the intrinsic worth of the person, as well as her labour; and democratic participation and economic redistribution.

Significantly, these development theories and policies are chiefly the domain of Western elite males and are manifest through the major power structures of the "development industry" – the IMF, the World Bank, USAID, OECD (Organization for Economic Cooperation and Development) and key UN development agencies. It should come as no surprise, then, that until very recently the dominant development frameworks paid little attention to women: development was for men. Even the New International Economic Order proposed by the developing countries at the United Nations in the 1970s had only one reference to women, and that was to their biological role. If women's voices were to be heard in the development debates, they were going to have to shout.

The acknowledged failure of the first development decade (the 1960s) and the emphasis in the second on "the poorest of the poor" and basic human needs made some development planners more open to women. The studies of this period clearly demonstrated that women were among the poorest sectors of the population. An understanding of their important role in child care, family health, and food production and preparation was key to the development of strategies for meeting basic human needs. During the 1970s there was increased attention to the world population "problem" – a case that clearly placed women on front stage as important actors. The emphasis throughout the period on economic growth led to a concern that women be more productively integrated into the economy. Economic growth, it was argued, could not take place without the participation of 50 per cent of the population. With the introduction of structural adjustment policies in the 1980s, women again became key as workers in the agricultural and industrial sectors, and as providers of health care and other services when government services were cut back. As Patricia Maguire noted, "So as the priorities shifted, the development industry found that it needed women."[2]

Both Third World and Western societies have long undervalued and underestimated the *reproductive* labour of women, that is, the work they do to reproduce and maintain the human race. At a personal level, the limited capacity of the (male) worker to function efficiently without the clean clothes, cooked food, and health and hygiene support traditionally provided by women is evident. Globally, Ruth Sivard estimates that this reproductive labour adds an uncounted one-third – or $4 trillion – to the world's annual economic product.[3]

Yet in most Third World countries it is women's *productive* labour – carrying firewood, fetching water, pounding grains – that forms the very backbone of national productivity, particularly in agriculture. The limits placed on women's productive labour by their arduous reproductive labour as well as the inefficiency of productive labour due to lack of training, credit, and appropriate technology became clear to those pushing the implementation of development programs based on economic growth and modernization. For these theorists and planners, integrating women in development became synonymous with increasing women's productivity.

A GLOBAL MOVEMENT FOR WOMEN'S LIBERATION

In the 1960s and 1970s the re-emergence of the women's movement had a significant impact on development debates – just as it had in every other major area of social and political relations. In Canada two key factors influenced this re-emergence: new education and work patterns for women and the growth of several popular movements. Over the course of the 20th century there were massive increases in the number of women entering the paid labour force. In the 1960s a university education also became accessible to large numbers of women. But in spite of these advances women still found themselves in low paying job ghettos and at the same time they remained responsible for most domestic work. More and more, however, the values and power structures of the late 1960s and early 1970s came under attack. Nancy Adamson, Linda Briskin, and Margaret McPhail described the situation in their book *Feminist Organizing for Change:*

These changes in women's work and educational patterns took place in the context of a series of popular movements in which everything was questioned – the student movement, the peace movement, the civil and native rights movements, the struggle for Quebec's independence and against increasing Canadian support to the U.S. war in Vietnam. Against the backdrop of these movements women began to explore their own situation, and their increasing consciousness of their own oppression politicized them.[4]

Women's political action in Canada took two significant forms within a wider and dynamic ideological discussion: the "institutionalized feminism" of groups, such as the Canadian Federation of University Women, that were lobbying for a royal commission on the status of women; and the grassroots feminism of locally based groups in universities, homes, and workplaces, with its emphasis on community organizing and consciousness-raising.[5] Feminists debated whether they wanted to enter the male world, transform it, or secede from it, and the richness and variety of their debates challenged and enriched the strategies and actions of all those working for improvements in the lives of women.

The experience of Canadian women paralleled that of women in Europe and the United States, where according to German sociologist Maria Mies the movements that developed in the context of major protest movements "were primarily cultural and affected mainly young, middle-class women."[6] At the community level internationally, women were organizing around issues of concern to them such as abortion and child care, while at the institutional level interest focused on women's role in development, women's studies, and the status of women.[7]

In the Third World, women's movements have a parallel and independent history.[8] Since the 19th century Third World women's movements have been an important force for change although, just as in the West, Third World women are only beginning to rediscover this history of organizing for change. There is increasing awareness of women's participation in nationalist and patriotic struggles, working-class agitation, and peasant rebellions. In Latin America both women of the elites and upper middle classes and those of the working classes have organized: the former in activities such as the marches of the "pots and pans" protesting Salvador Allende's socialist policies in Chile; the latter exemplified by the "Mothers of the Plaza del Mayo" protesting the disappearances of political activists organized by right-wing death squads.

Yet Third World women also have a history of organizing for their rights and liberation as women. In Sri Lanka women of the left parties formed the first autonomous women's feminist socialist group in 1948.[9] In Cameroon, the *anlu* was a form of traditional women's organization to protect their rights from encroachment by men; it was used successfully in the 1950s to prevent colonial administrators from interfering with women's land, agricultural methods, and teaching practices.[10]

As in the North, in the 1970s a grassroots movement of Third World feminists developed through the formation of autonomous women's groups or centres around particular issues. [11] In Jamaica, Sistren, a women's popular theatre group, began dramatizing women's oppression and providing assistance for poor women to organize around their problems. On the Mexican side of the Mexican-U.S. border, women organized to improve wages and benefits in the exploitative *maquiladora* (assembly) industries operated by transnational corporations with the blessing of the Mexican government. In India women's groups waged tireless campaigns against "bride-burning" – the harassment and eventual murder of young wives to extract larger dowries. *Manushi*, a women's magazine published in India, was a leader in this effort.

These women's groups often began in the face of great difficulties in securing support or funding and often lacked even the ability to meet openly to organize around women's issues. Z.M. Ahmad describes the special problems many women, particularly rural women, face in defending their interests and organizing themselves:

In most traditional cultures women seldom speak up in meetings when men are present, so that their views are frequently not taken into account in arriving at organizational decisions. Also, very few women are represented in higher level decision-making committees. In many cultures where seclusion is practiced, women have little freedom of choice in participating in organizational activities. They do not always control their own activities, even their decision on where to work being controlled by other household members – husband, mother-in-law, etc. – and this is equally true when it comes to making a decision on whether to join organizations, especially those which include male members. Finally it needs to be recognized that part of the struggle in which women are engaged is in opposition to the male members of their families, e.g. when women are beaten by their husbands, when men use up women's hard-earned money on drink etc. [12]

Women in the Third World saw themselves as needing to organize for power to solve the problems they were experiencing as women, but many of the groups saw their own situation as embedded in and inter-related with other relations of subordination: of class, race, and economic imperialism.

THE INSTITUTIONALIZATION OF WID

In 1970 Ester Boserup, a Danish economist, shook up the major international, national, and non-governmental development institutions when she published her critical and pioneering work *Women's Role in Economic Development*. [13] Boserup's work demonstrated that development was not only not helping women in the Third World, but that in many cases development projects were also contributing to a deterioration in women's status. She attributed this negative impact to *seems to be the case frequently in the failure of owl's programs*

a lack of knowledge about the economic – and particularly the agricultural – roles of women in the Third World, the negative impact on women of colonialism and the penetration of capitalism, and Western male bias in development planning. [14]

Boserup's work had a catalytic effect on women working in the development agencies, especially in the UN and USAID. In the early 1970s an informal network of female development planners, experts, managers, and academic researchers began documenting additional evidence of women's exclusion from development strategies and programs. The women in the Washington chapter of the Society for International Development, who had coined the term WID, began to formulate strategies for using the information they had collected to influence development policy. By 1973 the committee's successful lobby resulted in the passage of the Percy Amendment to the U.S. Foreign Assistance Act, which established as policy for USAID that women be integrated into development efforts. [15]

Along with these other international agencies, CIDA also began to show concern about WID issues in the early 1970s. In 1975 CIDA hired a Special Adviser on Women and Development and set up a modest Integration of Women in Development Responsibility Centre. The special adviser was to make sure the agency was sensitive to women's issues, provide expertise, and monitor the implementation of the WID strategy. This strategy was put forward by the CIDA President's Committee in 1977 as a "Statement of Policy Directives for the Integration of Women in Development" whose goals were "to ensure equal access to the benefits of social and economic development for men and women and to ensure that women participate in fact as agents and beneficiaries of socio-economic and political development equally with men." [16]

International Women's Year (IWY), proclaimed by the United Nations in 1975, was a key event that brought together for the first time development planners in the "development industry," government ministers, and women from the NGO sector to set out an action plan for WID. [17] The themes for IWY were peace, equality, and development. To discuss and develop a plan of action around these themes, an official conference hosted by Mexico involved 133 government delegations as well as inter-governmental bodies, UN agencies, and liberation movements. Running parallel to the official conference was the International Women's Year Tribune, which drew thousands of NGO representatives to a less formal round of seminars, discussions, and cultural events. The official conference produced a World Plan of Action and declared the UN Decade for Women (1976-85). Two additional conferences were held subsequently to monitor progress on the plan of action – one at the mid-Decade point in Copenhagen and an end-of-Decade conference in Nairobi. Again, as in Mexico, non-governmental conferences ran parallel to the official governmental conferences.

While the conferences provided important opportunities both for examining the situation of women around the world and for networking, the NGO forums also revealed some of the divisions within the international women's movement. Development planners and policy makers, especially those in major development institutions (and also in many NGOs), have considered feminism to be irrelevant to development programs for women. A dramatic example of this perspective was a quote that appeared in one of the issues of the Copenhagen NGO Forum newspaper: "To talk feminism to a woman who has no water, no food and no home is to talk nonsense."

Many of those involved in the work of the Decade were not feminists, and feminism itself does not have one coherent ideology. Kate Young described four major ideological variations in feminism, all differing in their analyses of the causes of women's subordination as well as in their prescriptions for change. [18] Third World feminists have criticized both the "development industry" and Northern feminists for their ethnocentric bias and their unwillingness to see the connections among race, gender, and class issues. The women's movements in the industrialized countries have concentrated on organizing around a limited number of issues affecting women in those countries – child care, reproductive rights, violence against women, and discrimination – and have not made the connection between those issues and more global structures of oppression. [19]

Northern women have also been criticized for trying to impose issues on Southern women. This, in its extreme, is seen as a form of cultural imperialism. At Copenhagen Northern women raised the question of female genital mutilation amid a storm of criticism from African women. While the African women agreed that female genital mutilation was an expression of male sexual violence against women perpetuated by women, they resented the issue being brought to the floor of an international forum by Northern women and declared their right and intention to determine their own strategies and priorities in their struggle for liberation in this and any other issue.

Although areas of conflict were still in evidence in Nairobi in 1985, over the course of the 1980s the basis for dialogue between Northern and Southern women had expanded. In Nairobi there were many more women from Third World countries than there had been in Copenhagen – and they were defining the issues and playing key roles in the conference. By 1985 it was clear that Third World women were constructing an indigenous feminist theory and practice that linked struggles against sexual inequality to other political struggles. [20] How did this experience of Third World feminists, in their theory and practice, understand the "women in development" approach?

CHARACTERISTICS OF THE WID APPROACH

The UN Decade for Women and its high-profile conferences were instrumental in promoting the WID agenda, as well as providing forums for discussion of alternative approaches. The major development agencies (World Bank, USAID, CIDA, European state development assistance agencies) adopted a common framework for their work with women, largely as a result of IWY in 1975. [21] But the approach by WID planners to the Decade's themes of "equality, development, and peace" shifted over time in relation to changes in development thinking and strategies in these major agencies. [22]

The emphasis of the early WID strategies was on equity – equality with men. In the words of Caroline Moser of the London School of Economics, this approach "identifies the origins of women's subordination as lying not only in the context of the family, but also in the relations between men and women in the market place, and hence it places considerable emphasis on economic independence as being synonymous with equity." [23]

The equity approach reflected the preoccupation of Northern feminists with equality, and it met with much resistance from development agencies and Third World governments. It required a redistribution of power between men and women and so has been dropped by the majority of implementing agencies. [24]

The greater emphasis in the second development decade – the 1970s – on the poor and especially the "poorest of the poor" led to an anti-poverty focus as the second WID approach. Here economic inequality between men and women was linked to poverty rather than subordination, and thus women's issues were separated from equity issues. [25] This shift also reflected a movement from "equality" towards "development".

Caroline Moser argues that in the 1980s there was a further shift away from an approach focused on anti-poverty to one emphasizing efficiency, which then became the predominant focus of the WID school. [26] According to this new approach, women need to be included in development activities to make the programs and projects more efficient. This shift occurred at the same time as there was a marked deterioration in the world economy and when the IMF and World Bank were advocating increased efficiency and productivity as two objectives of the structural adjustment programs. Thus these shifts in the rationale of WID programming should also be understood within a global political and economic framework for development policy. [27]

The shift in rationale from "equity" to "efficiency" is similarly evident in the evolution of CIDA policy. A 1977 policy directive talked about "equal access" to development benefits for men and women and women's participation as agents and beneficiaries "equally with men." By 1986 there is no mention of equality. Instead, "Development must involve men and women in order to be effective"; "Development must contribute to the realization of the full potential of women"; and "Women are to be included as both agents and beneficiaries." A letter from the minister of external relations introducing this policy notes that development cannot be achieved if it continues to ignore 50 per cent of a country's human resources.

By 1984 there was a strong commitment within CIDA to confront the institutional barriers to change with respect to WID and to deepen the agency's understanding of the issues. In that year a new WID director produced a policy paper,

Managing the Process of Change: Women in Development. Drawing on lessons in institutional change in other government departments, she outlined a structural perspective for understanding the impact of gender discrimination and proposed a systemic accountability model for combating its effect throughout CIDA. The paper notes that the integration of women in the development process was originally propelled by a concern for social equity but must also be seen as an issue of development effectiveness. Projects often fail if the perspectives of women are not taken into account. [28]

By 1984 CIDA also had a policy framework and action strategy for meeting its stated WID goal, "to ensure that the full range of its [CIDA's] development assistance will contribute substantively to the realization of the full potential of women as agents and beneficiaries of development." [29] The action plan was guided by several key objectives:

☐ to respond to the development efforts of Third World women.
☐ to achieve greater understanding of the existing multiple roles and potential roles of Third World women.
☐ to increase the participation of Third World women in the design, implementation, and evaluation of development interventions.
☐ to include women in CIDA programs and projects, in proportion to their share in the target group, to ensure that their existing level of participation is not reduced.
☐ to place particular emphasis on strategies to assist Third World women in generating and keeping income including those measures that alleviate women's time and energy constraints stemming from work demands in the household and their role in food production.
☐ to support special women's programs linked to overall development where special efforts are required to reach women because of cultural conditions or where separate programs are deemed necessary. [30]

The agency adopted both policy and operational objectives along with an organizational strategy to ensure that all of its branches took responsibility for implementation. In doing so, CIDA has been effective in institutionalizing the policy and Canada has gained a reputation internationally for its commitment to women and development. [31]

While WID built its policies on the pioneering work of Ester Boserup, who had argued that women were being harmed by the development process, Boserup did not question the dominant development model itself. That model – which encouraged export-oriented agriculture and industry, openness of the economy to foreign investment, and the transfer of financial and technical resources from North to South – was accepted as one that would promote economic growth.

The problem for women, the WID school argued, was that they were left out of this development process. Their domestic and agricultural labour was either ignored or undervalued. Training and other inputs such as new and more productive technology or access to credit were directed to men. At the same time this process of modernization destroyed women's traditional support systems and undermined their productive work. Without challenging the development model per se, WID proponents focused on two major causes for this gender discrimination: the Western male bias of development planners; and barriers to women's participation, such as traditional attitudes, limited education, poor health, and limited free time.[32]

Thus, because they saw Third World women as excluded from modern economic development, WID proponents sought ways to integrate them, usually through formal employment. Skills were required to prepare those women for such work, and so considerable emphasis was placed on education and training programs for them. Such programs have been geared not only to developing job skills but also to training for family planning, nutrition, and maternal and child health. With the increased concern about the population problem and women's education, the WID school drew close links between employment and fertility. Planners assumed, "Education and employment would simultaneously increase women's economic contribution and reduce fertility."[33] Because most development agencies carried out their work through development projects, guided by policy statements similar to those outlined by CIDA, their primary concern was to encourage the integration of women into those ongoing, large infrastructural projects. They also recognized that in some cases projects would have to be designed specifically for women.

The inadequacy of information about women's activities, roles, and status cross-culturally became a major focus for those encouraging WID analysis within the major development institutions, and throughout the UN Decade the collection of information about women became an important activity of the WID network. The work took the form of research into all aspects of women's lives, the reorganization of statistical data by sex, and studies to identify and quantify women's status in different countries.[34]

Out of this a new category of work came to the fore: gender analysis – the process of systematically analysing the sexual division of labour and the differing degrees of access and control that women and men have over inputs to their work, their work itself, and the products of their work. The analysis would be used as a basis for planning development projects and for making planners sensitive to the complexities of women's issues both internationally and locally in the Third World. In fact, the growth of WID work generated a parallel growth in "WID experts," women (mainly) paid to research and plan the integration of women in economic development projects. This group tends to speak for poor Third World women, and, in a sense, lives on their backs. These experts, from both the West and the Third World, speak at conferences, act as consultants, and undertake research and evaluations. Their motivations range from personal and professional opportunism to a genuine solidarity with and commitment to participate in the struggle against the oppression of those most oppressed: poor Third World women.

Agencies also recognized that the attitudes and skills of their own staff could influence the implementation of WID policies and strategies and in some agencies efforts have been made to increase the number of women in development posts, on the assumption that women are more sensitive to women's issues. USAID, the World Bank, and other major development agencies such as CIDA have all emphasized staff training programs in gender analysis. [35]

A FEMINIST CRITIQUE OF WID

For the major development institutions (from the World Bank to CIDA), the adoption of WID strategies provided a convenient rationale for the apparent failure of the development process to advance the cause of the poor over the past three development decades. With a glib and partial rationale, development planners reasoned that development projects had not succeeded because women were not being taken into account.

Yet, parallel to this increased attention to WID policies within CIDA and other development agencies, feminists from both North and South have advanced their own critiques, which in many respects expose the bankruptcy of the dominant development strategies for women as well as for the poor majorities of the South as a whole.

One of the problems is that although WID focused on poor Third World women, the relationship is something of a long distance affair, as the Indian feminist Anita Anand notes. [36] The work has largely been defined by Western women and their elitist counterparts in developing countries. Anand argues that as such WID falls prey to the fact that the development problem for the poor remains overseas while its solutions are imposed through the financial resources and skills of Northern institutions. As Asoka Bandarage puts it, "WID is *about* poor women in the Third World; it is not a force *of* those women themselves." [37] The critics of WID assert that any approach seeking to help poor Third World women must include those women themselves as architects and agents – not merely as beneficiaries.

While WID has contributed to the exposure of the negative effects of economic modernization on women, it is important to understand its limitations. The promotion of free trade zones and policies of structural adjustment by the World Bank, the IMF, and all major development agencies point to these contradictions.

The adoption of a WID approach by the major international development agencies has been entirely consistent with the efforts of one of those agencies, the

World Bank, to promote strategies that incorporate women on exploitative terms into the formal sector through employment in free trade zones. These are areas where national governments grant concessions (land, taxes, infrastructure) to encourage transnational corporations to establish facilities, most commonly for the production of garments, textiles, sporting equipment, electrical goods, and components for the electronics industry. The firms usually benefit from relaxed minimum wages, the absence of trade unions, and weak or non-existent health and safety legislation. Women usually find only short-term unskilled employment in these zones – work that tends to be hazardous to their health (they get eye damage from micro-chip assembly, damaged lungs from lint aspiration). Still, the major institutions see the income and employment generated by these industries as being in harmony with the WID strategy.

It is also important to note the roles expected of women in the structural adjustment programs advocated by the World Bank and the IMF. Peggy Antrobus states that while she had once argued that structural adjustment policies had failed to take gender roles into account, she later began to realize that these policies were "actually grounded in a gender ideology which is deeply and fundamentally exploitative of women's time / work and sexuality."[38] As an example she notes that the emphasis on export-oriented production leads to a concentration of government resources in that sector and a neglect of the sectors that produce for the domestic market, such as food production and distribution, where women predominate. Women are also expected to fill in the gaps left by the reduction in social services, especially in the fields of health and education.[39]

Even UNICEF, which has advocated adjustment with a human face, suggested that structural adjustment can promote efficient and effective social services through "self-help." UNICEF realized that this meant a shift of responsibilities to women, but noted, "While such an approach may increase the time costs for women it will place extremely modest monetary costs on the household and will lead to substantial savings in the public sector."[40] The institution did not discuss how women could combine these additional responsibilities with their acknowledged extremely important role in agriculture. Women's time, it would seem, is infinitely elastic. There is solid evidence that structural adjustment policies are profoundly inimical to women: The WID approach, with its emphasis on economic integration, is silent on this question.

The feminist critique of the failure of WID springs from the approach's philosophical and ideological roots in modernization theory and the liberal stream of feminism.[41] The central theme of the liberal branch of feminism is equality of opportunity and a strong belief in the role of the state in bringing about that equality. The branch sees inequalities between men and women as the result of aberrations within an otherwise just and equitable social system. Liberal feminists, therefore, do not see any need for a fundamental change of the economic and social order. Their vision includes a redistribution of opportunity to give women the access to the power and opportunities of men. The strategy concentrates on improving educational opportunities, changing socialization patterns, and removing legislation that discriminates against women. [42]

When this view is transposed into the WID school, sexual inequality in the Third World is ascribed to traditional values and male ignorance. [43] Strategies include, as in the North, legislative reform and attitude changes. In addition the strategies place heavy emphasis on intervention projects designed to provide basic needs and on work that will generate income for poor Third World women. The strategies also stress the incorporation of women into the paid labour force as the equals of men.

But as feminists developed their theory and practice over the past two decades, it became clearer that oppressive gender relations were deeply imbedded in all major institutions. The early optimism of women struggling for the reform of inegalitarian laws as the key to women's advancement yielded to a more realistic appreciation of how complex a project it is to change gender relations. These relations are a product not merely of laws and attitudes but also of the sexual division of labour, of family relations, of economic and power relations, and even of a woman's personal sense of identity.

By 1985 it was clear that there were serious weaknesses in the WID approach and in major projects specifically designed for women. Although many Third World women were significantly worse off than they had been at the beginning of the UN Decade, within the development bureaucracies there was still massive resistance to more pro-active ways of supporting women. Projects for women had suffered from a top-down planning approach, inadequate funding and managerial support, and a lack of data about women's real situations. The projects also tended to be small, scattered, and peripheral to the main thrust of agencies' country programs and plans. [44] In spite of these shortcomings, many feminists acknowledged that "these projects contribute to the increasing numbers of women becoming conscious of the 'woman's question'" through "providing women with skills, training, experience and a sense of power that they would otherwise have found difficult to obtain." [45]

Just as liberal feminists have not questioned the underlying socio-economic model in their own countries, WID proponents have not questioned the underlying development model promoted by the bilateral and multilateral agencies. It was assumed that this model would promote growth and bring benefits to men; therefore women, it seemed, would also benefit if they were incorporated into it. But the overwhelming evidence demonstrated that poor men have not benefited from current approaches, and in fact have been increasingly set aside on the margins of Third World economies and societies. Thus it seems equally clear to the critics of the model that incorporating poor women into this same system will not benefit those women.

Third World economies have been integrated into the international economy on an unequal basis. This has had negative consequences for the economy as a whole – consequences felt most sharply by poor women. Women are already integrated into their national economy, but on unequal terms through their unpaid domestic and subsistence labour. There have been few benefits for the women who have increasingly participated in the wage-labour force in the Third World, which entails "at best working as a factory or field labourer and at worst as a maid or a prostitute."[46] Given that women are integrated on unequal terms, "This further deepens the class, racial and national cleavages among women."[47] The WID school focuses on unequal relationships between women and men, and ignores these complex interactions of social class, race, and ethnicity, all of which combine to oppress women.

The WID proponents give no coherent explanation of the root causes of women's oppression. They propose economic solutions without a structural economic analysis of the problems women face. They are not clear about who will benefit from women's increased economic contribution and there is little discussion of the fact that when women move into waged labour they retain responsibility for reproductive and domestic work.[48] The approach does not even consider integrating men into domestic labour. Thus the approach assumes that women themselves – and not the relations between women and men – are the problem. The structures perpetuating oppressive gender relations are not an element of the WID analysis.

These strategies for economic integration have not worked in the North. Women in Northern countries have gained a large measure of legislative equality and have participated in the paid labour force in unprecedented numbers. But they still suffer from being shut off in job ghettos. They suffer from sexual harassment, rape, and other kinds of violence. They suffer from having to take full responsibility for domestic work and child rearing, and from lack of status. It is not surprising, then, that WID policies in Northern development agencies have also ignored these critical elements of gender relations.

The current international economic and political system depends for its continued existence on the exploitation of women's time, work, and sexuality. Maria Mies gives a detailed analysis of how the international capitalist system with its need for accumulation and its international division of labour oppresses women in both First and Third World countries.[49] Since the system is inherently exploitative of women, further incorporation into the system cannot be the solution. Equality of opportunity can never occur within the current structure; a radical transformation of capitalist patriarchal society is required for women to gain equality.

Feminist critics in both the North and South have acknowledged the tremendous contribution of the WID school in bringing to international attention the negative effects of development on poor Third World women. They question,

limits of its effectiveness in bringing about women's liberation,
ts lack of analysis of the roots of women's oppression, which leads
) faulty strategies.

D WORLD FEMINIST ALTERNATIVE

Th.. World feminists are also critical of WID and its liberal feminist assumptions. They maintain that Northern feminism has grown out of a particular historical and class context and is therefore not universally applicable. [50] A failure by many Northern feminists to recognize this context has led to criticisms of cultural imperialism and racist bias. The charge of cultural imperialism comes, for instance, when Northern feminists try to determine priorities and strategies for Third World women – around the issues of female sexual mutilation, for example. [51] Another example is the Northern analysis of the oppressive nature of the family. Third World women do not accept this analysis as universally valid: Some of them experience extended family relations as a support for their liberation rather than a limitation.

This clash led a number of Third World women activists to reconsider whether they would describe themselves as feminists. However, in workshops held in Bangkok (1979) and Stony Point (1980) Third World activists and academics affirmed their use of the word feminism and defined it in terms of two long-term goals:

1) The freedom from oppression for women involves not only equity, but also the right of women to freedom of choice, and to power over our own lives within and outside the home. 2) The second goal of feminism is the removal of all forms of inequity and oppression through the creation of a more just social and economic order, nationally and internationally. [52]

As a result of the dissatisfaction with the predominant WID focus on equity, an alternative approach to women's issues and their implications for development began to evolve. [53] It comes from the feminist writings and experience in grassroots organizations of Third World women and is based on empowerment of women through greater self-reliance and their own organizing activities. [54] Perhaps its best articulation comes from members of DAWN (Development Alternatives for a New Era), a network of Third World activists, researchers, and policy makers in their book, *Development, Crises, and Alternative Visions: Third World Women's Perspectives.* [55]

DAWN examines the development model assumed by the major agencies and argues that the strategies for overall economic growth and increased agricultural and industrial productivity have proved inimical to women. This is because gender relations oppress women and because many long-term economic processes have been harmful – or at best indifferent – to the needs of poor people. [56] A set of interlinked crises in the areas of food and fuel, financial and monetary disarray, environmental degradation, and demographic pressure has worsened the situation for poor people. Structural adjustment policies designed to try to restore the international economic balance have had devastating effects on poor people. Under structural adjustment programs women's employment may increase, but these increases come mainly in factories in free trade zones, on agribusiness plantations, and in the so-called informal sector. The cutbacks in social services have serious implications for increasing women's unpaid work in the home and decreasing access for women to health and education services.[57]

Reaction to the deepening economic crises has led to increased militarization, domestic repression, and foreign aggression, with the effect being fiscal cutbacks in other areas to support military expansion, vast numbers of women and children refugees, sexual abuse and rape, and the further entrenchment of a macho ideology.

At the same time women have developed a great capacity for creative response and have begun to organize and work together to improve economic conditions for themselves and others. Women in Northern India "hugging trees," for instance, have won concessions from government against clear-cutting contractors to maintain their right to fuel, timber, and other forest products. In Nicaragua, women's increasing involvement in political and economic organizations has strengthened their realization that without transformation of the sexual division of labour, there can be no real emancipation for women. During the 1980s, overcoming "machismo" was held up as an integral part of Nicaragua's revolutionary struggle. Women's experience has been that their subordination remains a problem in socialist societies.

It is necessary to build on these experiences and formulate a vision of the kind of society women want – and then develop strategies to get there. DAWN proposes a set of short-term and long-term strategies that will respond to the immediate situation that women find themselves in, as well as have the potential to transform some of the structures that oppress women. One important strategy is strengthening women's own organizations to further empower women.

The Self-Employed Women's Association (SEWA) of Ahmadabad, India, is one example. Ela Bhatt, originally the head of the women's wing of a male industrial trade union, was expected to improve the ability of male unionists' wives to support their husbands. Instead she developed what has become an independent "union" of self-employed women organized by occupation: rag-pickers, metal-workers, petty traders, load-carriers. SEWA developed strategies for bargaining with middlemen, dealing with police harassment, and providing mutual savings and credit. SEWA assisted with group purchase of imports and marketing. The women's confidence, pride, and economic self-reliance increased, as did their sense of the power of organization. When SEWA and its parent industrial union differed in analysis and strategy around an election issue, the women's organization

123

was strong enough to maintain its feminist perspective and disaffiliate from the men's union.

GABRIELA, in the Philippines, is a coalition of grassroots women's organizations with a clear feminist vision that supports increasing self-awareness and organized power for women. The organization has not hesitated to tackle problems of economic poverty, battering of women, and sexual exploitation in a manner that has combined the need to help poor women directly with the need to end the causes of women's exploitation.

DAWN argues that the perspective of poor and oppressed women is a unique and powerful vantage point from which to examine the effectiveness of all development programs and strategies. [58]

Because poor Third World women are among the most economically and socially disadvantaged women in the world, any assessment of development's success must be measured by their improved standard of living, access to dignified employment, and reduction in societal and workload inequality. The impact of development strategies on health care, sanitation, and provision of food, water, and fuel can best be assessed by starting with the views and experience of those Third World women who do the bulk of this work.

WOMEN AND DEVELOPMENT IN CANADA:
AN NGO PERSPECTIVE

The DAWN approach, both in the writing and in the workshops conducted at the 1985 Nairobi Forum, has had an important influence on feminists active within Canadian NGOs. Canadian voluntary organizations characterize their international development orientation as promoting participatory community involvement and being experimental and responsive to the needs of poor people. In theory, NGOs should therefore be more effective than government in responding to women's needs. Analysis of NGO practice, however, reveals little to distinguish their approach from that of most Northern donor governments.

A CIDA evaluation of Canadian NGO programs revealed "a strong tendency for most of the projects directed to women to be in the field of social welfare, home economics, child care and nutrition, or in a narrow range of jobs stereotyped as being good for women only." [59] Most NGOs publicly consider women to be a priority, but few of them have policy statements relating to women or gender relations. In a 1985 study undertaken by the Canadian Council for International Cooperation (CCIC), 70 per cent of the NGOs said they support activities related to women, and 75 per cent of these indicated they did not have guidelines for women's development either in project planning or evaluation. [60]

At the policy level an important exception has been the Women and Development Committee of the CCIC which has sponsored training workshops and joint NGO activities, including a study of the impact of NGO projects on women, a

124

workshop on Women and Food Production at the Nairobi conference, and a definitive policy paper, "Ensuring a Women's Perspective is Present in NGO Development Programs," which was accepted by the CCIC in 1988.

The CCIC policy paper draws from the DAWN framework and the analysis of the roots of Third World women's oppression for a set of NGO guidelines in the area of gender bias, criteria for development with women, feminist process, advocacy, and development education.[61] The policy notes that development for women should be planned and implemented using the framework of "women's practical and strategic needs."[62] Women's practical needs for food, shelter, clothing, and income for themselves and their families should not be separated from women's strategic needs to end their subordinate relationships with men and increase their power over their own lives. Several key Canadian NGOs have considered these strategic questions in the development of their programs and policies over the past decade.   ESSAY 1:

Match International, a Canadian NGO that focuses on small-scale projects for women, was created following the International Women's Year Conference in Mexico in 1975. Its goal has been "to create a direct link for action between Third World women and Canadians ... with a view to facilitating the full integration of women into the development process."[63] Small-scale projects were supported which "matched" the needs and resources of women in the Third World with those of women in Canada. By 1987, a major evaluation of Match had suggested that both changes in the development environment and the increased awareness of gender issues within the NGO community required a redefinition of its role. The study proposed a strategic orientation for Match to emphasize thematic activities based on an explicit analysis of women's struggle for justice and equality within given societies. It suggested that the themes should be based on strategic gender issues, such as structural barriers to equality and full participation in development, rather than practical gender issues, such as improved access to clean water and training. Exchanges, networking, policy advocacy, and information dissemination would constitute the core of its Canadian activities.

Other NGOs such as CUSO, Development and Peace, and Oxfam-Canada have supported animation and income-generating projects for women, but attention to women's needs has not spilled over into the NGO community at large, according to CIDA's evaluation.[64] This no doubt relates to some of the weaknesses of the NGO community identified in the North-South Institute review of the Canadian voluntary sector.[65] Canadian NGOs have a limited presence on the ground overseas and are therefore not always aware of the contexts in which they are working. They have not invested in research that would lead to effective policy development and staff training, and they have not been particularly effective in involving beneficiaries in project design. Given these factors in combination with preponderantly male field staff in Canadian and international NGOs, along with difficulties in reaching women in many Third World countries, it becomes apparent why the Canadian NGO record has not been more encouraging.

By the latter part of the 1980s there was a growing interest, particularly among women in the NGO community, in changing this situation, and in recent years several encouraging initiatives have taken place.

Match and Partnership Africa Canada (PAC) have collaborated on researching how Canadian NGOs can support the strategic and practical gender interests of Southern African women. This research is intended to culminate in Southern Africa women's organizations setting priorities for ways that Canadian NGOs can support their struggle, and in mechanisms to jointly plan and manage program implementation.

In February 1989 CUSO and Match organized a workshop to review CUSO's experience with gender and development. The product of the workshop was a gender policy as well as a program-planning framework incorporating gender issues. CCIC has developed programs for sensitizing and training Canadian NGO management and staff in the development and implementation of appropriate gender policies.

TOWARDS A "GENDER AND DEVELOPMENT" APPROACH

As a result of our experience in working with CIDA and with Canadian NGOs, as well as from our own critique of WID approaches, Canadian feminists working in development have begun to articulate an alternative analysis of the connections between women's issues and development issues. We speak as development workers who are rooted in a feminist perspective, and who bring this perspective to development programming. We have begun – and are by no means finished – to develop a gender and development approach and to formulate some clear conclusions.

A gender and development approach centres on the relations between women and men as the focus of analysis, rather than on women alone. It sees these relations as interdependent, rooted in different perspectives and experiences, and unequal. Both men and women are bound by these relations, which are, in the main, socially constructed. But because they are created by human beings, they can be recreated – transformed – by women and men.

The theory and practice of feminists in the last few decades have shown us that the struggle to transform the relations between women and men is long, complex, and often difficult. In this context, the feminist definition of the difference between the position and condition of women (their strategic interests as women, and their practical needs) provides a useful tool to analyse proposed strategies and programs. A gender and development approach emphasizes the need to combine both strategic and practical considerations in development work.

The insights gained from a feminist critique of the nature of dominant / subordinate relationships between men and women enable us to analyse and challenge other dominant / subordinate relationships: class, race, North / South, East / West, human / nature. A gender and development approach is rooted in feminism and reaches out to include class, race, and environmental issues. It seeks ways to redefine these relationships of "power-over" with non-hierarchical conceptions of power.

A gender and development approach is concerned about the process as well as the goal, the *how* as well as the *what*. It sees poor Third World women and other oppressed groups not as instruments or target groups but as architects, agents, and beneficiaries of development.

A gender and development approach is holistic, not segmented, which means that visions, strategies, and actions need to be examined from the perspective both of the world and the hearthstone; who scrubs the kitchen pots influences the world, and global policies influence the lives of women and men in remote corners of the world. The interactions of gender, class, race, and environmental issues are of concern in a gender and development approach: None is an independent variable, capable of being addressed without reference to or impact on the others. We are only beginning to learn how to work while keeping the intricacy of these interrelationships in focus.

We have seen that integration into the present development paradigm is not an answer for women or, indeed, for many other groups. A gender and development approach calls for an alternative paradigm, which seeks to transform radically rather than merely reform current social, political, economic, and gender relationships. Feminism informs our critique of WID and the growth-oriented policies of which it forms a part. From this perspective, we see that the present development paradigm is rooted in a particular view of the world that is linear, hierarchical, economistic, and male. All problems, relationships, and actions are understood within the context of this worldview, and yet that worldview is largely outside the scope of analysis because it is all-pervasive.

Scientists say that such a worldview or paradigm remains valid and unanalysed in spite of internal contradictions until, at a critical point, there is a shift in the paradigm, and collectively people move into a new way of understanding the world, with different assumptions. [66] Because women are for the most part left out of the current dominant paradigm, they are well placed to assist in this shift. The new paradigm will include women's contribution to a redefinition of what work is, and a social re-evaluation of work: productive and reproductive work, head work and body work, sustaining work and innovative work.

Canadian feminist development workers have learned that individual, or even collective action, is not enough; we must work to change the organizations and structures we live and work in. We know that the personal is political, and now, as development workers concerned about women, we are also learning that the organizational is political. Working more effectively on behalf of Third World women within our existing job descriptions in our existing organizations is at best a make-do, exhausting struggle with limited resources. It is burnout rather than social transformation.

The analysis of WID shows that we can change the policies and practice of organizations. Our institutions are what we make them, and through organized pressure from inside and outside, they respond to our priorities. To be effective in achieving our goals, we need to learn how to change organizations – from mission statements to hiring practice, from planning and implementation to organizational culture. Grappling with the responsibility and methodology of making organizations and institutions socially accountable is an essential part of shaping the new paradigm. It is not an adequate response to blame organizations – whether the World Bank, a corporation, a government, or an NGO – for the social harm they do.

Collectively, we permit our organizations to act irresponsibly because our strategies for change do not include adequate tools for organizational change. The feminist analysis of the WID experience is a rich field for improving our capacity in this area. It helps us to view organizations through new eyes, not as uncontrollable, inhuman entities, or objects of conspiracy theories, but as social constructions, shaped by the people who work in them and who use their products. If we conceive of them as social constructions, we can conceive of transforming them.

These elements of a gender approach are not necessarily original or unique. They are drawn from our work and our lives, our reading, sharing, and reflection, and represent a current understanding. The diversity of women's experience and our sharing and learning from each other will continue to inform both a gender and development approach and its contribution to the larger struggle of reformulating what we mean by development.

Notes

1. Gita Sen and Caren Grown, *Development, Crises and Alternative Visions: Third World Women's Perspectives* (New York: Monthly Review Press), 1987, p.28.

2. Patricia Maguire, "Women in Development: An Alternative Analysis 1984," mimeo, Center for International Education, University of Massachusetts, 1984, p.9.

3. Ruth Leger Sivard, *Women: A World Survey* (Washington, D.C.: World Priorities, 1985), p.1.

4. Nancy Adamson, Linda Briskin, and Margaret McPhail, *Feminist Organizing for Change: The Contemporary Women's Movement in Canada* (Toronto: Oxford University Press, 1988), p.38.

5. Ibid., p.29.

6. Maria Mies, *Patriarchy and Accumulation on a World Scale: Women in the International Division of Labour* (London: Zed Books, 1986), p.20.

7. Ibid., p.9.

8. Kumari Jayawardena, *Feminism and Nationalism in the Third World* (London: Zed Books, 1986).

9. Kumari Jayawardena, in ISIS (Women's International Information and Communication Service), *Women in Development: A Resource Guide for Organization and Action* (Philadelphia: New Society Publishers, 1984), p.23.

10. Karen Sacks, "An Overview of Women and Power in Africa," in *Perspectives on Power: Women in Africa, Asia, and Latin America*, ed. Jean F. O'Barr, Duke University Center for International Studies, occasional paper no.13, Durham, North Carolina, 1982, p.8.

11. Mies, *Patriarchy and Accumulation*, p.9.

12. See Z.M Ahmad, "Women's Work and their Struggle to Organize," in *Development: Seeds of Change*, No.4 (1984).

13. Ester Boserup, *Women's Role in Economic Development* (London: George Allen & Unwin, 1970).

14. Lourdes Beneria and Gita Sen, "Accumulation, Reproduction, and Women's Role in Economic Development: Boserup Revisited," *Signs*, Vol.7, No.2 (1981).

15. Kathleen Staudt, "Bureaucratic Resistance to Women's Programs: The Case of Women and Development," paper presented to the 76th Annual Meeting of the American Anthropological Association, Toronto, undated. p.4.

16. Elizabeth McAllister, "Managing the Process of Change 1984," Annex 1(A), CIDA, Ottawa, 1984. A number of activities were to be undertaken to ensure that the policy directives were implemented. By the early 1980s it was clear that this policy had made little impact on the agency, and in 1983 the agency hired a new WID director. She came from the public service and had a background in affirmative action programs for women and organizational change. Her analysis was that the previous policy directives had failed because they were based on an advocacy approach to organizational change rather than a systemic / accountability approach. She noted, "Such a program [following a WID policy] cannot be put into effect or monitored by creating a staff of specialists or by sending out orders to comply. The 1977 policy did both with little effect" (p.11).

17. Maguire notes that although the UN claims the IWY conference as the culmination of three other UN conferences on the environment (1972), population (1974), and food (1976), others argue that the UN continually excluded women from conference agendas (Maguire, "Women in Development," p.10). Maguire also notes the disagreement among UN delegates over the themes. Second World delegates maintained that there were no women's problems in socialist countries and that the capitalist system with its militarism

was responsible for women's problems, so peace was added to the agenda. Third World delegates added that development would increase women's status.

18. Kate Young, "The Four Feminisms," draft paper, unpublished, 1988.

19. ISIS, *Women in Development,* pp.67-68.

20. Amrita Basu, "Reflections on Forum 85 in Nairobi, Kenya: Voices from the International Women's Studies Community," *Signs,* Spring 1986, p.804.

21. Maguire, "Women in Development," p.13.

22. Caroline Moser, "Gender Planning in the Third World: Reaching Practical and Strategic Gender Needs," *World Development,* 1989; Maguire, "Women in Development." Moser has developed a set of five categories to describe policy approaches to Third World women: welfare, equity, anti-poverty, efficiency, and empowerment.

23. Moser, "Gender Planning in the Third World," p.24.

24. Moser, "Gender Planning in the Third World," p.26; Maguire, "Women in Development."

25. Maguire, "Women in Development," p.14.

26. Moser, "Gender Planning in the Third World," pp.30-31.

27. Ibid., p.31.

28. McAllister, "Managing the Process of Change," pp.3-4.

29. CIDA, *Women in Development: CIDA Action Plan,* Ottawa, 1986, p.4.

30. Ibid., p.8.

31. The basis for this statement is personal observation and comments by Canadian staff working in international agencies. Other reasons given for the success in institutionalizing the policy are the gender mix of staff and the commitment of the female officers in the branches to the policy.

32. Maguire, "Women in Development," p.13.

33. Ibid., p.14.

34. Ibid.

35. For the example of USAID, see Catherine Overholt, Mary Anderson, Kathleen Cloud, and James Austin, *Gender Roles in Development Projects* (Connecticut: Kumerian Press, 1985), p.xii.

36. Anita Anand, "Rethinking Women and Development: The Case for Feminism," *CUSO Journal,* 1984, p.18.

37. Asoka Bandarage, "Women in Development: Liberalism, Marxism and Marxist-Feminism," *Development and Change,* Vol.15 (1984), pp.495-515.

38. Peggy Antrobus, "The Impact of Structural Adjustment Policies on Women: The Experience of Caribbean Countries," paper presented to the UNDP / UNPA Training

Program on Women in Development, INSTRAW, Dominican Republic, November 28-December 2, 1988.

39. Ibid., p.10.

40. Quoted in ibid., p.20.

41. Bandarage, "Women in Development," p.498. For a detailed discussion of the philosophical roots of liberal feminism see Alison Jagger, *Feminist Politics and Human Nature* (Sussex: Rowman and Allanheld, 1983).

42. Adamson, Briskin, and McPhail, *Feminist Organizing for Change*, p.10.

43. Bandarage, "Women in Development," p.499.

44. Sen and Grown, *Development, Crises and Alternative Visions*, p.82.

45. Mies, *Patriarchy and Accumulation*, p.1; Sen and Grown, *Development, Crises and Alternative Visions*, p.46.

46. Bandarage, "Toward International Feminism," *Brandeis Review*, No.3, Vol.3 (1983), p.3.

47. Ibid., p.5.

48. Maguire, "Women in Development," p.24.

49. Mies, *Patriarchy and Accumulation*.

50. Bandarage, "Toward International Feminism."

51. Pepe Roberts, "Debate: Feminism in Africa, Feminism and Africa," *Review of African Political Economy*, double issue No.27 / 28 (February 1984), pp.175-184; Mamdana Hendessi, "Fourteen Thousand Women Meet: Report from Nairobi, July 1985," *Feminist Review*, No.23 (Summer 1986), pp.147-156.

52. Charlotte Bunch, *Passionate Politics: Feminist Theory in Action* (New York: St. Martin's Press, 1986), p.302.

53. See Sen and Grown, *Development, Crises and Alternative Visions;* Maguire, "Women in Development"; Moser, "Gender Planning in the Third World."

54. This view is also forcefully argued by women of colour in Canada. See Adamson, Briskin, and McPhail, *Feminist Organizing for Change*, pp.106-107, 239-240, and *Fireweed*, Summer / Fall 1984.

55. Sen and Grown, *Development, Crises and Alternative Visions*.

56. Ibid., p.16.

57. Ibid., pp.62-63.

58. Ibid., p.23.

59. CIDA, *Corporate Evaluation Study*, quoted in Tim Brodhead, Brent Herbert-Copley, and Anne-Marie Lambert, *Bridges of Hope? Canadian Voluntary Agencies and the Third World* (Ottawa: North-South Institute, 1988), p.129.

60. Lise Latremouille, "Women in Canadian Development NGOs: An Overview," Canadian Council for International Cooperation *Newsletter*, Vol.9, No.3 (August 1985), p.6.

61. Support for this approach appears in the literature of many NGOs. Whether they are able to implement it has not been fully documented.

62. See an elaboration of this framework in Moser, "Gender Planning in the Third World."

63. Quoted in "Evaluation of Match International Centre," prepared for Match International Centre and NGO Division, CIDA, Ottawa, July 1987, p.5.

64. Brodhead, Herbert-Copley, and Lambert, *Bridges of Hope?* p.129.

65. Ibid.

66. See Thomas S. Kuhn, *The Structure of Scientific Revolutions* (Chicago: University of Chicago Press, 1970).

FOUR

Wheat At What Cost?
CIDA and the Tanzania–Canada Wheat Program

Charles Lane

February 15, 1989
Open Letter to the Canadian People

We, the Barabaig of Tanzania, are a poor and troubled people. We are a pastoral minority dependent on our livestock for survival. Every day we strive to sustain our herds and secure a better future for ourselves and our children. We are few in number and live in scattered communities. We have little political power. We have struggled alone against great odds for many years. Few people understand our plight or are willing to help us. Our problems are great. We have failed to overcome them. We are asking for your help.

We live close to the land. It is an arid land where droughts are common. Many of our children suffer deprivation and die for want of better health care. Our livestock die also from lack of veterinary services. Our womenfolk walk many miles for water. They grind maize by hand using stones. Many of us are illiterate. Few people visit us to hear our problems and attend to our needs. Some of our leaders have tried to help us. However, not enough is being done to support our development compared with other Tanzanians.

Traditionally, we live on the plains that surround Mount Hanang in Hanang district of Arusha region. We have done so for well over a hundred years. Here we build our homes, herd our livestock, cultivate our plots, and live our lives. In colonial times we had our own Barabaig Native Authority and Chief. At that time we cleared the land to control the Tsetse fly. Today we burn the pasture to control ticks and improve the grazing. Some of the land is sacred. Our esteemed elders are buried here in graves that are tended and visited for generations. We value and respect the land. We want to preserve it for all time.

Our herds need forage, water, and salt. Our land has all these things. Without them we cannot survive. From as long ago as we can remember our land is being taken from us. People are continuously moving in to grow crops on our pastures. They take the best land which we rely on to sustain our herds. The loss of this land has resulted in the drastic reduction of our livestock and a decline in production that causes us great suffering. If our land continues to be taken we shall have to move away or perish. The choices for survival are few; either we accept the risks and hardships of migration or go and become paupers in the towns.

The largest tracts of land being taken from us are for the cultivation of crops. The government has taken more than 100,000 acres for a wheat scheme. The decision to take this land was made by non-Barabaig leaders. Official approval for this was given without our consent. We were just told the project needed the land and we would have to move. We have not been compensated for the loss of this land. A little has been paid to some of us, but only for the loss of housing, which has been offered too late, to too few people. To date no effective provision has been made for those dispossessed to go anywhere else and live.

Canada, through its aid program (CIDA), has been involved in the Tanzania-Canada Wheat Project for twenty years. In that time Canadian aid in partnership with Tanzania's National Agriculture and Food Corporation (NAFCO) has established a vast wheat-growing complex on the Hanang plains. The original plan was to cultivate seven farms of 10,000 acres each, totalling around 70,000 acres. This is the area we were told we would have to give up. Now we find NAFCO has obtained titles to more than 100,000 acres, 30,000 acres more than we had been advised. This was prime grazing land. We can ill afford to lose such a large area of pasture.

The growing of wheat on what was once pasture is destroying the environment. By stripping away the vegetation cover with mechanized cultivation, the soil is laid bare to be carried away by flash floods, creating deep gullies and silting up water sources and our sacred Lake Basotu. The area of land we are left with is generally less fertile and too small for our needs. It is becoming denuded by overgrazing. The vegetation has changed, making pastures less productive than they were before.

Widespread human rights abuses are associated with the conduct of the project. When moving us NAFCO have sometimes burnt us out of our homes without warning. In this way some people have lost all their possessions, including their food reserves. At other times they have ploughed around the homestead, making it impossible for us to come and go freely. When attempting to reach pasture, water, or salt by following traditional routes across the farms we are deemed "trespassers" and subjected to beatings and fines. We find it hard to resist this harassment as NAFCO call on the police and militia to enforce their will on us. Many of the graves of our elders have been ploughed up and are no longer recognizable. These sacred sites are very important to us as places of worship. It is there that we make offerings and call on God's blessings through the medium of our ancestors. This desecration is like the deliberate destruction of a church and graveyard in a Christian community in Canada.

Without success we have appealed in the past for help from our national leaders. We have asked the Canadian project staff and the Canadian High Commission in Dar es Salaam to help us. Despite their expressed concern little has changed for the better. In fact, the situation has got worse. Cultivation of disputed land continues. Beatings and fines continue. Some of the rights of way that were left open have now been closed completely. Lately, NAFCO have chosen to obtain Certificates of Title to the farms which exclude the two vital conditions for the provision of rights of way and the preservation of graves.

In 1984 the villagers of Mulbadau contested the taking of our land by NAFCO. The case succeeded in the High Court, but was overturned on appeal. It was ruled that the village did not have title to the land at the time it was taken from them. Individual claims to customary rights to possession of land, as recognized in law, were also denied to those few plaintiffs who testified in court as they happened to be of Somali origin and were thus not classified as "natives" with rights to possession of land in Tanzania.

Because of the continuing abuses of our rights, and the fact that the broader question of whether we have customary title to the land we occupied is still unresolved, we have decided to go back to the courts. We contend that NAFCO failed to adhere to the due process of law in acquiring this land and are thus trespassing on the extra 30,000 acres. We are demanding fair compensation for the loss of the land, the destruction of our homes, and the desecration of graves. We want restoration of traditional rights of way that will allow us to reach grazing, water, and salt as before. We want to establish once and for all that indigenous pastoral communities have customary rights to the land they occupy so that their future livelihoods may be protected by the law of the land.

Canadian aid is as much valued by us as other Tanzanians. We are not opposed to your involvement in the development of this country. In fact we would welcome your continued support for development in Hanang district. Our problems are with the project and its impact on our lives and land. Through this letter we want to inform you what is currently being done with your aid. You can see how you have been party to the wrongs inflicted on us. With what you now know we hope you will be moved to use whatever means are available to resolve the conflict in the name of justice.

We would also like you to consider how the wrongs inflicted on us might be redressed. We want our land back. We want our customary rights observed. We want no further destruction of the land. We would like a full and impartial investigation conducted into human rights abuses and those found guilty of crimes punished. Our hope is that you will be motivated to provide better human and livestock health facilities, and basic infrastructure and services would do much to overcome the underdevelopment we have endured. This is not a request for a few token projects, but a plea for a comprehensive development plan for the district. We want the opportunity to participate in our own development. In this way pastoralists can benefit as much as agriculturalists. Without your and others' support we are destined to remain a poor and abused people without a future.

You are a rich and powerful nation. You have the means to overcome your problems. Your aid has helped others, at home and abroad. You live far from us and know little of our problems in Tanzania. We hope that this letter will make you more aware of what is happening to us. Please join us in our struggle. Without an effective and positive response from you our cause can be lost. That is why we are appealing to you now. Our cry for your help is our last resort.

Gwaruda Gidabayokt
Gidamis Lugod
Bada Gilinya
Ako Gembul
Ng'ayda Baha
On behalf of the Barabaig people
Hanang district, Arusha region
Tanzania

❑

THE TANZANIA-CANADA Wheat Program (TCWP) has been acclaimed as a success in both Tanzania and Canada. Instituted by the Canadian International Development Agency (CIDA) in the early 1970s in co-operation with Tanzania's National Agriculture and Food Corporation (NAFCO), a state agency, the program set up seven huge and highly mechanized wheat farms on isolated pasture lands in northern Tanzania. By the early 1980s the author of a CIDA Annual Review was reporting that "Tanzanians thank God – and Canadians" for the program. [1] By the end of the 1980s it had certainly produced a lot of wheat. Yields were comparable to those on the Canadian Prairies and the 1989 output of the seven wheat farms was expected to be 50,000 tonnes – about 40 per cent of Tanzania's domestic demand. CIDA had declared the program a success and used production levels and financial data to justify support for similar forms of wheat production in Tanzania.

However, after nearly 20 years of funding and the investment of millions of dollars there is now evidence to show that the program has serious shortcomings. The high level of wheat production has been achieved at great social, economic, and environmental cost. A number of alternative economic and political analyses provide views that counter official publicity extolling the virtues of the program. Most importantly, the lives of the Barabaig people, herders who have lived for over 150 years in the area where the farms were assembled, have been severely damaged by the program – as witnessed by their moving "open letter to the Canadian people," which was delivered to Ottawa in May 1989.

BACKGROUND:
PARTICIPATORY RESEARCH AND THE BARABAIG

I worked directly with the Barabaig as a participatory researcher for about 18 months, from July 1986 to January 1988. The methodology of participatory research is more subjective than other kinds of research. The researcher becomes a member of the community and plays the role of catalyst and facilitator in exploring constraints and working to find solutions to identified problems. The work is shared by the researcher and the subjects of the research, but it is for the subjects to identify the topics they want researched. Throughout this process they retain power to direct the research in line with their needs and priorities. Each party contributes its own skills, knowledge, perspectives, and resources as appropriate, and by working together all parties follow through with ideas and try to reach constructive conclusions.

The ultimate purpose of this type of research is to apply the findings to identifying problems and constraints on well-being and work to overcome them by empowering people to deal with them through community action. It was through this process that the Barabaig raised the issue of land. They told me that progress on any other aspect of underdevelopment would be pointless unless they could secure rights to their land.

The Barabaig discovered that they do in fact have a right in Tanzanian law to possession of the land they have traditionally occupied. This knowledge encouraged them to engage legal counsel and contest the legality of land alienation. Also, in an effort to seek justice and the cessation of harassment and the continued alienation of their lands, the Barabaig traditional leadership decided to appeal directly to Canadians and bring international attention to their plight. By the time they delivered their open letter to Canada in May 1989 they despaired of ever benefiting from a positive response from the authorities in Tanzania.[2] After years of making representations to government and party officials without success, they had decided to prompt action that would ensure that their case would be judged on its merit in the courts; and they wanted to encourage CIDA to consider directly supporting Barabaig development as a redress to the wrongs inflicted on them.

THE BARABAIG: TRADITIONS, LAND, AND CULTURE

The Barabaig have occupied the plains that surround Mount Hanang for more than 150 years. They came to that area in a migration southward along the Rift Valley from the Serengeti plains and Ngorongoro highland massif.[3] There are some

[handwritten note: "I have suffered greatly cause not seen as contributing economically"]

30,000 to 50,000 Barabaig in the district.[4] Many of them still live in a traditional manner with strong adherence to the culture and customs of a pastoral way of life, which is in many ways similar to other Nilotic pastoral groups such as the Maasai of East Africa.

The Barabaig are distinguished from other groups by a unique and most important cultural feature. They bury their most highly esteemed elders with a *bung'ed*, which is both the name of the burial mound and the funeral ceremony associated with it. Only those elders adjudged by their clan peers to be sufficiently worthy can be buried in this way. Such a man must have displayed prowess as a herder in possession of many cattle, lived a moral life, exhibited wisdom in politics, and had many wives and children. Sometimes, but rarely, a woman is given such a burial. The corpse is stripped of all clothing and jewellery, wrapped in the skin of a sacrificial black bull and buried in a sitting position in a shallow pit. The ceremony involves thousands of people and costs what amounts to a fortune for the Barabaig, including as it does the slaughter of many livestock and the brewing of vast quantities of honey beer.

On the grave they build an earthen mound that eventually rises to a height of about three metres (three generations ago the mounds were made of stones); and for a period of nine months they hold celebrations at the grave site. The ceremony culminates when the eldest son of the first wife climbs the mound and offers a prayer. Before he descends he places his father's stick and sandals on top. The deceased man's clan is thereafter and forever responsible for the grave's upkeep. Clansmen will visit it for generations to appeal to their ancestor as a medium to *Aset*, their God. In this way the *bung'ed* acts as a lasting focus for their cultural and spiritual life. The Barabaig still visit the *bung'ed* of Gitangda in the Ngorongoro crater, a site remaining from the time when they occupied that land before being dislodged by the Maasai over a hundred years ago.[5]

Barabaig pastoralists regard their territory as the area centred around Mount Hanang in the Hanang district of Arusha region, which they occupied long before German colonists arrived in 1910. The area is divided by the Great Rift, which separates the Basotu high plains in the north and west from the lower Mangati plains to the south. The area is semi-arid with an annual rainfall of about 600 millimetres. Apart from the mountain forest on Mount Hanang, the vegetation is mainly acacia and commiphora woodland interspersed with open grasslands. The terrain is undulating with a series of depressions and many low hills and volcanic craters, some with permanent water. There are also two large salt lakes. The Barabaig exploit all these geographical features at different times. Their livestock benefits from forage, water, and salts found at the different locations, and many Barabaig move their herds and homes around the plains to make best use of the resources. This includes migrations up and down the Rift and congregation near persistent vegetation and permanent water in the dry season.

Like other pastoral groups they have a communal land-tenure system. Because of scarce and variable forage and water in their territory, they move their livestock in an eight-part seasonal rotation, which makes it necessary for all members of the community to have general access to the resources. But this general access is not uncontrolled. They manage the rotational use of pasture through traditional rules and institutions, which are effective means of maximum production and the conservation of pasture resources. The weakness of the system is that it does not traditionally provide for a ban on grazing when pasture is insufficient – a not surprising omission because until recently this was never the case. Interestingly, during a time of increased pasture shortage one Barabaig chief appointed by the British colonial administration did make a law in a customary manner that excluded habitation of the dry season refuge at Balangda. This law was generally accepted by Barabaig herders.

Traditional tenure arrangements tend to make pastures vulnerable to encroachment by outsiders. With growing pressure on land in the neighbouring Mbulu highlands, Iraqw farmers began occupying the most fertile areas of Barabaig pasture for cultivation. Until recently the Barabaig tolerated this intrusion: They had no customary notion of exclusion from their territory and no institutional means to prevent it. Faced with the expanding cultivation of their pastures they reacted in the traditional way, by moving away from the area of intrusion. But by the 1980s there were few places left to go, and it had become too late to return and reclaim the land they had left to others. This process of creeping alienation undermined the pastoral rotation by withdrawing from pastoral use the critical grazing areas where some of the most productive forage species are found.

This problem was compounded by the policies of the Tanzanian government, which has not only endorsed cultivation agriculture at the expense of traditional livestock production, but has also been directly instrumental in alienating the Barabaig from the land through the joint NAFCO-CIDA program.

By the mid-1980s the effect of this alienation on the Barabaig had become evident. A survey has shown that one Barabaig child in five was dying in its first year. Child nutrition and health had become significantly worse in the area near the wheat farms than in other parts of the country. The Barabaig also had very low literacy levels. Their hard life demanded a lot of work just to attain the most basic physical comfort and security. Women walked many miles for water and firewood and were also responsible for nearly all domestic duties, which included several hours a day grinding maize by hand, using stones. The men worked hard at tending the herds and generally looking after the well-being of the livestock.

Herd sizes were decreasing and by 1988 livestock holdings of communities neighbouring the seven program farms had declined to a third of their number in 1981. [6] Livestock production performance had become severely restricted by the loss of grazing resources and the lack of livestock extension services. As many as

40 per cent of the calves were dying. Of all cattle deaths, 76 per cent were attributed to tick-born diseases, and authorities made little provision for control of these diseases. Not one of the 19 dips in the district was operating, and some had not done so for up to ten years. Veterinary drugs were in short supply and sold at highly inflated prices on the black market. The effect of all of this was to limit herd growth and to deny sons their inheritance and the ability to establish households independently of their fathers.

One continuing Barabaig tradition causes great concern to Barabaig leaders and others and has a bearing on how the Barabaig are seen; indeed, it often prejudices other people against them and influences how they are treated. This is the custom of "ritual murder" in which certain non-Barabaig people are killed for financial reward and social esteem. The custom springs from the Barabaig's heritage of conflict, a history punctuated by battles with other groups competing for pastoral resources. Bitter animosity arising from years of harassment and oppression by neighbouring peoples and successive administrations is expressed through the cultural adaptation of rewarding with gifts and status those who kill an "enemy." Despite a reduction in hostilities, first brought about by colonial intervention, a legacy of antagonism persists to this day, reflected in a continuation of unlawful killings. [7]

In the past the Barabaig rewarded only those who killed in battle, a state of affairs no different than the awarding of military honours in other cultures. With the reduction in inter-tribal warfare the only opportunity to acquire status and reward to overcome poverty became the carrying out of a "ritual murder." Today poverty provides an economic imperative for those Barabaig without the social and economic means to advance themselves through the acquisition of livestock. Theft is another option exercised by young men: because they are unable to inherit viable herds sons steal livestock to acquire the means to become independent of their fathers.

Not unexpectedly, such practices are opposed by the Tanzanian government, and disregard for Barabaig rights is justified by the notion that the Barabaig are primitives. As a result the Barabaig have been denied development support. The practices have encouraged the government to alienate the Barabaig from their lands with scant regard, if any, for adherence to the due process of law. What is more important, surely, is to understand the roots of such unacceptable customs and work to assist the Barabaig to eliminate the behaviour – a process the traditional leadership has indicated it would support.

PERSISTING WITH OLD ORTHODOXY

The Barabaig, like other African pastoralists, have a form of common land tenure, looking on range land as the common property of the whole community. On a daily or seasonal basis individual herders make decisions to graze their stock at a particular place or time after assessing the possibilities of range productivity or considering a particular social requirement. It is the very practice of common property management that makes possible this variable use of range resources.

Because of the scarce nature of resources and the vagaries of climate, the Barabaig need to move around different areas at different times to make efficient use of the range. In these circumstances some land is left free of human habitation or livestock grazing for long periods, which allows it to be preserved from overuse or reserved for times of future need. This practice also makes common land vulnerable to alienation. People who do not understand pastoral grazing systems can be misled into thinking that pastoral land is vacant or under-utilized. This leads to the idea that pastoralists do not make the best use of land, which can in turn be used to justify their dispossession. This misconception is behind the thinking of governments and donors when land is taken for agricultural projects.

An independent study of Canadian aid to Tanzania by the North-South Institute stated: "The project (TCWP) has many of the characteristics of a frontier development effort. Traditional pastoralists, the Barabegs [sic], are being displaced and absorbed into the project as laborers. Previously *idle land* is being brought under cultivation."[8]

But, from what is now known about Barabaig land tenure, the pasture cannot be described as "idle." The Barabaig use land just as much as any farmer. Yet the belief prevails that pastoral use of land does not amount to true occupation and therefore does not proffer rights to it; and this belief justifies appropriation of pastureland without consideration for those whose lives depend on it.

The Tanzania-Canada Wheat Program is an example of a typical Canadian "frontier development" effort. Canadian history offers many examples of Native peoples being dislocated to enable others to farm wheat on what was tribal land. Like the Native peoples of Canada, the Barabaig have not found employment or rewarding lives on the land that once belonged to them. Less than ten Barabaig have jobs on the farms, which altogether employ more than 250 workers.

In reply to a report on the plight of the Barabaig the president of CIDA replied: "The report highlights the age-old African problem of the needs of farmers versus the needs of nomads."[9] The implication is that there is a qualitative hierarchy of land-use systems. As the argument goes, for the sake of development the more primitive pastoral systems will have to give way to more advanced forms of land use. This viewpoint was endorsed at a meeting in Canada convened to discuss the same issue, where it was suggested that there was a growing body of evidence showing that traditional pastoralism was a potentially productive and sustainable form of land use worthy of support. This was not accepted by a senior CIDA official who said, "We may still differ on the issue of whether pastoralists have to give way to farming."[10]

The Barabaig case is typical of a wider problem for pastoralists throughout

Africa. African pastoralists have long been accused of having land-tenure systems structurally incapable of efficient land use. The "tragedy of the commons" theory posits that private animals on communal pastures will inevitably lead to overgrazing and the degradation of pasture.[11] This has been a powerful force in the minds of government and aid agency officials, and the policy it suggests of taking over rangeland for other uses has been widely followed. As a result, many pastoralists, especially poorer and less powerful ones, have been denied access to their traditional rangelands, become more vulnerable to drought and famine, and suffered from underdevelopment. Also, because they have been denied access to pastures they have had to depend on a shrinking resource base. With their traditional land-use system disrupted, pastoralists have been forced to use land more intensely than would otherwise have been the case. As a result they get blamed for overgrazing, which again appears to support the contention that pastoral land use is destructive and further justifies disrespect for land rights and continued alienation.

However, recent advances in theory and better field research cast doubt on the "tragedy of the commons" as a useful explanation of traditional pastureland use. The "tragedy of the commons" assumes that collective users of the range are unable to co-operate in the effective and sustainable use of common resources. A more sophisticated analysis shows that if individual members of a group can negotiate with others to make rules for the use of resources, and if the group can create or collaborate with existing institutions to enforce such rules, efficient uses of common resources are likely to emerge (if they do not already exist) and be maintained. Such rules exist and are successfully operated by the Barabaig, who have a complex system that determines access, organizes use of resources, and protects rights to property.

Tanzanian agricultural policy and development practice have failed to recognize the value of pastoral land-tenure systems. Apart from the general principles embodied in colonial statutes, modern legislation has not provided legitimacy for traditional land rules. Land has been taken away from traditional pastoral management without effective legislation or legal precedent to protect that land. As a result, government action has created a situation of ruleless chaos – a true tragedy of the commons. In many places the government has tried to impose new types of land tenure more in line with the prevailing orthodoxy. These are generally in the form of discrete titles to farms and ranches that exclude the possibility of varied and peripatetic use of resources.

Given the nature of current developments in pastoral areas, as typified by the TCWP, it is doubtful that the Barabaig, and pastoralists elsewhere in Africa, can survive. Unless changes are made to the existing approaches to development in semi-arid areas of Africa, the pastoralists' skills and knowledge will be lost, and their abilities to sustain themselves will no longer be available for us to learn from.

Their demise may serve existing vested short-term interests in countries like Tanzania and Canada, but it is likely to eradicate a traditional system that is inherently more equitable, potentially productive, and ecologically sound. Denuded landscapes that can serve no future productive purpose for the growing of crops or pastoralism will be all that remain. Greater attention must be given to the traditional pastoral systems that have proved so effective in sustaining both livelihoods and the land through the good husbandry of natural resources.[12]

THE TANZANIA-CANADA WHEAT PROGRAM

Canadian interest in supporting wheat production in Tanzania dates back to 1968, when the Tanzanian government was looking for ways to become self-sufficient in wheat. Despite increases in its acreage under wheat, the country was only able to satisfy 60 per cent of demand. The Tanzanian government, expecting demand to increase at a rate of 8 per cent per year, was interested in finding ways to overcome the shortfall.

In response to a direct request from President Julius Nyerere, the first of a number of CIDA-financed and Canadian-staffed wheat-sector feasibility studies and planning missions went to Tanzania. The mission recommended the establishment of a research station in the country and suggested that the Tanzanian government acquire a farm at Basotu in Hanang district for the production of wheat. Canada made its first disbursement of wheat aid to establish a research station in 1970.

In November 1970 the Canadian and Tanzania governments drew up and signed a Memorandum of Understanding setting out the nature of CIDA support for wheat production in Tanzania for Phase I, 1970-75. This first phase involved Canadian investment for research facilities. Staff were posted to conduct the research, arrange for Tanzania staff training, and provide advice on the Basotu farm. CIDA's contribution was co-ordinated by Agriculture Canada, and the Tanzanian partners in research were the Tanzanian Research Organization (TARO) and NAFCO for production. Both bodies were parastatal organizations under the Ministry of Agriculture (KILIMO).

At the end of the first phase, consideration was given to abandoning wheat production at Basotu. Yields were low and irregular. However, after one farm manager achieved impressive production with the implementation of revised cultivation methods, the Canadian research team in Tanzania made a strong representation to CIDA to continue production. The new methods included improved water-conserving tillage, a change to a mid-February planting date consistent with the local production method, and the use of a new wheat variety called "Trophy." The plan to continue was accepted and Canadian advisers were placed on the farms to assist directly with production. Yields rose from just over 700 kilograms a hectare to more than 1.5 tonnes a hectare, which encouraged further research and development.

143

Then followed what has been called an "interim period" from 1976 to 1979 – a "period of waiting, anticipating, and planning Phase II," according to the author of a Canadian report outlining the history of the program. [13] Canada signed an agreement to provide 20 person-years of specialist support, running from July 1976 to the end of June 1981. The specialists were to assist KILIMO through NAFCO to produce wheat at Basotu and the newly acquired Setchet farm. In 1977 Manitoba Pool Elevators undertook a "Wheat Sector Study" and recommended, among other things, that CIDA give emphasis to the NAFCO farms at Basotu and Setchet "but without prejudice to other proceedings necessary to achieve an expanding and acceptable program in both wheat production and marketing." Their report made reference to the "Basotu area," defined to mean "all current and potential wheat land within an approximate 100 square mile area [259 square kilometres] in the vicinity of Basotu village." [14] The "proposed agronomic package" was initiated on the farms in 1976, becoming in effect an extension of the direction set by Phase I. The farm advisers at Basotu in 1971-75 reported directly to CIDA through the Canadian High Commission in the capital city, Dar es Salaam.

The documented "History of the Tanzania-Canada Wheat Programme 1967-1982" makes clear that in the "interim period" the expansion included the acquisition of land for first Setchet and then in 1978 the Mulbadau farm adjoining Setchet to the southwest. No mention is made as to why or how they were acquired. It can be assumed that land acquisition was the responsibility of the Tanzanian partners.

Dr. J.S.Clarke, Director of the Land Resource Research Institute of Agriculture Canada, gave an indication of how this might have proceeded after his visit to the area of the farms in 1978: "In spite of an understanding that this was to be a year of consolidation, the Tanzania farm managers had received orders earlier in the fall to expand the Mulbadaw farm to 4,000 Ha." [15] What appears to have happened was that KILIMO through its agents NAFCO acquired land in a somewhat ad hoc manner and on a far greater scale than was foreseen by CIDA, the district government, or Barabaig residents.

In Phase II, 1979-84, the research program completed the greater part of the work required to establish the "production package" on the farms. A large increase of $35 million in CIDA aid mainly took the form of equipment purchases. A Central Maintenance Service Centre (CMSC) was proposed to serve the farms. In this phase of the program the area of land under cultivation was to be increased by just over 50,000 acres, scattered over five farms. KILIMO stipulated that CIDA would be the exclusive donor to wheat production in Tanzania. Furthermore, as reported by a CIDA official, President Nyerere agreed with CIDA's suggestion to locate the scheme in Hanang district rather than at another location in a more remote area west of Lake Victoria / Nyanza. Nyerere also approved the expansion of wheat production into the Maasai pastures in the northern Arusha division of Loliondo, where land would be later acquired for cultivation by other organizations, including another parastatal, though the area would not be part of the Wheat Program.

Canadian aid was used to replicate the wheat farming practices of the Canadian prairies on the Hanang plains. Instead of accepting local limitations, let alone the rights and needs of the local Barabaig inhabitants, CIDA saw fit to construct seven large, technically sophisticated, capital-intensive and costly production units that would consume high amounts of energy. While it might be possible to maintain such production in Canada – though even here there is a growing body of opinion that such methods are destructive of the environment – events have shown that the same level cannot be sustained in Tanzania.

Canada's role in the program, then, was to be both substantial and long term. With the investment of an estimated $100 million, the program constituted one of the largest agricultural disbursements of Canadian aid, making it one of the biggest and longest term single-donor bilateral aid schemes in Tanzania. [16] The level of investment continued unabated to the end of the 1980s. By the end of 1989 only half of the total aid provided had been spent on the farms, with half of that going towards the purchase of capital equipment in Canada. After the completion of Phase II in 1984, the plans called for a Phase III to last until the end of 1992. In a supplementary report to CIDA, a Wheat Sector Study Team from Canada stated: "It is not realistic to anticipate Tanzania will become self sufficient by 1981, but that with continuing Canadian technical and financial assistance it is possible for this goal to be achieved by 2000." Yet, after 20 years of involvement, Canadian support would still be needed for at least another two years for the program to continue. The long-term prospect was that the program would not be able to continue if Canadian aid were withdrawn.

TANZANIAN LAND LAW

In Tanzania no one can own land. Because the Kaiser claimed all land in German East Africa (now mainland Tanzania), all rights to land have come into the "public domain" by way of the British colonial Land Ordinance of 1923. This instrument of law still provides the basis for assessing land rights in Tanzania.

Tanzanian law recognizes two kinds of title to land: Deemed Right of Occupancy, the right to possession of land, supported by customary claim as determined by the prevailing customary law of the area affecting those alleging title; and a Granted Right of Occupancy, which can be granted by the president (before independence it was granted by the governor), for a period of up to 99 years. This is regulated by statutory law. The case of *Nyagaswa v. Nyirabu* of 1985 ruled that customary tenure does not merely cease when statutory rights apply. They can only cease through due process of law. [17]

People can only be alienated from their land with the authority of the president. The 1967 Land Acquisition Act permits the president to acquire land in the public interest, including state-sponsored farming schemes. The Rural Lands (Planning and Utilization) Act of 1973 also allows for the identification and alienation of "planning areas" that are to be used for a specific purpose. Both statutes make provision for the compensation of unexhausted improvements, and re-allocation or resettlement options for those who previously occupied the land. The president may also revoke any Granted Right for a breach of condition pertaining to the title or in a matter of public interest.

The 1982 Local Government (District Authorities) Act provides that villages can be granted title to land by the district council acting as the legal authority. In this way villages can hold title to property and can sue or be sued as bodies corporate. Land use in a village is subject to overall control by the village council. The 1950 Land Ordinance Amendment provided that village land could not be taken without consultation with the "Native Authority," which is today the village council.

In 1985 the residents of Mulbadau village contested the taking of land by NAFCO in the case of *NAFCO v. Mulbadau Village Council.*" The appeal court ruled against the villagers on appeal from the high court because they failed to establish that their village had been allocated the land by the district council before the NAFCO occupation. Although the court recognized that this did not exclude a claim for customary rights to the land by individual villagers, it did rule against those few who testified to their customary title. The court did not accept that the five plaintiffs who appeared in court could adequately testify for the other sixty-two plaintiffs who were absent. Of those five plaintiffs who did testify, only one was claiming customary title. He was denied satisfaction because, being of Somali ethnic origin, he failed to establish that he was a "native" of the country as defined by the Land Ordinance and that he was thus entitled to occupy land legally in accordance with native law and custom. As a result the issue of whether the Barabaig could claim customary title to land by way of Deemed Right of Occupancy was not properly resolved.

There is nothing in Tanzanian law to say that the Barabaig's communal claim to Deemed Right of Occupancy for their common grazing land cannot be as valid as a claim for an individual. Like other forms of traditional land tenure, the claim is regulated by customary law. It follows then that the Barabaig should be able to successfully defend their customary rights to possession of land as a community, not as a registered village but as individuals within a community holding their rights in common consistent with customary law. The taking of any rightfully occupied land should only happen under due process of law.

THE BARABAIG LAND CLAIM

The Barabaig claim of customary rights to their land is supported by the fact that the land falls within the area defined by the Barabaig Native Authority in British colonial times. It could then be defended against unauthorized intrusion in the native court. After independence the Native Authorities were disbanded and customary rights have been widely infringed by encroachment and government appropriation.

Invariably, it has been the land with most agricultural potential that has been taken. These fertile areas are called *muhajega* by the Barabaig and constitute one of the forage regimes in the eight-part grazing rotation. Some of the soils of the areas covered by the TCWP wheat farms are so rich in nutrients that no fertilizers are needed on them. Exclusion from these areas has denied the Barabaig access to certain important and highly productive livestock forage species collectively called *nyega nyatka*. One grass, *megojiga* or "milk grass," which is particularly favoured by the Barabaig, has been completely eradicated from the area by cultivation. The TCWP alone covers 12 per cent of the district land area. More importantly, it covers the majority of the *muhajega*. If this exclusion is combined with areas lost to pastoral production by encroachment, and that infested with Tsetse flies in the south of the district, together with the salt pans of Lake Balangda Lelu and the Forest Reserve of Mount Hanang, it is clear how little access the Barabaig have to the vital resources they once occupied and understand to be their pastoral range.

The result of this is a decline in pastoral production and the over-exploitation of the areas that remain available for pastoral production. These areas in turn are becoming denuded by overgrazing, and forage grasses are being replaced by less productive weeds. Visual evidence suggests (and is confirmed by concerns expressed in program documents) that the mono-cropping of wheat on these soils has led to severe gully erosion. [18] In these ways the negative impact on the Barabaig economy and the environment is far greater than the area of land lost to pastoral production.

The Barabaig argue that they were never given notice of the proposed alienation, as required by the Land Acquisition Act. Very often the first they knew of their dispossession was when NAFCO employees started to plough around their homes and the Barabaig were harassed and accused of "trespassing." There are documented cases where Barabaig have been burned out of their homes without warning. [19] Although the authorities promised assistance for relocation, they failed to follow through. The dispossessed simply had to go and find other places to live. This caused overcrowding in some locations and forced some people to leave the district altogether. There have been reports of Barabaig migrating to the southern extremities of the country, and others have been moved as many as four times in attempts to find suitable places to live in the district.

Compensation was paid to some of those people who occupied the land before its acquisition by NAFCO. But the Barabaig argue that compensation has been extended to too few, and that it was too little, too late. The records show that beneficiaries were only paid for the loss of their houses. The compensation took no account of cultivated farm land or other unexhausted improvements. In the case of one of the seven farms, Gidagamod, the schedule for payment provided for TSh.728,955/– (about U.S.$7,000) to be divided among 89 households in Mogitu and Gehandu villages. This amounts to about only TSh.8,190/– (or U.S.$80) for each household. The beneficiaries do not include any of the many people who were dispossessed after the schedule was drawn up in 1988. Considering that the land was taken in 1982 and the payment was delayed for five years, the compensation did not adequately cover the loss or costs of relocation and rebuilding. It also failed to take into account the general loss of access to improved grazing and other pastoral resources.

Although some of the land was taken away as early as 1969, until the late 1980s NAFCO had farmed much of it with no more title than the possession of Offers of a Right of Occupancy. An offer is a stage in the process prior to the issue of a Certificate of Title. Such certificates are issued once the terms and conditions set out in the offer are accepted. These include the terms of the right, level of rents, and the nature of use to which the land will be put, as well as whatever exemptions and reserves out of the right apply. When the Barabaig first heard of the proposal for a large-scale wheat scheme they were told it would consist of seven farms of 10,000 acres each. This impression was also held by Canadians, and is confirmed by internal CIDA documents. An examination of the land records reveals, however, that the offers for the seven farms cover a far larger area than the Barabaig had been led to believe – a total of 99,077 acres. In addition, the program has occupied a piece of land for the Central Maintenance Service Centre (CMSC) to which there was no offer issued.

The offers were made for the maximum permissible term of 99 years, and they set out the conditions under which full title could be accepted. In all seven offers the conditions for the exemption and reservations out of the right for "all existing public roads, rights of way and highways crossing the land" would apply. In addition it was stated, "The occupiers shall respect any grave existing within the boundaries of the right." In the late 1980s NAFCO acquired seven Certificates of Title for all of the farms, and one for another area described as "Basotu" for 205.5 hectares, which most likely represents the area covered by the CMSC. It was therefore only in May 1988 that NAFCO obtained any title to the land at CMSC. The increase in total acreage of the seven offers is 2,123 acres. With the Basotu title of 508 acres, the total additional acreage for the eight titles is 2,631 acres. In 1979, when NAFCO formally requested permission from the district to alienate land sufficient for seven farms, it originally requested a total area of 72,500 acres.[20] The total area of the combined titles is now 101,917 acres – 29,417 acres more than asked for and than the Barabaig were expected to accept. Both NAFCO and CIDA officials argue that the original figure of 72,500 acres only referred to arable acreage but there is no evidence to support this contention. Official documentation makes no mention of 29,417 acres for "housing, workshops, roads and ancillary services."[21]

Another matter of great concern is the exclusion from the titles of the two conditions for provision of rights of way and respect for graves. In this way the titles differ from the offers, where these two conditions were specifically stipulated. It can only be assumed that the exclusions were arranged by NAFCO to outmanoeuvre the Barabaig so that they would fail in a case to defend their customary rights to the disputed land.

Although they have continually protested to government and party leaders about the enforced alienation of what they regard as their rightful territory, the Barabaig have been defeated by the autocratic use of authority and, at times, physical force by law enforcement bodies.[22] Protests and appeals to government and party leaders proved to be ineffective.

By the end of the decade the Barabaig were almost despairing of ever being able to stop the continuing take-over of their land. However, on the advice of counsel from the Legal Aid Committee of the University of Dar es Salaam they were still attempting to test the legality of the alienation of land by NAFCO in the courts. In two cases contesting the taking of land for the Gawal, Gidagamod, and Waret farms they sought the return of the extra 30,000 acres in excess of the original area applied for, redress for abuse of rights, restitution of rights of way, and the restoration of graves. To avoid what happened in the Mulbadau case they obtained high court rulings allowing the 17 plaintiffs (three of whom are signatories to the Open Letter) to represent all those others who have similarly been hurt by the loss of land.

This may not be enough to ensure that justice will prevail. In what could only be described as a cynical attempt to undermine the Barabaig case, the Tanzanian government used its executive authority to circumvent judicial process. In July 1989 the prime minister, Joseph Warioba, issued an order extinguishing customary rights to land in the areas adjacent to the wheat farms. The order was framed so as to be effective from February 1987. The Barabaig responded by contesting the legality of the order along with the other claims. Their counsel argued that the order was unconstitutional because it purports to extinguish entrenched native rights without due process of law – as well as violating a basic principle of international human rights law and natural justice because of its retroactive effect. The international human rights monitoring group Africa Watch stated that the order also breached the African Charter on Human and People's Rights, to which the Tanzanian government is a signatory.[23]

If the order was allowed to persist it would render void the Barabaig claim to the disputed land, because they would be deemed to have had no customary rights to land at the time of filing suit against NAFCO. This turn of events would create a major travesty of justice. The very existence of the order, however, could be construed as an implied admission by the government that the Barabaig had customary title to the land at the time they were dispossessed, and thus an invalidation of NAFCO's authority to take over the land the way it did. A Barabaig failure to win the case would deny them and other pastoralists in Tanzania the legal precedent they need to protect their lands from wrongful alienation.

The use of such measures against a cultural minority to simply persist with a development project must surely cause CIDA and the Canadian government considerable discomfort. The only possible justification for defending the project against Barabaig interests is if it makes a great and necessary contribution to the national good. Sadly, recent economic analyses reveal this not to be the case.

ECONOMIC ASSESSMENT

The Tanzania-Canada Wheat Program has had a number of internal evaluations.[24] Until 1980 only one economic analysis had been done because before then there was a "lack of consistent and reliable data upon which to estimate the costs and revenue accruing to" the program.[25] For a long time the studies gave a positive picture of the program's economic performance. A "Project Evaluation" done in 1980 arrived at a cost / benefit ratio of 1.59 and a net value of $19.5 million to Tanzania. The internal rate of return to the capital employed in the program of nearly 40 per cent indicated that it was a "very profitable investment for the Tanzanian economy."[26] The evaluation estimated that local production of wheat would save nearly $1 million of the cost of importing the same amount of wheat from abroad in the years 1979-84. Even when an attempt was made to calculate an "estimated social cost-benefit" ratio, which included "some families [who] were displaced from the farms area and will have their income opportunities affected by this action" – but did not include aid grants as they are "not borne by Tanzanian society" – the results were found to be "well above the opportunity cost of capital."[27]

This initial positive assessment was promoted by both Canadian government ministers and senior CIDA officials despite later studies that gave a negative picture. Not only did these politicians and bureaucrats deny that there were anything but positive results, but they also tried to revise negative assessments and even went so far as to misquote others in a positive light. The initial findings of a cost-benefit analysis done in 1985 by Prairie Horizons Ltd. were so negative that CIDA asked the firm to provide an additional report giving details of the production and import cost-analysis used.[28] CIDA gave both reports to another consultancy firm, Michael Mascall and Associates, to test whether "the assumptions, methodology, and analytical techniques used ... were reliable and sound."[29] Despite recommending that several parameters used by Prairie Horizons be changed, the

Michael Mascall report stated: "As very few changes have been suggested by MMA for the commercial viability and financial analysis, MMA does not expect any significant changes from the results obtained by PH."[30]

The final report of the cost-benefit team reconfirmed what had already been found:

The results of this study indicate that wheat production on the Hanang farms is profitable from the viewpoint of the farms given the price and cost structure that have been in place, and the farms are likely to remain profitable unless major changes in costs or prices occur. However, from the standpoint of contributions to, and resources used within, the Tanzania economy the Project is shown to be uneconomic. In strict economic terms, the costs have exceeded the benefits and this is likely to continue through to the year 2000.

In *economic terms* these results mean there should be better ways to use the aid and scarce foreign exchange which has been used in wheat production....

Judged against economic criteria, the Project appears to be very expensive for Tanzania in terms of resources used up and foregone economic opportunities.[31]

In the second half of the 1980s members of the Department of Agricultural Economics at the University of Manitoba undertook a number of independent studies drawing on both existing data from the original evaluation and new material to assess the program's economic performance. They also added another dimension by comparing small-holder production with the large-scale mechanized production of wheat as represented by the program.[32] The purpose of the studies was to test the efficiency of resource use and find out whether it makes economic sense to grow wheat by the methods employed on the program compared with small-holders using oxen, and relative to the direct importation of wheat from the world market.

Both Canada's secretary of state for external affairs, Joe Clark, and its minister for external relations and international development, Monique Landry, responded to one of these studies by reasserting the official line:

An analysis of the economic viability of wheat production in Tanzania, published in March 1989, *does not conclude it is uneconomic.* The three supply systems in Tanzania are compared – small-holder, large-scale mechanized and imported. Small-holder production is the most profitable and can be marketed efficiently in most areas.... Large-scale mechanized production is efficient in serving the inland market. Because of high transportation costs, imported wheat is only cost-effective when sold in coastal markets accessible to the port of entry. (Emphasis added.)[33]

But scrutiny of the studies provides another viewpoint. The economic analysts from the University of Manitoba argue that an economic analysis that "examines all costs and benefits from the point of view of society as a whole" is more valid than a financial analysis that imputes only those "costs and returns as faced by the individual or firm" in a commercial setting. [34] By employing just such an analysis they show that, contrary to previous evaluations used to justify continued support for the program, large-scale mechanized production had a negative net financial profitability of TSh. 1,050 / 60 per tonne, and a minus benefit-cost ratio of 0.94.

They also point out that when accounting for the previously "sunk cost" of aid and accepting that it has an opportunity cost to the nation's economy, together with other costs previously excluded from calculation, the program had extremely negative results. Small-holder production was both financially and economically profitable, while large-scale mechanized production was unprofitable, particularly if the calculations include the cost of transporting wheat to the distant market in Dar es Salaam, where most of the wheat is consumed. Furthermore, they found that large-scale mechanized production was economically unprofitable compared with direct importation of wheat from the world market. This led them to conclude that the program "is not economically viable nor does it make effective use of domestic resources in saving foreign exchange for Tanzania to use large-mechanised wheat production to satisfy the domestic demand for wheat in the coastal market." [35]

The implications of these findings is that the program is diverting resources from being employed for economic gain elsewhere. It also raises the question of why CIDA supported and continued to defend large-scale mechanized wheat production in Tanzania when it is clear that a more efficient and more substantial contribution to the Tanzanian economy would have been investment in small-holder production. This is not just a reflection based on hindsight. Small-scale producers were already well established in Tanzania: in the Njombe district to the south, and in the Arusha region, particularly in the Iraqw divisions of Mbulu district. [36] CIDA could have found this out itself if it had commissioned a thorough economic analysis including this alternative system of production and consistent with the scale and importance of the aid being contemplated by CIDA officials. The support of small-holder production would have also been consistent with Tanzania's development policy for peasant advancement. Also, its development may also not have resulted in inflicting much hardship on the Barabaig.

The fact that government ministers, CIDA, and NAFCO did not concede to the economic realities of the program means that other imperatives must have influenced their interest in persisting with the program. Decisions to maintain this inefficiency and failure to redirect resources to more productive activities depend on considerations that go beyond economics. To fully understand how it is that CIDA became so embroiled in a project with so many apparent flaws it is necessary to know something of the political context from which it arose.

TANZANIAN POLITICS AND CANADIAN AID

In 1961 the Tanganyika African National Union (TANU) accepted power from the British mandate under the leadership of party chairman and president Nyerere to lead the country into independence; and after the union with Zanzibar the Republic of Tanzania was formed. Ever since the Arusha Declaration of 1967 the country has expressed a commitment to socialism and self-reliance – which seems to mean more a freedom from the international capitalist market than independence from foreign aid, as though they are different. The declaration was followed by a "villagization" program that required all Tanzanians to settle in villages. The banner cry was the doctrine of "ujamaa," a Kiswahili word that means familyhood and has been used to embrace the political ideal of communal living and production.

The policies of *ujamaa* were implemented harshly on those, like semi-nomadic pastoralists, who resisted settlement because it was unsuitable for their particular form of production. The state also nationalized many private enterprises and assumed control of the "commanding heights" of the economy. Consistent with this ideology the state began to act as producer with the establishment of parastatal production corporations in the industrial and agricultural sectors. Organizations like NAFCO were entrusted to set the standard for production and achieve national self-reliance.

In the decade after independence, Tanzania's economic performance was encouraging. Development for the rural-based majority of the population involved in agricultural production seemed assured. Favourable climatic conditions enabled the country to become a net exporter of food. However, food security was threatened by a "crisis" in the 1970s. Food production per capita fell 8 per cent between 1970 and 1978. [37] To make up the shortfall Tanzania was forced to beg food aid and enter world grain markets at a time of high prices. In the 1970s, food grain imports averaged 200,000 to 300,000 tonnes annually. [38] The value of cereal imports rose tenfold and foreign reserves were severely depleted. By 1981 Tanzania's foreign reserves amounted to only U.S.$1.4 million, a level equivalent to two days' cover. [39] Because of this the country became more dependent on aid, so much so that by 1980 foreign aid accounted for 70 per cent of the Gross National Product. [40] Self-reliance, a pillar of the nation's development strategy, was thus undermined. It was for these reasons that Tanzanian development policy stressed self-sufficiency in food.

In this period Tanzania, the one-time darling of the aid community, began to be criticized for its poor economic performance. The Tanzanian government attributed the economic decline to "external shocks" to the economy over which it had no control. A series of droughts, unprecedented world oil-price hikes, declining terms of trade for Tanzania's exports, the cost of the war against Idi Amin in Uganda, and the collapse of the East African Community gave credence to this

153

view. However, the World Bank attributed the decline to structural weaknesses in the economy created by a failure to adequately invest in the agricultural sector. [41]

Other critics pointed out that economic decline was matched by growth in the public sector. The country's bureaucracy doubled in size between 1970 and 1976 and by 1980 accounted for 16 per cent of national income. [42] This growth was not matched by performance. Early gains in the fields of education and health were mitigated by shortages, low prices for produce, inefficiencies, and corruption – all leading to what has been described as "the end of a dream." [43] The disruptive effects of "villagization" and the failure of the bureaucracy to deliver services to the rural population forced peasants to withdraw from willing co-operation with government directives and form what Goran Hyden called an "uncaptured peasantry." [44] Others argued that the state was using socialist ideals to legitimize centralized control by bureaucratic elites to overcome peasant resistance. [45] Instead of shifting policy to favour peasant production the government consistently looked to the state sector to bypass peasants. [46] Parastatal corporations such as NAFCO were seen as "quick-fix" solutions to food self-sufficiency and a recalcitrant peasantry. [47]

For its part, Canada had become a generous supporter of Tanzanian development. From as early as 1970 Tanzania was Canada's top recipient of aid and by the late 1980s constituted Canada's largest program of bilateral aid in Sub-Saharan Africa. [48] This most-favoured position is said to have originated in the level of Tanzania's needs, its status as a most-poor country, its membership in the Commonwealth and Frontline States, and in support of Nyerere's socialist experiment. CIDA's rhetoric supported the notion that aid disbursements to Tanzania were being made to alleviate the poverty of the poorest members of society in one of the world's poorest countries.

However, in an analysis of Canadian aid to Tanzania Linda Freeman revealed that economic interests and not political considerations determined the extent and nature of Canadian aid. [49] Large-scale, capital-intensive, technologically sophisticated schemes not only provide a market for Canadian goods and services, but also offer jobs, travel, training, and access to the means for private accumulation of wealth for Tanzanian officials. An alliance is thus struck between Tanzanian bureaucratic elites and Western capital. Freeman supports this contention by detailing aspects of Canadian "tied aid." More than 80 per cent of Canadian aid to Tanzania has been tied to procurement of Canadian goods and services, and two-thirds has consisted of "value added" in Canada. [50] Despite the disparity of wealth between the two countries, between 1970 and 1979 Canada enjoyed a net trading surplus of $73 million with Tanzania. [51] Between 1968 and 1975 overseas sales for International Harvester, the major supplier of machinery to the Wheat Program, expanded the company's sales outside North America from one-fifth of the total to a third: a true breadwinner for Canadian industry.[52] In this way the TCWP has clearly had more to do with the hegemony of Western capital than socialist development in Tanzania.

More than 20 per cent of Canada's aid to Tanzania between 1961 and 1980 was associated with wheat.[53] Between 1975 and 1980 Canada gave over 86 per cent in the form of wheat food aid, which amounted to 139,462 tonnes at a cost of $22.3 million.[54] In addition to $100 million directed to the TCWP, $1.7 million went towards construction of the infamous automated bread factory in Dar es Salaam.[55] One explanation for the emphasis on wheat by Canadian aid has its origins in Canada's acknowledged expertise in this field. The choice of wheat might also be justified as support for Tanzania's policy for food self-sufficiency. However, wheat only accounts for 1 per cent of Tanzania's food-crop consumption and 2 to 3 per cent of its preferred staples production.[56] Yet wheat makes up more than ten times the level of internal demand of imports for preferred staples.[57] It has the largest trade deficit of all other cereals and in the 1970s constituted a third of cereal imports by weight.[58]

The importance of wheat has less to do with the need to feed the country's population and more to do with satisfying the needs of a growing class of town dwellers. Most Tanzanians do not eat wheat; they rely on maize and other traditional cereals. The Barabaig only eat wheat when it is provided as famine relief. The interest and investment in wheat have their origins in a cheap food policy for Dar es Salaam, where most of the nation's decision-makers reside and where failure to satisfy demand could lead to political unrest. The town dwellers with a growing taste preference for bread and other products of wheat flour are not the poorest people in the country. The program therefore bypasses the truly needy people in Tanzania by both its method of production and the marketing of its product.

Wheat, then, is a "luxury" that cannot be justified by the nation's development objectives.[59] The Canadian administrations of the past two decades have willingly complied with a policy that accommodates this anomaly because it suits their own implicit agenda for capital accumulation. In this way the political expediencies lead to the construction of a "wheat trap." The trap occurs when a country is caught up in a process that leads to the "entrenchment" of wheat by creating a dependence on outside influences and resources that make disengagement from external forces difficult – in other words, dependence on Western capitalism.[60]

Both governments pay lip service to the policy of self-reliance, yet the program has actually created a massive dependency on Canadian financial aid, expertise, and equipment. It was originally planned that Tanzania would provide for fuel and replacement of farm machinery, but because of foreign-exchange constraints the World Bank had to step in and pay for machinery replacements on the Basotu and Setchet farms. In 1972 CIDA also provided $32 million for fuel. Again in 1981,

155

another $375 million was needed that amounted to 58 per cent of export earnings although it only brought in half as much volume as in 1970.[61] Given the impoverished nature of the Tanzanian economy, it is unrealistic to expect that Tanzania will be able to run the Wheat Program without continued external support. Canadian program staff admitted privately that they believe the farms will fail to sustain production at anything like the current levels for more than a year after the withdrawal of Canadian support.

THE CANADIAN RESPONSIBILITY

From what is now known of CIDA's support for the TCWP, it can be seen that the Canadian aid is perpetuating underdevelopment. The program has little to commend it. Contrary to Tanzania's chosen development objectives it has created dependency rather than self-reliance. In economic terms it has contributed a net loss to the Tanzanian economy. From the perspective of the people who have been displaced to make way for the wheat farms the program has proved disastrous. Their lives have been ruined. They have lost vital land resources and what is left to them is being degraded. When judged against broader development objectives the program has failed to adequately address issues of justice, equity, participation, and ecological sustainability.

The program offers an example of how development can go wrong when an inappropriate model is used in a country unable to resist the lure of aid – a country that can ill afford the consequences of expensive mistakes. Without major reforms, even the program's own objectives of Tanzanian food self-sufficiency and economic viability are unlikely to be satisfied. Unless changes are made to the method of production, continued mono-cropping of wheat will ultimately destroy the land, which will have no future productive use.

Because both CIDA and NAFCO have an interest in persisting with the status quo, it is likely that the only means by which the Barabaig will receive a fair deal is through the pressure of public opinion in Canada forcing the Canadian government and CIDA to take up the challenge and convince their Tanzanian partners to make the necessary changes to bring about justice.

The program persists because of implicit agendas, if not explicit policies, that favour Western capital in alliance with vested interests in Tanzania. Responsibility for its ultimate outcome and effects must rest as squarely with donors as with the recipients of development projects. It is not enough for CIDA to say that "land use and administration are internal matters for a sovereign government, and ones in which outsiders may only play an indirect role" when it is clear that CIDA played a direct role in determining the type of project it would fund, which in this case created underdevelopment and penalized a minority group in the name of aid.[62] It is not enough for program staff to say "We are wheat farmers, and I am here just to grow wheat" and absolve themselves from responsibility for what their Tanzanian partners are doing.[63]

In law an omission can be as significant as an act. Turning a blind eye to human-rights abuses is not a worthy response, nor is the misuse of program resources and equipment for private gain. But by the end of the decade CIDA was still convinced the farms would be economical at some point. The aid agency seemed satisfied with limited attempts to help the Barabaig and with taking a hands-off approach to the legal issues of land title and minority rights that its own project had created.

Surely CIDA has to accept its responsibility and fully exercise its "indirect role" to construct a new political climate: one that will allow both governments to over-turn what has become a disastrous project in resource management, with a painful human cost.

Notes

1. Quoted in Linda Freeman, "CIDA and Agriculture in East and Central Africa," in *The Politics of Agriculture in Tropical Africa*, ed. Jonathan Barker (Beverly Hills: Sage, 1984). p.108.

2. For a report of the delivery of the open letter in Canada, see Charlotte Montgomery, "Kill CIDA 'albatross,' herders tell Canada," *The Globe and Mail*, May 8, 1989, p.A11.

3. Mcl. Wilson, "The Tatoga of Tanganyika," *Tanganyika Notes and Records*, No.33 (1952), p.35.

4. It is impossible to be more accurate than this as ethnic origin has not been recorded in a Tanzanian census since 1956.

5. M. Borgerhoff Mulder, D. Sieff, and M. Merus, "Disturbed Ancestors: Datoga History in the Ngorongoro Crater," *Swala*, Vol.2, No.2 (1989).

6. D. Gitganod, "What Value is a Cow?" paper presented at East African Pastoral Land Tenure Workshop, Arusha, Tanzania, December 1-3, 1988.

7. In traditional Barabaig custom these killings were not unlawful.

8. R. Young, *Canadian Development Assistance to Tanzania* (Ottawa: North-South Institute, 1983), p.67 (emphasis added).

9. Letter to President of International Institute for Environment and Development (IIED), London, August 31, 1988.

10. Minutes of meeting with Vice-President of CIDA for Anglophone Africa Branch, Hull, Quebec, April 28, 1989.

11. G. Hardin, "The Tragedy of the Commons," in *Managing the Commons*, ed. G. Harden and J. Baden (San Francisco: W.H.Freeman, 1977).

12. The author is indebted to Jeremy Swift for assistance with this analysis; see Charles Lane and Jeremy Swift, "Pastoral Land Tenure in East Africa," a report of a workshop convened by the Institute of Development Studies, University of Sussex, U.K., in Arusha, Tanzania, December 1-3, 1988.

13. This quote and much of the information relating to the history of the program were obtained from J. Nielsen, "History of the Tanzania-Canada Wheat Programme 1967-1982: A Report to Complete a Portion of the Requirements of a Contract Between the Department of Supply and Services, Government of Canada on behalf of Agriculture Canada," Ottawa, 1982.

14. Ibid., p.49.

15. Ibid., p.66.

16. This estimate was made by C. Carter, D. Frank, and R. Loyns, "Wheat in African Development: The Case of Tanzania," a paper presented to the Annual Conference of the Canadian Association of African Studies, Carleton University, Ottawa, May 10-13, 1989.

17. See R. James, *Land Tenure and Policy in Tanzania* (Nairobi: East African Literature Bureau, 1971); and R. James and G. Fimbo, *Customary Land Law of Tanzania* (Nairobi: East African Literature Bureau, 1973).

18. See M. Fenger, V. Hignett, and A. Green, *Soils of the Basotu and Balangda Lelu Areas of Northern Tanzania* (Ottawa: Agriculture Canada, 1986). This publication was produced in co-operation with the Government of Tanzania under the auspices of CIDA, Agriculture Canada, and the Tanzania-Canada Wheat Project.

19. Survival International, *Urgent Action Bulletin*, January 1990; *African Watch News*, March 12, 1990.

20. This was by way of letter NAFCO / ARA / WP / 59 from NAFCO to the district authorities, August 21, 1979.

21. Correspondence to the author from CIDA.

22. See I. Shivji and R. Tenga, "Ujamaa in Court," and "NAFCO's Reign of Terror," *Africa Events*, December 1985, pp.18-20,21.

23. "Tanzania: Executive Order Denies Land Rights; Barabaig Suffer Beatings, Arson and Criminal Charges," *News from Africa Watch*, March 12, 1990.

24. The evaluations were done by private Canadian consultancy firms engaged by CIDA.

25. J. Stone, "Project Evaluation: A Case Study of the Canada-Tanzania Wheat Project," University of Guelph, quoted by Young, *Canadian Development Assistance to Tanzania*, p.67.

26. Ibid.

27. Ibid., p.70.

28. This was explained to me by one of the evaluation team members.

29. Michael Mascall and Associates, "Report on the Evaluation of the Benefit / Cost Report," and "Production Cost Analysis of the Tanzania Wheat Project Reports," Prairie Horizons Ltd, Ottawa, August 13, 1986.

30. Ibid.

31. "Final Report of the Benefit / Cost Team on the Tanzania Wheat Project," submitted to the Natural Resources Branch, CIDA, by Prairie Horizons Ltd, Ottawa, November 1986.

32. Carter, Frank, and Loyns, "Wheat in African Development." The senior member of these studies was directly involved in the original cost-benefit analysis.

33. Letter to Warren Allmand from Joe Clark, June 16, 1989; and letter to Christine Stewart, M.P., from Monique Landry, June 12, 1989.

34. Carter, Frank, and Loyns, "Wheat in African Development," p.17.

35. Ibid., p.24.

36. P. Raikes, "Peasant Wheat Production in Four Districts of Tanzania," University of Dar es Salaam, Tanzania, Economic Research Bureau paper 70.3.

37. L. Freeman, "CIDA, Wheat, and Rural Development in Tanzania," *Canadian Journal of African Studies,* Vol.16, No.3 (1982), pp.479-504.

38. Ibid.

39. Ibid.

40. Young, *Canadian Development Assistance to Tanzania.*

41. J. Boesen et al. (eds.), *Tanzania: Crisis and the Struggle for Survival* (Uppsala: Scandinavian Institute of African Studies, 1986).

42. Freeman, "CIDA, Wheat, and Rural Development."

43. Young, *Canadian Development Assistance to Tanzania.*

44. G. Hyden, *Beyond Ujamaa in Tanzania: Underdevelopment and an Uncaptured Peasantry* (London: Heinemann, 1980).

45. A. Coulson, *Tanzania: A Political Economy* (Oxford: Clarendon, 1982).

46. Freeman, "CIDA, Wheat, and Rural Development."

47. Young, *Canadian Development Assistance to Tanzania.*

48. Freeman, "CIDA, Wheat, and Rural Development."

49. Ibid., pp.479-504.

50. Ibid.

51. Ibid.

52. Ibid.

53. Young, *Canadian Development Assistance to Tanzania.*

54. Young, *Canadian Development Assistance to Tanzania;* and Freeman, "CIDA, Wheat and Rural Development in Tanzania."

55. For a thorough critique of this project see A. Coulson, "The Automated Bread Factory," in *African Socialism in Practice: The Tanzanian Experience*, ed. A. Coulson (Nottingham: Spokesman, 1979). See also Robert Carty and Virginia Smith, *Perpetuating Poverty: The Political Economy of Canadian Foreign Aid* (Toronto: Between The Lines, 1981), pp.71-74.

56. Carter, Frank, and Loyns, "Wheat in African Development."

57. Ibid.

58. Young, *Canadian Development Assistance to Tanzania.*

59. Freeman, "CIDA, Wheat, and Rural Development."

60. See Gunilla Andrae and Bjorn Beckman, *The Wheat Trap: Bread and Underdevelopment in Nigeria* (London: Zed Books, 1985), where the authors document the case against wheat in Nigeria. Although the Nigerian case can be distinguished from the Tanzanian, there are enough similarities in the process of wheat dependence to make a comparison valid.

61. Freeman, "CIDA, Wheat, and Rural Development."

62. The quote is from correspondence to the author from CIDA.

63. The quote is from an interview with farm staff.

FIVE

Canadian NGOs and the Politics of Participation

Brian K. Murphy

She believed that, in an ideal world, the working classes would rule the country, but she had no desire to ask any of them to tea.

John Mortimer, *Paradise Postponed*

IN GUATEMALA between 1980 and 1983, a military campaign in the highlands destroyed 440 Indian communities. Government troops killed tens of thousands of peasants and displaced one-and-a-half-million people. Many fled as refugees to Mexico but most were forced into militarily-controlled model villages or "strategic hamlets". Canadian aid to the government of Guatemala was suspended, and since then non-governmental organizations (NGOs) and churches have consistently argued against the resumption of this bilateral aid.

In late 1987 the Canadian government decided to re-establish its bilateral assistance program with Guatemala, and in February 1988 the Canadian International Development Agency (CIDA) organized a meeting with Canadian voluntary organizations to seek their advice about how these funds might best be used. It was a small meeting including about 20 agencies that receive Canadian government funds for their activity in Guatemala. But a number of organizations working in Guatemala were not in attendance; for several years these groups had declined to accept funds from the Canadian government for security reasons – that is, to protect the lives and work of project partners – because it was known that the government sometimes shared Canadian project information with the Guatemalan government and the U.S. embassy.

The decision to resume bilateral aid had been severely criticized by some agencies, including the Canadian Council for International Cooperation (CCIC) and the

Inter-Church Committee on Human Rights in Latin America (ICCHRLA). Yet the ground rules established at the beginning of the 1988 consultation meeting indicated that there would be no time spent discussing the wisdom of the actual decision to resume bilateral funding. The meeting therefore quickly covered the surface of the issue: amounts of money to be made available to the Guatemalan government, the various models being considered for the fund, the general types of work currently being carried out, and the needs to which new funds might be applied.

At one point a worker for a major Protestant church questioned the implications of the decision to support the Guatemalan government, given the articulated concern in the room "to assist the poorest of the poor". She spoke of the dangers of supporting organizations and welfare projects associated with the Guatemalan government and of the military campaign against rural organizations, especially those representing the people who make up 80 per cent of Guatemala's countryside. She wondered how funds could ever get to those "popular" organizations working for real change, social justice, and self-determination for the poor.

We will call this worker "Jane." Her question was a good one, a necessary question, demanding a response not only from CIDA but also from her agency colleagues. There was a tense silence; uncomfortable glances were exchanged, with some impatient tongues clicking off the few seconds before an executive of one of the largest agencies, his voice an uneasy balance between a scold and a tease, boomed, "Come on, Jane, what do you want? ... a revolution?"

The tension was broken. The laughter that washed away the discomfort also buried the question that had been asked and quickly faded back to the businesslike chatter of the meeting, which wound up as politely as it had begun. Nothing had happened.

Nothing had happened, but everything had happened, including the formulation of the key question facing Canadians and Canadian agencies trying to form a vision and a practice for the future: *"What do you want? ... a revolution?"* This is a critical question for two reasons.

First, as will be evident from close reading of the other chapters in this book, the *possibility* of a revolution may be debatable but it is clear that little less than global revolution is *sufficient* if the Earth's poor are to achieve the justice and life they deserve. It even appears probable that such a revolution is necessary if the planet itself, let alone the billion of absolute poor, is to survive the mounting military and environmental cataclysm threatened by the concentration of wealth and power in hands accountable to no higher order than the concentration of power itself.

Second (and this should be a compelling reason even without the imperatives of survival), in every society in which Canadian voluntary agencies work today, there are significant movements organizing for fundamental change in political and economic relationships – between the powerful and the powerless, between the rich and the poor, between autonomous nations and the major international powers – that determine the political evolution of nations and the destinies of entire peoples. In many Third world nations these movements are made up of the majority of the people, or at least the majority of people far enough removed from the grim line between life and death to articulate such a choice.

Sometimes these are national liberation movements, such as the African National Congress (ANC) in South Africa, the South West African People's Organization (SWAPO) in Namibia, or the Farabundo Martí National Liberation Front – Democratic Revolutionary Front (FMLN-FDR) in El Salvador. But most often they are coalitions of so-called "popular" organizations – organizations run by communities of people in their own interests. These include labour and farm-workers unions, associations of small farmers and other small producers, co-operative federations, associations of teachers, health workers, and other professionals, women's organizations, non-government human-rights commissions, and in some cases religious "base communities".

Such movements exist as part of the "development" and essentially *political* landscape in which international agencies carry out their work. The relationship with these movements and the political and economic issues that the movements are trying to resolve is inevitably a central issue for critical reflection, and choice. It must therefore be a focus of any discussion of the role of Canadian international development agencies in the dynamics of global poverty and the struggle for global justice.[1]

THE INTERNATIONAL "NGOS": WHAT'S IN A NAME?

Any discussion about NGOs must begin with an explanation of the meaning of the very term. It is ironic, but revealing, that "non-governmental organization" does not tell us what an NGO *is*, but rather what it is *not*: it is not a government organization. The term NGO originated in the United Nations system and maintains wide use throughout the world, north and south, resisting continuous efforts to replace it with a more positive term. It is normally used only to refer to agencies active in international development, peace, human rights, environment, and development education.

Why would this denotation be required? Perhaps because the NGOs support or implement programs for which governments are normally thought to be responsible; and they often do these things in co-operation with governments, relying to a large degree on government funds. Therein lies much of the significance, and the contradictions, of the NGOs.

NGOS AND THE VOLUNTARY SECTOR IN CANADA

While a critical analysis of the Canadian NGOs depends on an understanding of the role they play in the wider world, it first requires an understanding of their evolution in Canadian society.

163

Canada's international development NGOs are just a small part of a larger sector, the so-called "voluntary sector", which has a long and significant tradition in Canadian life. Participation by Canadians in the life of their communities through voluntary action is an important defining characteristic of what it is to be a Canadian. The most visible examples are organizations like the United Way that are themselves fundraising coalitions of scores of voluntary organizations run by local citizens to provide social services within the community. There are also the large national charities dedicated to, for example, medical research and treatment of diseases such as cancer, diabetes, and heart disease. Similarly, there are the large service clubs, like the Rotary, Kiwanis, or Lions clubs, with chapters in the smallest of rural communities. Another huge segment, in fact the largest single category, is the voluntary action component of the churches, including all religious and spiritual institutions.

Behind these large organizations – part of our lives for so long that we take them as part of the landscape, like the ubiquitous service club welcome signs across small-town Canada – is a vast tapestry of smaller local organizations set up by ordinary people to assist neighbours in need and to develop the community so that it provides opportunity and quality of life to more of its members.

At the same time there are thousands of organizations set up by and for people who feel a "special interest" due to their exclusion from mainstream society, including the mainstream voluntary sector. They have created their own mechanisms to respond to needs not met by society at large and to advocate for fuller participation in society. Such organizations are usually created by specific communities of people, most often on the basis of race and ethnicity, gender, or class, and often on the basis of all of these discriminating factors at once. Therefore we see ethno-specific and women-specific crisis intervention and community service centres, legal aid clinics, anti-poverty groups, literacy centres, advocacy groups of welfare recipients and the unemployed, tenants unions, shelters for battered women and their families, support groups for victims of sexual crimes such as rape and incest, support groups for addiction victims, and mutual support structures created for, and usually by, the disabled.

"Voluntary" activity falls under both a legal definition and a popular conception of the charity (a definition also including certain kinds of cultural and educational activity). There are more than 55,000 incorporated charities in Canada (that is, one charity for just slightly more than every 470 Canadians) and well over five million Canadians – one in four adults – participate in community action through these organizations, contributing an estimated one billion hours of unpaid labour, the equivalent of 500,000 full-time jobs, to voluntary activity every year.[2]

This does not represent all voluntary action, of course. Not all active community groups are "registered", nor is all spontaneous community activism that occurs continually throughout the length and breadth of the land. Only a group with a "charitable" purpose, in the sense of social service and "charitable good works", can be registered as a charity (which allows the organization to collect tax-deductible donations). The statistics for (and privileges of) registered charities leave out a broad range of voluntary groups whose purpose is advocacy or political action, such as organizing for civil liberties, human rights, social justice, global peace, or fundamental economic and social change.

When all these types of social participation are considered, voluntary action makes up a very significant component of Canadian cultural life and of socio-economic activity within Canadian society. Some estimates have it that in pure economic terms the voluntary sector accounts for fully 4 per cent of the gross national product (GNP).[3]

The international organizations, or NGOs, make up only a tiny proportion of the tens of thousands of organizations in the Canadian voluntary sector. Only about 220 organizations fit the definition in the 1988 North-South Institute study.[4] The international NGOs range from scores of small religiously-affiliated and community-based fundraising and public education organizations to large Canadian organizations whose names are almost as well known as the Rotary Club. The best known would include Oxfam-Canada, USC Canada, and CUSO; church-based agencies such as the Mennonite Central Committee, the Canadian Catholic Organization for Development and Peace (CCODP), Canadian Baha'i International Development Services, or the Council of Muslim Communities in Canada; the Canadian arms of international institutions such as the International Red Cross and UNICEF; the Canadian fundraising branches of large U.S-based multinational agencies such as CARE, Foster Parents Plan, and the evangelical World Vision; and patriated but originally foreign-based agencies, such as Save the Children-Canada or Aga Khan Foundation Canada, which are developing as authentic Canadian agencies in their own right.

There is also a range of lesser known agencies that have a firm base of support built gradually over several years: for example, INTER PARES, Horizons of Friendship, MATCH International, or Plenty Canada. More recently we have seen the creation of unique organizations that are as much national action networks and coalitions as NGOs per se. An example is Tools for Peace, a network of community-based committees in support of development actions in Nicaragua. Some organizations have a significant regional base, such as SUCO, Fondation Jules et Paul-Emile Léger, or Organisation canadienne pour la solidarité et le développement (OCSD) in Quebec, or Farmers for Peace and Change for Children in Alberta.

Normally included among the 220 to 240 NGOs are international departments connected to larger Canadian institutions, such as the Canadian Labour Congress, the Canadian National Institute for the Blind, the Co-operative Union of Canada, the Association of Universities and Colleges in Canada (AUCC), the YM / YWCA, or the Council of Provincial Organizations of the Handicapped (COPOH) through its affiliation in Disabled Peoples International.

The international NGOs represent a broad and disparate grouping of agencies.

Their distinctions may be more significant than their commonalities. [5] At the same time this sector, including as it does major churches and large national institutions as well as fundraising branches of large international organizations, is significant beyond its numerical size. The amount of money these few organizations raise and spend is considerably higher than their proportionate numbers within the voluntary sector would predict.

To understand the work the NGOs do, and where their money comes from, they must be placed in the larger context of the Canadian voluntary sector in its relation to government and the wider society. As a general rule the voluntary sector in Canada carries out actions in support of individuals, groups of individuals, or entire communities, which government at various levels – municipal, regional, provincial, or federal – is unwilling or unable to carry out. In most cases, where the activity has generated at least "special interest" support, and therefore political collateral, the activity receives some financial support from government. In many cases the organizations have paid staff, and in the case of major charities and social services they have well-paid and secure "professional" staff. In this sense the voluntary sector is not entirely voluntary at all, and is a major employment sector in Canada.

Still, a great deal of the work carried out within this sector remains voluntary and is in fact subsidized by citizens who donate time, material, goods, and other resources to ensure that activities are carried out. Even within large voluntary agencies, the "stewards" of the organizations – boards of directors, committees, patrons – are volunteers, and by law receive no remuneration. Similarly, private donations, often a large proportion of the financial resources of the voluntary organization, are by definition voluntary contributions. In this sense this sector, once entirely sustained without government support, continues to be legitimately called a "voluntary" sector. This is true even with the growing financial involvement of the public sector in many fields of volunteer activity. Some of these fields, especially in the social services, are almost entirely government-funded, because many *community* organizations deliver *government* services more cheaply and more effectively than any government bureaucracy could ever hope to do.

What has been unique in this relationship between community and government is that the activity itself has usually been generated through social activism within the community. Programs that first develop as a systematic community-based (or "voluntary") response to community needs later give rise to political demands within the community for better resource allocation from the government. As a result it has become expedient for the government to support voluntary community services because they generate low-cost political capital for the government.

This shift gained critical momentum with the "social participation" and "Just Society" strategy of Pierre Trudeau's first government – an attempt to harness, if not co-opt, the social activism of the late sixties and early seventies. The trend now characterizes the social-service field to such an extent that government at all levels prefers to *create* (directly or indirectly) government-funded "voluntary" organizations rather than government-run social-service bureaucracies.

At the same time there has been a parallel shift in which the advocacy and activism of voluntary agencies have been reduced to the institutionalized pattern of annual negotiations with various levels of government for secure funding and program priority status. This has happened at the expense of the militancy and the political activism that is essential to bring about the social change implicit in the original mandate of the organizations in question.

Political action in the voluntary sector has become virtually restricted to lobbying government for funds, for political legitimacy, and for fiscal policies and priorities that promote the organizations and programs of specific sectors. This has meant that for reasons of institutional maintenance and security (and not incidentally the security of paid workers), organizations and even movements have developed pragmatic partnerships with government as an extension of government programs and priorities within specific communities, rather than operating as an authentic nexus of community-based social action. There remains some give and take in the relationship, but due to conventional illusions of who is giving (the government) and who is taking (the community), there is rarely rigorous debate and struggle in what has become a comfortable symbiotic relationship. But the givers and takers are in reality entirely the reverse of conventional premises: The government is in fact taking from the community; and it is the community that is giving; the workers (paid and unpaid) and those nominally served by the sector in question are subsidizing the government and society as a whole through volunteer activity.

There are many negative effects of this evolution that relate to the quality and effectiveness of programs. But three aspects are particularly germane to this discussion:

☐ The first is the extent to which these trends have been incorporated into the general shift to "special interest" politics within liberal democracy in the last two decades. This is a trend ("governing-by-Gallup") in which vision, planning, and a guiding social and ethical ethos are replaced by the politics of personality and party, and a vulgar preoccupation with simple power: getting it, exploiting it, keeping it.

☐ The second is the disenfranchisement of the truly marginal and voiceless. These are persons and groups who are unable to consolidate as a sufficiently powerful "special interest" to make themselves heard in the din of special interests, or whose voice has been appropriated by an elite of "community leaders" and a compliant voluntary sector – an anti-establishment establishment. This establishment is courted, contracted, and paid by government to speak in the name of particular target groups in society, while the truly marginal remain invisible and powerless within an increasingly segmented society.

An example of this is the extent to which radical (or "root") responses to the vulnerability of women to isolation, poverty, and violence are blunted by the creation of minimal mainstream services that individualize the problem and speak for the "victim". Similar developments have occurred in the welfare and housing areas and, most recently, in the field of literacy. A more comprehensive example is the dominance of upper-middle-class and professional males in an emerging "ethnic" establishment that is gaining a voice in urban Canada; this is testimony to a minimal pragmatic (and grudging) opening in the circle of male-dominated political-economic power in the country, but it does nothing to confront the real barriers of race, gender, and class that condemn 25 per cent of Canadians to a lifetime of poverty within a permanent underclass.

☐ The third is the institutionalization of the voluntary sector around two seemingly contradictory phenomena: competition for scarce public dollars, and mutual self-interest in the public promotion of the voluntary sector. There is within the voluntary sector intense competition to secure a "fair share" of the budget pie. At the same time there is a surface of genial co-operation among the established players in this game, the thriving organizations whose political base is solid and whose maintenance strategy includes promotion of their own organization through promotion of the voluntary sector itself and of their own leadership within it.

The net result of these three effects – special interest politics, disenfranchisement of the poor and marginal, and the institutionalization of the voluntary sector in patterns of competition and self-promotion – is an almost complete removal of the voluntary sector from the populations, communities, and persons that it evolved to represent and serve. [6] This result is combined with a corresponding deterioration of the significant potential that voluntary agencies present to society, a role promoted by the authors of the study carried out by the North-South Institute (NSI): "to continuously shape and reshape the vision of a more just social order." [7]

This is the context in which international NGOs operate. The dilemmas integral to voluntary agencies are critical to the international NGOs. Questions of mandate, of relevance, of independence – essentially questions about whose interests are ultimately served by the activity of the NGOs and how well these interests are served – all begin here, and in the way that the NGO sector has evolved over the past several decades.

THE EMERGENCE OF THE INTERNATIONAL NGOS

The first NGOs in Canada developed before 1960 as branches of international and multinational organizations, themselves originating in the experience of post-World War II war-relief efforts (for example, CARE in Europe, Oxfam in Greece). Their purpose had been entirely charitable and involved the distribution of aid, and sometimes services, such as emergency medical care or inoculation, usually carried out through official local government channels or multinational (especially UN) programs.

After 1960 more NGOs formed. Again these were often affiliated with foreign agencies or were extensions of the pastoral missions of international church bodies. Increasingly, however, Canadian organizations expanded their focus to include notions of social development, at least to the extent of trying to replicate institutions associated with advanced development in the industrialized nations: for example, higher education, medicine, intensive agriculture. This meant moving from the mere delivery of surplus goods (usually food) as charity for the destitute, to the delivery of personnel and material to build institutions and advanced methodologies for the nations in which they lived.

By 1970 the limits of these strategies were apparent. The fabric of cosy notions about post-colonial development was unravelling, with economic collapse, natural disaster, and civil war competing with each other as scourges of the growing majority of absolute poor. It was becoming clear, largely through the critique of theorists and activists from the Third World, that the assistance being "transferred" to the Third World was not reaching the poor and that the poor were not being assisted to secure or exploit this assistance. New NGOs with these insights began to emerge, with a focus on the community-based self-help approach that has become the commonplace of NGO literature over the last two decades. Increasingly these NGOs were created by Canadians and related to specific Canadian communities of interest.

Most of these new NGOs came into their own at the same time as the broader voluntary sector began to expand its government funding and move towards its present place as a close partner of government. The proliferation of international NGOs was, in part at least, the result of this trend. At the same time, the growth of NGOs drew upon the very strong commitment of some of the most forward-looking senior officials within the Canadian government and CIDA. This was a commitment borne of their conviction (for many a political as well as professional conviction) that long-term social change in the Third World was dependent upon grassroots development, local community-based organizations (the local "voluntary sector"), and related socio-political movements. CIDA officials recognized that this work could better, and more safely, be supported through a dynamic Canadian voluntary sector than directly by the Canadian government, because the "popular" sector in most Third World countries was more politicized than in Canada and the relevant social movements were confronting national governments that the Canadian government was formally bound to respect.

At the same time Canadians were developing an awareness of the increasingly grim problems of survival and development in scores of Third World countries. Many Canadians came to accept the responsibility of the industrialized countries to try to resolve the growing disparities between North and South. Public support increased for interventions by CIDA and by the better-known NGOs.

There were many reasons for this gradual change in awareness, which began in Canada as early as 1956 with Canada's role in the Suez Crisis and the subsequent acclaim of Lester Pearson. That period had a clear impact on the self-deprecating Canadian consciousness – the beginning of the myth of Canada as the quiet peace-maker on the turbulent world stage. The events merged with the impact of the struggle for Algerian independence, the Cuban Revolution, and the world-wide attention paid in the early 1960s to the struggle against apartheid and the problems of the British Commonwealth in dealing with the white supremacist regimes in South Africa and Rhodesia. Certainly the unmasking of imperial America, especially as it thrashed around in Southeast Asia but also in such adventures as the 1965 intervention in the Dominican Republic, allowed a loss of innocence that permitted a new consciousness to emerge from the numb isolation of the post-Korea 1950s.

The last few years of the sixties and the early seventies saw an intense flash of radical political action in Canada, on both national and international issues, deeply influenced by events and movements sweeping the United States and Europe. Vietnam abroad and "apprehended insurrection" and the War Measures Act at home were searing experiences for a new generation. Images from other events – like the 1967-70 Nigerian Civil War and the plight of stranded Biafra, the bloody war of secession between East and West Pakistan that led to the creation of Bangladesh in 1973, the devastating drought in the Sahel in 1973, the U.S.-inspired coup in Chile that same year, and the growing attention to liberation movements in Latin America, Southern Africa, and Asia – all encroached upon and reshaped public consciousness.

Probably nothing was as profound in its impact as the creation of the Organization of Petroleum Exporting Countries (OPEC) and the ensuing "energy crisis". This "event" influenced people's daily lives through the rising cost of a gallon of gas to power the automobile, the very symbol of affluence, and gave real substance if not coherence to the notions of "global village", interdependence, and the international economic order. The inflation of the 1970s and the world-wide recession that followed into the early 1980s consolidated this awareness for Canadians, along with an anxiety and a sense of vulnerability.

Canadian NGOs evolved within this context. What is key is that while most NGOs were beneficiaries of this change in consciousness (many actually exploiting the images of misery to raise funds), only a few organizations, and especially the churches, were active agents in the process of consciousness-raising. Through concerted organizing and development education, these NGOS supported the creation of a dynamic network of community-based and church-based activism devoted to public education, cultural action, lobbying, and solidarity work, as well as linking communities and providing material support to Third World movements.

Coalitions of the mainstream Christian churches actually created or supported the creation of organizations such as the Latin American Working Group (LAWG), GATT-Fly, and Ten Days for World Development, as well as formal "committees" (with full-time staff) on issues such as human rights and refugees. Church NGOS such as CCODP developed extensive community education programs and publications. Secular NGOS such as CUSO and Oxfam took the lead in developing local committees and funding support structures for regional education and organization.

A broad network of community-based learner centres was created, providing a resource base for much of the local international public education and activism of this period and playing a critical role in supporting and developing many people who eventually went on to key leadership roles within the NGOS. Some of these centres, such as the Development Education Resource and Information Centre (DEVERIC) in Halifax, One Sky Cross Cultural Centre in Saskatoon, and the International Development Education Resource Association (IDERA) in Vancouver, became regional clearing houses for alternative international print and film materials in support of major educational programs. The Development Education Centre (DEC) and the Cross Cultural Communication Centre (CCCC), both in Toronto, played a leadership role in this field. DEC and CCCC not only served as national resource and distribution centres for books, films, and other resources, but also developed innovative animation and workshop techniques and promoted much needed critical research and policy analysis, often in collaboration with alternative book publishers such as Between The Lines.

Independent regionally-based national coalitions such as the People's Food Commission emerged with new strategies for public education and participation; at the same time INTER PARES was developing the Common Heritage Schools Program and creating international linkage mechanisms such as Women's Health Interaction (WHI). Regional structures co-ordinated through the Canadian Council for International Cooperation (CCIC) facilitated collaboration among these varied activities.

This education and advocacy role over a period of fifteen years may have been the most significant activity and contribution of the NGOS, with more lasting effect than the millions of dollars the NGOS used in programs in the Third World in the same period. [8]

The result was a rising Canadian awareness and concern, which provided a solid and growing base of support for the activity of NGOs in the Third World.[9] The new focus was translated not only into a lode of private donations to support this work but also into the political capital necessary to gain an ever-increasing pool of funds from the Canadian government. It allowed increasing participation in the policy debates on Canada's own official development assistance program (ODA). Finally, it enhanced the role of the most clearly political NGOs to intervene (with mixed success) in Canada's broader foreign policy.

With this impact in mind, it is worthwhile examining in some detail the size of the NGOs and their significance in relation to Canada's overall development assistance effort. Most of the 220 to 240 organizations and institutions were created after 1970; fully 16 per cent of the NGO respondents in the NSI study were formed between 1980 and 1985 and this rapid growth of the sector has continued.[10] The agencies are also growing larger, with average Canadian-based staffs doubling from six full-time equivalents in 1975 to eleven in 1984. The NGOs employ an estimated 2,500 full-time Canadian-based staff, with perhaps another 500 paid staff working overseas. Co-operants – Canadians placed as "volunteers" in technical support positions in Third World institutions – number about 5,000, and there are another 500 annual short-term exchanges through groups such as Canada World Youth. There are also an estimated 6,000 missionaries overseas, about 3,000 of them engaged in development rather than pastoral or evangelical work.[11]

There are, then, about 12,000 Canadians working with the NGOs on a full-time paid or vocational basis. There are another 40,000 Canadians directly involved with the NGOs on a strictly volunteer basis (excluding donors and members of specific institutions such as the YM / YWCA or the churches).[12] These figures must be balanced with the knowledge that the NGOs vary tremendously, ranging from the many having but the tiniest of budgets (including no access to CIDA funding) and virtually no full-time staff, to those with budgets in excess of $25 million annually, and with Canadian offices employing scores of people. Of the 97 agencies that submitted financial data to the NSI study, fully 36 per cent had budgets below $250,000; 24 per cent were between $250,000 and $1 million; another 24 per cent were between $1 million and $5 million; and 16 per cent had budgets over $5 million.[13]

The agencies connected to large institutions or to the churches have access to much greater resources, and larger international program delivery networks than the smaller unaffiliated or non-sectarian organizations. And of course there are the large agencies reporting to foreign head offices, usually of U.S.-based multinational charities, international churches, or evangelical institutions, whose reportable budgets in Canada form only one part of a larger economic and political reality (25 per cent of the agencies responding to the NSI study were affiliates of, and at least partially responsible to, foreign-based institutions).

The NSI study calculated the total resources of the NGO sector in 1984-85 at about $525 million, of which almost $280 million was raised from private (or non-government) sources. CIDA contributed $245 million, which represented more than 11 per cent of its entire Overseas Development Assistance allocation for that year. [14] This was a significant increase on the $37.6 million provided through NGOS eight years earlier in 1976-77 (which was then only 3.9 per cent of total ODA). CIDA's contribution had increased to $87.5 million (6.7 per cent of ODA) in 1980-81, and $143 million (8.6 per cent of ODA) in 1982-83. [15]

While CIDA's contribution of $245 million to the programs of NGOS represented about 11 per cent of Canada's ODA, the total of $525 million used by the NGOS represented *fully* 20 per cent of a total $2.38 billion, public and private, dedicated to international development activity in the same period. [16] Clearly the NGO sector has become a significant participant in the Canadian international development arena. The Canadian NGO sector was also impressive internationally, second only to Switzerland in percentage of ODA channelled through NGOS, and third behind the United States and West Germany in both absolute dollars of government funding and absolute dollars of private donations. [17]

While both private and government contributions have continued to increase at substantial rates, the ratio of government to private funds increased to about 50:50 by 1984, from an already quite high 40:60 in 1974. [18] This trend further reflects the growing "partnership" between government and the voluntary sector in Canada, a trend that has been dramatic in the international development field. This merger of interests has reached the extent that some NGOS have become implementing extensions of government (what the NSI refers to as "social entrepreneurs"), mere "managers" of programs selected or created by the Canadian government and other multilateral institutions, devoid of authentic local relationships or primary programming with local groups. In fact, it is the smaller agencies and a few large agencies, which have historically insisted on lower government funding ratios to protect their independence, that keep the apparent government funding ratio to NGOS at an artificially low level.

In the case of the very largest and often most powerful of the NGOS, such as World University Services of Canada (WUSC), CUSO, CARE, Foster Parents Plan, and World Vision, the ratio of government funding is much higher than 60:40, often reaching to 75 or 80 per cent and sometimes as high as 90 per cent. The NSI study describes the concentration of government funding within the NGOS, showing that only 25 agencies (or less than 20 per cent of the total studied) received a significant amount of bilateral or "country focus" funding, with well over 50 per cent of the total going to just five agencies: CARE, UNICEF, WUSC, CUSO, and CECI (Centre canadien d'études et de coopération internationale). In the field of "service contracts" to implement or manage government projects, a category separate from "country focus" project grants, WUSC on its own accounted for 80 per cent of the NGO total in the period studied.[19] A more recent CCIC study ranks 13 NGOs based on active CIDA contracts held as of spring 1989. At that time these 13 organizations were implementing, among them, 95 CIDA projects worth over $277 million.[20]

This pattern of funding has serious implications for the independence and relevance of the NGO programs. More significant, in the long term, is an increasing divergence of opinion and principle among the international NGOs about the autonomous role of NGOs.

CANADIAN NGOS AND THE THIRD WORLD:
WITH WHOM, AND FOR WHAT?

There are many ways to categorize the international NGOs and the activity they support. The most conventional framework, essentially descriptive and donor-centred, distinguishes five main categories of overseas activity: relief and emergency assistance; development assistance projects; placement of personnel; material assistance; and child and family sponsorship. All of this activity was fairly evenly distributed among Latin America and the Caribbean (38 per cent); Asia (25.7 per cent); Anglophone Africa (21 per cent); and Francophone Africa (15.2 per cent).

Among 129 NGO respondents in the NSI study, the largest proportion of resources (58.9 per cent) was devoted to development assistance projects, that is, to providing direct financial and technical support for the improvement of social services and production.[21] This large category breaks down into various activities: health, nutrition, and population, including water and sanitation (20.6 per cent); education and human resource development (28.6 per cent); agriculture and food production (18.7 per cent); institutional support and management (14.4 per cent); economic and financial support (13.5 per cent); miscellaneous production, in areas such as energy, forestry, industry, mines, and fisheries (1.9 per cent); and non-productive projects in communications and transportation (0.3 per cent).[22]

The remaining categories receive about equal emphasis. The placement of Canadians overseas makes up 12.6 per cent of NGO overseas activity. This involves placing and supporting co-operants in technical or professional support roles in productive projects (such as agriculture or forests), human services (health, education), commerce (small business, micro-enterprise), or infrastructural development (energy, planning). Placement is a specialized activity concentrated among a very few large institutions, such as CUSO, WUSC, or CECI, and smaller NGOs such as SUCO, Organisation canadienne pour la solidarité et le développement (OCSD), and the Mennonite Central Committee (MCC). Also included in this category are the short-term linkage programs such as Canada World Youth and Crossroads International.

Relief and emergency assistance in response to natural disaster, war, or protracted crisis (such as drought and famine) makes up another 10.5 per cent of NGO activity. While a number of agencies such as the Red Cross and some church-based NGOS are highly specialized in this role, virtually all agencies are involved to some degree. It is an area experiencing renewed growth after a time when it was less emphasized because of its short-term focus. The new emphasis is due in part to the ever-increasing vulnerability of hundreds of millions of the poorest and most destitute persons on the planet to the devastation of war and to the natural and technological disasters that have laid waste the productive environment that once sustained and nurtured life. As a result there are increased funds availabile from CIDA and from Canadian donors stung by the images of starvation and misery on their television screens.

Child and family sponsorship activity, much criticized in recent years, still represents 9.3 per cent of NGO activity.[23] In fact, sponsorship is less a specific overseas activity than a technique for raising funds in Canada, and is a practice limited to only a few Canadian agencies, such as Foster Parents Plan of Canada. Increasingly funds raised this way are channelled to local social welfare organizations for the benefit of communities in the name of, but not the sole benefit of, specific children or families.

A final category, "material assistance", makes up the remaining 8 per cent of NGO overseas activity and involves the acquisition and delivery of materials, such as medical, agricultural, or building supplies. This activity is prevalent in agencies with a specialized capacity but is carried out to some small extent by most NGOs as part of their larger focus.

To understand the variety of agencies – and their distinctions – it is necessary to define their mode of operation and the forms that their assistance programs take. A minority of Canadian agencies are "operational", that is, actually implementing projects in the field, with or without local involvement. Of the sample of 51 projects evaluated by the NSI study, only 15 (29 per cent) were implemented by Canadian NGOs, while another 14 (27 per cent) were implemented by international affiliates; and 22 (43 per cent) were implemented directly by local community-based or national (so-called "indigenous") NGOs, with support from international NGOs.[24] Many Canadian NGOs are merely involved in raising funds to be channelled to projects operated by an international parent. This is a model common within the Protestant and Evangelical churches, and some of the large U.S.-based institutions. But, as the figures show, the most common model for the autonomous Canadian NGOs is to provide funding and other resources in direct support of the work of local "partner" NGOs (community-based or national) in Third World countries (and sometimes NGOs serving regions).

Another kind of program, which overlaps with the original framework, is the placement of personnel within government or parastatal institutions or projects, or within the programs and activities of the voluntary or NGO sector. About 12.6 per cent of activity fell into this category.

Finally there is the specialized Canadian-based activity commonly known as "development education". This is activity aimed at deepening public awareness and commitment towards resolution of the major global problems of poverty, violence, war, underdevelopment, environmental degradation, and social and political injustice, including human-rights violations. Although over 75 per cent of the NSI respondents were involved in some development education, only about 10 per cent of total staff resources were dedicated to it. Only 3 per cent of funds received by the NGOs from CIDA were earmarked for public education activity.[25] Most NGOs restrict "education" to their efforts to raise money, including newsletters to their donors describing projects in the field. This narrow "project" focus and firm notions of the non-political role of "humanitarian" agencies have led to a self-restricted role for most NGOs in terms of public education and advocacy. As a result, the commitment to development education beyond this project-oriented and donor-specific approach has been limited to a small minority of agencies.

These few agencies have often linked their development education programs to some support for a final category of activity that we can call *solidarity activism*. This is the point where international development action meets activism for change *in Canada* as well as in the remote Third World.

Solidarity activism is advocacy, political education, and community organizing to connect people and communities in common cause on related local and global issues. This includes lobbying the Canadian government about its foreign policy on specific international situations; and mobilizing groups of Canadians to provide material and political support for liberation movements (such as the South African anti-apartheid movement), revolutionary processes (the Sandinista revolution in Nicaragua), and human-rights activists and organizations in the most repressive of regimes (Chile, El Salvador, or Indonesia). The work also involves promoting and supporting international linkages and mutual support relationships between peoples, communities, organizations, and movements – relationships based on a common vision of global justice, common cause to solve shared problems, and common methodologies to bring about local and global change.

DEVELOPING A CRITIQUE:
PARTNERSHIP AND PARTICIPATION

Individual NGOs may incorporate a range of these activities. It is the emphasis among the types of action that distinguishes the various agencies and groupings of agencies. More importantly, it must be recognized that these categories are descriptive and one-dimensional: political maturity, clarity and depth of analysis, and the *quality* of intervention provide the real distinguishing mark among the agencies. The fundamental element that distinguishes agencies and their work is the *nature and quality of the relationships* formed in developing priorities and strategies, and the *quality of local participation* within the specific context of an agency's programs and projects.

These qualitative factors have recently received closer scrutiny by development theorists. In an influential series of papers David Korten adopted a "social learning" framework dividing international NGO activity into three "generations" representing a spectrum of potential interventions available to NGOs: relief and welfare, small-scale self-reliant local development, and sustainable systems development. [26] Korten's analysis derives from management and organizational theory and is based on experiences assisting USAID (an agency of the U.S. government) in the application of social learning theory in the Philippines and Thailand. [27] His analysis is limited and is more useful at the descriptive than the strategic level. While he accurately describes some of the learning experience of the NGOs, Korten bases his generations and his analysis of present possibilities on the insulated institutional experience of the NGOs themselves, rather than on an analysis of changes in the external conditions and experiences of the objects of all this learning: the poor themselves. Korten therefore misses the critical fact that the poor have not experienced their poverty any differently through the long learning process of the NGOs; the poor have merely experienced the NGOs differently, as the NGOs have stumbled from analysis to analysis, theory to theory, and from new strategy to newer strategy. There is little in his prescription to provide hope that this trend will change.

Tim Brodhead, one of the authors of the North-South Institute study, adapts and simplifies this framework, not to provide a definitive description of reality but to clarify the critical choices facing NGOs. [28] He creates a matrix that distinguishes three basic functions – service delivery, education, and public policy – and explores activity within these functions along a three-stage spectrum according to the primary role perceived by the agency: Stage I is the provision of relief and welfare; Stage II focuses on funding or implementation of self-help projects; and Stage III concentrates on collaboration with local agents for change as a facilitator or catalyst in specific aspects of the change process. Brodhead points out that all of these activities are valid and respond to real needs. In many agencies all three of these stages co-exist, within some degree of harmony, but with varying priorities placed on the different activities. These "stages" manifest an evolution in the maturity and analysis of the NGOs, and the emphasis within any NGO is an indicator of its dynamism and relevance.

In a related essay exploring some of the difficulties NGOs face, especially the properties of working relationships, Charles Elliot provides a description of the extent to which these emphases can be in conflict *within* organizations, with intense analytical debate and competition for resources on the part of protagonists promoting one or another kind of activity.[29] The roots of this conflict lie in divergent visions of the role of the NGOs – and essentially in whether the NGO is merely a neutral humanitarian intervener or a political partner fully engaged and committed to a long-term struggle for social change.

In fact, the data indicate that the resources of most Canadian NGOs are concentrated in Stage II activity (local self-help projects).[30] We also are seeing growing attention and resources being focused once again on Stage I (emergency relief and welfare) in areas of natural disaster or extended conflict. It is useful, therefore, if we wish to formulate possible new directions, to examine the Stage III "catalytic" role, which Brodhead defines as the primary option, or next step, for NGOs.

The focus in Stage III is on developing new qualities of relationships and new actions in the context of these relationships, and on NGOs taking "strategic decisions about the optimum use and leverage of their limited resources and influence."[31] The emphasis is on NGOs adapting to new realities and choosing to take on more critical roles in the dynamics of social change within a turbulent global political economy.

The characteristics of such a role are vague. But the role clearly transcends the limited one of provider of money and material for projects and partner NGOs, a role increasingly taken on by Northern governmental and multilateral agencies, and requiring, in any case, less proliferation of NGO bureaucracy, not more.[32] And it certainly transcends the role of project implementation, because increasingly this has become the function of local Southern NGOs, institutions, and community-based organizations. This is true even for basic relief and reconstruction, let alone the much-touted self-help projects, which, by definition, are increasingly implemented by local voluntary sectors, popular organizations, or non-government structures such as co-ops, unions, and federations (a fact that should be taken as a measure of success by those agencies that have promoted the development of sustainable Third World NGO sectors).

The theorists cited here, among others, are calling for an approach that transcends the very project-based orientation itself.[33] But a new catalytic or facilitation role of Northern NGOs largely remains to be defined, in conjunction with Southern NGOs. Brodhead sees the creation of "a new international division of labour … in which northern and southern NGOs both have essential parts to play if common goals are to be attained, in which neither has sole power, and one might add, the risks in working for change are more equally shared."[34] The role of Northern NGOs would involve collaborating with Southern NGO partners as equals – through, for example, "bridging" or "levering" other supports such as credit, training, legal aid, or facilitating links to related institutions and actions in other parts of the world. Central to this vision has been a preoccupation with communications and the democratization of information flow; collaborative research, analysis, and dissemination; and action networking.

Integral to this conceptualization is a commitment to a strategy of *mutual support* in which the collaboration among NGOs has the articulated quality of nurturing and supporting each other's local actions as manifestations of mutually shared global goals. This concept of mutual support has been most clearly developed within the political analysis and empowerment strategies of the feminist movement, which has been the single most influential intellectual and ethical stream in planting the seeds of a transformation within the activist voluntary sector, largely because its strategies and analysis have been extremely effective in moving forward the activist agenda. [35]

Another critical component is an emphasis on *constructive advocacy* in the national and international policy arena. As Tim Brodhead puts it, this emphasis counters the negative local effects of "the preponderant control exercised by industrialized countries in the multilateral system and in the management of the global economy." Central to this formulation is the imperative that in their development education and policy advocacy, the NGOs "move beyond an awareness of the implications of interdependence in the spheres of trade, finance, and resources, to a broader concern with the imperatives of global survival: environmental protection, demilitarization, and greater justice and equity in the use of the world's resources, as the building blocks of a sustainable future for humanity." By broadening their approach in this way, NGOs will "find common cause not just North / South but also with popular movements and social forces within our own societies." [36]

This transformation is an absolutely critical goal, articulated by Brodhead, among others. [37] The possibility that such a transformation could occur forms a fundamental point of departure for discussion of the distinctions among Canadian NGOs, and the imperatives of the future development of the NGO sector in Canada. Brodhead declares:

The truth is that for many, perhaps most, NGOs the aid nest is comfortable, familiar and secure. We have not fundamentally challenged the premises of aid, as we have not fundamentally challenged each other. But in a changing environment … this comfortable consensus is likely to fragment…. The breakdown of the polite fiction that as NGOs we are really all in this together will force us to ask ourselves what business we are really in. [38]

MISSION, MANDATE, AND MYTH:
LIMITATIONS TO THE ROLE OF CANADIAN NGOS

The actions of the NGOs, and the capacity they have to change and adapt, emerge from their individual histories. The goals that inspired their formation also determined the structures that evolved to meet their goals. The NGO activities reveal a pattern that coincides with the theory of generations or stages. At the same time there is overlap within these stages and within the organizations themselves.

The first NGOs developed as Canadian branches of organizations whose purpose was the distribution of aid and emergency care to the stricken and destitute; later they often tried to replicate "modern" development through the delivery of personnel and material to build institutions and advanced technical and technological methodologies. By the beginning of the 1970s the failure of these strategies to even minimally combat the poverty of the large majority in the Third World was increasingly apparent. By the mid-1970s the concept of "appropriateness" of intervention was emerging: appropriate technology, appropriate health care, appropriate agriculture, culturally-appropriate social methodologies – what Ivan Illich calle the "tools of conviviality." Part of this trend was the conviction that self-help projects could more "appropriately" be identified, controlled, and carried out by local groups than by agency staff or volunteers from the donor countries. This may seem a self-evident conclusion now, but history is always blessed with more clarity than is experience.

Ultimately, new NGOs, and some of the older ones, developed an emphasis on promoting and supporting the NGO sector in the various regions of the world where they were active, accepting the role of providing funds and other resources for the local partner organization, which would now own and operate the local program and projects.

NGOs gradually gained more experience in the field (even the oldest of these organizations was very young and except for some fine pioneers the current workers are still, essentially, the first full generation of international workers in Canada).[39] As relationships developed, so did the understanding of the Canadian NGOs of the complex issues confronting their NGO partners. They began to appreciate the critical global factors that affected the lives of hundreds of millions of poor in the Third World and were completely out of the hands of the governments of the Third World, let alone the local partner organizations themselves.

Prompted by their Third World partners as well as the increasingly sophisticated analysis of the NGOs themselves, the new role emerged, of development education: public education on global development themes, to try to influence Canadian perceptions and policies. Some of the Canadian NGOs, in co-operation with a broader global network of NGOs, brought to Canada such international issues as the New International Economic Order (NIEO), the baby-food campaign, the preservation of genetic seed resources, and the campaign against proliferation of dangerous and expensive pharmaceutical products.

Some Canadian NGOs were developing increasingly longstanding and committed relationships with Third World NGOs, relationships characterized by mutual education as the Northern and Southern NGOs developed to some extent "together". The relationship between a small group of Canadian agencies and the Jamaican popular education group Sistren is an excellent example. Since 1980 Sistren, a collective of Jamaican working women, has had a significant influence on popular theatre and popular education in Canada, while its own activism against poverty and violence in Jamaica has received ongoing support from the Canadian NGOs.

It was not such a big step, then, for these Canadian NGOs to focus their analysis on the local as well as global issues facing the poor and the marginal in the places where they worked, and to bring back to Canada increasingly specific issues for their public education program. These NGOs began to focus education on themes such as apartheid in South Africa, human-rights abuses in Chile, the "dirty wars" in Central and South America, and the war-induced starvation in Eritrea and Tigray. They also looked at "structural" issues such as the increased landlessness caused by intense cash-cropping and the concentration of ownership of land and wealth throughout the Third World, or the international division of labour and the general political and economic powerlessness of the poor.

This structural analysis also led some of these NGOs, with the prompting of their Third World partners, to focus on similar issues endemic in Canadian society, particularly the problems of farmers and other primary producers and Native people. Unique Canadian initiatives began to transform the limits of development education: the People's Food Commission (1978-80) carried out public hearings across the country on Canada's food industry and its effects on farmers and the consumers; the Family Farm Consultation (1979) brought Canadian and Third World farmers together for two weeks to analyse ways to confront the crisis of the disappearing family farm; NGOs, particularly the churches, Oxfam, and CUSO, participated in the Berger Inquiry on the impact of the proposed Mackenzie Valley pipeline on the environment and local culture. [40]

The growing sophistication of these NGOs, and their increasing focus and analysis on specific issues and situations, also generated a capacity to formulate a critique of Canadian international development programs and foreign policy in general. Promoting political action and lobbying aimed at the Canadian government has therefore become part of the development education activity of some of the NGOs.

This broadening of analysis and purpose and the increase in Canadian activism have been limited to a relative few agencies and have ultimately become a point of strong disagreement, not only between the agencies and their primary funder, the Canadian government (through CIDA), but also within the mainstream of the NGOs themselves. Even the most politically active of NGOs are now less involved in activism specifically relating to Canadian social issues than they were in 1980. At the same time, their activism in foreign-policy issues has increased and become much more sophisticated and sustained.

CIDA has been very sensitive to the lobbying of the NGOs and the use of government funds to directly or indirectly criticize government policy. This has been especially true since the concentrated campaign against the reopening of bilateral aid to El Salvador in 1984-85. The relationship between the NGOs and CIDA has begun to reach a fundamental turning point, largely though not solely as a result of the role of the activist NGOs in making formal presentations to parliamentary committees, during which the NGOs effectively represented not only their own interests and development priorities but also alternative political perspectives on the history and the future of Canada's relations with the Third World.[41] This led to a gradual and informal process of renegotiating the "partnership" between CIDA and the NGOs, as CIDA began to implement a fundamental restructuring of its priorities and operations as a result of its own policy review and the recommendations that emerged from the committee hearings themselves.

This renegotiation will inevitably continue through the 1990s and set the stage for the critical role of NGOs to begin the next century. Given the close relationship of the NGOs with government programs, and the NGO dependence upon government funding, the autonomy and political and social relevance of the NGO sector will be largely determined by how successfully the NGOs are able to redefine their own special role in a changing Canadian context. It is in this light that the divergence among the NGOs becomes quite significant.

There has always been tension within and among the Canadian NGOs about their "political" role. This tension has most clearly played itself out in debates within the major umbrella organization, the Canadian Council for International Cooperation (CCIC), which includes about one-half of the 220-plus Canadian NGOs. These debates have often been about policy positions the council should take in the name of its members: for example, about the position taken against the resumption of bilateral aid to El Salvador. Just as often the debate has centred on ongoing internal issues such as the role of the CCIC in supporting regional structures for development education or in sustaining major co-operative programs among the NGOs themselves. These differences among the NGOs have never been clear-cut and ongoing interest in co-operation has, at least until recently, prevented a polarization of the divergent views about the role, and self-interest, of this sector.

At the same time that the NGO sector in Canada has matured (with the noted contribution from the Third World NGOs), the capacity and base of the Third World NGOs themselves have become increasingly sophisticated and politicized, largely due to their confrontations with the grim deterioration of the quality of life and an increasing polarization of political forces in their communities. One example of this tendency is the National Federation of Sugarworkers (NFSW), based on the island of Negros in the Philippines. The NFSW has fought against the extreme deprivation of its members caused by their forced dislocation from the land and traditional employment after the collapse of the sugar market, and the sugar plantations that employed them, in the early 1980s. Rather than accept dispersal, starvation, and more decades of serfdom at the hands of large landholders, the sugarworkers developed a strategy for land reform that would allow the displaced workers to occupy small family plots on sections of the former sugar plantations. The plan included technical and training supports to assist the former agricultural labourers to develop the skills to become viable and self-sufficient farmers. To implement this strategy the NFSW had to develop a range of capacities, including not only project design and implementation but also program administration, political organizing, legal advocacy, international outreach for solidarity, and security and protection in the face of police intimidation and death squads acting for the landholders.

To sustain their efforts, and similar efforts by politicized groups in the Philippines, the NFSW joined with over 30 other NGOs and "popular" organizations to form the National Council for Peoples' Development (NCPD). This coalition was set up not only to support local grassroots efforts but also to work at the national and international levels to promote the goals, and the safety, of member organizations and their communities. Similar comprehensive programs and coalitions have emerged throughout the Third World, in countries such as Malaysia, El Salvador, and Jamaica. Major regional grouping have also emerged in Southeast Asia, Southern Africa, the Caribbean, and Central and South America. These regional coalitions are acting both as networks to assist and sustain local work and as international advocates for a deeper political relationship and a new kind of solidarity and long-term commitment from the international NGOs.

The issues confronting these partner NGOs have become more and more complex: the deterioration of local economies; the destruction of the productive environment; the shrinking amount of land available to landless and homeless poor; lack of capital and markets to promote development and expansion of sustainable productive activity; entrenched hostility of local elites and international economic interests to community-based production and economic activity; intensified militarization of society and human-rights abuses; and curtailment of political and civil rights.

These local NGOs also must contend with working in countries staggering to maintain the semblance of national integrity and with governments alienated from the mass of the people and their day-to-day lives. These nations are struggling to manage debt loads that have taken on the quality of economic "dark holes", with interest rates performing the role of gravity sucking into the international centres of capital the meagre surplus of the productive and creative labour of the nation.

This is the historical point at which Canadian NGOs had arrived by the beginning of the 1990s. But they did not begin together and certainly did not arrive together, nor did they experience this history the same way. The point at which an NGO entered this stream of events, and the analysis and motive for action it had at that time, to a large extent determined its structure and capacity for action and change, although experience altered virtually all organizations to some extent. It is these differences that ultimately contributed to the increasingly clear divergences.

An NGO that for 30 years has seen its mission as the delivery of goods and services to the poor and destitute has an ethos, experience, and a rationalized "delivery" structure to sustain this capacity. It will have generated a core of workers and volunteers who have formed and been formed by this experience. This history and structure are its strength, but also its limitation. The increasing millions of destitute people around the world give impetus to continue in this charitable work despite the mounting evidence of its limitations.

There are limits as well in the histories of other NGOs: an NGO established for some 25 years with the primary purpose of recruiting and placing personnel within institutions and programs of Third World governments, local non-government institutions, or programs of the Canadian NGO itself; or an NGO of similar age that concentrates on the design and implementation, in co-operation with the Canadian and host government, of infrastructural projects such as well-drilling, or of formal and informal education; or an NGO with no particular mission, but which contracts its services to manage the projects or programs of the Canadian government or multilateral agencies in specific countries; or finally, a small NGO, just 10 years old, which has developed by raising funds for partner NGOs to implement small-sized or medium-sized local projects in fields such as agriculture or primary health care, and devotes some resources to education materials and activity within its donor base or community.

All of these examples are composite, but real. Each NGO has a history, an impetus, an experience, and a structure, including a funding base, that reinforce the basic activity in which it is engaged. This is a strength; it is also a limitation.

None of these NGOs are beyond change. A changing funding climate, for example, can change almost any institution, as can the trauma of the real experience of the work in the field. But we have seen the trend to a voluntary sector that is competitive for scarce resources, in which government plays a dominant role as funder and an increasingly pro-active role in determining program directions. In such a milieu, when the original mandates of the organizations involved have lost relevance and the organizations themselves have lost some of their original impetus and moral force, there develops an inertia. This is an inertia of experience, of analysis, and of structure, which is an impediment to identifying and creating new roles and new methodologies. This inertia remains a constant limitation on the capacity for renewal within the NGO sector.

LIMITS OF RELATIONSHIPS

A critical element in the evolution of the Canadian NGOs has been the nature and quality of the relationships they have formed over the years. It is often these relationships, and what the NGOs have learned through them, which have prompted the organizations to adapt to new situations and take on new roles.

Some Canadian agencies, as the primary deliverers of social welfare or infrastructural projects, create their own institution and structures, usually with the blessing if not the active collaboration of the host government. Clearly such organizations form a different quality of local relationships and have a quite different experience with the country than those organizations that constantly renegotiate a mutual relationship with local NGOs, community-based organizations or structures, and popular organizations, to support their work and goals.

Canadian NGOs see and understand the situation of communities and countries through the eyes and experience of those with whom they work. An NGO that relates primarily to government officials and departments will take on the analysis and point of view of official (and essentially *national*) positions and priorities. The focus will be on national development goals, base-level social services, and state stability and security. Not least it will be on the consolidation of the interests and political and economic power of those who form or support the governing class. [42] This experience and analysis will be very different from that of NGOs whose primary relationships are with popular organizations such as farmers' federations, workers' unions, or co-operatives. Those NGOs will experience the lives and efforts of the local groups, which will be mobilizing and organizing and, through their own vision and efforts, attempting to change the basic circumstances of their life and work, often in an atmosphere of neglect or harassment on the part of an ineffectual and even hostile government.

The intimacy and quality of the relationships of an NGO determine the intimacy and quality of insights; the variety of relationships determines the complexity and comprehensiveness of the insights; the mutuality and commitment implicit in the relationships, and the strategic properties of the relationships, determine the depth and dynamism of the analysis.

Clearly, the histories and experiences of the NGOs involve different types and ranges of relationships. The donor / recipient relationship, the service / client relationship, the bureaucratic relationship, the professional relationship, the political relationship: these are all different, with very different properties and very different levels of trust, commitment, and intimacy. The relationships nurture quite different views of reality, views of the needs of the people, and perceptions about the role of an international NGO.

These differences can be seen most clearly, perhaps, in examples like El Salvador or Guatemala, where the state's relationship with the civilian population is

185

both authoritarian and paternalistic. Canadian NGOs working in collaboration with the governments (military or civilian) there experience a reality radically different from that of NGOs working with base organizations. By "base organization" I mean those legitimate and popularly-based membership organizations (such as farmers' unions, self-help associations, or human-rights organizations) that are operating legally and openly in activity to promote the social and economic welfare of their members. In El Salvador and Guatemala, along with their poverty, these organizations have experienced constant repression, disappearances, and murder at the hands of the government and the military. Canadian NGOs that support base organizations constantly share the lived experience of ordinary people struggling for a decent life, as well as the fear and grief caused by the disappearance or death of friends and relatives. Because the Canadian NGOs must constantly negotiate with the local groups about local perceptions of needs and the nature of programs, they remain in constant contact with the reality of the countryside as experienced by the people whose lives will actually be affected by their support.

An NGO that chooses to work with the militant political organizations of opposition movements or liberation fronts will develop insights informed by the experience of people in those organizations. Such groups work to transform the very structures that the government and the prevailing dominant forces are pledged to defend. Depending on the specific context, this work often cannot be supported using funds raised from CIDA, because the work confronts national realities that Canada must respect diplomatically even while disapproving on moral or ideological grounds. Some NGOs choose to use their own privately raised funds to directly support communities-in-opposition in open conflict against the entrenched economic and political elites; these organizations even more clearly share an experience and analysis unique to their commitment and capacity to support these communities.

This complete range of activity and relationships exists within the Canadian NGO sector working in Central America. Similar examples exist where Canadian NGOs work around the world, for example, in Southeast Asia in countries such as Malaysia, Thailand, the Philippines, or Indonesia.

Aside from these distinctions, the interests and analysis of the NGOs working through church-based organizations vary from those that have relationships with secular NGOs. The role of church-based and religiously-affiliated agencies is complex. These agencies, extensions of formal institutions with defined religious belief systems and social goals, exist to extend those beliefs and goals internationally. The nature of this intervention is not necessarily insidious, no more so than the equally biased and self-interested secular intervention of government-to-government bilateral aid. But the role of the churches requires more critical scrutiny than the polite commentary usually offered. The need for scrutiny arises not only because of the churches' clear vested interests and the extent of their power in the secular as well as the spiritual realm, but also because they are among the wealthiest and most politically influential international institutions in the world.

A good example of this complexity is the role of U.S.-based Protestant fundamentalist agencies in Central America. The relationship of these agencies to the New Right in the United States, and even with the agencies of the U.S. government, is an important issue in the region. This is especially true in Guatemala where fundamentalist Christian groups have been instruments of government passification and anti-insurgency programs in areas of conflict, and intimate connections have existed with key actors in the Guatemalan military and government. Similarly, the role of Catholic agencies such as the U.S.-based Catholic Relief Services (CRS) and CARITAS is ambiguous and constrained by the opposition of the present Pope and the conservative Roman Catholic hierarchy to the role of the popular church and the radical manifestation of the theology of liberation, and the increasing politicization of church bodies and personnel. [43]

These distinctions about the bases for Canadian NGO relationships in the Third World are important, and in many countries they are critical. There is an increasingly fundamental alienation of the majority of the people, bitterly poor, from government and the tiny economic (and sometimes ethno-religious) elites for whose benefit all decisions of state are manipulated, and whose power and control over the state is defended by an entrenched military establishment. While in most countries this conflict takes place in the political arena, the reaction of governments to ever stronger popular opposition has been an increasing militarization. Today up to 200 wars rage at any one time, most in the Third World. Virtually all of these wars are not between nations, but between internal factions within nations, and most commonly between governments and their people, between political-economic elites and a politically and economically marginal majority, between the state military apparatus and the organized guerrilla forces of a suppressed popular opposition. Open socio-economic conflict has become the norm in the political evolution of the Third World. This reality demands that we radically reassess prevailing assumptions about global justice and international development.

Third World elites are wealthy beyond imagination. The countries of the Third World, rich in natural and human resources, are not inherently poor but, rather, systematically impoverished, including both the majority of their people and the social apparatus of state. This situation benefits the economic interests of those whose wealth and economic power are internationalized, in the form of capital and control of production. These interests include economic elites in the Third World who have gained their wealth (over generations going back to the late 18th and early 19th centuries) by appropriating national resources and the labour of the poor and integrating them within the interests of international capital. [44]

In the 1970s, most international development workers, influenced by the vestiges of anti-colonial rhetoric and the ravages of the international economy, saw simply the rich nations of the North pitted against the poor nations of the South. There were no agents of this unjust system, no clear actors, only nations, governments, and an international system that had to be changed. The ultimate expression of this paradigm was the 1980 report of the Brandt Commission, *North-South: A Program for Survival,* which played on the self-interest and fear for survival of the industrialized North to argue for a voluntary reform of the international economic order.[45] Yet this simplistic analysis does not begin to explain the world.

It is not merely the nations of the North that benefit from the present economic order. In both the North and the South, economic elites (who largely control governments and state apparatus) are in conflict with the majority in the South, an opposition made up of poor and marginalized people whose economic and political birthright has been expropriated. This opposition includes new nationalist movements representing cross-class alliances, which perceive that the interests of the majority can be served only within new formulations of national economic and cultural autonomy.

In this light, conventional assumptions about the good (or even lesser evil) of providing bilateral support to the nations of the South, that is, to national governments and national strategies, clearly demand re-examination. NGOs, which historically have worked to a large extent in the context of, if not always in direct collaboration with, government programs and national strategies, must participate in this re-examination. Such analysis can never be absolute and the choices of the NGOs can never be unambiguous, given the complex world in which we live and work. But this reality demands clear and strategic choices by the NGOs about their role and participation as the next stage of history unfolds.

The NGOs need to examine the quality and nature of the relationships they form within societies in conflict, and the limits implicit in the vested relationships that already exist.[46] Notions of pluralism and neutrality will be put to the test as the issues surrounding such choices become more clearly debated.

LIMITATIONS OF IMPACT

Much is made of the impact of development programs and projects: about such things as accountability, effectiveness, getting "value for the dollar". One reason is that NGOs are preoccupied with fundraising, meeting the expectations of funders, and questions of image and credibility. At the same time there is considerable uniformity, duplication, and even mediocrity in the sector. The North-South Institute study itself is a warning that the relevance, methods, and quality of the programs of NGOs are increasingly coming under question from the Canadian government, from the Third World NGOs themselves, and from the general Canadian public as more NGOs compete for a limited pool of charitable dollars.

In this context attention to impact at all stages of an NGO's work is both inevitable and essential. At the same time, impact and effect are always complex. Identifying and choosing – let alone measuring – effects involve value judgements and complex interests and perceptions. These values and interests are much more difficult to identify and analyse than the effects chosen as the goals of the work.

A program might have as its stated goal the development of productive economic projects so that poor families can become economically self-sufficient. One indicator of the success of the enterprise would be its permanence and the income generated for each family. But such a project can be an economic "failure", and still have a significant positive effect on those involved as long as the assistance provided sustains ongoing efforts to organize and resist disintegration of the community. In a situation of trauma and crisis can more be expected? In fact, in the real world, where poverty and economic dislocation are the norm, so-called productive projects rarely are "successful", because small local enterprise has virtually no chance of long-term success. If such success was possible for the ordinary landless poor, the poverty would not exist in the first place.

The real goal of such projects should be to organize people economically and politically so they can understand their situation and begin to work together to change it. In this situation the very fact of productive engagement, of creative activity, can sustain a family and give it the hope and courage to continue. What is the price of the dignity that comes from work, and from joining with others in the community to challenge the structures that cause poverty and condemn one's children to a bleak future? How do we measure impact when the process of long-term social change is slow and spans several lifetimes? In this context the notion of impact often seems merely bureaucratic.

The emphasis on impact also often ignores the lessons learned along the way by those who are trying to achieve the desired goals. The perceived "failure" to achieve economic viability in specific community projects may mask significant learning within the community about the local and national factors that prevent their economic self-sufficiency, and the possibility of new strategies to confront these factors, including sustained political action. Project impact analysis tends to occur outside an articulated historical perspective or analysis. Without a clear historical understanding of communities, and their evolving political, cultural, and economic context, the real impact and potential of program or project interventions are obscured.

These are limitations that all NGOs face. Yet it is essential that they work to understand the impact of what they do. And the most significant issue is not really whether NGOs "think small", or take the challenge of influencing broader phenomenon; or even whether they choose to put their resources into responding to "symptoms" of poverty, or take on frontline work to confront the "causes". There is a larger question about the historic impact of the international NGOs, which places these choices in a context that allows such choices to become more clear.

It is increasingly evident that the net effect on literally billions of humans, many now dead, of some 30 years of development assistance from North to South has been disastrous. Not merely negligible, but negative. The world is not a better place. There are more poor, in absolute and proportionate terms. Most critically, there are more landless and homeless people who have not gained in their struggle against poverty. They have lost their land and only means of self-subsistence and employment in the increasingly commodity-based and cash-oriented societies fostered by the industrialized countries.

In the past 30 years the Southern countries have been drawn further into an international economy that concentrates the ownership of land and commerce and drains the natural wealth and surplus, transferring from the Third World the capital required to build autonomous countries capable of meeting the needs of their peoples. This system has developed the industrialized nations, *not* the countries of the Third World. While some individuals in the South have become fabulously wealthy, the real flow of wealth has been North, not South.

The international development establishment has based its strategies on the same assumptions that move the international economic systems that have created this imbalance: that the development of Third World nations is predicated on "stable" societies and governments, a small, technically-competent and affluent middle class, a relatively cheap labour force, low social expenditures, and competitive integration in a world economy. This economy is characterized by specialized exports of intensive agricultural products and natural resources, and the importation of manufactured goods and commodities, including food, for local markets.

The national and international development institutions have been an integral, and explicit, part of this development strategy. These include, especially, multilateral institutions such as the World Bank and the International Monetary Fund, which are controlled by the governments of the largest Northern economies, and the major UN agencies such as the Food and Agriculture Organization (FAO) and the United Nations Development Programme (UNDP). Government agencies such as CIDA, which to a large extent share the same economic assumptions, have been integral in this system, through the socio-economic strategies they support. And to the extent that Canadian NGOs have worked as partners of the Canadian and Third World governments, they too are complicit in a system which is not working for the poor, and cannot work for the poor.

What then is the impact of the NGOs? And to whom are they accountable beyond the Canadian government, which provides the bulk of their funds? The NGOs have an obligation to develop a critical analysis both of the effects their interventions could have in the future, and of the limitations of their impact to date.

Above all the NGOs need to become more accountable to those in whose names they have justified their very existence as "humanitarian" organizations. To do this they will have to scrutinize their vision of the world and of themselves, their vision of the future, and the role they wish to play in that future. They will have to re-evaluate their values, their own self-interest, and their motivation and commitment to the work of promoting social change in solidarity with the poorest of the poor.

LIMITATIONS OF VISION

What we see as *necessary* is largely determined by our experience of what actually is. What we see as *possible* is very much determined by our understanding of what once was, and how it has been changed. The role we envisage for *ourselves* in promoting change to create that which is possible is determined largely by our experience of ourselves and others as active possibilities, as agents of change in the world we live in. The combination of these elements – the necessary, the possible, and ourselves – makes up the essence of vision.

This is true of individuals and it is true of the organizations that individuals create and sustain, such as the NGOs. This is how the NGOs were developed. Activists working together have created mechanisms to challenge conventional patterns of thinking and assumptions about what is tolerable or "natural" in the world. They have worked together to give substance to their vision of justice and a humane quality of life.

Many would agree with the authors of the NSI study that the very essence of the voluntary sector, and therefore of the NGOs, is to "continuously shape and reshape the vision of a more just social order." NGOs should strive to affirm and renew the vision that defines their mission, guides their action, and justifies their mandate. However, just as vision enables, and stimulates, it can also hinder and impede. There are not some who have vision, and others who do not. We all have a vision of ourselves and our society, of the world and the future. The places where we live and worship and study and work are also based in a vision. And so are the NGOs.

The vision of an NGO is affirmed and renewed by its history, experience, and relationships. It is a social vision, formed and reformed continuously in action and dialogue with partners in Canada and in the Third World. But vision is also limited in this way. The limits of experience of the NGO will finally limit the vision it forms and nurtures. Ultimately the vision of the entire sector, the so-called "NGO Community," is limited as NGOs interact and reinforce the increasingly conventional wisdom and assumptions that underlie their structures, methodologies, and preoccupations.

The prevailing vision within the NGO sector is largely implicit and unarticulated. It is revealed in practice rather than gleaned from the rhetoric of the NGOs themselves. On the surface there is some common vision, but the extent to which this is a "lowest common denominator" can be seen in the findings of the North-South Institute study. The researchers used responses from the 129 NGOs that actively participated in their study (about 60 per cent of the total number of 220 Canadian NGOs identified) to generate "articles of faith," 11 basic statements that define the NGOs according to the self-perception of the NGOs themselves.[47] The NSI grouped these statements into five principles: altruism, autonomy, participation, efficiency, and co-operation.

These qualities reveal an internal vision of the NGOs, about themselves as institutions, but say little about how they see the world or the future. Other more fundamental aspects of vision need scrutiny, the most significant of which is the view of the world that allows the NGOs to nurture a vision of themselves as neutral, humanitarian, and altruistic.

There is a longstanding yet implicit debate within the NGO sector about the extent to which the work of the NGOs, or even development assistance in general, is "political". A few NGOs, after intensive and difficult internal debate, have quite explicitly defined their work as political and risked criticism by trying to articulate some political vision. The largest majority shun political discussion and insist on an apolitical, humanitarian, and neutral status and role, not only in their overseas programs but also in their place within Canadian society as well. This position is taken not just for individual NGOs but as a statement about the very essence of the NGOs and of the voluntary sector itself.

This is clearly a question of vision. It is *the* critical question of vision, which joins definitions of history, and of the future – of what is necessary and possible – with definitions of the NGO role as agents of change. The political nature of NGOs, their neutrality in the contexts in which they work, locally and globally, is the fundamental issue as the NGOs search to redefine their role. Some would have the question only whispered in the inner halls of the NGO establishment, a private matter to be resolved privately within individual NGOs. Some see it as a pragmatic question, already answered in the choices of the NGOs and largely determined by the perceived need to be apolitical and non-controversial in order to receive funding from the government and the Canadian public.

But the real question about neutrality, as it always has been, is not whether it is desirable for NGOs to be neutral and apolitical, which is a question of values; but whether it is possible, which is a question of fact. In the world described in this book, neutrality is not possible. Any choice to act, to intervene, or any choice not to act, is a political choice, and the actions chosen are political actions. This is not a statement of opinion; it is a definition of reality. This is clearly seen in the examples used previously. If we act in El Salvador or Guatemala, in Southern Africa, or in the Philippines, we are clearly choosing sides; when we choose relationships, we are engaging politically with political actors, since in the politically charged milieu, all action is political, and all actors are carrying out political choices.

It is unfortunate that this debate does not unfold in a coherent fashion. The extent to which NGOs explicitly recognize, or deny, the political nature of their activity defines the limits of their vision of the world and their role as agents of change. It defines the limits of their capacity to intervene in the world in the decades ahead.

The prevailing position, which values neutrality as a positive quality and denies the political nature of the NGOs and their work, forms a severe constraint on the relevance and impact of the NGOs. Ultimately, because they will be unable to make critical and politically aware choices, this limited vision will relegate the NGOs, at best, to a benign but marginal role in the world. At worst some will play a malignant role as agents of the very global social and economic forces that have created the conditions of poverty, deprivation, political repression, militarism, and environmental degradation experienced by billions throughout the world.

Sithembiso Nyoni, of the Organization of Rural Associations for Progress (ORAP) in Zimbabwe, places this question in a critical light when she states that the role of international NGOs is to support the poor in their efforts to eliminate their condition of underdevelopment, "a condition," she reminds us, "which originates from outside the poor community." But she also reminds us, "We cannot reverse the process of underdevelopment by using the same tools, methods, structures, and institutions, which were used to dominate and exploit the poor."[48]

For Nyoni this point is absolutely critical, and for reasons that the NGOs must always keep foremost. The NGOs "have to be constantly aware that they are fighting against an internationally well-organized system of domination and exploitation. This system would rather see the poor removed from the face of the earth than see them change their situation or have them gain real power over their own fate." Nyoni calls for the "international NGOs which are committed to the liberation of the poor" (and this would include, at least ostensibly, the Canadian NGOs) "to examine very seriously their role in promoting inappropriate models of 'international developmentalism'." She believes that this self-examination can best be carried out in "honest dialogue with the indigenous NGOs and those they represent."[49]

Finally, as if to set the stage for such dialogue (her comments were made to international NGOs at a symposium in England in 1987), Nyoni asks, "As NGOs, are we not also guilty of perpetuating dual economic and social systems for the poor nations by advocating self-help for the poor in our development programs, while permitting the state to continue helping only the rich?"[50]

Nyoni is challenging the NGOs to take a hard look at their histories, their structures, their relationships, their real impact, and most fundamentally their vision of themselves as political actors and agents of change. And, implicitly, she is challenging the NGOs to examine their mission, their commitment, indeed their very will to act.

LIMITATIONS OF COMMITMENT

Commitment, by which I mean a *defined will and determination to act*, certainly exists in the NGOs. The extent of this commitment, and the ideas or objects to which it is attached, may not be defined in the abstract, but clearly it is manifest in the "practical" world of global problems and NGO programs and priorities – that is, in the actions of the NGOs. A definition of the commitment of the NGOs can be inferred from actions in the real world, by what they choose to do and choose not to do. The issue is not simply the type of work organizations choose to do, which "generation" of activity they emphasize. These can have their own validity, although we can value some activities more highly than others, and it is important to develop the analytical tools to make such judgements. But a larger issue is the one related to vision and neutrality.

An essential element of commitment is the *shedding of neutrality.* To what are we committed, and what is the quality of this commitment? Are NGOs committed to the ideal of equality, and to the creation of justice? Are they committed to working towards the eradication of the conditions of economic and social injustice, and the causes of poverty? To whom are the NGOs committed? Are they committed to the poor and to the oppressed? Does this commitment mean that the NGOs consider themselves to be accountable in their actions to the poor and the disenfranchised, and to the organizations in the Third World created to act in the name of the poor?

Many NGOs seem to operate on the assumption that "the poor will always be with us," a premise upon which much charity is based. Real charity, however, is not based on profane and fatalist considerations, but rather on a profound ecological insight: an injury to one of us is an injury to all; exploitation of the least of us, diminishes us all; freedom and peace for "the one" are only possible through freedom and peace for "the other".

Our first commitment is to ourselves. Our actions are always self-interested. Pure altruism is an illusion. We act to improve our condition, which includes our environment, and therefore to improve the condition of the world in which we live. If our vision has an ecological quality, we will act with others in our own self-interest, and we will do so in our own name, not in the name of others. This element of commitment leads to critical distinctions among organizations like the NGOs.

The NGOs act in their own interest and that of the people who provide the vision and impetus. Their first commitment is to themselves, to their own survival and physical and spiritual well-being. If an NGO has an analysis that sees the interests of all of us on the planet as integrally connected, and specifically sees the interests of Canadians and our society as interdependent with that of the people of the Third World, the quality of commitment will be clear, firm, and uncompromised by artificial distinctions between commitment to self and commitment to others. If an NGO has concluded out of its own sophisticated self-interest that the condition of the world is intolerable and dangerous (to itself as well as to the clearly exploited billions on the very edges of existence) and demands fundamental change, that conclusion will lead to a commitment towards change, and towards the struggles of oppressed people. This is a different commitment from that of an

NGO limited to a view that the suffering of the disadvantaged and unfortunate should be relieved through the generosity and support of those who have enough.

These distinctions exist among people, and they exist among the NGOs. They arise not merely from analysis of the wider world, but from our social and political relations here in Canada. Our visions for the world we live in, and our commitment to action in that world, emerge from our sense of who we are and what we want for ourselves and for our own society. Ultimately, the mature and dynamic NGO will be willing to focus on a vision of Canadian society and to articulate and incorporate a vision of justice in Canada and of a just Canada at work in the world. This will inevitably implicate the NGOs in choices about their role and commitment to action not only "out there", but also at home in the Canadian society of which they are an integral and quite significant part.

These choices will involve forming new relationships and new coalitions, finding "common cause not just North-South but also with popular movements and social forces within our own societies," with wider coalitions among social activists and organizations acting as agents of change in areas such as environment, peace, economic justice, and human rights within the Canadian and the international context. Such choices are political as well as ethical.

The North-South Institute report on the NGOs declares:

Their freedom to function implies that NGOs can do what governments cannot, ought not, or will not do – supporting human rights for example, or working in politically 'difficult' areas like Eritrea, or asking questions about the impact of large-scale projects on the environment, and so on. But the *will* to do so derives ... from a vision of development rooted in values and choices. It is this willingness to explore alternatives and to experiment with new initiatives which makes NGO autonomy valuable and worth protecting.[51]

Will Canadian NGOs be willing to broaden their commitment – their will and determination to act – in this way? Do they have the vision to assess and renew their mission? Do they have the capacity to redefine their mandate as popular organizations? Do they still have the resilience to tolerate and transform ambivalence and conflict? Do they have the capability to exploit these dynamic tensions – to transcend contradiction and ambiguity when it is possible, and to live with these inevitable qualities when it is not?

The short answer is, yes, some will do so, because "We simply have no choice."[52]

Some are struggling to do so even now, in response to the challenge of both their experience and their partners and colleagues. Others will not, because it is not within their vision, not within their capacity, or not perceived to be in their interest. Some NGOs are committed to discovering new roles and strategies, and new NGOs with different visions and commitments are being created. These NGOs are

challenging long-held assumptions about a "community" of purpose and commitment within the NGOs. Such a development may disturb some, but the short history of the NGOs, and varying reactions to the trends in the Canadian voluntary
sector towards parastatal status and institutionalization, make this divergence
healthy and inevitable.

The NGOs have passed at least two watersheds, once in the early 1960s when
they moved beyond relief and charity to social development, and then in the
mid-1970s when they matured in their partnerships with local counterparts and
began to bring home the lessons of the Third World. By the 1990s they had arrived
at a third watershed, a new stage in their evolution. With this stage will come the
possibility of not only a more dynamic role for Canadian NGOs in the Canadian
context but also a new quality of Canadian activism in the area of international
co-operation. Such a development would herald a welcome new era for the NGOs,
an era that is long overdue.

THE END OF CONSENSUS

Brent Herbert-Copley quotes Nelson Rosenbaum in pointing out that the U.S.
voluntary sector "celebrates" the "values of pluralism, diversity, and individual-
ism." Herbert-Copley believes this maxim applies to Canadian development
NGOs as well. He adds, "Within this community, 'strength in diversity' has always
been part of NGOs' claim to both effectiveness and legitimacy."[53] A similar observation, that the voluntary sector expresses "an ideal of pluralism," is made at the
beginning of the NSI study.[54]

In Canada, the quintessential pluralistic society, such claims not only are taken
for granted, but also take on a sacred value that is rarely challenged; they are inter-
nalized and reflected in the rhetoric and self-image of our institutions, including
those of the voluntary sector. But what of this pluralism? If it is merely a descriptive term, meaning that there are a lot of different kinds of people and organizations around, and that they are all more or less allowed to exist, the term is generally accurate, although somewhat redundant. But when we speak of an "ideal" of
pluralism, I question whether we have not moved more into the realm of self-serving myth than onto the high plateau of principle.

There is a plurality but general homogeneity among mainstream agencies in
the voluntary sector, to the extent that many have become relatively secure extensions of government programs. Marginal groups can emerge and compete within
the market of special interests, but it is really a milieu based on the survival of the
fittest and only those most able to generate a base and forum within the mainstream are able to compete and survive.

Yet new agencies emerge precisely because needs are not being met by the
mainstream public or voluntary sector, and because people continue to be cut off
from access in this "pluralistic" society. Those agencies created to "respond" to

these marginal groupings have the right to register as charities but have no guarantee of funds or public support; in fact they often receive hostile neglect from both the government and the social-service mainstream and find it very difficult to survive.

The history of the anti-violence organizations of the feminist movement is just one example. Even after years of lobbying and public education it is extremely difficult to secure adequate funding for programs for women who are victims of the violence of men: for rape-crisis centres, incest intervention programs, or shelters for battered families. This may not be surprising in a country that has so long resisted a commitment to justice and equity for women, but it shows the limits of "pluralism".

Similar limits exist within the field of international development. For example, there are formal constraints imposed by the Canadian government that inhibit government support to NGO activity in several countries, such as Vietnam. NGOs working in these countries are held in suspicion by the Canadian government, as are those who support the social programs of opposition groups working in conflict zones of countries in political transition, such as the Philippines, Eritrea and Tigray, or El Salvador (just as there were sanctions against direct Canadian support to the African National Congress [ANC] and South West African People's Organization [SWAPO] for almost 30 years prior to early 1990).

Even further marginalized are those Canadian organizations that agitate, mobilize, and engage in the politics of social change. Such organizations can exist unmolested only as long as neither their purpose nor their methods are perceived as radical, that is, as having the capacity to promote, let alone achieve, significant political or economic change.[55] These judgements are made in secret by cabinet ministers and by the Canadian Security and Information Service (CSIS) or the RCMP. They are sufficiently broad to justify, since the early 1970s, harassment of a variety of community organizations and NGOs; political parties such as the NDP and the Parti Québecois; churches; magazines such as *Canadian Dimension* and *This Magazine;* lesbian and gay men's organizations; feminist coalitions; and especially organizations in the peace movement. Activists in organizations of Sikh or Palestinian Canadians also know only too well the limits of Canadian pluralism. Yet when these cases become public, even on the floor of the House of Commons, there is rarely significant public outcry – the pluralist instinct of the Canadian people is not so deep as to be offended by attacks on those presented as a threat to "national security".

Pluralism often means a smug tolerance among the powerful – a kind of non-aggression pact which presumes that "I won't question or criticize what you are doing, if you don't question me," while otherwise it's every man (usually quite literally) for himself. Pluralism rarely means appreciation for other experiences or a commitment to dynamic interaction among viewpoints to challenge assumptions

197

and improve ways in which we intervene in the world. Rarely does it extend to a commitment to nurturing and defending the right of the most marginal in our society, or the world, to actually participate in this pluralistic theatre of ideas and activism.

The principle of pluralism as it is defended today is essentially a utilitarian construct. It promotes a norm of tolerance and mutual existence among a self-defined majority. Its purpose is to maintain the strength and survival of the defined group by tempering internal conflicts. It does not reflect a commitment to the participation of those who do not share membership in, and the values of, the majority group. Pluralism sustains and defends an implicit common denominator, such as economic interests, ideology, ethnicity, birthplace, or gender; it rarely promotes an openness to other experiences, backgrounds, or beliefs. The limits to pluralism are defined by the most powerful, and the commitment to pluralism rarely survives divergence among, or a challenge to, the self-interests of those who espouse it.

It is not surprising, therefore, that we are beginning to see a more clear divergence and distinction among the NGOs. Nor is it surprising that we are seeing many of the most prosperous NGOs using the ideal of pluralism, of tolerance – a kind of moral relativism and social agnosticism – to deflect criticism and debate, especially on the issue of the political nature of the NGOs. One of the most prevalent arguments against Canadian NGOs becoming more political is the notion that the politicization of NGOs threatens the very ideal of pluralism. This view arises from an assumed connection between pluralism and political neutrality, and the position that both are essential qualities of the NGOs and their programs. A common form of this argument, seen, for example, in debates about the role of the NGOs in Central America, is that the poor are powerless, non-political victims manipulated by radicals and agitators – a vast pluralistic majority caught between the forces of two inflexible extremes. This view sees political commitment, radicalism, and politics itself as a cause of the problems of the poor, rather than as the result of generations of systematic exploitation and repression of the poor.

The NGOs are marked by a self-imposed constraint of pluralism and neutrality, and a fear of being perceived as "political". Yet this is a sector whose primary partner is its own government, which provides over 50 per cent of the funds (and in the case of some of the largest and most prosperous, upwards of 85 to 90 per cent of the funds) and one of whose primary implementation partners on the ground is the local government itself. Clearly the NGOs are already fully politicized; it is merely that to this point in the history of Canadian NGOs, this politicization has been (with a few notable exceptions) more or less uniform, and entirely implicit.

In reality, it is not the politicization of the NGOs to which some object. It is the *explicit* politicization to which they object, and especially the critique of the limitations of the politics that characterize much of the activity of the NGOs. Yet even this is beginning to change. The 25th-anniversary annual general meeting of CUSO, in November 1985, heard a prediction that we were approaching "the end of consensus" among Canadian NGOs – "the breakdown of the polite fiction that as NGOs we are really all in this together."[56]

In fact, there probably has not been a real consensus since the early days of NGO activism – since the transition began from Stage I to Stage II and the expansion of the NGO sector started to develop. This is because the transition from Stage I to Stage II was in fact a *political* transition in itself. Clearly not all NGOs made this transition; and some of the newer NGOs that entered this spectrum in the second wave entered as stage II organizations and were motivated by a new politics that had already transcended the political paradigm of the established institutions, and of CIDA and the Canadian government itself.

The polite fiction has been maintained, not so much for idealistic reasons as for practical reasons, having to do with the mutual need for promotion of the NGO sector and fear of public response to overtly political goals and messages. But, as predicted, we are beginning to see the breakdown of this fiction, as many NGOs offer more public critique of the role of Canada internationally and argue for a closer link between global social issues and issues at home. Some organizations have called for attention by the Canadian government and NGOs to human-rights or environmental protection, for a more pro-active role in Southern Africa or Latin America, for tighter controls on the sale of Canadian-made materials for military purposes, or for structural economic reform. It is increasingly difficult for NGOs in general to avoid taking positions on these issues; and all positions are not the same.

The most significant impetus behind this change among the NGOs has been the urging from their partners for them to take on this more activist role. A critical element in the divergence among Canadian NGOs, therefore, has been the varying quality and nature of their Third World relationships and the form that the commitment to these relationships has taken.

We are now seeing Canadian NGOs working on different sides of issues and conflicts in the same countries. This is most clear in situations where some NGOs have chosen to work in collaboration with a national government while others are supporting popular organizations that are confronting the policies of the government and the authority of the state. The NGOs in question have inevitably come into conflict more and more directly as the political choices they have made are openly challenged.

El Salvador again provides a recent example of this. In 1984 the Canadian government decided to re-establish its bilateral aid program with the government of El Salvador through the creation of a device called the Canadian Development Fund. The fund is generated through sales of Canadian-donated fertilizer to middle-level agricultural producers in El Salvador. The profits from the sale of the fertilizer belong to the government of El Salvador, which is the indirect marketer of the fertilizer itself. In an agreement with Canada, these profits are placed in a special "counterpart" fund which is then used to support development projects submitted to a projects board. The agreement is explicit: all projects are subject to the approval of the government of El Salvador, and all project information must be available to the government.

The renewal of bilateral aid and the specific mechanism of the counterpart fund was opposed by most NGOs working in Central America, at the request of many of their partners in El Salvador. It was also opposed by the assembly of the CCIC. Yet when it was time to implement the project, a Canadian NGO, the Canadian Hunger Foundation (CHF), which had no experience or relationships in Central America, let alone in El Salvador itself, agreed to become manager of the counterpart fund. In effect, over the virtually unanimous opposition of colleagues within the NGOs, the Canadian Hunger Foundation contracted to manage a Canadian bilateral aid program with a government notorious for its abuse of its people, including years of mass killings and systematic violations of basic human rights. The response of the CHF to the opposition it faced from other NGOs was to cancel its membership in the CCIC.

Within two years the CHF entered a similar arrangement with the Canadian government to manage a bilateral program in the Philippines, called the Philippines Development Assistance Program (PDAP). Again the CHF acted against the opposition of several Canadian NGOs, especially within the church-based Canada-Asia Working Group (CAWG). On this occasion, however, the opposition among Canadian NGOs, while intense from some agencies and their Filipino partners, was considerably less broad-based, and the debate among the NGOs was tense and heated. Several major Canadian and Filipino NGOs opted into the mechanism, and both they and CIDA were outraged at the objections of the Canadian dissenters. The CCIC was able to take no formal position, playing instead a mediating role among its membership in the absence of a clear consensus.

The role of CIDA and Canadian NGOs in the Philippines remained a very intense issue. Perhaps one reason for the divergence of viewpoints and positions was that the experience of most Canadian NGOs in the Philippines was quite new at the time. Several agencies had only begun to develop programs in the Philippines when CIDA increased the bilateral funds available to NGOs willing to work in there in the wake of the uprising against Ferdinand Marcos and the election of Corazon Aquino. There was neither any particular sophistication in the experience of the NGOs in the Philippines nor a history of long and deep relationships upon which the Canadian agencies could rely for guidance in developing their own analysis.

At the same time, because of the conflict and open debate, and the clear manner in which issues were drawn, the CCIC was ultimately prompted to implement a program investigation and consultation involving both Canadian NGOs and local Filipino organizations. The investigation led to a new co-operative program mechanism, the Philippines-Canada Human Resource Development Program (PCHRD), controlled jointly by Canadian and Filipino NGOs and funded by CIDA. While the many issues around the role of NGOs in the Philippines were not resolved through this process, and the PDAP continued to operate as a separate program, there was still significant progress made, and the base was laid for an ongoing dialogue among Canadian NGOs and between Canadian NGOs and their Filipino counterparts, as well as with CIDA.

These examples illustrate how in the increasingly political and polarized contexts of many of the countries where the NGOs work, their choices bring them into political debate with CIDA, and with one another. There are growing differences among NGOs in the ways in which they analyse and respond to specific situations and conflicts and in the political risks they are willing to take in these kinds of situations.

A complex, but similar situation is the stark Ethiopian crisis, where some NGOs took positions in support of the struggles of the people of Eritrea and Tigray, while the Canadian government was trapped in its support for the government of Ethiopia, with whom it maintained diplomatic relations. Again some NGOs argued with the Canadian government that assistance provided to the people who had been ravaged by war and drought and forcefully relocated to the Ethiopian savannah was a humanitarian imperative; others concentrated their support on the people in Eritrea and Tigray, arguing that support to those relocated through the government of Ethiopia was in fact tacit political support to the government and its relocation policy.

The responses of different NGOs to the grim and complex situation of displaced people and returning refugees in Guatemala is another example. Thousand of peasants, most of them Indian survivors of the massacres committed by the Guatemalan military in the early 1980s, have been forcefully relocated by the military into controlled zones and communities, where the men are forced into compulsory paramilitary civil patrols, to "defend" their communities from subversive elements. Most of these communities are continually on the brink of starvation and illness because productive activity has been disrupted by the strife and dislocation. Many Canadian NGOs, with the concurrence of partners in Guatemala, refused to participate in programs in these areas, programs operated under military supervision and control; other NGOs, with support from the Canadian government, continued to provide such assistance, arguing that their humanitarian assistance is non-political. The Canadian government, meanwhile, pleaded no such innocence, justifying these programs with the very political rationale of the need to provide international support to the besieged Christian Democrat government itself.

As Guatemala staggered towards its national elections in the fall of 1990, besieged by the rising hundreds of political assassinations, the folly of this approach became apparent even to its authors in the U.S. state department, which issued a stunning condemnation of Guatemala's human rights record in February 1990, to coincide with the annual deliberations of the United Nations' Commission on Human Rights in Geneva. Canada finally began to alter its policy, never once acknowledging the now proved validity of the unwavering critique it had received for ten straight years from the small circle of NGOs that had consistently resisted Canada's policy regarding this bloodied country.

In all of these cases, the divergence of analysis is dramatic. When the opposition of some NGOs includes directly confronting bilateral policies of the Canadian government and CIDA, this forms another locus of dissension within the NGOs, since some NGOs are quite eager to absorb the millions of dollars made available to those willing to work with CIDA in these countries, while other NGOs oppose the allocation of any bilateral aid whatsoever.

There are rare examples of Canadian NGOs forging their way in critical areas, expressly independent of Canada's foreign policy and the mainstream of NGOs. An excellent example is the work, unique among Canadian NGOs, of the Mennonite Central Committee (MCC) in Vietnam, one of the countries blacklisted from support by Canada and other Western nations. Another example is the lead taken in the early 1980s by such organizations as the Canadian Catholic Organization for Development and Peace and Oxfam-Canada to work independently of CIDA in Guatemala during the worst of its repression, a period still referred to by Guatemalans as *la violencia*. The decision was enhanced by the unique independence of their funding bases. A final example is the lead some agencies took in the mid-1980s, co-ordinated with CCIC, to secure and direct increased CIDA funding in Africa both in the Horn of Africa where the Ethiopian conflict raged, and in the Frontline states of Southern Africa, especially Mozambique and Angola, both regions where CIDA had been reluctant to become heavily engaged due to the complex political ambiguities and the diplomatic hazards.

Another difference among NGOs is the priority that a few of them place on public education and solidarity, and probably most critically, the extent to which they are committed to challenging the policies and practices of the Canadian government, multilateral institutions, and major private-sector interests such as agribusiness, the pharmaceutical industry, the arms industry, or the banks, as they impinge on the prosperity, health, safety, and security of people throughout the Third World and in Canada.

An example is the participation of Canadian NGOs in international coalitions such as INFACT to combat the practices of Nestlés in marketing powdered milk formulas for babies. These products are not only extremely dangerous in those areas where the water to mix the formula is itself the leading cause of infant illness and death, but using them also discourages breastfeeding, the safe and single most important nutritional asset for newborns. Another example is the activity led by coalitions like the International Defense and Aid Fund for Southern Africa (IDAFSA) and the Taskforce on the Churches and Corporate Responsibility to pressure Canadian financial, religious, educational, and professional / labour institutions to withdraw their investments from South Africa as part of international pressure to bring an end to the apartheid regime in that country.

In addition to these long-term involvements, some NGOs have participated in lobbying the Canadian government. They have opposed plant breeders' rights legislation, which would consolidate the global monopoly over seed patents by multinational petrochemical and agribusiness conglomerates. They have lobbied against similar legislation to protect the multinational pharmaceutical giants from the competition of manufacturers of incredibly cheaper generic drugs. They have urged the Canadian government to adopt strong positions to revise the structural adjustment policies of the World Bank and the International Monetary Fund.

An entire movement for alternative national policies that would discourage militarism and promote peace has grown up in Canada, with participation from some NGOs. NGOs active in this area have taken a direct stance against government support and subsidy to Canada's arms industry in the sale of military equipment to Third World regimes, particularly Indonesia, and Canadian involvement in the military support provided to these regimes by the U.S. government.

This transition sharpens the political role of the NGOs but is only in its formative stage, not yet clearly articulated. Such a transition will imply a major departure from the mainstream of the NGO world, a divergence from clear paths and from old assumptions on which the NGO sector has been built – and to this point, has thrived. It will mean risk, and there is no assurance that any new way will bring more success. But there is no alternative. The experience of the NGOs in the world tells us, as do Third World partners, that "Quite simply, we have no choice."

TOWARDS THE FUTURE: AN OPEN CONSPIRACY?
Is there a vision that defines a consolidated role for NGOs in the next stage in the political and economic evolution of the planet? Certainly a vision has begun to form among some people working within the Canadian NGO sector.

A common element among those calling for a redefinition of NGO action is a notion of the voluntary organization as a kind of conspiracy on the margins of society and on the margins of the imagination. The word *conspiracy* comes from Latin words that mean to "breathe together" and combines the notion of mutuality of life and existence with the image of hope. Groups and coalitions emerge in the voluntary sector as an active mutual expression (breathing together) of vision and hope for different ways of doing things, and for different conditions of life for people. Most significant in this local conspiracy is always a more active vision of the quality of participation – economic, political, social, and cultural – by all members of society, and ultimately by all peoples and societies on Earth. Another essential aspect of this kind of conspiracy is that it is a public manifestation of this active vision.

This last aspect was critical in the original emergence of the voluntary sector: The activity of a group was an open declaration of a new quality of participation in society and a challenge to existing patterns of exclusion and exploitation. Significant elements in the voluntary sector were, in an uncoordinated fashion, an *open conspiracy* to bring about social change.

This element has diminished with the recent trends within the voluntary sector in Canada: the degenerative effects of special issue politics, disenfranchisement of the poor and most marginal, the pro-active incursion of government into the voluntary sector, and the institutionalization of interests and action. These trends have also influenced the development of the international NGOs, narrowing their community of interests and fragmenting their strategies and goals.

The vision emerging in the revitalization of the NGOs involves a revitalization of the very roots of NGO action: a new sense of the possibility of a profound, dynamic, and broad-based *open conspiracy* for change – at home in Canada and abroad in the wider world. [57]

A conspiracy, because this vision sees action based in broad coalitions in a movement of people and groups committed to the ethic of mutual support and co-operative action (an ethic largely created and shared in the long struggles of the feminist movement), breathing together, sharing life, action, and hope. A conspiracy, because this movement can be inspired by a coherent and articulated vision of participation and justice in the world, and by a clear critique of the economic and political structures that contribute to injustice, human misery, and planetary degradation – and that annually kill tens of millions, especially in the Third World. A conspiracy because the goal would be fundamental social change. [58]

An open conspiracy, because the movement foreseen will be based on shedding neutrality. The conspiracy will be a political conspiracy, which is critically aware not only of the political quality of these issues but also of the essentially political nature of our social existence and that of our organizations. The movement will be a public and open movement, clear in its witness to the human condition and in its declaration of alternatives. Central to this open and political quality will be the formulation and assertion of a new politics, an open politics committed to promoting active and full participation and transcending the utilitarian paradigm of special interests and the concentration of power.

Some NGOs could have a role as catalysts in such a movement, and in nurturing and sustaining it, and ultimately of being transformed by it to become themselves more clearly popular organizations in the movement for change. Many already have the analysis and the vision. These NGOs have relationships in the Third World with scores of groups with a similar vision and years of sophisticated experience in the development of broad-based popular movements. These partner groups could help us achieve similar levels of organization here in Canada.

Canadian NGOs also have developed co-operative international and multisectoral relationships involving activists in the social justice, economic development, environmental, peace, and human-rights fields, and involving NGOs and popular organizations from around the world: Europe, Asia, Africa, and the Americas. These relationships comprise a potential informal international structure for sharing of information, analysis, resources, and experience – and ultimately, for sharing international action. Finally, these NGOs have, among them, a large base among the Canadian public, which if consolidated through a co-operative commitment and strategy could be mobilized within a dynamic social activist movement in Canada.

Are the vision and hope expressed in this conclusion too optimistic? The forces of inertia in the NGOs are strong; and the interests and capacity of the powerful to prevent fundamental change are often irresistible. How can optimism be justified? My response is that I do not consider the conclusions laid out here as optimistic. I am not predicting outcomes, but presenting possibilities, which emerge directly from the history and evolution of the NGOs themselves.

The roots of the open conspiracy that I propose are the historical possibility present at this point. [59] These possibilities and options have been created in the experience and choices of the NGOs and in their direct interaction with history and with the partners with whom they have built relationships and commitments over years. History – and the partners of NGOs in the Third World who are intent on actively participating in history – will continue to make demands on Canadian NGOs. Some NGOs, indeed several, have the real possibility of making the transition to the role and quality of participation I have described. It is their historical possibility to do so. Will the NGOs seize this moment? Do they have the vision and the capacity? Do they have the will and determination to act? Do they, ultimately, see it in their self-interest?

We began this chapter with a question prodded by a church activist: "What do you want? ... a revolution?" We end with other questions. The answers will be created by individuals and groups in their personal visions and actions – and by history.

Notes

1. It is impossible here to provide an intensive description of the Canadian NGOs and their history. Fortunately, within the NGO sector there is an inclination towards self-examination, an inclination reinforced by the NGOs' need to define their relevance and impact to secure support from funders, both public and private. As a result there is a basis, and some data, on which we can begin to develop a critical framework of the role of the NGOs. The most recent manifestation of this introspection has been a process led by the

North–South Institute (NSI). The report of this process, in Tim Brodhead, Brent Herbert-Copley, and Anne-Marie Lambert, *Bridges of Hope? Canadian Voluntary Agencies and the Third World* (Ottawa: North–South Institute, 1988), delineates some of the crucial institutional issues facing Canadian NGOS. This material is concise and can be consulted by those interested in a broad understanding of the evolution of the NGOs, and especially the NGOs' perception of themselves and their roles and choices as they face an uncertain future.

2. Brodhead, Herbert-Copley, and Lambert, *Bridges of Hope?* pp.ix–x; "More Than Five Million Canadians Volunteer Services: StatsCan," *The Ottawa Citizen,* August 29, 1989, p.A5.

3. See David P. Ross and Peter J. Usher, *From the Roots Up: Economic Development as though Community Mattered* (Ottawa: Bookstrap and the Vanier Institute of the Family, 1986). For up-to-date statistics and analysis of the scope and impact of the voluntary sector in Canada, contact the national umbrella of voluntary agencies, National Voluntary Organizations (NVO), Ottawa, and the Canadian Council on Social Development (CCSD), Ottawa.

4. Brodhead, Herbert-Copley, and Lambert, *Bridges of Hope?* p.9.

5. For details of the individual NGOs, see Canadian Council for International Cooperation (CCIC), *I.D Profile: A Who's Who and What's What of International Development,* revised edition (Ottawa: CCIC, 1986), 316 pages.

6. There do not exist many coherent analyses of the alienation and loss of vision and mission of voluntary agencies due to the difficulties associated with government funding. Readers can refer to the excellent work of Roxana Ng, who develops such an analysis in the specific context of immigrant women in Canada; see, for example, *The Politics of Community Services: Immigrant Women, Class and State* (Toronto: Garamond Press, 1988); and "State Funding to a Community Employment Centre: Implications for Working with Immigrant Women," in *Community Organization and the Canadian State,* ed. Roxana Ng, Gillian Walker, and Jake Muller (Toronto: Garamond Press, 1990). Important groundbreaking work in this area was done a decade earlier by Linda Harasim, who was at that time based in the Participatory Research Group, Toronto; see, for example, "Issues in the Politics of Funding: Community Organizations and the State in Advanced Capitalist Society," a presentation to the International Forum of Participatory Research, in Lubljana, Yugoslavia, April 12–22, 1980 (unpublished).

7. Brodhead, Herbert-Copley, and Lambert, *Bridges of Hope?* p.x.

8. For a thorough and concise analysis of this 15-year period, see Jean Christie, "A Critical History of Development Education in Canada," *Canadian and International Education,* Vol.12, No.3 (University of Calgary, 1983). The treatment of the significance of development education in Brodhead, Herbert-Copley, and Lambert, *Bridges of Hope?* particularly in Chapter 5, is perhaps the strongest element of that report; for instance, the study reports, "Officials at CIDA argue that one of the most important impacts of Canadian

NGOs has been their effect upon Canadian government policy – for example, in terms of CIDA's funding of development work in areas previously considered 'off limits', such as Eritrea and Tigray, South Africa or parts of Central America" (p.113).

9. This growing awareness and concern was confirmed in various studies and polls. For example, "A Report on Canadians' Attitudes Toward Foreign Aid," CIDA / Adcom Research Ltd, Hull, 1980; "Financial Support for Non-Profit Organizations 1984: A Study of the Behaviour and Attitudes of Canadians, Narrative Report," Toronto, 1984; and "Canadians and Africa: What Was Said," a report of a nation-wide survey to the Canadian Emergency Co-ordinator (February, 1986).

10. Brodhead, Herbert-Copley, and Lambert, *Bridges of Hope?* p.20.

11. Ibid., p.22. The report clarifies in another place (p.10) that, "Despite the importance of religion and missionary work in the early days, most Canadian development NGOs – 72 percent – could be defined as secular, only 13 percent as 'religious but non-denominational', and 14 percent as 'denominational'."

12. Ibid., p.22.

13. Ibid., p.9.

14. The CIDA contribution includes relief and emergency assistance and programs (including implementation contracts) shared with CIDA's own bilateral division (ibid., p.24).

15. Ibid., p.23.

16. Ibid., p.24.

17. Ibid., p.26.

18. Ibid., p.58.

19. Ibid., pp.10-11,58,60.

20. In addition to CARE, UNICEF, WUSC, CUSO, and CECI, the 13 NGOs listed include CCODP, OCSD, Horizons of Friendship, as well as the Association of Canadian Community Colleges (ACCC); the Societe de cooperation pour le developpement international (SOCODEVI); Canadian Hunger Foundation (CHF); the African Medical Research Foundation (AMREF); and the Canadian Organization for Development Through Education (CODE, formerly OBC: the Overseas Book Centre). See CCIC, *The Political Scene: The Limits of Partnership*, Ottawa, May 1989, p.5.

21. Brodhead, Herbert-Copley, and Lambert, *Bridges of Hope?* pp.14-16.

22. A further 2.6 per cent of the NGO "development assistance projects" funded by the Special Programs Branch of CIDA apparently defied definition and are simply listed as "Unknown".

23. For the critiques, see "Please do not sponsor this child," *The New Internationalist,* May 1982; and "SIMPLY ... why you should not sponsor a child," *The New Internationalist,* April 1989.

24. Brodhead, Herbert-Copley, and Lambert, *Bridges of Hope?* p.132.

25. Ibid., p.17.

26. David C. Korten, "Third Generation NGO Strategies: A Key to People-Centred Development," *World Development* (Supplement: "Development Alternatives: The Challenge for the NGOs"), Vol.15 (Autumn 1987), pp.145-159.

27. Ibid., p.157, n.21.

28. Tim Brodhead, "NGOs: In One Year, Out the Other?" *World Development* (Supplement: "Development Alternatives: The Challenge for the NGOs"), Vol.15 (Autumn 1987), pp.1-6.

29. Charles Elliot, "Some Aspects of Relationships Between the North and South in the NGO Sector," *World Development* (Supplement: "Development Alternatives: The Challenge for the NGOs"), Vol.15 (Autumn 1987), pp.57-68. The first two sections of Elliot's paper are particularly challenging in their description of the limitations of the Northern NGOs. The later sections are less useful in that: 1) he accepts that there is a natural working dichotomy between the donor agency and the recipient local NGO, a norm that needs to be changed; and 2) he assumes that the local NGO is always of and with the intended "client" group, and that the client group forms a defined "community," assumptions which quite often prove to be false.

30. "Recognizing that any effort at rigid categorization of NGOs risks oversimplification, we may nevertheless describe mainstream northern NGOs as what Korten (1987) calls Second Generation organizations." From Brodhead, "NGOs: In One Year, Out the Other?" p.2.

31. Ibid., p.1.

32. The trend towards increased direct government involvement in the programs of local NGOs, known as "direct funding" (to distinguish it from indirect funding through international NGOs) was explored extensively by a Task Force of the CCIC; see "*Mind If I Cut In?": Report of the Task Force on CIDA-NGO Funding Relationships* (Ottawa: CCIC, 1988). Brodhead, Herbert-Copley, and Lambert, *Bridges of Hope?* also examines the "direct funding debate"; see pp.135-139.

33. See, for example, Brian K. Murphy, "Learning on our feet," *The New Internationalist*, May 1988, pp.12-13; and other articles in the same issue.

34. Brodhead, "NGOs: In One Year, Out the Other?" p.5.

35. The key role of feminism within NGOs is not surprising, because the voluntary sector has relied on unpaid and underpaid labour, providing women therefore with a little more parity and influence than in the mainstream (an analysis whose irony is not missed by women, especially when they note that men still predominate in the higher paid executive and public roles even within the voluntary sector). Added to this is the growing awareness that in virtually every situation of injustice and deprivation, women (and children) are the primary victims, and men are the primary agents; this very fact gives credibility and moral force to the healing and creative strategies developed by women.

36. Brodhead, "NGOs: In One Year, Out the Other?" p.4.

37. For example, see Christie, "A Critical History," in which her starting point is the assumption, "The purpose of development and of development education is fundamental structural change in society." Just as the authors cited here have adapted a stage or generational framework to categorize development activity in the field, Christie earlier used an evolutionary framework to categorize development education activity into four basic (and co-existing) types, the fourth of which is "solidarity work, which – conceptually at least – assumes that the forces which oppress Third world people operate also in Canada, and that it is in our own interests to oppose those forces – both at home and abroad." See also Brian K. Murphy, "Canadian NGOs and Political Activism," *CUSO Journal,* 1986, pp.2-3; Brian K. Murphy, "El Salvador: A Canadian Looks in the Mirror," *Canadian Dimension,* Vol.20, No.6 (November 1986), pp.28-32; and Brian K. Murphy, "The Pan-American Game: Canada and Central America," *Canadian Forum,* Vol.LXVII, No.776 / 777 (February / March 1988), pp.9-13.

38. Tim Brodhead, "NGOs: The Next 25 Years," in *CUSO Journal,* 1986, p.22.

39. The pioneers include Murray Thompson, adult educator and peace activist, who was Executive Director of CUSO and Director of Project Ploughshares before he became Director of the Peace Fund of the International Council for Adult Education (ICAE); Nancy Pocock, of the Canadian Friends Service Committee, with her life-time commitment to the human rights of refugees and the displaced; Lotta Hitschamanova, founder of the Unitarian Service Committee, one of the first NGOs; the late Roby Kidd, international educator and one of the founders of the International Council on Adult Education; and the late J. King Gordon, who was a founder of both CUSO and the Group of 78, among many accomplishments in seven decades of activism.

40. See Christie, "A Critical History."

41. See House of Commons, *Independence and Internationalism: Report of the Special Joint Committee of the Senate and the House of Commons on Canada's International Relations* (Ottawa: Queen's Printer, 1986); and *For Whose Benefit? Report of the Standing Committee on External Affairs and International Trade on Canada's Development Assistance Policies and Programs* (Ottawa: Queen's Printer, 1987).

42. This observation projects no value; the bias described will prevail regardless of the "politics" of the specific government in question: right or left, revolutionary junta or military dictatorship, hereditary rule or liberal democracy.

43. See Penny Lernoux, "The Pope and Medellin: Casting out the 'People's Church'," *The Nation,* August 27 / September 3, 1988; also Penny Lernoux, "The Papal Spiderweb," Parts I and II, *The Nation,* April 10 / April 17, 1989, based on her book *People of God* (New York: Viking, 1989).

44. For a fuller examination of this theme, specifically pertaining to Central America, see Murphy, "The Pan-American Game." An excellent and moving primer of this dynamic is

Eduardo Galeano, *Open Veins of Latin America: Five Centuries of the Pillage of a Continent*, trans. Cedric Belfrage (New York: Monthly Review Press, 1973).

45. Willy Brandt et al., *North-South: A Program for Survival: The Report of the Independent Commission on International Development Issues under the Chairmanship of Willy Brandt* (London: Pan Books, 1980).

46. This theme has begun to be explored by the Canadian agencies, animated by the CCIC, notably in its groundbreaking conference in spring 1988, "Conflict and Development in the Horn of Africa." Sandra Pentland, the organizer of the conference, and Gayle E. Smith, the author of its background paper, developed a "Concept Paper" (S. Pentland / G.E. Smith, September 1988, unpublished) on this theme for the CCIC and interested international agencies.

47. Brodhead, Herbert-Copley, and Lambert, *Bridges of Hope?* p.29. In virtually all areas the NSI study found the NGOs deficient in matching practice with rhetoric and self-defined articles of faith; in weighing these findings readers should note that the "articles of faith" were generated from a partial and self-selected sample of the NGOs, with 91 Canadian NGOs (about 40 per cent of the total) choosing not to respond. At the same time, while the conclusions of the study were based in part on field studies of a sample of 51 projects from the participating agencies, many of the general conclusions emerged from reflection on the activity of the entire sector, not only on those who actively participated in the study.

48. Sithembiso Nyoni, "Indigenous NGOs: Liberation, Self-reliance, and Development," *World Development*, Vol.15 (Autumn 1987), pp.55-56.

49. Ibid., p.56.

50. Ibid. This recalls the clever but insightful quip, sometimes credited to cartoonist Johnny Hart, that ODA is merely the transfer from the poor of rich nations to the rich of poor nations.

51. Brodhead, Herbert-Copley, and Lambert, *Bridges of Hope?* p.70.

52. Brodhead, "NGOs: The Next 25 Years," p.23.

53. Brent Herbert-Copley, "Canadian NGOs: Past Trends, Future Challenges," *World Development*, Vol.15 (Autumn 1987), p.21.

54. Brodhead, Herbert-Copley, and Lambert, *Bridges of Hope?* p.ix.

55. I am reminded of Rick Salutin, writing in *This Magazine* several years ago: "If you are doing anything worthwhile with your life you must assume you are being watched, or worse, by the RCMP. This could only be avoided by ceasing to do anything worthwhile with your life. This is too high a price to pay."

56. Brodhead, "NGOs: The Next 25 Years," p.23.

57. This concept of an "open conspiracy" first emerged almost a decade ago as result of work and discussions with several persons then working in community and adult education activity in Ottawa and Montreal; among others, Guy Côté, who introduced me to the

concept, Ruth Baldwin, Mike Kelly, Brian Rowe, Lance Evoy, and Jean Christie. For another exploration of the theme see Murphy, "El Salvador."

58. I have recently become aware of a quite different formulation of this concept as developed by H.G. Wells in a 1928 monograph, *The Open Conspiracy: Blue Prints for a World Revolution*. Wells' formulation presumes an infiltration of state institutions by an enlightened elite in order to influence these institutions from within to promote an "inescapable" program towards a world federation, a "World Federal State." My own use of the idea of an open conspiracy is radically different, in that it suggests a strategy to confront and transform, rather than infiltrate, the elitist structures, national and global, which lock the poor and oppressed in their condition. There is nothing in the analysis presented in this chapter that should be seen as derived from Wells' vision or from the World Federalist movement itself.

59. This sense of historical possibility or imminence is shared, at least by some, within the wider activist and internationalist community in Canada. See, for example, David Cayley's essay on the significance of the June 1988 Citizens' Summit Conference in Toronto, "View from the Summit (Has Everyone Suddenly Gone Sane?)," *The Journal of Wild Culture,* Vol.1, No.4 (Winter 1988 / 89), pp.9-14. From extensive interviews he conducted for a four-part documentary on the Citizens' Summit for the CBC radio program "Ideas," Cayley concludes, "It is clear that the goals of world peace and sustainable development can only be achieved by a mass movement. It is also clear that the pre-conditions for such a movement now exist.... The question then becomes: can such a movement actually sustain itself?" (pp.13-14).

SIX

The Environmental Challenge: Towards a Survival Economy

Richard Swift

IN THE THIRD WORLD the environment is more a matter of the stomach than of the head or heart. While thought and passion motivate ecological protest from the Danube to the St. Lawrence, the defence of local ecosystems in the rainforests and highlands of Africa and Latin America is a matter of immediate survival – especially for people living on the margins of the cash economy, who depend on access to natural resources rather than paid employment. And for millions of people the twin scourges of desertification and deforestation have made an already tenuous way of life next to impossible.

The importance of the environment as the basis of life itself has gradually made it onto the agenda of government and non-government organizations concerned with international development. The Canadian International Development Agency has adopted environmental criteria as a major focus of its development program, on paper at least. In December 1988 CIDA commissioned a comprehensive study, *CIDA and Sustainable Development,* which recommended a whole series of steps by which the agency could contribute to a more sound ecological approach to development programs.[1]

Sustainable development has quickly become the catch phrase of the day, adding itself on to the fine phrases and vague commitments of previous development initiatives of the 1970s and 1980s. The approaches of those initiatives – including the New International Economic Order and the Brandt Report – failed to arrest the deteriorating economic position of the international poor. Will it be any different with "sustainable development"?

The problem has always been akin to the dilemma of having your cake and eating it too. The health of the Third World's natural environments has traditionally taken a back seat to a preoccupation with rapid economic growth, and mere economic growth is taken as evidence that a country is "developing" – no matter how unevenly the benefits are spread. Pollution was simply the price of development.

Until quite recently, according to the prevailing logic, concern for the environment was a luxury that the Third World could not afford. Ecological health was something only the Northern middle class had time to worry about. This position was clearly stated by Indian prime minister Indira Gandhi (before the tragic chemical leak in Bhopal) when she proclaimed: "Environmental safeguards are irrelevant: poverty is our greatest environmental hazard."[2] Not surprisingly, Third World leaders point to the massive environmental problems of the industrialized countries, with their "wastefulness and rampant consumerism," and complain about "unwarranted interference in their countries' affairs by Western environmentalists."[3] At the October 1989 Commonwealth summit in Kuala Lumpur, Malaysian prime minister Mahathir Mohammed charged: "Unfortunately, the line taken by environmentalists is to lay the blame on poor countries and seek to force them to slow down their development in the interest of restoring the environment which the rich have polluted."[4]

As the report of the World Commission on Environment and Development pointed out, the same Western-backed development processes that have led to some gains – a falling infant mortality, increased life expectancy, increased literacy, increased global food production – have also led to disturbing environmental trends: productive dryland turned into worthless desert; forests destroyed; species disappearing; unsafe water; the spread of toxic substances from industry and agriculture into the human food chain and underground water tables; in general, new forms of pollution.[5]

The ecological costs of destructive development in the Third World can no longer be confined there. The depletion of the ozone layer (which protects the earth from cancerous ultra-violet rays) is only one of a series of environmental problems where effects and thus solutions lie outside any national boundaries.

The destruction of the Brazilian and other tropical rainforests is having a negative impact on global climatic conditions. These fragile and complex ecosystems with their layers of trees and climbing vines are not only home to an incredibly varied array of vegetation and wildlife but also a source of livelihood for thousands of people. They play a vital cooling role – acting as a kind of air conditioner for the world's climate. Tropical deforestation – bulldozing the rainforest to build dams and cattle ranches – is aggravating the global warming trend known as the "greenhouse effect," by releasing carbon stored in trees and by reducing the capacity of forests to convert carbon dioxide into oxygen. In June 1990 an international research group led by the Washington-based World Resources Institute reported that Third World countries were accounting for 45 per cent of greenhouse gas emissions.[6] This adds to the problem created by the industrialized world's cars

214

and factories, which spew forth waste in massive volumes, enough to heat up the global climate. Scientists are predicting widespread flooding of low lying areas and coastal cities all over the world by early in the next century if current climatic warming continues. [7]

Even in the unlikely event that conventional approaches to development succeed in providing a Northern middle-class lifestyle to a significant portion of the Third World, the effects on the environment would still be catastrophic. The vision of all Chinese citizens having their own ozone-depleting refrigerators is a Northern environmentalist's nightmare – but why shouldn't they have them, if we do? If the Third World rises to present North American per capita energy use, global energy use in the next century would multiply by 14 times. [8] But it seems far more likely that the next century will see the dismantling of untenable levels of Northern affluence.

Economic growth still holds pride of place within the ideology of national development held to by most Third World bureaucrats and politicians. It also retains its hold among the grey suits at the International Monetary Fund who more than ever lay down the ground rules. The idea of economic growth is at the root of the foreign-exchange machine that gears Third World state economies to meeting foreign-debt obligations and obtaining the hard currency needed to support a growing governmental system. Without this foreign exchange the comforts of life enjoyed by middle-class city dwellers and the expensive weapons systems demanded by the military would be difficult to obtain.

In fact the post-colonial state, especially in Africa, has far outgrown the ability of the population to either support or control it. Most often Third World states operate not in the interests of peasant majorities or low-paid industrial workers but of a narrow political clientele of landowners and bureaucrats. This is the political background that must be considered when analysing the argument that a concern for protecting the environment is going to get in the way of development. Such development must be evaluated by the degree to which it meets or undermines the basic needs of poor people.

It would be a mistake, however, to see the problem as one of lack of development. Growth rates in many Third World countries have been respectable: 2.8 per cent a year overall between 1965 and 1984. The problem is not so much a *lack* of development as it is the *kind:* a development that destroys both the economic and the ecological viability of the smallholder and landless peasants as well as of the urban poor crowding into the Third World's exploding cities.

It is simply not possible to push the idea of sustainable development while insisting also on debt repayment, favourable access to minerals and agricultural resources for transnational corporations, and cuts in the public sector and lower levels of social spending by Third World governments. Such an economic model is bound to focus not on environmental safeguards but on achieving a better trade and payments balance – the kind of policy package known as "structural adjust-ment". The notion that the same ideologies of industrial growth that created the environmental crisis can bring about "sustainable growth" is, in the end, not only puzzling but also dangerous.

BRAZIL: SHUTTING OUT THE POOR

There is probably no place on earth where the glare of publicity has illuminated the "environment vs. development" controversy as much as in Brazil. Rock stars and environmentalists from around the world have flocked to Brazil to lend their support to the international campaign to preserve the rainforests of the Amazon basin, which make up over half of Brazil's national territory. Brazilian political fig-ures such as ex-president José Sarney have been quick to denounce the hypocrisy of environmentalists from countries that long ago sacrificed environmental con-siderations for industry and affluence.

In Brazil the "development" of the Amazon rainforest has been mainly fueled by a speculative land boom underwritten by tax concessions, which has resulted in the establishment of some 350 large cattle ranches – many of them over a half-mil-lion acres in size. As biologist Susanna Hecht points out, this land grab accom-panied by massive burning of the forest is destroying more development than it is creating: "In the Amazon much more employment and small-scale industrial development are linked to extractive industries – timber, rubber, brazil nuts, palm hearts and the like – rather than agriculture."9

The reasons for rainforest destruction have far more to do with the pattern of development of Brazilian society, which has resulted in widespread landlessness and poverty in the south and northeast of the country – problems that are now being exported into the Amazon. Brazil has adopted a model of development or "modernization" primarily based on large-scale cash-crop farming and export-oriented industrialization. This model creates wealth for a minority, but for most it leads to the twin consequences of poverty and environmental decay.

Within this process, for example, the country has become highly dependent on motor transport, to the point that, by 1978, 96 per cent of its passengers and 70 per cent of its freight moved by road.10 Yet Brazil has no domestic sources of oil. To get around the problem of dependence on expensive imported oil (which contributes to the country's huge foreign debt) the government has introduced the production of ethyl alcohol (ethanol) derived largely from sugarcane, which it hopes will meet 75 per cent of all liquid combustible fuel needs by the end of the century. This form of energy farming is a windfall for the 250 families that control two-thirds of sugar production in the country.

As in the case of the Sahel in Africa (and many other parts of the Third World) large-scale commercial farming leads to the best land being taken away from small-scale peasant farmers who grow food crops for local consumption. Between

1974 and 1979, 362,000 acres of land went over to cane farming largely at the expense of the food crops, such as corn and rice, that the poor depend on.[11] According to one critic, "In a country where an advantaged 20 per cent of the population owns almost 90 per cent of the automobiles and a disadvantaged 50 per cent spends at least half their income on food, the policy decision … comes perilously close to choosing between allocating calories to cars or to people."[12]

The environmental consequences of the dependence on road transport are staggering. Although gas from alcohol is less polluting than petroleum-derived gasoline, its production leaves behind a toxic waste that has polluted many of the country's rivers. But the most significant environmental impacts are indirect. The gasohol program reinforces an already highly inequitable pattern of land distribution and has forced small Brazilian farmers off the fertile land in the south and into the fragile ecosystem of the Amazon where they practise slash and burn agriculture, converting forest to low-grade farmland. These small farmers must not only eke out a precarious existence on unsuitable land but also compete with large cattle-ranching companies that serve lucrative urban and foreign markets.

In the long run the soils in the Amazon region are not able to sustain either type of agriculture. It's a vicious circle: The thin tropical soils cannot long sustain livestock production, so more forest has to be bulldozed to meet export quotas. As a result, a precious resource – to both the world's climate and local livelihoods – is being wasted with no possibility of a stable land-use pattern emerging to take its place.

The Amazon is the most dramatic example of a trend that can be identified throughout the Third World. In East Asia, another forest "trouble spot," an estimated 5,000 hectares of tropical forests were being destroyed each day by 1990, in a cycle of abuse that begins with big logging companies clearing roads and misusing their concessions and in the process creating access for poor villagers who further clear the forests for farmland. In Thailand, government policy is blamed for the decimation of mainland Asia's largest intact rainforest – which contains about 80 per cent of the world's remaining teak stands.[13]

The more their traditional means of survival are undermined, the more people are forced to degrade the environmental resources they have at hand (land, soil, water, trees) just to get by. Environmental pressures shape social structures and vice versa. According to a study done by Robert Chambers for the Institute of Development Studies in England, "Both resource-poor lands and forests are exploited by urban, commercial and rich country interests (especially for ranching and logging) … often in non-sustainable ways. It is convenient to blame the poor for deforestation, degradation of fragile soils, overgrazing, erosion, and desertification. In fact, they are often victims in the scramble to exploit public and common resources in which the rich and powerful get in first."[14]

AGRICULTURE: PROFITS AND DESERTS

Despite the oft-heard argument that the environment must be sacrificed to feed hungry people and that the hidden hand of the market will result in a "trickle down" effect, most of the growth in Third World economies has been geared to the export of raw materials and agricultural produce and has contributed only incidentally to meeting the basic needs of the poor. As with the case of Brazil, most undirected modern development leads to the polarization of wealth within Third World societies as well as to intensified pressure on local ecosystems. The result is the worst of both worlds: no solution to poverty and continued devastation of the environment.

The combination of soil exhaustion and the monopolization of agricultural resources (credit, land, market access) by commercial farming has resulted in the near collapse of smallholder agriculture in much of the Third World. An example is the desertification that has caused widespread starvation in the Sahel countries of Africa. The semi-arid Sahel region stretches across Africa from Senegal in the west through Mauritania, Mali, Burkina Faso, Niger, Chad, Sudan, and Ethiopia to Somalia and Northeast Kenya in the east. This huge region has witnessed some of the worst suffering and hunger in the past two decades.

In the mid-1970s British journalist Martin Walker visited a village in drought-stricken Mauritania and reported: "Something seemed to be missing, and it suddenly occurred to me that there were no children following us. In most villages in Africa, a white man strolling around bears a long train of giggling, thumb-sucking children. But here not one child had the strength to play or to follow or even to wave away the flies that crawled on his sores." [15]

Television pictures of this kind of tragedy from Mali to Ethiopia have led to an avalanche of donations from shocked Northern viewers. Yet generosity has seldom been accompanied by an understanding of causes. Often, a failure of the rains in combination with the Third World farmer's lack of scientific know-how in maintaining soil fertility seems reason enough. The solution is seen as food aid followed by a modern approach to agriculture.

But in fact it is the emphasis on commercial agriculture – often for the export of luxury foods or cotton to the European market and particularly the spread of peanut farming in West Africa – that has undermined the traditional semi-nomadic agriculture of the region and pushed poor farmers and pastoralists onto marginal lands. This in turn has increased the pressure on the carrying capacity of these marginal lands. The result is overgrazing, deforestation, and the abandonment of traditional land-use patterns that had for centuries preserved a delicate balance of people and nature in an inhospitable semi-arid environment.

The system of migration that had allowed the region to support a relatively large population was discouraged by national governments that wanted to maintain control of nomadic peoples. A number of other factors came into play, including fast population growth, widespread overgrazing, soil erosion and desert encroachment, and "agricultural practices that emphasized short-term profit at the expense of long-term sustained yield." [16] The growth in commercial farming aiming its products at urban markets often meant that food was widely available in more prosperous parts of a country while starvation became common in the semi-arid zones.

The problem was not lack of food but people who had been slowly deprived of their ability to grow their own food – and yet had no money to participate in the modern market economy that was evolving and producing food on a commercial basis. The traditional local methods of dealing with failure in rain-fed agriculture – storage of surplus from good years, moving, the sale of animals, and dependence on the extended family – also suffered the restrictions and distortions of modernization.

The story is the same throughout much of the Third World. In the words of the Italian philosopher Sebastino Timpanero, "For too long the ruling classes have attributed to 'Nature' ... the inequalities for which the organization of society is responsible." Market-oriented modernization of agriculture has placed poorer farmers on the margins of the national economy as well as undermining local soils and vegetation. In Ethiopia much of the best land has gone over to state farms to grow the coffee and other export crops that will earn the foreign exchange necessary to fight a series of murderous civil wars. Just as in the Western Sahel, in Ethiopia the pressures of "commercial agriculture organised by the foreign companies" displaced the nomadic Afars from their traditional pasture land in the Awash Valley, leading to a "struggle for survival in the fragile uplands which degraded the ecosystem and led to the starvation of cattle and the nomads." [17]

Official Canadian aid dollars helped underwrite the Ethiopian government's controversial scheme to resettle 1.5 million highlanders in the sweltering southern lowlands – a program that ignored the underlying problems of commercial monopoly over fertile land and the ongoing military conflicts in the region. Also, as Canadian environmentalist Patricia Adams points out, "Resettlement is already having devastating environmental effects.... Most of Ethiopia's remaining forests are being cleared, robbing that country of scarce fuel and fodder and of a barrier to the encroaching desert." [18]

But perhaps the failures and controversies surrounding Ethiopian resettlement have taught the Canadians who fashion aid policy a valuable lesson. There are some positive signs. For example, the Canadian government threatened to cut off aid to Ethiopia's neighbour Sudan unless there were peace negotiations to end that country's civil war and efforts made to effectively tackle the environmental and hunger crisis that gripped the south of the country. This shows a willingness to recognize the connection between famine and militarism. A next step would be recognition of the way the commercial monopoly over the most valuable environmental resources increases the vulnerability of poor people.

In Mexico the government neglects the highland rain-fed agriculture on which most poor *campesinos* depend and instead supports large-scale, irrigated commercial farms, particularly in the northwest. The farms are geared to producing luxury crops for the U.S. market. The highly inequitable *latifundia* system of landholding throughout Latin America – where land ownership is concentrated in huge estates – has meant ever larger numbers of poor farmers clinging precariously to thin mountain soils while large tracts of fertile estates go unused. According to one estimate, some 2.5 per cent of landowners with holdings of more than 250 acres control nearly three-quarters of the earth's land resources. [19]

The ecological costs of such a landholding system are not hard to calculate. Poor farmers must use already marginal land beyond its capacity to yield returns and destroy local forest cover and irreplaceable watersheds for firewood. One result has been a fuelwood crisis in the Third World, which is a barometer of how a degraded environment taxes the energy of the poor, its primary victims. Fuelwood is so scarce in Gambia, for example, that gathering it takes 360 woman-days a year per family. The situation is similar throughout the Sahel. In Nepal and in parts of the Andean region of South America the amount of time and labour that has to be devoted to gathering fuelwood seriously disrupts household production.

The economic rationale of large-scale export-oriented agriculture is that it creates a prosperous commercial sector with spin-off effects for the rest of the economy. A main canon of this approach is the old workhouse ethic of making the poor more productive. But the approach ducks the issue of distribution of benefits that has always plagued undirected market solutions to economic misery. Most profits never leave the narrow circle of big farmers who dominate the commercial sector. Even these surpluses are squeezed by the prohibitive costs of chemical farming and an international price system rigged against Third World producers. In 1986 Tanzania managed to double its production of cotton, but after the cotton price dropped by 50 per cent in the same year the potential gains were wiped out. [20] In Guatamala, "Of the US$40,000,000 per year earned from cotton exports, about three-quarters left the country in the form of pesticides, spray planes, tractors, and so on, used as 'inputs' for growing cotton in a capital-intensive way." [21]

So the export-oriented model degrades the environment either directly through the unregulated use of agricultural chemicals and heavy machinery or indirectly by forcing poor farmers to over-exploit marginal land. It also fails to make these ecological sacrifices more palatable by delivering on its economic promises.

INDUSTRY AND THE TECHNO-DISASTER

Early on the morning of December 3, 1984, some 40 tons of lethal methyl isocyanate escaped from a storage tank in Union Carbide's pesticide manufacturing facility in the southern Indian industrial centre of Bhopal. In a matter of minutes the town was turned into a stifling gas chamber, and by the time the deadly clouds had cleared, 2,500 people had choked to death. Another 17,000 were permanently disabled. Some 200,000 people had been exposed to the poisonous gas.[22] There was an incalculable toll of birth defects, tuberculosis, and lowered resistance to diseases like chronic asthma.

The people of the shanytowns clustered around the now silent Union Carbide plant are still haunted by the events of that day. As the Indian journalist Vasanta Surya reported:

The children in the shanytowns of Bhopal have a new game. One plays the "mother," another the "father." Just as they have settled down for the night with their "children" around them, one shreiks, "Gas aagayi hai" (the gas has come). Then they all leap up, thrash around, choke, and fall "dead."[23]

Although Union Carbide blamed the accident on "sabotage," the U.S.-owned company agreed to pay $470 million to the Indian government to compensate the victims. It remained unclear how much of this rather modest sum (compared to the billions that were demanded) would filter down through a less than sympathetic Indian bureaucracy and into the hands of the families of those who died and those who were still suffering. Demonstrations by Bhopal victims and their supporters over bureaucratic foot-dragging were suppressed by the Indian police; and Union Carbide was able to manoeuvre to have the Bhopal case heard in an Indian court, rather than in a U.S. court where much higher damages would likely have been awarded.

After four years of extensive legal wrangling the half million plaintiffs of Bhopal ended up with less than one-sixth of the $3 billion originally demanded – about $2,000 a victim. The people of Bhopal were outraged at this paltry settlement and thousands of victims demonstrated their disgust on the streets of Bhopal and other Indian cities. As Osgoode Hall law professor Brenda Crossman points out: "The ruling sends a clear message to multinational corporations with investments in developing countries. Seeing Union Carbide escape the full costs of Bhopal is no incentive for them to invest in occupational health and safety precautions. They will feel free to have local populations run whatever risk is involved in their activities."[24]

Bhopal is just the tip of the iceberg. Transnational companies are involved in all manner of hazardous ventures in Third World countries. They are building nuclear power plants, constructing massive dam projects, undertaking large mining and mineral-processing ventures, and investing in manufacturing that uses dangerous chemicals and produces hazardous wastes. In most Third World countries health and safety regulations inside plants are either non-existent or weak. Environmental standards to govern industry are just starting to be taken seriously. Most Third World governments are so desperate to attract investment that companies are in a good position to reduce their costs by saving on expensive pollution controls and health and safety equipment for workers.

The situation recalls the days of the early industrial revolution in Europe and North America when the word of the captains of industry was law. Workers are often not trained to deal with dangerous jobs and surrounding communities are unaware of the risks involved. Yet it is left to workers or local communities to challenge cost-cutting on worker safety and environmental standards; and the very act of challenging corporate activity can be risky under political systems where dissent means "subversion" and inevitable involvement with the police.

One of the most dangerous industries, and one spreading rapidly across the globe, is the manufacturing of chemical poisons for use in agriculture. The record of the producers of agricultural chemicals is among the worst on worker safety, on the dumping of dangerous and polluting wastes, and on looking after the health interests of the communities that surround the sprawling chemical complexes. Low wages, growing markets, and lax environmental and safety regulations make for tempting investment opportunities for the corporate giants that dominate the world market in agricultural pesticides and herbicides.

The problem is that the real costs are borne by workers and farm hands who suffer occupational diseases and by the residents of the communities that surround the plants. Those costs include the deteriorating water and air quality throughout the Third World.

David Weir, in his 1987 study *The Bhopal Syndrome,* documents the dangers of pesticide production from "the Nile to Mexico" and identifies Brazil as a likely site for a future Bhopal – "with its sprawling industrial complexes and fast-growing population." Weir states, "Accidents are, after all, bound to happen. On February 25, 1984, for example, in Cubatao (known as 'pollution valley') near Sao Paulo, gasoline leaking from a pipeline exploded, setting off fires in a nearby shantytown. By the time the fires were put out, at least 500 people were dead."[25]

But industrial techo-disasters are not restricted either to Brazil or to the chemical pesticide industry. They run the gamut from nuclear plants situated on earthquake fault lines to the production and distribution of unsafe pharmaceuticals to unsuspecting Third World consumers. Industrialization on the cheap is leaving vast areas of the Third World with a dreary legacy of poisoned rivers, dead fish, fouled air, and sterile soil.

The full impact of the techno-disaster can only be understood by looking at the astounding rate of chemical poisonings in the Third World. Some two million people a year suffer from chemical poisoning, the majority as a result of the use of agricultural chemicals. Even more will suffer from the long-term carcinogenic effects of the agricultural chemicals. Already there are 40,000 fatalities a year – a kind of "Bhopal of the fields".

THE ENVIRONMENTAL CATECHISM

As the writer André Gide put it when he witnessed the effects of French colonial policy in Africa, "In the colonies it is always the most beautiful ideals that are covering the most shameful practices."[26]

Gide's words might well be applied to the concept of "sustainable development," which forms the centrepiece of the report *Our Common Future* by the World Commission on Environment and Development (known as the Brundtland Commission after its chairperson, the former Norwegian prime minister Gro Harlem Brundtland). The Brundtland report is an impressive piece of work: at once a documentation of how far down the road to planetary destruction the human species has come and a clarion call to action to turn back and find another road – a better way. The new development buzzword, sustainable development, now echoes from village development projects in remote parts of the Third World to the plush offices of the World Bank in Washington, D.C.

In Canada too sustainable development holds centre stage. The government founded an Institute for Sustainable Development located in Winnipeg. In early 1989 CIDA funded a series of roundtable discussions organized by the prestigious Institute for Research on Public Policy (IRPP) to explore ways in which Canadian aid can "more effectively support sustainable development in developing countries."

These roundtables brought officers from some of Canada's major banks and corporations with substantial Third World investment together with a range of non-government organizations and critics of past environmental practices of both the government and the private sector. The IRPP produced its report *CIDA and Sustainable Development* out of these consultations and made a series of recommendations designed to push CIDA in the direction of greater concern for the environment.

Not surprisingly, the discussion about environmental responsibility remained vague and agreement on specifics was elusive. Sustainable development is a bit like peace – everyone is for it as long as it fits their own particular definition. Both the strength and the weakness of the Brundtland Commission's notion of sustainable development are that it assumes a consensus based on the idea that conflicts of fundamental values remain outside the terrain of its investigation or at best can only be expressed in general philosophic terms. For example:

Yet in the end, sustainable development is not a fixed state of harmony, but rather a process of change in which the exploitation of resources, the direction of investments, the orientation of technological development, and institutional change are made consistent with future as well as present needs. We do not pretend that the process is easy or straightforward. Painful choices have to be made. Thus, in the final analysis, sustainable development must rest on political will.[27]

The report concludes, with a refreshing note of realism, "We are aware that such a reorientation on a continuing basis is simply beyond the reach of present decision-making structures and institutional arrangements, both national and international."[28]

If you strip away the diplomatic language, what is being said is simply, "We have a toxic waste crisis, degradation and depletion of resources, and a threat to the global climate – that the present arrangements of political power simply cannot or will not handle." The hidden sub-text is that those people who have the greatest power to change things are those with the greatest stake in the way things are. For those who regard the Third World as primarily a place to make money, sustainability must first of all mean their continued ability to do so. If this can be made compatible with a healthy environment then so much the better, but this compatibility will never be the primary starting point.

In doing its work the commission bent over backward not to offend any major economic powerholders. It simply assumed that a whole range of patterns of behaviour by major institutional actors that have consistently degraded the environment can be either benign or environmentally friendly. An expanded role for transnational corporations; chemical agriculture; nuclear power; the (equitable) exploitation of non-renewable resources; new technologies as saviours: These were all part of Brundtland's recipe for "sustainable development" and a new era of non-polluting economic growth. Instead, what seemed most likely to emerge from the Brundtland Commission was an ideology of environmental managerialism – a technocratic fix for a problem created by technocratic development.

The Brundtland approach emphasizes the weighing up of environmental costs as a part of proceeding with any development project. The emphasis on planning "tools" like cost / benefit analysis and environmental impact assessment runs very much in the direction of measurability and quantification. In his evaluation of this approach, Michael Redclift worries that it will have more to do with evaluating techniques of implementation than with scrutinizing the effects of overall policies. Redclift points out the way in which environmental managerialism hides its political biases:

The underlying assumption of environmental management is that long-term political interests in the 'environment' are convergent. Sustainable development – unlike almost any other sphere of human activity – can be achieved through seeking consensus rather than conflict.... In most LDCs promoting conservation objectives implies much more interference with poor rural people, whose environmental activities are designed to secure a livelihood rather than profit.... By locating the structural problems of underdevelopment in geographical space, usually in areas inhabited by the poor, environmental managerialism does not raise distributive issues in the development agenda, but serves to obscure them behind technocratic 'solutions'.[29]

In developing their notion of sustainable development the commission members correctly sought to break down the barriers between economics and environment. They offered some sensible ideas about making production environmentally sensitive – that is, recycling, use of alternative energy sources, conserving and enhancing the resource base, and making food security a priority.

But in breaking down the distinction between economics and environment the commission also opened the door for vastly differing interpretations of sustainable development. Each page of *Our Common Future* cries out for a radical reorientation of the very meaning of economic development. Yet those who manage the Third World debt, who control most of the land, or who have privileged access to mineral and timber resources can provide a thousand reasons why such a reorientation is both impractical and unsustainable. At the end of the day there is no getting around the political struggle between those who support the poor of the Third World and their right to a secure and sustainable livelihood and those who will continue to promote the hard-ball economics of megaprojects and profit margins.

Perhaps the impressive achievements of the Brundtland Commission can strengthen the hands of the poor. The danger, however, is that a vague notion of sustainable development will simply become a new dressing in which to smother the same old ideas about a development that neither protects the environment nor meets people's basic needs.

The World Bank's conversion to the environmental faith is a case in point. According to World Bank president Barber Conable, "If the World Bank had been part of the problem in the past, it can and will be a strong force in finding solutions in the future."[30] The World Bank – one of the major sources of development capital for Third World economies – has come under heavy criticism for its environmental negligence. It has bankrolled a number of questionable projects in Brazil, such as the giant Polonoreste road-building and agricultural colonization scheme that is destroying an area of unique rainforest the size of Britain.

The Bank has taken some positive steps, such as increasing the number of staff doing environmental assessment and making loans to support national environmental institutions in Brazil. Still, the environment is a long way from the top of its agenda when it decides which projects to fund. Careers in the Bank are not made by slowing down the momentum of projects and loans by being picky about the environment.

Factors such as increasing exports, the effect on balance of payments, and enhancing the ability of a Third World government to service its debt obligations weigh much more heavily in project and loan selection. Factors such as the future of the tribal peoples so often victimized by bank projects or maintaining species diversity in fragile ecosystems may be all very nice; but, as Canadian David Hopper, the Bank's vice-president in charge of policy and planning, points out: "Let's face it: You can't have development without people getting hurt."[31] Hopper, who is responsible for environmental policy at the Bank, contends that while the World Bank may become more eclectic in the type of project it funds, it is "not going to go small scale."[32]

The best we can hope for, perhaps, is that the World Bank will be dragged reluctantly into a recognition of the harmful effects of its activities on the environment and of the need for some compensation for the thousands of "development refugees" created by its large-scale infrastructural projects (dams, major roads, extractive industry development) throughout the Third World. After years of pressure the World Bank did after all agree to take responsibility for the resettlement of some 23,000 such refugees displaced by its thermal power projects in India.

The addiction of the World Bank and the other multilateral development banks to a series of megaprojects is built into both the ideology and the bureaucratic momentum of these institutions. Any major shift from gigantic water diversion and hydroelectric projects, big ranching developments, mineral development, deforestation for timber exports, and massive agricultural colonization schemes like those in Ethiopia and Indonesia would challenge the very rationale for these institutions.

Their top-down procedures are such that funds must be dispersed in multi-million-dollar lump sums to prestigious and high-profile projects. To disperse and administer funds to thousands of small-scale grassroots projects – a prerequisite for safeguarding environmental resources while meeting people's basic needs – would seem a bureaucratic nightmare to development bankers.

Another institutional obstacle is the Bank's widely held assumption that private-sector partners and their drive for profits are the real motor of economic development. Even its programs that exclude the private sector, such as support given to socialist governments (China and Ethiopia) tend to be for megaprojects that aim primarily at improving the country's competitive position in the world economy. For the World Bank, success is measured by a project's impact on a range of criteria set at the level of the national government: for instance, effects on gross domestic product, balance of payments, development of an industrial base, or changes in debt position.

A truly sustainable development would call for a completely new set of criteria measured at the local level and starting with enhancement of regional ecosystems and a project's ability to provide a stable livelihood for people in a particular area. Such an approach would at least provide the beginnings of a definition of an alternative model of ecodevelopment. The current approach of even the most enlightened technocrats is to start from a project based on national criteria and when they finally get around to questions related to the environment the situation becomes simply a matter of how to ameliorate the most negative effects of the project.

An ecological development would base project design on the possibilities embedded in regional ecosystems and work out ways in which environmental resources could provide for local human needs in a manner sustainable in the long run. It would be out of the question for projects designed in this way to lead to the destruction of whole ecosystems or result in the displacement of local populations – the "development refugees" produced by the current megaproject approach.

THE CANADIAN RECORD

In the 1990s, can we expect more coherent leadership from Canada's international aid program on the questions of environment and development? There is at least some potential here, because Canadian aid is not tied to the same set of influences as that of the multinational development banks. In addition, a program of direct aid means less emphasis on quick returns on loans tied to the earning of foreign exchange. Certainly the Canadian government has made the rhetorical commitment to sustainable development.

But Canadian foreign-aid policy is shaped by a mixed bag of motivations. One of the Canadian goals is to secure a measure of political influence and achieve its own foreign-policy objectives in the Third World. More importantly, the government insists that 80 per cent of CIDA bilateral aid dollars be tied to the purchase of Canadian goods and services. This not only costs Third World recipients some 20 to 25 per cent more than if they were to purchase goods on the open market but also ties them to Canadian technologies and ways of doing things that may or may not be appropriate and environmentally sound. [33] Despite recommendations from the Parliamentary Task Force on North-South Relations and other critics to untie Canadian aid, the government has remained committed to the commercial path, which makes its aid program saleable politically to the Canadian business constituency.

Still, CIDA has at least flirted with trying to gear its development assistance towards ecodevelopment. Canadian policy makers have been influenced in this direction by a number of international initiatives that preceded the Brundtland Commission report, including the UN conference on the Human Environment in Stockholm in 1972 and a World Conservation Strategy formulated in 1980 to try and get commitments from national governments around the world in favour of sound environmental policies. CIDA responded first by getting together with the federal Department of the Environment in 1975 to try to hammer out a coherent environment-development strategy. The agency"s "country program" in El Salvador was to be a test case for this strategy, but the project never got off the drawing board and past the "long theoretical paper" stage. It seems to have become lost in a bureaucratic maze, besides floundering at least partly under the impact of El Salvador's civil war.

In 1980 the International Institute for Environment and Development in

Britain evaluated CIDA's record on environment and development. The study found that CIDA's environmental efforts were "sporadic and piecemeal":

The report stated that a lack of political will on the agency's part was indicated. The study team concluded that CIDA lacked the commitment to incorporate environmental concerns into its projects and programs, that it did not have a systematic process to assess the impacts of its activities, and that it was lacking in environmental expertise, training and issue awareness. [34]

Since then CIDA has attempted to integrate environmental evaluation as part of its regular project criteria. It has tried to follow the standards set forth as part of the federal Environmental and Assessment Review Process (EARP) – although it has resisted the kind of public review of projects called for under EARP guidelines. There is no doubt that many of the aspects of development that are destructive to the environment are beyond the power of CIDA to change: the global economic situation and the resultant pressures on recipient governments to make anti-ecological decisions so they can pay the interest on Third World debt, for instance. Still, critics of Canadian aid feel that the agency could have done better in devising a coherent strategy for environment and development. According to a Pollution Probe study, "The lack of any overiding policy commitment to ecodevelopment, the lack of any provision for public review or consultation and other shortcomings are disappointing and may have been modified if CIDA had consulted the public in formulating the strategy." The study argued that CIDA's approach to environmental issues was aimed at being "flexible" and "practical" and in accordance with the realities of existing priorities rather than providing a more integrative, "holistic approach." [35] Environmental considerations were left competing with a range of other pressures for how to make the best use of Canadian aid dollars.

Despite a flurry of policy initiatives following the Brundtland report, major foreign-aid decisions continued to be shaped both by financial commitments to business and ideological commitments to technocratic modernism and structural adjustment – commitments that far outweighed those to the environment. CIDA's partnership with the export-hungry Atomic Energy of Canada Limited in the financing (through a $4.7 million CIDA grant) and installation of a commercial food irradiator in Thailand is a good example. There was no public review of the project and CIDA's internal environmental screening was little more than a casual checklist that found no environmental impacts whatsoever. Yet other researchers have pointed out potential dangers from low-level radiation at all stages of the project.

A letter sent to Thai prime minister Chatichai Choonhavan from a coalition of Canadian environmental organizations argued that irradiated food had not been legalized in Canada and that a Canadian undertaking to import irradiated Thai mangoes and shrimp was highly questionable. A 1987 parliamentary committee concluded that sufficient proof of the safety of irradiated food did not exist and recommended that all moves to ease regulation of irradiated food across the country be stopped. The coalition pointed out the dangers associated with the exposure to the Cobalt-90 used in food irradiation both for Thai workers at the facility site and for those involved with the disposal of radioactive wastes from the irradiator. Citing tests on children carried out by the National Institute of Nutrition in India, the coalition documented the negative evidence of the health impact (a chromosomal abnormality called polyploidy) on children of eating irradiated food. It also stressed the numerous negative impacts shown up in tests on animals. [36]

Whatever the final judgement on the safety of irradiated food, the Thai case shows the dangers to environmental well-being of mixing commercial and developmental criteria when deciding on foreign-aid projects. The project came about partly because the AECL was looking for new products and new customers after the market in its CANDU nuclear reactors crashed following the nuclear catastrophe at Chernobyl. But CIDA involvement in this quest seriously jeopardized Canada's commitment to sustainable development.

Canadian aid policy has also not been immune to the lures of megaproject development. Dams have traditionally been a CIDA specialty. In Haiti the agency helped underwrite a dam project in the Artibonite River Valley that would have flooded nearly 10,000 acres of some of that country's most fertile agricultural land. Fortunately, local resistance and a French counterstudy showing that the agricultural output of the valley was 40 per cent higher than the projected benefits from the two dams delayed the project. The report found that flooding would destroy lands that could feed 60,000 Haitians annually. Like many such projects, basic food crops of corn, congo peas, and sweet potatoes as well as the preservation of the valley ecosystem were all to be sacrificed for national development goals. [37]

The grand "engineering of nature" associated with dam development also provides lucrative contracts for those parts of the private and public sectors that specialize in this area. A classic case is CIDA involvement with Chinese plans to dam the Yangtze River. If it goes ahead the proposed Three Gorges dam will be the world's largest hydroelectric project. CIDA funded a $17.5-million feasibility study of the project, to be carried out by a consortium of Canadian companies. Canadian officials hoped that their involvement would give "Canadian companies an edge in the bidding for the financing, equipment and engineering that would follow a decision to build." [38]

Several of Canada's leading engineering firms – including Lavalin Inc., SNC Group, and ACRES International – became involved in carrying out the feasibility study and would benefit from the billion-dollar construction boom if the project went ahead. According to Vaclav Smil, a University of Manitoba geographer who has written several books on energy use and development in China, "The Canadian participation is about money – it's just greed. There's nothing altruistic. It's revolting. These private companies are using public money to get the big foot into the door."[39]

In China the damming of the magnificent Three Gorges stretch of the Yangtze has been the subject of controversy and debate for decades. On the one hand there is the majestic beauty of a stretch of river that has inspired poets and writers for centuries. On the other there is the uncertainty about how the high costs, capital imports, and loan commitments will distort the Chinese economy, about the ten cities and one hundred thousand acres of intensively cultivated farmland that will be submerged, and the three hundred thousand to one million people that will have to be relocated. There is also concern about the project's unknown environmental impacts on rates of erosion, fish stocks, local soil fertility, and the silt load of the river.

According to Patricia Adams of Probe International, the consequences of the Chinese megaproject could be catastrophic. In an interview Adams stated that the financing would have to come from the World Bank. But "Every penny is going to have to be paid back. If it turns out that this dam is a boondoogle – if it silts up, if it doesn't function, if the turbines get damaged by the silt – it's not going to be an economically viable project."[40] To make matters worse, the dam is located in an earthquake-prone zone, which raises fears of a catastrophe of unimaginable proportions should the huge walls be ruptured.

Proponents of the project discuss its potential to control periodic flooding that has taken thousands of lives this century, as well as the massive generation of reliable power to fuel the ambitious Chinese program of industrial development. The abandonment of Maoist economic prescriptions that emphasized decentralization and privileged rural development in favour of top-down industrialization and market reforms has created a desperate need for new energy sources. Relatively clean hydro power seems attractive when compared with a dramatic increase in burning fossil fuels.

Whatever the final decision on Three Gorges, the massive dam is a classic megaproject case. As Brock University biologist Michael Dickman points out, "A lot of the energy produced is not going to the poorer people or farmers, but is going to the large cities like Shanghai to be used for air conditioners and refrigerators and freezers and stoves." According to Dickman, "The people displaced are the ones who will bear enormous social costs and they will get very little benefit."[41] What does CIDA's involvement with Three Gorges have to say about the agency's commitment to the much-touted principles of sustainable development laid out in the Brundtland Commission report? It would seem that sustainability could be better guaranteed by support for much smaller-scale hydro developments – the Chinese domestic hydro industry has built 90,000 such installations – in combination with a program for conserving energy and helping to improve China's poor record of energy efficiency. Again, commercial motives appear to stand in the way of CIDA fully embracing a philosophy of sustainable development.

Not suprisingly, the feasibility study results concluded that construction was indeed practical and recommended that work on the site begin as early as 1992. Fortunately, massive public pressure in China resulted in cooler heads prevailing and the project was shelved for at least five years so more studies could be conducted. Still, with the tense political situation in China environmental protest is likely to become increasingly dangerous for those who challenge top-down bureaucratic schemes like Three Gorges. In the wake of the 1989 massacre of pro-democracy demonstrators in Tiananmen Square, one Lavalin executive tried to reassure Canadians that the events in China were the kind of repression that had happened throughout the centuries and were really not something to get too upset about: a case of business making strange bedfellows.

CANADIAN COMPANIES AND RESOURCE DEVELOPMENT

Much of Canadian bilateral aid to the Third World is targeted at resource sectors in which Canada is strongest at home. Canadian companies seem to be in a good position to export our "know-how" (and the problems that go with it) to Third World countries. But the domestic environmental record of the timber, pulp and paper, hydro, and mining industries does not provide much assurance about the stewardship of Third World environments.

CIDA's environmental record on forestry projects, for instance, has been questionable. One 1981 study said that in Indonesia, "CIDA has since 1974 been carrying out a massive forest resource inventory, including aerial photography of more than one million square kilometres of the country and costing $20 million. Unless there are parallel efforts to forest management, this work provides a type of information which may only accelerate the pace of forest destruction."[42] CIDA's involvement with an "industrial forestry program" in Peru raises similar questions. Much of that project was carried out in sensitive rainforest areas of the Pichis / Palcazu / Pachitea region of the country, an area that contains soils of low fertility. According to reports from the Food and Agricultural Organization and the World Bank, the soils are "highly acid with high aluminium saturation." They are "deficient in nutrients, and consequently limit the forest's natural regeneration capacity."[43] One of the reasons that CIDA gave for supporting this program is the "positive effect on the development of Canadian forestry equipment exports for use in timber extraction and mechanical transformation."[44] This project, which dates from the days before sustainable development became a serious concern for CIDA, again illustrates a clash between commercial and environmental pressures.

In the mining sector in the Third World, large Canadian companies like Inco, Falconbridge, and Cominco have major investments, which also help integrate Third World export economies into production for the global mineral markets. It is almost impossible for a major mining development to not severely disrupt local environmental conditions and indigenous ways of making a living. A good example is the Marcopper Company on Marinduque Island in the Central Philippines. Marcopper is a partially-owned subsidiary of the Canadian mining giant Placer Dome Ltd. of Toronto. Placer Dome's partner in Marcopper was the Performance Investment Corporation, controlled by the family of corrupt Filipino dictator Ferdinand Marcos. The government of Corazon Aquino took over Marcos's share of Marcopper after the dictator was thrown out of power in 1986.

For almost 13 years Marcopper dumped up to 30,000 tons of mine tailings a day into shallow Calancan Bay.[45] According to Sister Aida Velasquez of the Secretariat for an Ecologically Sound Philippines, Marcopper has "crushed and powdered about half of a mountain and transferred it into Calancan Bay ... transforming a once bountiful fishing ground into a desert with compacted mine tailings. In the process, fishermen and their families numbering about 20,000 have been impoverished."[46] Local fishers have been protesting Marcopper's destruction of the environmental resources on which their survival depends since 1974.

Finally, in April 1988, the Aquino government's Department of the Environment issued an order to stop the dumping. According to Sister Velasquez, "Within 24 days the water in the bay started to clear up and the fish catch started to increase." But pressure from the company and union got the Filipino government to overturn the order and Marcopper resumed its dumping of tailings. Sister Velasquez feared that before the mine was spent it would endanger the fishing grounds that the quarter-million people who live on Marinduque Island depended on for their survival. The Marcopper operations employ 1,500 people and the company owes $33 million in back taxes to the government of the Philippines.

Unfortunately, the public sector is not immune from environmentally questionable practices in the Third World. Canada's publicly-held oil company Petro-Canada is involved in a project to push through an oil pipeline and associated road construction in Yasuni National Park in Ecuador. Environmentalists and Native rights activists are concerned not only about the environmental impacts of this project but also that the newly constructed roads will expose the Huaorani Indians who inhabit this region to an invasion of land-hungry colonists that will threaten their way of life.

Canada has a long way to go if we are to present ourselves as a model for sustainable development in the Third World. Whether in official development assistance or investment by Canadian companies, the record calls for more vigilance on the part of those Canadians who truly believe in ecodevelopment. If CIDA is serious about addressing the ecological crisis graphically illustrated by the Brundtland Commission, rethinking the primarily commercial motives behind many aid projects should be a priority. It may not be possible to please the Canadian business community and save the planet from ecological destruction at the same time.

The utterances of CIDA president Marcel Massé indicate that we may be moving in the opposite direction – closer to the U.S. and IMF prescriptions in favour of painful structural adjustment policies that sacrifice the Third World poor. For CIDA President Marcel Massé, "Structural adjustment is a high priority" and "an essential prerequisite to a prosperous future." For Massé, "The structural adjustment imperative implies two things: First, we must need to consider moving away somewhat from the project-by-project approach of the past towards more policy-based aid; and second we and other bilateral donors must work in closer co-ordination with key international institutions, such as the World Bank and IMF."[47] The underlying message is produce more for the international market and you will prosper. But the questions that have always dogged this strategy – who will prosper and at what cost to the environment – remain unanswered.

The past five decades of development experience make clear the folly of ignoring questions about the distribution of benefits in order to enhance pure productivity. It seems equally unfortunate that in this era full of praise for the triumph of market forces and the obvious collapse of top–down planning, "productivity" may prove a more potent bureaucratic buzzword than "sustainable development".

DEFENDING THE SURVIVAL ECONOMY

The past two decades have witnessed a grassroots explosion of ecological consciousness and direct action on the part of Third World peoples fighting to save the environment. For many years environmentalists had few examples of movements that actively defended fragile ecosystems against the resource-intensive development strategies of private companies and national governments. It seemed that the vast indigenous experience in working out a careful balance between human production and nature inevitably gave way before the onslaught of a narrow technocratic science in the service of power and capital.

The pattern of development that concentrated commodity production in urban-industrial enclaves and exported resources from the hinterland to earn foreign exchange went virtually unchallenged. That pattern extracted an ever-growing tribute, laying waste to vast areas of rural hinterland and eroding the natural resource base that was the future of development. Across the political spectrum of the Third World there was a commitment to industrial development unqualified by concern for sustainability.

The few sane voices that cast doubt on such an approach found themselves literally crying in the wilderness. As early as 1928 Mahatma Gandhi proclaimed: "God forbid that India should ever take to industrialism after the manner of the west. The economic imperialism of a single tiny island kingdom (England) is today keeping the world in chains. If an entire nation of 300 million took to similar economic exploitation, it would strip the world bare like locusts."[48]

Gandhi's perceptive warning was ignored and the dominant ideology of development swept across India as quickly as anywhere else. Yet it was in India that one of the first stirrings of resistance in defence of the environment took place. The

233

Chipko movement – where local hill tribes literally embraced the trees to prevent their felling by commercial timber interests – started in the Himalayan state of Uttar Pradesh. The movement quickly spread to preserve the ecological stability of major upland watersheds in Northern India. Chipko inspired the Appiko movement in Southern India, where local survival economies are based on multi-purpose, mixed-species forests. The Appiko movement began to actively promote the preservation and enhancement of those forests. Both groups opposed the commercialization of the resource through replanting of monoculture forests for narrowly commercial purposes.

All across the sub-continent movements and action groups sprang up to oppose disruptive mining and timber development. Results have been mixed. One of the major successes occurred in the Doon Valley, where popular resistance to limestone quarrying led to a Supreme Court decision severely restricting the area where quarrying is allowed. Elsewhere protests have been ignored or smashed. The construction of dams and big river valley projects that cause extensive flooding of fertile land, deforestation, and the creation of thousands of "development refugees" also became a major point of environmental resistance. One of the most infamous of these projects is the building of the Narmada Dam supported by the World Bank – a project that would displace some 67,000 indigenous people from their homelands. The dominant pattern of resource-intensive development tends to turn renewable resources into non-renewable ones. This is happening with heavily mechanized industrial fishing fleets that are destroying the Indian in-shore fishery on which hundreds of communities depend for their livelihood. Here too resistance is growing.

Action to defend local environments has been taken by many indigenous tribal groupings from Bangladesh and the Philippines to the Americas. Action has been taken by the rubber-tappers of the Brazilian Amazon or the movements of South Pacific islanders against French nuclear testing or the dumping of Japanese nuclear wastes. Indigenous peoples are by both way of life and philosophy close to ecological values, but as with many others in the Third World these people remain invisible to the market economy. According to Jayanta Bandyopadhyay and Vandana Shiva writing in India's *Political and Economic Weekly:*

They are perceived as poor and backward if they eat self-grown nutritious millets and not commercially produced, commercially distributed processed food. They are seen as poor and backward if they live in ecologically suited, self-built housing from local natural resources like bamboo, stone or mud instead of cement concrete bought from the market. They are seen as poor and backward if they wear indigenously designed handmade garments of natural fibre instead of mechanically manufactured clothes.[49]

This invisibility to official society makes indigenous people particularly suscept-ible to the arrogance of megaproject planners who proceed to turn a culturally rel-ative poverty into absolute misery. Those who do not resist are forced into a fight for survival at the margins of society – in the slums of Third World cities or as landless labour in rural areas.

The active groups see resource-intensive development and its consequences not as a threat merely to the quality of the environment but to their immediate eco-nomic and physical survival. The environment is a life and death issue. In this sense they differ from environmentalists in the industrial world, whose physical survival is usually not at stake – at least in the short run.

In the industrial world environmental protest has focused on the cumulative effects of concentrated industrial pollution. In the Third World the struggles tend to be more around issues of resource exhaustion and degradation. If the Brazilian rainforest is destroyed the half-million Indians, rubber-tappers, or harvesters of Brazil nuts who depend on it for their livelihood have no savings to fall back on. They have no unemployment insurance or job retraining schemes to get them back on their feet. They are part of a large number of people in the Third World who derive their sustenance from a survival economy directly dependent on access to environmental resources. For their very survival they rely on soil fertil-ity, ample vegetation, clean water, abundant fish and game. It is understandable why they are have been so tenacious in their struggle to defend these resources against those who would despoil them in search of a quick profit that the survival economy will never see let alone benefit from.

In Brazil the rubber-tappers are the first line of defence in the Amazon. The roadblocks set up by the rubber-tappers union have saved thousands of acres of luxuriant rainforest from the bulldozers of Brazilian cattle barons who seek to "develop" through destruction. But the price they must pay is high. Just before Christmas in 1988 a leader of the rubber-tappers, 44-year-old Chico Mendes, was shot down in front of his home in the jungle town of Xapuri. Mendes's fame caused a world-wide outcry and demands for the arrests of the prominent ranching fami-lies involved in his murder. Less well known are the thousand other killings since 1980 of peasant leaders, church workers, nuns, lawyers, and trade unionists by pro-development forces. All have been documented by Amnesty International.

The Brundtland Commission report on the environment calls for wide public information and input into decision-making that affects the environment. The fate of Mendes and others who are fighting the dual battle to protect the environ-ment and to introduce a sustainable and people-centred approach to development shows the price that must be paid for such development. Halfway around the world in the eastern Malaysian province of Sarawak, government authorities have thrown a hundred or more of the indigenous Penan people in prison for trying to resist the destruction of their rainforest home by commercial logging interests.

The Penans, one of the last tribes of hunter-gatherers left in the world, are also using road blocks to stop timber companies and politicians who own logging concessions. In 1987 the same Malaysian government rounded up and charged members of the Penang-based environmental group Friends of the Earth as a threat to national security. In other parts of the Third World official intimidation and unofficial violence have made sustainable development a very risky business indeed.

There have also been environmental organizations that are coming together to press for sustainable development at the national level of Third World societies. The strength and forthrightness of such groupings are often dependent on the political space allowed by a particular government. The bureaucratic state inherited from colonialism and often ruled by just one party becomes simply a vehicle to enforce the interests of the narrow military and business circles that control the economy. The economic weight of a modern state with its demands for high salaries and the latest military gadgets crushes the ability of poor societies to pay the bills. The legitimacy of this kind of government is shaky at best. So those on top fear the least hint of criticism.

In some cases, such as that of Indonesia and most of Africa, environmentalists must be extremely careful not to be perceived as anti-government and this influences the bluntness of their criticism. But in some societies such as Brazil they have even witnessed the formation of small Green political parties. In Asia the Pesticides Action Network and in the South Pacific the Movement for an Independent and Nuclear-Free Pacific are examples of regional environmental networks that transcend national boundaries to provide mutual support and exchange information and analysis.

The more urban-based environmentalism provides the possibility of building alliances with and between those involved in the immediate defence of the survival economy. The urban activists must also try to address the deterioration of environments in Third World cities. Between 1920 and 1980 the Third World's population doubled, yet that of Third World cities grew by ten times to almost one billion people. The environmental conditions in Third World cities due to lack of proper sewage systems and pollution-control regulations present staggering public health problems. In Calcutta alone it has been estimated that 60 per cent of the population suffers from respiratory diseases related to air pollution.[50] An urban-based environmentalism in the Third World must tackle some daunting problems.

Urban environmentalism also creates possibilities for bringing together a scientific and institutionalized ecology with the traditional environmental knowledge derived from intimate contact with an ecosystem – all with the purpose of implementing a truly sustainable development. The social movements that are emerging must learn to make selective use of the technological products of industrial society. In this they are seeking alliances with environmentalists and non-government agencies in the North, with people dedicated to the critical use of such tools to forge a grassroots strategy of ecodevelopment. Canadian aid policy is best judged by whether it contributes to or impedes this process.

There is a growing body of literature and experience that demonstrates that ecodevelopment is not only desirable but also quite possible. Indeed, it is actually going on. There are hundreds of small-scale development projects that work to stabilize the survival economy and the environment on which it depends. There can be real progress even though no foreign exchange is earned and there is minimal impact on the national debt. Health standards can be improved for both people and livestock. Small-scale irrigation can be installed or proper drainage developed where needed. Soils can be upgraded and agricultural productivity increased. Groups such as the Oklahoma-based World Neighbors organization and dozens of other non-government organizations have experienced success using such techniques. What is required is an empowerment of local people and a low level of dependence on expensive inputs (whether technology, supervision, or chemical fertilizers) from the outside. It also helps if such people are not sitting on some valuable resource that a multinational corporation or government planner thinks should be developed for them.

Robert Chambers of England's Institute for Development Studies, after studying five projects put together in what are considered resource-poor conditions in different and diverse parts of the Third World, argued that "ecologically vulnerable people" need new forms of development. He suggested that sustainable development projects would "put livelihoods first, enabling people to gain secure and decent livings for themselves and for their children, where they are, and with the resources they command." Chambers argued that people-centred development projects "are political and ecological safeguards against pillage and ecological degradation by commercial interests and the rich":

When poor people have secure rights and adequate stocks of assets to deal with contingencies, they tend to take a long view, holding on tenaciously to land, protecting and saving trees, and seeking to provide for their children.... Their time perspective is longer than that of commercial interests concerned with early profits or of conventional development projects concerned with internal rates of return.[51]

This notion of a survival economy based on relative regional self-sufficiency and community development could prove crucial for the future of the industrial world as well. Here too a range of non-destructive technologies and decentralized economies could form an alternative to the unsustainable political economy of waste. Global resources that could be shared equitably are being gobbled by an industrial machine that is simply out of control.

What is clear is that while they might want to minimize environmental costs,

CIDA and the other major development institutions of the industrial world are unwilling to alter their commitment to an export-oriented model of development – a model that at its core is hostile to the environment. Nor has this model proved successful in meeting the basic needs of the poor.

While there may be some short-term conflicts between transforming the material well-being of poor people and a healthy ecosystem, in the long run these interests are indivisible. For the sake of fairness and the health of the planet, we need to change course and design a survival economy that meets basic needs. We need a political economy that allows for cultural diversity and a quality of life that goes beyond the ethic of "what you own is what you are".

Notes

1. Jim MacNeill, John Cox, and David Runnalls, *CIDA and Sustainable Development: How Canada's Aid Policies Can Support Sustainable Development in the Third World More Effectively* (Halifax: Institute for Research on Public Policy, 1989).

2. Quoted in David Weir, *The Bhopal Syndrome: Pesticides, Environment and Health* (San Francisco: Sierra Club Books, 1987), p.60.

3. Ross Laver, "Who Pays the Bill," *Maclean's*, September 17, 1990, p.76.

4. Ibid., pp.76–77.

5. World Commission on Environment and Development (Brundtland Report), *Our Common Future* (Oxford: Oxford University Press, 1987), pp.2–3,5.

6. Laver, "Who Pays the Bill," p.77.

7. Anthony Milne, *Our Drowning World* (Bridgeport, Conn.: Prism Press, 1988). Milne provides a frightening look at a global warming trend that he predicts will seriously disrupt the lives of millions.

8. Lester Brown et al., *The State of the World* (Washington: W.W. Norton, 1989).

9. Alexander Cockburn, "Trees, Cows and Cocaine: An Interview with Susanna Hecht," *New Left Review*, No.173 (1989).

10. Michael Redclift, *Development and the Environmental Crisis: Red or Green Alternatives?* (New York: Methuen, 1984), p.114.

11. Ibid., p.115.

12. W. Saint, "Farming for Energy: Social Options Under Brazil's National Alcohol Programme," *World Development*, Vol.10, No.3 (1982).

13. Philip Smucker, "Trees 'Ordained' in Forest Fight," *The Globe and Mail*, July 13, 1990, pp.A1,A7.

14. Robert Chambers, "Sustainable Rural Livelihoods," Institute of Development Studies Occasional Paper, Brighton, 1987.

15. Quoted in Richard Franke and Barbara Chasin, *Seeds of Famine* (Totawa, N.J.: Rowman and Allanheld, 1980), p.11.

16. A.R.E. Sinclair and J.M. Fryxell, "The Sahel of Africa: Ecology of a Disaster," *Canadian Journal of Zoology*, Vol.63 (1985).

17. Jayanta Bandyopadhyay and Vandana Shiva, "The Political Economy of Ecology Movements," *Economic and Political Weekly* (India), Vol. XXIII, No. 24 (June 11, 1988), p. 1230.

18. Patricia Adams, "Canada's Foreign Aid Flouts UN Environmental Plan," *The Gazette* (Montreal), June 20, 1988.

19. Redclift, *Development and the Environmental Crisis*, p.33.

20. *CUSO Advocate*, December 1989.

21. Michael Redclift, "Redefining the Environmental 'Crisis' in the South," in Joe Weston (ed.), *Red and Green: A New Politics of the Environment* (London: Pluto Press, 1986), p.89.

22. Weir, *Bhopal Syndrome*, p.44.

23. Quoted in Weir, *Bhopal Syndrome*, p.159.

24. Brenda Crossman, "The Tragedy of Bhopal: Adding Insult to Injury," *The Globe and Mail*, March 2, 1989, p.A7.

25. Weir, *Bhopal Syndrome*, p.85.

26. Quoted in Franke and Chasin, *Seeds of Famine*, p.226.

27. World Commission on Environment and Development, *Our Common Future*, p.9.

28. Ibid., pp.22–23.

29. Redclift, "Redefining the Environmental Crisis," pp.96–97.

30. Bruce Rich, "Conservation Woes at the World Bank," *The Nation*, January 23, 1989.

31. Quoted ibid., p.90.

32. Quoted in Janine Ferretti and Trevor Wickham, "The World Bank's Environmental Reforms: Rhetoric and Reality," *Probe Post*, Fall 1988.

33. Patricia Adams and Lawrence Solomon, *In the Name of Progress: The Underside of Foreign Aid* (Toronto: Doubleday, 1985).

34. J. Ferretti, P. Muldoon, and M. Valiante, "CIDA's New Environmental Strategy," *Probe Post*, Winter 1987.

35. Ferretti and Muldoon, "CIDA's New Environmental Strategy," p.31.

36. Letter from Probe International et al. to the AECL, Sept. 8, 1988.

37. Patricia Adams, "Dam Busters," *The New Internationalist*, May 1988.

38. James Rusk, *The Globe and Mail* (Report on Business), April 27, 1988.

39. Ellie Kirzner, "Selling China on Yangtze Gamble," *NOW Magazine* (Toronto), July 21–27, 1988, p.9.

40. Ibid.

41. Ibid.

42. Arthur Hanson and Bernard Wood, *Canadian Aid and the Environment* (Ottawa: North-South Institute, 1981).

43. Correspondence from Peggy Hallward of Probe International, Toronto, to David Mattey, Peru Desk, CIDA, Ottawa, December 14, 1987.

44. CIDA, "Forestry Development Program: Canada / Peru," Ottawa, April 1981.

45. Vyvyan Tenorio, "Philippines Pollution Row Leaves Marcopper Operations at Standstill," *The Globe and Mail* (Report On Business), May 3, 1988.

46. Sister Aida Velasquez, "The Role of Citizens in Sustainable Development," address, Secretariat for an Ecologically Sound Philippines, Manila, The Philippines.

47. Marcel Massé, "Adjustment in Perspective: Notes for Remarks to an International Colloquium on Structural Adjustment and Social Realities in Africa," Institute for International Development and Cooperation, University of Ottawa, November 17, 1989.

48. M.K. Gandhi, *Young India*, December 20, 1928, p.422; quoted in Bandyopadhyay and Shiva, "Political Economy of Ecology Movements," p.1224.

49. Bandyopadhyay and Shiva, "Political Economy of Ecology Movements," p. 1230.

50. J. Hardoy and D. Saterhwaite, "Third World Cities and the Environment of Poverty," *World Health Forum*, Vol.8 (1987).

51. Chambers, "Sustainable Rural Livelihoods," p.6.

SEVEN

Missiles and Malnutrition: The Links Between Militarism and Underdevelopment

Esther Epp–Tiessen

In a Cairo slum a mother cradles a whimpering infant in her arms. The child has diarrhea – the result of impure water – and is severely dehydrated. She will probably die within hours because the parents have no money for medical care. Three older children, pale and thin, huddle together in the corner of their small shack. Several kilometres away at the seaport, dock-workers unload a new shipment of military transport trucks.

In a Salvadorean village a group of women and men take turns hoeing beans on their co-operative farm. The co-op is a new venture. Its aim is to help local people reduce their dependence on a few exploitative produce merchants. As they hoe they sing and laugh, while young children dart among the rows of beans. Several days later, the tortured bodies of two co-op members are found beside a road leading out of town.

UNDERDEVELOPMENT and militarization: These pressing Third World problems are frequently treated as two separate issues. But high military spending is one of the reasons for inadequate health care and the lack of other social services. The drain on foreign exchange caused by arms imports contributes to the promotion of export-oriented agriculture – a strategy that benefits a small elite but is disastrous for the majority. People who pursue models of development that threaten the powerful, or who challenge the legitimacy of the existing order, are often confronted by the barrel of a gun. In short, militarization is both a cause and part of underdevelopment. The two realities go hand in hand.

In the late 1980s world military spending stood at U.S.$1 trillion (Can.$1.2

trillion) a year or $1.9 million a minute. The global military establishment, including support functions, accounts for 5.6 per cent of the world's Gross National Product and employs about 26 million people in the armed forces alone. An estimated 57,000 nuclear weapons are stockpiled worldwide, and they contain a thousand times the explosive power used in all wars since the introduction of gunpowder six centuries ago.

Especially sobering is the pace of militarization in the Third World. In 1960, military governments ruled 22 of 78 independent developing countries. By 1988 the number of countries ruled by the military had almost tripled, to 64 of 113, or 57 per cent. From 1960 to the late 1980s, military spending by Third World countries rose five-fold in constant prices. In 1987 Third World countries accounted for 17 per cent of global expenditures.[1] By 1987 developing countries were absorbing 82 per cent of the world's arms transfers.[2] Moreover, many of them were now in the business of manufacturing their own armaments. Brazil, China, South Africa, Argentina, India, and North and South Korea now supply their own armed forces and sell a wide range of military commodities on the foreign market. As increasing militarization engulfs the Third World, the goal of just development for the poor becomes more and more elusive.[3]

The militarization of the Third World means not only that lives are being lost, but also that the remaining life is brutalized. It means that people are hungry and ill and unemployed because resources that could be used to tackle these problems are being used to purchase arms and support armies. It means that drastic measures are being instituted to release money to pay for arms, the burden placed on those who are already poor. It means that persons who advocate a different political and social order, one in which the poor participate in shaping their own destiny, are subject to harassment, detention, torture, and even murder. Most of all, it means the sustaining of a world system that enriches the North while further impoverishing the South.

A significant event in the process of linking militarization and underdevelopment was the establishment by the United Nations in 1978 of a Group of Experts to study the relationship between disarmament and development and to bring forward recommendations for advancing both goals. The Group of Experts has promoted the position that militarization hinders development because it uses up resources that are needed for social and economic development. Its assumption is that if there was a reduction in military spending by the industrialized nations, the funds released would be available for development assistance. In other words, if there were disarmament, there could be development.

Although the UN Group of Experts has helped to advance thinking on these matters, its analysis has not gone far enough. Rather than simply impeding the process of development by the misuse of resources, militarization actually contributes to and maintains underdevelopment by establishing the conditions that allow the developed North to continue underdeveloping the South. Militarization is an integral ingredient of a global order that ensures economic and political dominance for the developed countries and subordination for the underdeveloped.[4]

The means of this militarization are many, from the transfer of arms and arms technologies to the establishment of military bases on foreign soil. And in much of this Canada's own military industry has its own role. Indeed, just like many other nations of the North, Canada seeks to capture its own part of the action and is thereby complicit in the continuing process of domination and underdevelopment.

THE TRANSFER OF ARMS

The most important way in which the Third World has been militarized has been through weapons transfers. The leading world powers began transferring arms to Third World governments around 1960, when rebel victories in Vietnam, Cuba, and Algeria forced the U.S. State Department to turn its attention away from the Soviet menace in Europe to the threat posed by revolutionary movements in the developing countries. First through aid, and later through sales, the United States sought to strengthen Third World governments and elites so they could resist these movements. The Soviet Union soon followed suit.

Military spending by the Third World grew phenomenally in the next 30 years, and the biggest expense was imported arms. Between 1960 and 1987 the developing countries imported $400 billion in military goods from the industrial regions.[5] During 1982, the peak year for international trade deals, arms agreements with a record value of $46.8 billion were signed by Third World countries.[6] In the early 1960s the value of arms imports by the developing countries amounted to less than one-third the value of foreign aid they received. By the 1980s Third World countries were spending more on arms imports than the total of all economic assistance given them.[7]

The percentage of global arms transfers destined for the Third World grew as well. In 1963 Third World nations absorbed 50 per cent of world arms transfers; by 1975 they took in 75 per cent.[8] In 1982, according to the U.S. Arms Control and Disarmament Agency, the total of global arms transfers to the Third World reached 82 per cent.[9]

Until the mid-1960s the two superpowers accounted for almost all arms sales to the Third World. In the late 1960s, France, Great Britain, and West Germany joined the race. From 1976 to 1979 these five nations accounted for 89 per cent of all arms sales to the developing countries.[10]

Beginning in 1980 a new group of secondary suppliers emerged, taking over a significant chunk of the Third World arms market. This group includes Canada,

Belgium, Czechoslovakia, Poland, Spain, Sweden, and Switzerland, as well as Third World suppliers such as Argentina, Brazil, Israel, North and South Korea, and South Africa. In the 1980 to 1983 period, during the boom years of the arms trade, this group of second-tier suppliers captured 30 per cent of the Third World market share.[11]

Since 1982 the estimated value of the international arms trade has oscillated, with 1987 sales totalling $45 billion.[12] Part of this is due to world recession, and to the fact that many countries are still trying to absorb the massive purchases they made between 1979 and 1982. But equally important is the fact that more and more military trade deals are being made clandestinely and are not recorded. Revelations of under-the-table arms deals like Irangate suggest that the black market in weapons is booming.

THE TRANSFER OF ARMS-MAKING TECHNOLOGY

The developed countries also contribute to the militarization of developing countries through the transfer of arms-making technology. This transfer enables Third World countries to produce and even export their own armaments and has led to the emergence of indigenous arms industries in a growing number of Third World nations.

The transfer of arms-making technology works step by step. It begins with the construction of maintenance and repair facilities to service components assembled locally. This is followed by the local manufacture of components using imported raw materials, usually under some kind of licensing agreement with a partner in the North. A third step is the local production of components using domestic raw materials. The ultimate and final step is to produce armaments using local research, design, and development. Instances of this last stage are quite rare.

The annual value of major weapons produced in the Third World grew steadily after 1950 and declined only after 1980. In 1950 Third World production was valued at $2.3 million (in 1975 U.S. dollars); in 1984 the value was $1.2 billion. Between 1980 and 1984 the total value of major weapons produced in the Third World was 25 times higher than that between 1950 and 1964.[13] Despite this phenomenal growth, Third World arms production still only accounts for a fraction of global military production.

There are several reasons why both the developed and developing countries seek the transfer of arms-making technology. For the North, technology transfer is a way for industry to cut costs, avoid export restrictions, and gain access to embargoed markets, in South Africa for example. For the South it is a way to ensure a steady supply of arms, to avoid the danger of being suddenly cut off by a major supplier. It is also a means of achieving at least a modicum of political independence from the supplying countries.

MILITARY TRAINING

A third way that the developed countries foster the militarization of the Third World is through military training programs. Unlike arms transfers and the transfer of arms-making technology, military training does not add to a nation's stock of war material. However, it does provide the rationale or justification for these kinds of transactions, and it enhances the efficiency and effectiveness of the country's new military capabilities. In addition, military training impresses upon the trainees an ideology and worldview that, among other things, has a profound influence on development within their own countries.

The United States is the world leader in providing military training to Third World personnel. U.S. training programs emerged after World War II alongside the provision of surplus weapons and became available to any government prepared to climb aboard the anti-communist bandwagon. In the late 1950s, when the concept of counter-insurgency gained currency, the number of officers from developing countries at U.S. military academies soared. Between 1950 and 1986 the United States trained 457,675 personnel from the Third World. [14]

Britain and France have also developed extensive military training programs. Canada, as a member of the Commonwealth, offers military training to states in Africa and the Caribbean.

Soviet training programs lag behind those of the Western nations. Between 1955 and 1985 the Soviet Union trained 69,680 military personnel from the developing countries. [15]

Military training programs do much more than teach military personnel how to use new weapons or how to instil discipline in the rank and file. A fundamental objective is political indoctrination. [16]

Miles Wolpin notes that the U.S. military training program revolves around several key themes:

- the legitimacy of "civil" (or stable) rather than civilian government;
- the promotion of development through corporate investment that receives subsidies, tax breaks, and other forms of protection from the state;
- the liberalization of trade;
- a denial that capitalism is exploitative;
- a faith in Western and U.S. leadership; and
- a diabolical portrayal of communism. [17]

Besides communism, the program includes among the evils to be eliminated: nationalism, leftist revolution, insurgents and their allies, political dissidents, and radical elements.

The goal of the U.S. military training program is to convince Third World

245

military leaders that they should adopt and defend a capitalist open-door development strategy – one favourable to the exploitation of markets and natural resources by foreign concerns, even though its priorities "flatly contradict ... development oriented towards self-reliance and the satisfaction of basic human needs."[18] The program is a way for the United States to gain the loyalties of elites who can safeguard U.S. interests, often at the expense of the poor of the world.

MILITARY BASES AND FOREIGN MILITARY PERSONNEL

Alongside these other means of militarization is the establishment of military bases and the positioning of military personnel in the Third World. In 1987, 84 countries had foreign military forces operating on their soil. Worldwide, some 1.8 million personnel were serving abroad. The Soviet Union led with 730,090 troops permanently stationed overseas, while the United States had 492,500 forces detailed abroad.[19]

The superpowers and their allies control virtually all of these foreign facilities. The United States has the most elaborate system, with over 300 major naval and air bases covering some 2 million acres, besides a whole host of lesser installations. The total number of U.S. bases worldwide has declined since the 1960s because of the country's reliance on long-range intercontinental ballistic missiles and missile-firing submarines, as well as its new satellite-observation techniques. Nevertheless, despite recent proposed reductions, foreign bases are likely to remain an important component of U.S. and Soviet strategic planning for a long time to come.

These foreign bases not only distort socio-economic development in the host countries but also heighten the potential for conflict throughout the world. They bring Soviet and U.S. military forces virtually "nose to nose" in many regions of the world, thus risking confrontation. They also draw host countries into the geopolitical struggles of the major powers and make them vulnerable to attack. The storage of nuclear weapons and the docking of nuclear-capable ships at U.S. bases in the Philippines, for example, make that country a target for Soviet missiles in the event of nuclear war. Foreign bases and personnel also increase the possibility of direct intervention by the major powers in situations not to their liking.

CANADA'S ROLE IN THE ARMS TRADE

As ally and largest trading partner of the United States, Canada has long supported the broad strokes of one superpower's foreign policy, including its history of foreign intervention. While sporadically mounting independent positions (such as trading with Cuba during the U.S. economic boycott), for the most part Canada has accepted, and often endorsed, U.S. military action and doctrine in the Third World. Moreover, successive Canadian governments have reinforced the

U.S. definition of the Cold War, doing their part to feed the largest and most widespread military buildup in history.

Yet the most direct way that Canada contributes to the militarization of the globe is through military exports. During the 1980s the export of Canadian armaments grew rapidly, due mainly to the Reagan arms boom. Between 1980 and 1985, Canadian military exports rose from $722 million to $1.9 billion, an amount exceeding Canada's combined exports to Central America and Africa and representing nearly 5 per cent of the annual world arms trade.[20] After 1985 Canadian arms-export totals fluctuated in a tighter international market, but remained high relative to a decade earlier (see Table 1).

Three-quarters of all Canadian arms exports go to the United States. Since the late 1950s Canadian military production has been governed by the Canada-U.S. Defence Production Sharing Arrangements (DPSA), which have had two major implications for the structure of the Canadian military industry. First of all, Canadian companies have been largely limited to producing components for U.S. weapons rather than complete weapons systems. Secondly, Canadian military commodities have been allowed access to the U.S. market, with the proviso that Canadian sales to the United States balance with U.S. sales in Canada.

During the Vietnam War and the arms boom of the 1980s, Canada benefited from this reciprocal trade arrangement. At other times Canadian military sales have slumped. Over all, Canada has imported more than it has exported: By the end of 1987 the total "balance" in cross-border weapons trade was $3 billion in favour of the United States.

Without the opportunity to achieve a surplus in military trade with its neighbour, Canada has sought to market its military goods elsewhere. Though not a major competitor in the race to arm the Third World, Canada has been trying hard to corner part of that market. During the 1980s direct Canadian sales to the Third World averaged about $150 million a year, with peaks of $250 million in 1982 and 1986. The sales had increased from $55 million as recently as 1979.

Canadian direct sales, however, only tell part of the story. A significant portion of Canadian exports to the United States is incorporated into U.S. weapons systems that eventually end up in the Third World. Because a portion of U.S. military production goes to the Third World each year, presumably the same portion of Canada's share in that production goes there as well. In 1985, when Canadian sales to the United States amounted to $1.6 trillion, an estimated 10 per cent or $160 million worth was re-exported to the developing countries.[21] Including this kind of indirect transfer, Canada's total sales to the Third World were worth $300 million to $400 million annually by the end of the 1980s.

Although this amount appears small next to the massive arms deals made by the major powers, it is no less disturbing that a concerted effort is being made by politicians, bureaucrats, and industrialists to increase Canadian military exports, particularly to the Third World. Two government reports issued in 1987 called on Canada to increase its long-term military-production capabilities. The traditional way to do this is through more military spending on Canada's own defence forces and more exports to the United States. However, with budget restraints placing limits on these two options, the reports point to the markets of Europe and the Third World as holding the most promise. [22]

A host of government programs and agencies was set up to provide incentives and assistance to Canadian companies. After 1959 the Defence Industry Productivity Program (DIPP) provided grants for research, development, production,

Table 1

Canadian Military Exports 1959-1989

($ million)

Year	United States	Europe	Other*	Total
1959-1969	2,418.8	439.8	207.0	3,065.6
1970	226.5	41.2	68.5	336.2
1971	216.3	67.2	53.0	336.5
1972	175.0	73.7	51.7	300.4
1973	198.8	72.8	37.6	309.2
1974	150.0	45.6	84.9	280.5
1975	188.5	58.6	33.7	280.8
1976	191.1	113.1	31.9	336.1
1977	314.1	76.0	163.9	554.0
1978	267.0	129.6	87.9	484.5
1979	367.7	145.6	55.0	568.3
1980	481.7	142.1	97.9	721.7
1981	826.6	149.4	174.8	1,150.8
1982	1,027.9	157.8	248.4	1,434.1
1983	1,207.4	128.6	145.2	1,481.2
1984	1,360.5	243.1	149.8	1,753.4
1985	1,644.2	154.0	104.5	1,902.7
1986	947.0	196.2	244.8	1,388.0
1987	1,281.0	351.0	169.0	1,801.0
1988	900	n/a	193	1,093
1989	966	n/a	376	1,342

* This category primarily represents sales to the Third World, although some sales to Australia and New Zealand may be included.

SOURCE: Department of External Affairs.

Table 2
Defence Industry Productivity Program
Total Expenditures

Fiscal Year	Current $million	1979 Constant $million
1978-79	52.2	52.2
1979-80	57.9	52.6
1980-81	94.9	76.1
1981-82	154.9	115.6
1982-83	132.0	93.1
1983-84	144.2	98.2
1984-85	152.7	99.8
1985-86	181.5	113.7
1986-87	189.4	113.9
1987-88	232.8	134.6
1988-89	248.6	138.9

SOURCES: Public Accounts of Canada; Industry, Science and Technology Canada; Consumer Price Index, Statistics Canada.

and marketing of goods destined for export. Like Canadian military exports, DIPP contributions took off in the 1980s, with the program's budget increasing by five times in ten years (see Table 2). By 1989 total annual DIPP payments stood at $250 million.

The Defence Programs Bureau of the Department of External Affairs was established to provide marketing assistance to Canadian arms exporters. The DPB organizes international trade fairs, carries out market analysis, and supports bilateral research, development, and production agreements for the industry. In addition, the Canadian Commercial Corporation, a crown corporation, was set up to arrange prime contracts on behalf of foreign governments and Canadian firms. Other government agencies provide export financing, insurance, and additional export promotion.

Even more disturbing than the governmental encouragement given to the business of military exports is the manner in which the Department of External Affairs' permit system operates. On paper, "close control" of the export of military goods and technologies is to be applied to:

- countries that pose a threat to Canada and its allies;
- countries involved in or under threat of hostilities;
- countries under UN Security Council sanctions; and

countries that persistently engage in human rights violations, unless it can be demonstrated that the goods in question are unlikely to be used against civilians.[23]

While External Affairs seems to conform to limits imposed in the first and third categories, it has engaged in a loose interpretation of the second and fourth categories. Canada has repeatedly sold military equipment to governments engaged in hostilities, among them Indonesia, Pakistan, Guatemala, and Honduras. Canada continued to sell arms to Britain during the war over the Falklands and to the United States during the Vietnam War. Of the 45 known probable recipients of Canadian arms between 1980 and 1984, more than one-third were involved in hostilities during that time. It appears that, rather than denying permits in instances where there is armed conflict, Canada's policy is one of choosing the conflicts, and the side in each conflict, which it is prepared to support.[24]

Canada also has an unenviable record of approving sales to governments that engage in human-rights violations. On numerous occasions permits have been granted to known human-rights violators, including South Korea, Chile, the Philippines, and other countries recognized by Amnesty International and the United Nations Commission on Human Rights for their poor human rights records. Indeed, during the period 1984-88 Canada approved permits for the export of military goods to 21 of the 32 Third World countries acknowledged as persistent violators of human rights (see Table 3).

One rationale given is that certain kinds of strategic equipment, such as radios and computers, are unlikely to be used against civilians and therefore should not be subject to the same close scrutiny as equipment viewed as "specially designed for military purposes." A second rationale is that even human-rights violators have legitimate defence functions to perform. Little consideration, it seems, is given to the fact that strategic communication and surveillance equipment such as computers and radios can indeed enhance a government's ability to subvert the human rights of its citizens, and that *any* kind of equipment sold to a human-rights violator lends a measure of moral and political legitimacy to that government.

Another problem with Canada's export-control system is that Canada relinquishes control over the final destination of a particular commodity after it has left Canada. While end-use certificates are required to certify that a particular commodity will be used for the intended purpose in the intended country, these do not apply in instances where Canadian components are used in the manufacture of larger weapons systems. Thus, aircraft engines produced by Pratt & Whitney Canada have gone into the Italian helicopters shipped to Sudan and Somalia in the war-torn Horn of Africa, into the U.S. helicopters supporting El Salvador's counter-insurgency effort, and into the Swiss aircraft used in the Iran-Iraq war. Indeed, Canadian military equipment is present in almost all the world's current war zones and trouble spots.[25]

Although Canadian government officials are embarrassed by revelations of where Canadian military hardware ends up, they argue that Canada's responsibility for its military goods ends once the goods have been delivered. Regulations are there to prevent a resale of the goods as they are, rather than their transformation through manufacture. In this policy Canada differs from the United States, which claims the right to withhold permission for equipment that may be re-exported, even if it is incorporated into another system outside the United States.[26]

Perhaps most disconcerting about the permit system as it applies to military exports is the secrecy that shrouds the granting of these permits. On the grounds that divulging information to the public violates commercial confidentiality and

Table 3
Annual Values of Canadian Military Export Permits
to Human-Rights Violators
($ thousands)

Country	1984	1985	1986	1987	1988*
Chad	–	–	219	–	–
Chile	10,185	7,420	6,182	1,175	–
Colombia	5,026	–	4,057	310	–
El Salvador	–	4	–	–	–
Ethiopia	3,000	–	–	–	–
Guatemala	–	15	–	–	–
India	16,820	33,551	35,655	30,007	82,950
Indonesia	17,795	14,176	3,238	8,598	–
Korea, South	56,094	29,641	25,475	102,009	161,972
Mauritania	–	3,000	3,000	3,000	–
Morocco	8,000	5,047	1,036	11	–
Pakistan	45,564	23,345	2,063	73,129	1,125
Paraguay	25,000	1	–	–	–
Peru	46,000	150,521	2,000	7,376	3,048
Philippines	10,604	58	3,258	38	–
Syria	1,000	–	441	–	–
Togo	–	–	3,000	3,000	–
Turkey	2,220	17,804	11,363	112,225	17,057
Uruguay	–	3	1	–	–
Zaire	–	–	3,000	3,000	7,527

* To May 1, 1988.
SOURCES: *Hansard*, June 29, 1988, p. 16941; Ruth Sivard, *World Military and Social Expenditures 1987-88*, and earlier editions.

compromises the competitive position of Canadian companies, the Canadian government refuses to divulge the details of permits granted. Unfortunately, this secrecy lends little credence to the statement that Canada's policies on military exports are marked by restraint and careful consideration.

Canada's ambition to get in on the action of the international arms trade stands in stark contradiction to another key Canadian foreign policy, namely, the pursuit of international security and the peaceful settlement of disputes. Increasingly, the promotion of Canadian military exports flies in the face of Canada's image as an international peacekeeper. Given that Canadians value that image, what motivates us to get involved in an activity that can only heighten international insecurity? Indeed, what motivates the developed nations in general to promote the militarization of the globe?

WHAT'S IN IT FOR US?

The reasons for the North's push to militarize the South represent a web of interrelated political, strategic, and economic motives.

In brief, the superpowers are interested in developing and maintaining an international political environment in which they can pursue their own long-term interests. The major and intermediate powers, including Canada, usually have more immediate economic benefits as their goal. Yet they too, because of their close alliance with the United States and their integration with the international capitalist system, also stand to gain in the long term from the existing global political and military order.

The superpowers are primarily concerned about establishing a military presence in a certain region, directing another country's policy decisions, or consolidating a sphere of influence sympathetic to their own economic, political, and ideological perspectives. The famous quotation by a Lockheed official – "When you sell an aircraft, you buy a political partner" – supports this. Despite the trend whereby a number of developing countries purchase arms from both Soviet and U.S. blocs, most developing nations are armed by one of the superpowers or its allies and are thus drawn into informal alliance systems.

Certain regions have special significance for the superpowers. Northern Africa and the Middle East, which control access to the Suez Canal, have great importance for both the Soviets and the Americans. The Indian Ocean and Pacific Basin, because of their importance as trade routes, their untapped mineral, agricultural, and forest reserves, and the populous nations found here, also hold major strategic interest for both the United States and the Soviet Union. In recent years both nations have poured billions of dollars of arms into these regions. They have also initiated technology transfers and military training arrangements and negotiated the establishment of military bases there, purely to safeguard their own interests.

Strategically, access to reliable sources of petroleum is crucial for the developed nations to maintain current levels of industrial production and international pre-eminence. Arms transfers and other military transactions are a way to maintain guaranteed access to oil. According to one study, between 1968 and 1973 the world's top ten oil producers received 30 per cent of all French and 48 per cent of all British major weapons exports.[27] Between 1975 and 1980, 13 OPEC countries accounted for over 40 per cent of the arms imports of all the developing nations.[28]

In addition to oil, military arrangements also provide the "cash" with which industrialized nations pay for other strategic minerals such as bauxite, chromium, manganese, platinum, and cobalt. These minerals are essential for the production of war material as well as basic consumer goods, yet most of them are found in greatest supply in the Third World. Five of Africa's six largest military importers and eight of its ten highest military spenders are also major mineral exporters.[29]

There are also basic economic motives underlying the militarization of the South by the North. The capitalist powers need to ensure an environment that permits them to carry on their own business interests with a minimum of difficulty. Their basic objectives are: 1) to market goods produced either at home or in overseas plants; 2) to invest surplus funds; and 3) to gain access to cheap raw materials and labour. Because these interests clash with the demands of Third World peoples for justice and self-determination, resistance movements have spread throughout the world. By providing weapons, technology, training, and in other ways facilitating the militarization of Third World societies, the United States in particular tries to create the kind of conditions that will allow it to carry out its business exploits while keeping a lid on popular opposition.

Recent history is replete with examples of how the United States has bolstered oppressive dictatorships or helped to overthrow democratic governments so that its own political, strategic, and economic interests can be preserved. Two examples of its aid to dictatorships are its longstanding support for the Shah of Iran and Ferdinand Marcos of the Philippines – though as it turned out, no amount of U.S. military assistance short of direct military intervention could buttress these two dictators from the opposition of the local population. An example of an overthrow of a democratically-elected government was the CIA-engineered military coup that brought down Salvador Allende in Chile in 1973.

For Canada, as for other middle-level traders, the primary motivation behind arms exports to the developing countries is the foreign exchange to be earned. Military exports also resolve some of the contradictions relating to the "logic" of arms production. Because of insufficient local demand for certain military commodities, producers look to the international market to justify the longer production runs that can cover initial capital investments. The Third World is a highly desirable market for Canadian producers, because there is no reciprocity requirement as there is with the United States. Exporting arms and arms components is also a way of preventing lay-offs and plant closures in Canada, as well as of maintaining repair services and the manufacture of spare parts.

But even though potential profits are Canada's primary rationale for promoting military exports, there *are* strategic factors at work. For instance, permits for the export of certain military commodities are more likely to be granted to countries with which Canada has an ongoing trade relationship or is interested in fostering closer political and economic ties. More important, the integration of the Canadian defence establishment with the U.S. military-industrial complex guarantees that Canadian activity is directed by U.S. interests. An officer in the Export Control Division of the Department of External Affairs stated openly: "If we are to enjoy the benefits of unimpeded access to U.S. technology, we must make sure it is denied to countries where the United States does not want to go."[30] In other words, the Canadian government gives careful consideration to ensure that the export of Canadian military commodities does not undermine U.S. policy.

In addition to this, because of Canada-U.S. defence integration, the very commodities themselves embody certain military strategies; they are not neutral. Canadian-made weapons components are used in U.S. nuclear weapons, in equipment for U.S. interventionary forces, and in arms shipped by the United States to its client states, including some of the world's most repressive regimes.

By producing for and buying from the U.S. military machine, Canada becomes implicated in the military policies that its weapons sustain. Researcher Ernie Regehr states:

The fact that Canadian industry makes components for the F-111 bomber obviously does not make Canada responsible for the U.S. raid on Libya, but the Canadian industry's extraordinary dependence on sales to the U.S. and identification as part of the U.S. defence industrial base does imply an overall endorsement and support of the general military policies of the United States.[31]

Thus, Canadian involvement in the international arms trade serves to consolidate U.S. hegemony in the world.

According to Marek Thee of the International Peace Research Institute in Oslo, "The main function of militarism today as a global force is the defence and preservation of the exploitative *status quo* between the North and South, the rich and the poor countries."[32] Militarism is thus the big stick, wielded worldwide, to beat back those who would challenge the existing global economic order. How does this happen? What are the mechanisms whereby this process occurs? There are several, including the role of debt, the pressure to produce goods for export, the policies of institutions like the International Monetary Fund, and increased state authoritarianism and repression.

MILITARIZATION AND UNDERDEVELOPMENT

Most developing countries must import military equipment, whether complete weapons systems or components. These imports result in a serious drain on precious foreign-exchange reserves and contribute to a country's debt.

By the end of the 1980s, arms imports accounted for fully 25 per cent of the Third World debt burden. Indeed, the value of arms imports of developing countries accounted for 40 per cent of their debt increases between 1975 and 1985.[33]

Military imports divert foreign currency away from essential imports such as food, agricultural implements, medicines and health-care equipment, and industrial machinery. This happens not only at the time of transfer but also far into the future. The purchase of a jet fighter, for instance, necessitates ongoing expenditures for spare parts and servicing as well as the construction of additional airports, the extension of runways, and the installation of navigational and control systems. Even weapons provided as gifts impose maintenance, operational, and infrastructural costs that can be overwhelming.

One of the reasons that a growing number of nations have ventured into arms production is to save on foreign exchange. But in many instances there is no saving. It is often more expensive to buy unassembled parts than to purchase a complete weapon or weapons system.[34]

There are licensing fees and royalties to be paid. In addition, even relatively simple arms-producing facilities set up in a developing country are highly dependent on imported inputs. A U.S. government study revealed that between 53 per cent and 80 per cent of the cost of installing M-16 machine-gun factories in developing countries over a five-year period was for imports. All the countries involved had at least an incipient industrial base to begin with.[35]

A special problem with military-related imports is that they generate no income to help pay off loans. Unlike industrial machinery, which can be used to produce clothing or appliances for exports, military commodities cannot improve the balance of payments. They either are used up or become obsolete.

Besides the debt incurred when arms are imported, there is another important, if more indirect, link between militarization and the foreign debt of developing countries. The escalation in U.S. military spending during the Reagan years was a key factor in the huge U.S. deficit. This deficit prompted higher interest rates, which in turn resulted in higher payments for debtor nations. The cruel irony is that the peoples of the developing world are helping to finance the guns that are frequently turned against them.

By aggravating debt as well as by structuring economies towards export and inviting the harsh austerity measures of the International Monetary Fund, the militarization of Third World societies contributes indirectly to greater hardship and suffering for those who are already poor. More directly, it exacerbates local disparities within those societies.

Local military industries, which are being established in a growing number of developing countries, tend to draw on the highly skilled few rather than the unskilled majority. In fact, many countries rely on foreign technicians and advisors to supply the necessary expertise. Disproportionately high wages in turn stimulate a standard of living way out of line with that of the general populace. The result is the formation of little islands of militarized wealth amid a sea of poverty. Indonesia's "high tech" industry and Iran under the Shah are examples.

Additionally, military establishments drain the hinterlands of resources and income for their own benefit. This is not unlike the way that resources flow from the less developed nations to the developed ones. Because military imports are paid for primarily by the export of commodities that are produced in the rural areas, the peasantry ends up paying for goods used by a small elite of military bureaucrats and industrialists to build up local military production. Peasants also pay for the imported luxury items consumed by this elite and by foreign-service persons. Few, if any, benefits ever return to the countryside.

Foreign military bases also exacerbate local disparities in a particular way. Within the communities that develop alongside military bases, the economic benefits generated by the bases usually accrue to a small minority. In Olongapo City, a rest and recreation centre next to the U.S. Subic Naval Base in the Philippines, U.S. marines spend $466 million each year. The major part of this wealth ends up in the pockets of the owners of Olongapo's 500 bars, discos, lounges, and nightclubs.

The women who work in these establishments, and who are required to provide sexual favours to their customers, receive abysmally low wages, and sometimes only commissions on the drinks they sell. They may earn a fair bit when an aircraft carrier is in port, yet several "good" days can be followed by weeks of little business at all. The base thus sustains a social system that enriches a few while keeping the majority of workers dependent and impoverished. The base has also virtually destroyed the local fishing industry, disrupted the life of an indigenous tribal group, and debased the moral fibre of the community with prostitution, organized crime, and drug trafficking.

AUTHORITARIANISM AND REPRESSION

In the increasing number of Third World countries where political power is militarized, there is a high level of authoritarian rather than participatory decision-making. There is a high reliance on coercion to enforce decisions and a systematic violation of human rights. Voting is restricted, the press is censored, organizing activity is closely monitored and often prohibited, and there is frequent resort to arbitrary arrest, torture, disappearances, and extrajudiciary killing. In 1988, 58 of 64 military-controlled governments exercised repression in its most extreme forms. [36]

Although development is usually conceived of in terms of socio-economic indicators such as infant mortality rate, literacy rate, and GNP per capita, human rights is also an essential component. Where people are prevented from freely exercising their political rights there is no assurance that the benefits of development will be evenly distributed. Indeed, the main reason for repression in most of these countries is to maintain a system that enriches a small minority and to prevent popular movements from gaining sufficient strength to threaten that system. Yet a basic prerequisite of sound development is that all members of society be guaranteed an opportunity to voice, and work towards the fulfilment of, their needs.

There is a high correlation between governments that persistently violate human rights and those that pursue a right-wing open-door development strategy tending to attract investment and political support from Western market economies. [37] Despite severe human-rights abuses, such countries are rarely reprimanded or subjected to diplomatic pressure from nations espousing the principles of freedom and democracy. [38] While the U.S. government has been quick to criticize the Soviet Union for its poor human-rights record, it has leveled similar criticism against Brazil, Indonesia, Chile, and other countries where the United States has significant economic and political interests. Indeed, the flow of U.S. military hardware to such regimes carries on. Canada, likewise, has not gone out of its way to refuse military commodities to human-rights violators.

The relationship between militarization, underdevelopment, and repression is a cyclical one. Militarization, especially as it is encouraged and supported by arms transfers, deepens poverty, oppression, and underdevelopment in the Third World. As people rise up in protest against these injustices, governments resort to repression to maintain social control. More military equipment is required to break up demonstrations and strikes, to arrest, torture, and kill dissidents, and to wage counter-insurgency campaigns. This in turn invites greater economic hardship, which invites more dissent, which invites more repression – and so on. The very arms that are supposed to provide security in fact deliver insecurity.

Militarization contributes to underdevelopment in the Third World by compounding the foreign debt of developing economies, by gearing production towards export and away from urgent local needs, by contributing to dependence on the IMF and other Western-dominated banks and lending agencies, by exacerbating local disparities, and by promoting authoritarianism and repression. Through these mechanisms, the militarization of the Third World serves to reinforce the structure and dynamic of a world hierarchy of power as we know it. At a very basic level, militarization makes for underdevelopment by integrating the developing countries into a global economic order in which they are destined to be the losers.

CANADA AS VICTIM

Although Canada bears some responsibility for a militarized world, it is also, ironically, a victim of militarization and underdevelopment.

Politicians and bureaucrats argue that increased military production will invigorate Canadian industry and bring greater prosperity to all Canadians. In truth,

Canadian military production plays a part in our own industrial underdevelopment and general economic malaise.[39] The reasons for this relate to certain dynamics within Canada. Much of it has to do with the reality of military spending, and the symptoms of these same ills can be found in other developed countries as well.

In many ways, Canada is more like a Third World arms importer than a First World arms exporter. Because of the development of the Canadian military industry in relation to the U.S. military-industrial complex, Canada must purchase major weapons systems while mostly selling components and parts. Even the material we do produce remains heavily dependent on U.S. capital and technology. We build using foreign designs, with foreign machine-tools and sub-components, often under foreign licensing agreements.[40] The situation is analogous to that found in some of the semi-industrialized countries of the developing world.

The ramifications for Canadian independence are disturbing. Just as Third World countries find themselves pressured by scarce foreign currency to accelerate the export of raw materials, divert lands into the production of cash crops for exports, and welcome foreign investment, a similar dynamic occurs in Canada. Our dependence on U.S. capital and technology for military production, as in other areas of industry, invites greater U.S. control of our own economy. The resources that could and should be used to meet the needs of Canadians increasingly flow south.

The Canada-U.S. Free Trade Agreement brought in by the Progressive Conservative government after the fall 1988 election only heightened this problem. According to the government, the agreement would give Canadian manufacturers secured access to the U.S. market at a time when pressure for trade protectionism was mounting within the United States. The trade-off, however, was that Canadians would have to give up any lingering controls over their natural resources, which would increasingly be mobilized in support of U.S. arsenals and economic policies.[41]

While there may be some immediate economic gains, long-term development cannot be secured by this kind of strategy, especially when the future benefits of closer links with the U.S. economy are far from assured. At the same time, the free trade agreement adds pressures to make military production more central to any Canadian industrial strategy. While the agreement in general views government subsidies to industry as unfair competition, and thus prohibits them, support to military industry is an exception. To ensure a defence industrial capacity, both sides reserve the right of public intervention in military industries, particularly the right to subsidize them. This policy could mean that when the federal government contemplates regional industrial incentives, the only instrument available will be the subsidization of military industries – resulting in a built-in prejudice towards using military production as an instrument of industrial strategy.

Despite the government argument that "defence programs ... make a significant contribution to overcoming regional economic disparities," 10 of the top 20 military contractors in the country are found in Ontario and 7 are located in Quebec.[42] Similarly, U.S. prime contracts, that is, sales directly to the Pentagon, are heavily concentrated in companies in Central Canada. The government award of the CF-18 fighter aircraft-maintenance contract in 1987 to Canadair of Montreal, when Bristol Aerospace of Winnipeg came in with a lower bid, confirms that rather than "overcoming" regional disparities defence contracts actually compound them.

There are other ways that Canadian military production contributes to underdevelopment, rather than development, within Canada. Although military industry is justified, indeed promoted, because it supposedly creates jobs, jobs, and more jobs, this reasoning remains more myth than reality. First of all, because of Canada-U.S. Defence Production Sharing Arrangements and their stipulation of reciprocity in military trade, there can only be as many jobs created by military exports bound for the United States as there are jobs lost. In other words, for every job created by the manufacture and export of a particular military commodity, there is another job lost because of the corresponding purchase of a U.S. product.

Secondly, recent studies have shown that military spending is not an effective means of creating employment. A Canadian Union of Public Employees study looked at the number of jobs created by the spending of the Department of National Defence in 1983-84 compared to the number of jobs that might have been created if the same amount of money had been added to consumer spending. While military spending resulted in 146,641 jobs, the same amount spent by Canadian consumers in the fields of health, transportation, construction, communications, education, and consumer goods would have created 257,844 jobs.[43] Clearly, if the Canadian government wanted to give priority to job creation as a means of economic development, it would have much greater success if it found ways to encourage consumer, rather than military, spending.

Besides job creation, another rationale for military spending, especially in the field of research and development, is that there will be a spin-off effect for the civilian economy. One of the major arguments used for Canadian participation in SDI (Star Wars) research is that it will lead to major breakthroughs in the fields of medicine, computer technology, and communications. While occasional spin-offs do occur – the production of canoes made from Kevlar, a lightweight material designed for space, is one example – they are hardly sufficient justification for the high capital investment in military research. A growing number of studies conclusively demonstrate that the companies making innovations in civilian production are not military-related firms but companies doing civilian product development. Those who argue for increased military spending because of the spin-offs that might occur are like the farmer who, "anxious to fatten the chickens, increases the feed to the horses so that more of it spills over the edge of the trough, thus giving the chickens more scratchings to forage."[44]

Finally, there is the problem of the opportunity costs of military spending. When public resources are spent on military needs, this means that those resources are not available for low-cost housing, health care, or public transportation, for instance. During the 1980s, when needs for day care, research into AIDS, and increases in social assistance were crying to be met, the federal government increased the military budget by 50 per cent above inflation.[45] This can only be considered a tragic distortion of a nation's priorities.

THE CONTINUING BLIGHT – AND NEW POSSIBILITIES

Two concurrent events in the closing days of the 1980s spoke of very different horizons for the majority of the world's people who live under physical or political oppression.

The first event, the collapse of the Ceausescu regime in Romania, was a sign of hope – that dictators can still be deposed and that the overwhelming will of the people remains a potent force. The role of the military did not go unnoticed, in both its international and domestic forms. Unlike previous occasions of resistance to doctrinaire Communist Party rule in Eastern Europe, the Soviet armed forces did not intervene in Romania, just as they stood distant from the dramatic changes involving other members of the Warsaw Treaty Organization during the second half of 1989. Moreover, a turning point in the fate of the Romanian political elite came when the army refused to turn on its own people. Regardless of the eventual outcome of a tumultuous period in the Balkans, the overthrow of another oppressive government was marked as a step forward for humankind.

The U.S. invasion of Panama brought different tidings. It served notice to the peoples of the Third World, and particularly to those of Latin America, that, despite the changes in Eastern Europe, the Pentagon was still open for business. It demonstrated what Mexican writer and diplomat Carlos Fuentes has called "the United States' arrogant rejection of negotiation and law in its own sphere of influence, Central America and the Caribbean."[46] The blatant disregard of international law, brought to the fore during the Reagan administration, was to remain official U.S. policy, as was the preference for military over diplomatic or economic foreign-policy initiatives. The invasion also illustrated both the new focus of the Pentagon's attention and the kernel of its *raison d'être* for the 1990s – the pursuit of "low intensity conflict," the euphemism for fighting wars in the Third World. Finally, the event threatened, through what Fuentes terms "the basic rules of international symmetry," to pressure the Soviet Union to return to the policies it had only recently let slip: spheres of influence and military intervention.

The Panama invasion, therefore, was both a warning and a lesson to the Third World. The events of Eastern Europe, whatever their effect on East-West relations, will not necessarily translate into changes along the North-South axis. At the beginning of the 1990s, militarization in particular remains a blight throughout the developing world: Death, injury, and other consequences of conflict or military occupation continue to be a pervasive and devastating part of daily life.

The consequences of militarization for development in the Third World, and secondarily in Canada, are complex and defy easy solutions. Moreover, the enormity of the problem tempts even concerned persons to despair. Still, there are possible measures that, if adopted by the Canadian government, would represent steps towards less militarization and thus also less poverty and oppression for the peoples of the world.

To place meaningful restraints on its own military exports, as well as to push for controls on the international arms trade, the Canadian government should, as a minimum, take the following steps:

- Prohibit *all* arms exports to governments identified as human-rights violators. This would limit the capacity of repressive regimes to violate the basic human rights of their citizens. It would also deprive them of the legitimacy that comes from an arms-trade deal.
- Provide full public disclosures of all Canadian military exports and subject these to annual public review. This would ensure greater restraint in the granting of export permits.
- Terminate grants and subsidies (especially under the Defence Industry Productivity Program) to military industries seeking markets outside Canadian borders. This would remove much of the incentive behind the export of military commodities.
- Exercise control over the ultimate destination of military components produced in Canada. This would prevent instances in which Canadian goods are exported, built into larger weapon systems abroad, and then used for purposes and under circumstances repugnant to Canadians.
- Work to place the control of arms transfers on the agenda of international disarmament efforts. This would alter the present situation wherein no existing international forum addresses the problem of the global arms trade. [47]

To provide for the economic well-being of Canadians the government should also explore alternatives to current military production. Removing the country from the Canada-U.S. Defence Production Sharing Arrangements, converting existing military production capacities to civilian production, and channelling resources now used for military purposes to human needs, would move Canada towards the prosperity that military production promises but fails to deliver.

Given the rampant militarization and desperate need that characterizes much of the world, the vision of peace with justice remains an elusive dream for many peoples. Yet the pursuit of the above measures by the Canadian government would represent courageous and concrete steps towards limiting the cancerous growth of militarization and the social and economic underdevelopment that it breeds. At the very least, Canada could set an important example that other industrialized nations would be encouraged to follow.

❑

MILITARISM AND THE GULF WAR

The U.S.-led war against Iraq that started in January 1991 was both a legacy of Cold War militarization and a beacon of a born-again Pentagon role in the post-Cold War era. The legacy was clear enough: Iraq had been given the capability to invade and annex Kuwait by a decade of direct and indirect arms supplies. The supplies had arisen from superpower attempts to manipulate power balances in a very unstable region and from commercial weapons sales of middle powers dependent on exports to maintain military industries for Cold War scenarios. As for the born-again military role: The United States was able to unleash its massive arsenal on Iraq because, with the tailspin of East-West tensions, the troops and weapons were no longer needed in Europe. The weapons that faced each other across the Arabian desert sands had been designed to fight in the fields of Germany.

Yet Operation Desert Storm also introduced a new era to supersede the Cold War. As American political analyst Michael Klare has argued, while the Cold War era was characterized by U.S. supremacy in the military, economic, and political spheres – a period that Klare labels "Pax Americana I" – the Gulf conflict inaugurated a new era to be characterized by continuing U.S. military supremacy without the equivalent political or economic strength – "Pax Americana II". (*The Nation*, February 11, 1991.)

In responding to the August 1990 Iraqi invasion of Kuwait, the U.S. government had at least two strategies: to pursue a multilateral, diplomatic strategy that would ultimately concede power to the peoples within the Middle East; or to impose a unilateral U.S. solution through the threat or use of military force, which would leave the United States the unchallenged regional hegemonic power. The White House chose the military option, killing thousands of Arabs in the process. Not coincidentally, the strategy also supports high levels of military spending in the industrial sector – those that produce weapons – where the United States still retains some international advantage.

Canada, its economic future now inextricably linked to the United States by the Free Trade Act, has a stake in U.S. economic and, ultimately, military success. The most unpopular prime minister in Canadian history was well aware of this; despite clear public hesitancy and opposition he unilaterally committed Canadian troops to deployment and eventual fighting in the Persian Gulf. The use of Canadian fighter aircraft to ride shotgun for U.S. bombers over Iraq or the made-in-Canada components of the many sophisticated and highly lethal U.S. weapons that pounded Baghdad and Kuwait only served to emphasize the integration of Canadian military troops and industry into the U.S. system. At the same time, in abandoning its role as a major United Nations peacekeeper to become a minor adjunct to the American warrior, Canada squandered the years of good will it had built with the Third World. In its eagerness to go to war alongside the United States, Canada may have burned intercontinental bridges behind its march.

For the Third World, the Gulf War raises the spectre of a unipolar, militarized world ruled by the Pentagon. Well aware of Saddam Hussein's brutalities – his propensities are far from unique in countries of the South – many people of the less developed world were nevertheless drawn to his defiance of the North. One commentator summed up Third World reaction in this way: "It is not just Islamic peoples who feel frustrated by the course of the war and fearful of its outcome. In India, Central and South America, and Africa, President Bush's new world order looks suspiciously like old-fashioned imperialism, and President Saddam's windy rhetoric sounds like a heroic defence of the downtrodden." (*Manchester Guardian Weekly*, February 10, 1991.)

But the Third World's downtrodden will not be the only losers in a triumph of the U.S. military will. The era of Pax Americana II would remove any vestiges of a peace dividend, of the conversion of resources squandered on the military to more socially beneficial and needed purposes. Instead, the industrialized economies, and especially the North American trading bloc, will be further drained to sustain an inflated military machine stationed around the world, or at home, ready to intervene anywhere.

The 1990s could become a decade of even greater militarization and violence, when Rambo leaves the videoscreen to stalk the earth. In response, says Michael Klare, "Those who oppose this emerging praetorian culture have no choice but to make antimilitarism the defining theme of progressive politics in the 1990s."

Notes

1. Ruth Leger Sivard, *World Military and Social Expenditures 1989* (Washington: World Priorities, 1989), pp.5,12,19,20-21,46,50.

2. U.S. Arms Control and Disarmament Agency, *World Military Expenditures and Arms Transfers 1988* (Washington: U.S. Government Printing Office, 1989), p.7.

3. See Ruth Leger Sivard, *World Military and Social Expenditures 1987-88* (Washington: World Priorities, 1987).

4. This position is advanced by a number of articles in Mac Graham et al. (eds.), *Disarmament and World Development*, 2nd ed. (Oxford: Pergamon Press, 1986); see Robin Luckham, "Militarism and International Economic Dependence," pp.43-70; Nicole Ball, "Third World Militaries and Politics," pp.17-39; Mary Kaldor, "The Military in Third World Development," pp.71-100. See also Marek Thee, "Third World Armaments: Structure and Dynamics," *Bulletin of Peace Proposals*, Vol.13, No.2 (1982), pp.113-117.

5. Sivard, *World Military and Social Expenditures 1989*, p.21.

6. Michael T. Klare, "Who Reaps Benefits of Third World Arms Sale Boom?" *Current News*, January 9, 1985, p.12-F.

7. Ruth Leger Sivard, *World Military and Social Expenditures 1986* (Washington: World Priorities, 1986), p.12.

8. Mary Kaldor and Asbjorn Eide (eds.), *The World Military Order: The Impact of Military Technology on the Third World* (London: Macmillan, 1979), p.5.

9. See Table 1 in "Disarmament and Development: Security in an Interdependent World," North-South Institute *Briefing Paper*, No. 9 (Ottawa, May 1985), p.4.

10. Michael T. Klare, "The Transformation of the International Arms Trade," *Ploughshares Monitor*, March 1985, p.7.

11. Ibid.

12. Sivard, *World Military and Social Expenditures 1989*, p.12.

13. Michael Brzoska and Thomas Ohlson (eds.), *Arms Production in the Third World* (Sweden: SIPRI, 1986), p.7.

14. Sivard, *World Military and Social Expenditures 1987-88*, p.13.

15. Ibid.

16. Miles D. Wolpin, "Military Dependency Versus Development in the Third World," *Bulletin of Peace Proposals*, Vol.8, No.2 (1977), p.139.

17. Ibid.

18. International Peace Research Association, "The Impact of Militarization on Development and Human Rights," *Bulletin of Peace Proposals*, Vol.9, No.2 (1978), p.173.

19. Sivard, *World Military and Social Expenditures 1987-88*, pp.12-13.

20. Ernie Regehr, *Arms Canada: The Deadly Business of Military Exports* (Toronto: James Lorimer, 1987), p.17.

21. Ibid, p.19.

22. *Ploughshares Monitor*, September 1988, p.20.

23. Regehr, *Arms Canada*, p.141.

24. Ibid, p.148.

25. See "Armed Conflicts in the World 1989," *Ploughshares Monitor*, December 1989, pp.14-15.

26. Regehr, *Arms Canada,* p.144.

27. Jan Oberg, "Arms Trade with the Third World as an Aspect of Imperialism," *Journal of Peace Research,* Vol.12, No.3 (1975), p.226.

28. Eboe Hutchful, "Trends in Africa," *Alternatives,* Vol.10, No.1 (1984), p.118.

29. Luckham, "Militarism and International Economic Dependence," p.195.

30. Quoted in Regehr, *Arms Canada,* p.142.

31. Ibid., p.183.

32. Marek Thee, "Militarism and Human Rights," in *Militarism and Human Rights* (Geneva: Commission of the Churches on International Affairs, World Council of Churches, 1982), p.10.

33. Sivard, *World Military and Social Expenditures 1986,* p.5.

34. Signe Landgren-Backstrom, "Arms Trade and the Transfer of Military Technology to Third World Countries," in Asbjorn Eide and Marek Thee (eds.), *Problems of Contemporary Militarism* (London: Croom Helm, 1980), p.244.

35. Peter Lock and Herbert Wulf, "Consequences of the Transfer of Military-Oriented Technology on the Development Process," in Pradip K. Ghosh (ed.), *Disarmament and Development: A Global Perspective* (Westport, Conn.: Greenwood Press, 1984), p.113.

36. Sivard, *World Military and Social Expenditures 1989,* pp.20-21.

37. Tamas Szentes, "The Economic Impact of Global Militarization," *Alternatives,* Vol.10, No.1 (1984), p.61.

38. Richard Falk, "Militarisation and Human Rights in the Third World," in Eide and Thee (eds.), *Problems of Contemporary Militarism,* p.215.

39. See Regehr, *Arms Canada,* pp.159-189.

40. Ibid., p.174.

41. *Ploughshares Monitor,* December 1987, p.3.

42. *Ploughshares Monitor,* March 1988, p.14.

43. Regehr, *Arms Canada,* p.170.

44. Ibid., p.168.

45. *Ploughshares Monitor,* June 1988, p.4.

46. Carlos Fuentes, "US – Keep Out," *Manchester Guardian Weekly,* February 11, 1990.

47. See Regehr, *Arms Canada,* pp.190-217, for an excellent discussion of alternatives that Canada could explore.

EIGHT

A Native View of Development

Pam Colorado

TO THE NATIVE American, tidelines, mountain tops, connections, and communications – any place or moment where energies meet – are considered to be sacred and to offer the opportunity for growth, learning, and development. That is why European invaders of the Americas were greeted warmly. In fact, the initial xenophilia of Native people represented more than a kindly mindset, it was a manifestation of indigenous science – a search for truth that is holistic and embodies objectivity, the natural world, spirituality, and the feminine in its paradigm.

Had the Spaniards, British, or any other European nations arrived here with more than "profit" in their minds, they would have become acculturated, educated, and nationalized into the various First Nations. This process would have ensured the acquisition and understanding of Native mathematics, astronomy, medicine (including surgical skills) comedy, drama, music, and art. In short, European colonists would have become true Americans and in so doing would have acquired a science far advanced over the nascent positivist approach.

This is not a moot point. Indeed, the "Americanizing" of European colonists could have maintained conventions that were natural to the Americans: the pristine ecosystems, economies built on co-operation and sharing, and societies organized to integrate rather than alienate. Moreover, the acculturating process would not have destroyed the European but rather awakened a sleeping tribal knowledge that was similar to the Native American. For example, before contact both women and nature figured prominently in the tribal science of European and Native people.

This is not to suggest that tribal people have not abused the earth; we have. But it has been the exception, not the norm, and when the environmental report card of the Native is compared with that of the Westerner, the winner is clear.

But Europeans did not integrate with the land and cultures indigenous to the Americas. Instead, the interests of capital and nation states combined with the forces of church to precipitate the global disaster we now face. Worse yet, this destruction, driven by the linear application of Newtonian science, was called progress, civilization, and development, and the people of Canada and the United States believed it.

As a Native woman charged with the responsibility to write about "development" and "environment," I can tell you it is not an easy job. For my people, family, land, and way of life have suffered immeasurably from the various schemes of Western "developers." Chicago's Newberry Library estimates that nearly 80 million Natives were exterminated in the fires of European colonialism. Yet the juggernaut, now sublimated into institutions and people's hearts, goes unnoticed.

As evidence of this fact, you can travel the length and breadth of the entire North American continent and not see a single monument or marker to the millions of Native people sacrificed to "development." Similarly, in property law, deriving from the English Common Law, "Land Improvement" means stripping the land of all natural topographical features – flora, and fauna.

By now you, the reader, may be wondering if this chapter is yet another rage-filled lament of a disenchanted Indian. It is true, I do feel pain, I do feel grief, but mostly these feelings are for our children and our land – yours and mine. And I grieve for our failure to communicate because I believe that most Westerners, given the opportunity to experience the joy, power, and wisdom of the indigenous science, would make powerful allies in reversing the forthcoming fatal effects of development. And that is what this chapter attempts to do – create a space for our cultures to meet and usher in a new paradigm of "development," one characterized by authenticity, integrity, a sense of relatedness, and deep concern for our children and planet.

NAUI OLLIN, FOUR MOVEMENT GEOMETRIC EXPERIENCE

I did not feel the change until I heard my heart pounding and had to stop. My lungs, like old bellows, gasped for air. Small wonder, I am in the mountains of Mexico – over 7,000 feet above sea level. And today, a dream is coming true. I am ascending the pyramid of the sun. Teotihuacan – the place where the fires always burn; seat of universal knowledge; home to Azteca and origin of Canada's Iroquois – my people.

Now, I am clearing the last step to the brown volcanic rock top. The sun is in its zenith and I am lightheaded. My nose is sunburnt and the skin on my cheeks is beginning to tighten. I kneel. When the moment comes, I lay down an offering for ancestral spirits and reach out to the four directions.

The wind picks up. Words, new to me, come to mind. "Amerrikua," original name for North America – land where the wind blows. "Hahnahuac," eagles, the people from the Great Lakes to Nicaragua. "Nicaragua" really – meaning the "Eagle stops here." I am dazed. Never in years of study have I been able to find even one tribal language with a term big enough to include all Native nations. Even my own language seems to reinforce the isolation and alienation visited upon us by European invasion and genocide. "Hahnahuac" the word feels good; it feels right; I whisper it to myself, trying to hold on to the image.

Then, yielding to the onslaught of the noise and presence of a dozen or so young school boys on a class trip to the pyramids, I rise and make my way to the stairs on the west side.

The sun warms the back of my head. At the top of the stairs I pause and gaze to the distant Cerro Colorado. This is the sacred mountain, and it marks the point on the horizon where the Pleiades star cluster sets. In an instant I understand why our own old people in Ontario look to Pleiades when they set Mid-Winter or turning the ashes ceremonies. This is our new fire for a new year. Other scattered images, thoughts, teachings, and customs from home begin to connect in this place. Walking through a gestalt-like experience, I move down the first level of the pyramid.

By the second level, my knees begin to quiver with strange electrical energy. I am afraid I am going to fall. Suddenly, it is very still.

The face of Xilonem, Aztec woman, elder, and friend, comes to my mind. She has literally returned from the jaws of death. Healing herself through traditional medicine, Xilonem begins in her retirement years the greatest work of her life – sharing the traditional science, geometry, wisdom, and beauty of Azteca. Earlier this morning she told me:

The Native mind is scientific because it is open to everything. It is not dogma, limiting a mind when the mind cannot be limited. That is the power of indigenous science …

It is science because all things are related, nothing is apart, so we have to study all things …

Energy is like art, pure energy. The most pure is when you get in touch with the origin of people and who made the people!

Geometry is how energy gets into the form of things. I am touching beautiful energy. The more science, the more spirituality, getting to know what you know and love what you know.

All nature lives by the same laws. The earth lives because of the mind of the human beings.

These words seem to steady the energy in my legs, so I continue down the steps. Two steps later I am halted again. Strong gusts of wind throw me off balance and

I have to lean forward to prevent falling. As I do so, my eyes focus again on the distant mountains.

Voices, voices in the wind begin to speak
Who are you?
   I answer, in Oneida and in the old way; they seem to hear.
Who are your children?
   Again I respond.
Who are your other relatives?
   Here I mention people, including plants, animals, and other beings who have helped me or are close in some other way.
What do you want here? What do you seek?
   I seek the wisdom and the strength of mind to bring out the traditional teaching to heal the people and the earth.
What will you do with it?
   I want to heal the planet and our people.
That is good. How will you do it?
   By bringing it out of the earth and returning it to the earth through the people. I can do this with your help.
We will help you.
   Now, who are you?

Struggling inside for an answer, the anxiety fades as a slow smile moves across my face. I know, I know, I know. I have known all along!

   Light in my step, I move down off the pyramid – hips swinging gently, arms loose and natural at my side, my feet meet the earth.

THE BIRTH OF WESTERN DEVELOPMENT

Columbus had a geometry too. In fact, it was his knowledge of geometry that got him to the New World; created the conceptual framework for modern-day development theories and saved his neck when the crew wanted to mutiny.

   Physicist Kounosu explains:

Before [Columbus] European sailors were navigating along coasts using land marks for their guide – It was good enough for Mediterranean trade and even going along the African Coast to get to India. They did draw maps, pointing out land marks for the benefit of novice navigators.

   But a remarkable thing happened in the 15th Century. Map makers started to draw lines on maps. Perhaps it was just convenience in copying maps. But lines had a significant mental effect.... Namely, if you keep drawing a line of your course – say at a certain speed for a certain time period – you get an idea of where you are on the map. You do not need land marks for that.

Not only that, the geometry of drawing lines on maps gave an extension of vision in imagination.... One can set one's course and organize the trip ahead of time. Of course the geometry was all in the imagination, and mental construction, there was a great deal of uncertainty and unknowns. But the geometry enabled a group of people to talk and think about future events and plan for collective action that deserves to be called science.

Kounosu says that Columbus learned the navigation science and was confident that he could navigate without land marks. Columbus had another tool for navigation. He had also learned from Arabic science that the earth is like a sphere, and since the Arabs also knew the radius of the sphere, Columbus could predict that India was some 40 days of sailing in the distance.

That was the secret of Columbus. He did not tell anybody but sold his idea of bringing back gold.... That is how European colonialism and modern imperialism started.

You may wonder why nobody before Columbus thought of an Atlantic navigation. The ships were there, all they had to do was sail west for a month and a half, why didn't they do it?

The reason had to do with the confidence that science (technology) gives. In the middle of the ocean European sailors were not that confident. Only Columbus had the nerve. In fact, the crew tried to mutiny but could not kill Columbus because without his science-technology they might not be able to find their way back to port.

I cite the "Geometry of Drawing Lines on a Map" because I want to point out that science-technology is mental if not spiritual or religious. It has to do with imagination, worldview, and confidence and goes beyond a matter of "knowledge." It is a part of empowerment and very much psychological.

The problem is, we have trouble with too much confidence that our science has in itself (arrogance) and receives from the public.

Science is useful for empowerment and liberation of the oppressed. The difference is, whether the imagination / science is large enough to encompass the whole or not. When Martin Luther King said, "I have a dream," he had a big geometry, big enough to encompass all the human race. It was not a fragmented local geometry like that of Columbus: his only meant gold to bring back home.

To make a big geometry (map, vision, dream) many connections have to be made.

INVASION

The authentic Native mind is extraordinarily clear and strong. Sophisticated mathematical protocols – the sacred geometry – structure solar energy so that thought processes complement – the dynamics of the pyramid. The pre-Columbian sages correctly anticipated and prepared for the holocaust of European invasion. We can see evidence of this foresight in the rapid formation of tribal confederacies; that is, the Iroquois and Powhatten and the closing of centres of knowledge. Medicine Wheels of North American and Meso American pyramids all were abandoned. Thus, the power of these places could not be accessed by invaders who were neither prepared nor worthy of such sacred wisdom.

This aspect of Native character – the ability to turn away from great power – has bewildered and enraged the Western profiteer. Later, "Indian laws" of Canada and the United States would be filled with proscriptions against the "reckless give away" rituals of Native tribes. Nonetheless, on the precipice of invasion, a time of great fear, Native people left their traditional source of strength. How was this possible?

The answer lies in the mathematics and geometry of the Americas, which were powerful enough to generate predictions in cycles of tens of thousands of years. The confidence engendered through such science permitted Native people to do many amazing things; including walking away from the pyramids for 500 years. Another example is seen in the leadership of Aztec Chief Montezuma. Before the arrival of the Conquistadors, the calculations of Aztec scientists indicated that the Hahnahuac would enter a period of "nine hells," each "hell" representing an Aztec century of 52 years. This 9 times 52 equals 468 years – the length of time until the new sun. It was further anticipated that the completion of the 9 hells would be followed by 13 heavens ($13 \times 52 = 682$ years). This period would be ushered in by a "new sun," which happened in 1987.

Montezuma knew this; he also knew that it would be neither possible nor desirable to stem the waves of people coming from Europe despite the nearing horrors. So, in counsel with other leaders, Montezuma established a policy of xenophilia.

One delegation of leaders that Montezuma met with was the Iroquois. About every six years leaders of the Great Lakes-based people travelled to Mexico for counsel. Even though the Northeast is a long way from Mexico, the vast distance was bridged through family ties and practice. You see, the Iroquois had migrated out of the southwest, Azteca, lands thousands of year earlier; the route, language, and customs were known. Thus Visits of State were also a renewal of relationships and completion of cycles – two critical elements of indigenous science.

Native science is distinguished from Western science in a third way – the import of female energy. Unlike contemporary leaders in the West, the chiefs who visited Mexico were selected and removed from office (when necessary) by women – clan mothers who had observed the chief from childhood. These women appointed men who were humble, wise, compassionate, and willing to work. The chiefs did not travel to other nations without approval of the clan mothers and upon their return home they reported in to the women.

When the last delegation of Iroquois chiefs got to Mexico, the Spanish had already arrived, bringing with them a level of savagery unknown to the Americas. As the 1961 version of the *American Heritage Book of Indians* (p.138) puts it:

They [Indians] died in massive numbers from measles, smallpox, cholera, and tuberculo-sis, from starvation, incredible overwork, from desperation, from sheer horror at inhuman-ities they could not believe even while they were happening. They died drunk, they died insane, they died by their own hands; they died, they said, because their souls were stolen. They vanished in such numbers that African Negroes could not be shipped in fast enough to take their places. Their children were born dead, from syphilis; or their women, rotted with syphilis, became unable to bear children at all.

And so they went mad and rebelled and fought ... and the *Indios bravos,* the wild Indians, filled with dread, became only wilder still.

Despite the horrific circumstances, the Chiefs worked on to formulate policy that would guide our people through the next 500 years. The guiding principles of this policy were:

☐ Non-Natives would be greeted as relatives.
☐ Traditional knowledge would be protected.
　■ the pyramids, temples, rock rings, and other powerful sites of knowledge and research would be closed and traditional teaching would go under-ground.
　■ the knowledge would be scattered; to this end, intertribal delegations from across the Americas would cease to meet.
☐ Upon return home, the Iroquois would initiate scientific protocols to encour-age or attract the "agricultural European." It was believed that European farm-ers would be less warlike and more respectful of the Earth and people than the Spanish.

Why did the Native nations assume a policy of pacifism when they could easily have overpowered the Europeans? Because a fundamental tenet of all indigenous sciences requires that development decisions be made on the basis of *long-range* sustainability. To Iroquois, "long-range" means seven generations. The number seven correlates to the stars in Pleiades which are visible to the naked eyes. It is understood that the earth derives from this constellation and all development emulates or synchronizes with this original pattern of development. For the Aztec relatives, the mathematics of seven generations is projected across 28,000 years.

Given this kind of worldview, the nemesis of Western development – that is, local or short-term rationality that creates long-term, global insanity – is impossible.

Thus, in the interests of the long-term survival of the land and the children, American Indian leaders made the decision not to fight the European colonizers. Occasionally, in the fury of wave upon wave of genocide, Indian tribes did fight but only in the extreme moments was the vision of global peace lost. Besides, we had another dream or geometry to hold on to. That dream was the knowledge that the "world would turn back," that the wisdom and science of Native people would return again in the new sun. A wait of 468 years was insignificant to Natives to whom time and space are one.

NINE

Mass Media Worldviews:
Canadian Images
of the Third World

Eleanor O'Donnell

> Western society, biased toward the objective mental mode of experience, tends to be
> blind not only to the power of images but also to the fact that we are nearly defense-
> less against their effect.
>
> – Jerry Mander, *Four Arguments for the Elimination of Television*, (1978)

THE MASS MEDIA are not just our main information source. They are our main
source of images and ideas about ourselves and the rest of the world. They define
the limits of our knowledge and understanding more broadly and persuasively
than do our educational systems, research institutes, governments, or churches.
The mass media define the terms of our debates, and in large measure determine
what we care about or can imagine. As agents of social control, the media are
closely tied to other power elites, and are as powerful as the coercive forces of the
police and the military.[1] People most likely to be taken in by the media are those
who are unaware of their influence or ties with other power elites.

This susceptible group is by no means restricted to the many hundreds of millions of uneducated people world-wide. Children and youth are susceptible,
agreed. But so are those who believe they personally are too sophisticated or too
well educated to be influenced, say, by television, because they watch little or any
of it themselves – "usually only PBS or *The Journal*," with their children only
watching *Sesame Street* and other educational television. Other likely marks are
those who might define themselves as too "Canadian," too far removed from mass
culture, too creative, too politically astute, too traditional, too non-conformist, too
busy, too well travelled, or too well read to be influenced.

Many of these people feel superior to the rest: They are unconnected to the masses of people, untouched by the hopes and dreams and humour and nightmares of the majority. On an average day, 79 per cent of Canadians view TV at least once.[2] For most people, television is their main information source.

We need to not only acknowledge the media's awesome power but also regularly and methodically examine and decode its messages. We need to try to understand the process of image-making ... and then work to create new social relations, with new images and ways of seeing, experiencing, and understanding.

THE IMPACT OF MEDIA

To prove the indelibility of media images and their power over our imaginations, television critic and former advertiser Jerry Mander asked his readers to try an experiment similar to this: Try to form a picture in your mind of your mother. Your father. Most of us can call up this picture quite readily. Then, Mander says, bring to mind the image of Coca Cola. Mickey Mouse. Brian Mulroney. Wayne Gretzky. Princess Diana. Are you able to picture a Barbie Doll? G.I. Joe? The McDonald's Golden Arches?

Did any of these images appear? "If so," says Mander, that is proof that once media images have entered your brain, "They remain in there. They live in there together with all the memories of your life." The brain's storage system does not differentiate between images of fictional characters and people you really know. Pictures of Big Bird or Brian Mulroney are retrieved as easily as those of your mother or father.

In the experiment, Mander then asks his readers to try to erase the image of Coca Cola from their minds. Delete the image of Princess Diana. Make Mickey Mouse go away. Can you do that? "If so, you are a most unusual person," he says. "Once television places an image inside your head, it is yours forever."

Advertisers know this and so do political advisers and other groups interested in results. Empirical research used by advertisers suggests that human beings actually "think" in images. Advertisers (and politicians) don't care at all if you know that advertising is fictional. According to Mander, "They make very little effort to fool you about that, because whether or not you know it is fictional, the image of the product goes into your head. From then on, you've got the image and there's no letting it go."[3]

Advertising is the *lingua franca* of the media – the common language of commerce through which different peoples around the globe can understand one another. The Spanish cognate of the word advertising – *propaganda* – reveals its true nature. The grammar and syntax of advertising determine the shape of our news-cases, "in-depth" documentaries, magazine articles, sports specials, and fashion spectaculars. The TV news format we now take for granted – with anchor teams, cut-aways to worldwide, "on-the-spot" correspondents, mixed in with in-studio comments, panels, sports, and weather – was initially designed by marketing consultants to boost ratings.

Understanding the form, content, ownership, control, and interests of the news and information media also helps us understand how world injustice, waste, and poverty are perpetuated. We need as well to examine the mass media's relation to the structures and messages of other institutions that confer meaning in our society – the education system and the training, intellectual, religious, or ceremonial institutions that confer prestige, authority, or identity.

A media analysis should also not overlook the implicit and explicit messages of apparently insignificant but widely syndicated filler or curiosity items: cartoons; household hints, business briefs, or beauty tips; jokes; fashion news; tourist items; escape literature. Taken together, these messages exert a tremendous power over our collective imagination. In the aggregate they assign us our place in our own imaginary world and in the "real" world. For example, children's expectations are closely shaped by what they see, especially toy advertising and sex-role stereotyping – and the effect can be seen in the games they play and the actual occupations that girls and boys eventually choose.[4]

Not only has one sex been stereotyped; other cultures, even entire nations are pigeon-holed. For instance, Bangladesh has been defined by the humiliating and offensive term "basket case of the world." Individually or collectively we are all given our place – as women, aboriginal peoples, members of minority groups, as the privileged, as whining nationalists, risk-takers, as achievers or Junior Achievers, doers, winners and losers, as Canadians or Quebeckers.

When we begin to explore how we see ourselves and how we are seen – what effect *Anne of Green Gables* has in Japan or *Reader's Digest* in Canada – only then can we break out of the cycle of being exploited to the full ourselves (including even those hard-working young professionals who never watch TV), perpetuating the status quo, and passing along the exploitation to others "less fortunate," to the ultimate benefit of our exploiters.

What place in the imaginary world do the media assign the "Third World"? Most people think of a poor country. The accepted image is that in the Third World there is only misery; the land is parched and good for nothing, there is no food to eat, diseased children grow up in filth, poverty, and illiteracy. The places we imagine are grossly overpopulated, and the brutality of daily life is so commonplace that only the most unbelievable of atrocities become significant.

The inequalities we recognize within these countries are almost understandable, given the "swollen" populations, the primitive facilities, the widespread ignorance and lack of technical know-how. The general population has no experience in governing themselves. Every once in a while a crisis erupts and suddenly thousands of screaming, howling mobs are seen, direct by satellite, on our televisions.

Paradoxically, these pictures stored in our minds are both true and untrue, accurate and misleading. The actual wealth of the Third World – found, for example, in the cultures, histories, and the very land itself of subsistence societies

– is invisible to the "Western" eyes that equate wealth with accumulation, especially capital accumulation. Another kind of Third World wealth – as seen in the obscene personal empires of such former corrupt dictators as the Shah in Iran, Marcos in the Philippines, Somoza in Nicaragua, or Bokassa in the Cental African Republic – is vaguely attributed to the "corruption" somehow endemic in the Third World and not in any way intrinsically linked to Western interests.

Still another kind – the wealth of natural or created beauty – is prized by Western travellers as if it were not noticed or valued by local inhabitants. Visitors derive particular satisfaction when their adventures (usually photographed) have been completed before *other* tourists spoil another Wonder of the World. The Easter, Hawaiian, Caribbean, or Galapagos islands, Tibetan mountain villages, Brazilian rain forests, or Zimbabwean temples were all "done" by tourists long, long ago; their images have been commodified and marketed separately from their social surroundings. The great pyramids of Egypt or India's Taj Mahal fit into our "tourist curiosity" category and bear no relation to these huge, poor / rich countries that we hear so little about.

We recall the misery, starvation, immense natural beauty, social chaos, insurrection, and repression as images, impressions. Causal relationships are often unstated when we receive the messages, and therefore they become difficult to identify later, too. They begin to be more easily identified, however, if we look at how they got in our minds in the first place.

For Canadians the principal medium that frames our worldview – our understanding of everything, of wars, peace, history, the future, the environment, danger, glamour, sorrow, prestige, humour, normalcy, decency, depravity – is American. Some 10,000 of the 12,000 hours of television that Canadian children watch by the age of 12 will consist of U.S. programs. Of the 52,000 hours of English-language TV available to the average teenager each year, 80 per cent of the programming chosen will be foreign. Francophone teens will spend more than half their viewing time watching foreign programs. [5]

In peak viewing hours, 60 per cent of what English-speaking audiences in Canada watch is fiction: comedy, suspense, and drama. (About 95 per cent of this is foreign.) [6] The implicit and explicit messages of prime-time fiction, then, inform Canadians about ourselves and our relation to the rest of the world. Mark Starowicz, a creator of the CBC current affairs programs *As It Happens* and *The Journal*, says Canada is "an electronically occupied country," an "emerging Third World electronic culture":

Television is an information medium not just in its newscasts.... In our police dramas, we convey a sense of our streets, the state of our courts, the values of our justice system ... the family, attitudes towards divorce, single parent families, relationships between parents and children.... A television set is virtually a 24-hour disseminator of social information. [7]

278

The foreign domination of our media is not restricted to entertainment. A study commissioned by the Department of External Affairs discovered that close to 60 per cent of the international news media coverage we receive has no reference to Canada. [8]

Virtually all the information we receive through the media is packaged as a commodity to be consumed. Networks "feed" their affiliates news "packages" that are retransmitted to consumers. Television's one-way transmission ensures that it will not be seriously challenged by viewers or altered by discussion. News features are quickly cooked up by adding one or two fresh ingredients to an assemblage of already processed ingredients ("Perfect Every Time!"). We consume "sound bites." The bites are already digested for us when we consume *Reader's Digest*, which we devour – it's the leading Canadian paid-circulation magazine in the country. [9]

FICTION AND REALITY

On April 14, 1986, regular Canadian television programming was interrupted for a live broadcast from the U.S. White House, in which President Ronald Reagan announced that U.S. fighter jets were bombing Libya. The interruption was followed by images of U.S. soldiers spraying (fake) bullets from automatic weapons on Arabs – a promotional ad for a Chuck Norris film. The week following the [real] Libyan raid, the [real] U.S. president commented that he had just seen *Rambo*, and that if he had seen the film before the Libyan raid he "would have known what to do." In January 1990 U.S. soldiers in Panama and officials in Washington defined their mission in that Central American country in TV police show idiom, vowing to "take out" the head of state Manuel Noriega.

The fictional MacGyver's television adventures have him launch a secret, unauthorized attack on a Central American government post to rescue imprisoned friends. Jessica Fletcher of *Murder, She Wrote* travels to the Soviet Union, solves a murder at a dinner party with the Gorbachevs, and at the end of the program raises her eyebrows, smiles, and good-naturedly smuggles microfilm out of the country.

FRAGMENTATION OF STORIES

As long as news stories are seen as unrelated, the superficial contexts they are given will guarantee passing interest and lasting confusion. Donald Lazere writes, "One issue at a time gets singled out for headlines and possible legislative action and then gets shuttled out of sight." This process usually gives the false impression that the problem has been resolved. [10]

"Outdated" media stories from the 1960s include "The Brain Drain" of Canadian intellectual talent to the United States; massive opposition to nuclear tests and Canada's arming itself with nuclear weapons; a famine in Biafra; the consumer movement inspired by Ralph Nader's exposure of careless design and planned obsolescence; the "industrial incentive" strategy of government funding business start-ups and giving them tax holidays of one to thirty years; the Sharpeville massacre in South Africa.

Old news from the 1970s includes foreign control of the Canadian economy; Canadian nationalism in education and culture; government "rescue" of indebted companies; the Women's Liberation Movement; the energy crisis; the unemployed and unemployment; law-breaking and abuse of power by security agencies; a CIA-sponsored military coup in Chile and widespread Canadian opposition to bank loans to Chile; drought and famine in Africa's Sahel region; Vietnam; Iran; the Soweto massacres and "suicides" of Blacks in detention in South Africa.

Items from the 1980s that have "already been done": technological change and threatened job security (1970s "unemployment" reframed); the homeless; stock market failures, a "recession," bankruptcies of major financial institutions and other business failures, followed by more government "rescues"; "privatization" (of some of the same companies that received "incentives" and "rescues"); opposition to U.S. aid to El Salvador and to human-rights abuses there; world "terrorism"; turmoil in the Philippines; a U.S. war against the Nicaraguan government and support of repressive regimes in the rest of Central America; a famine in Ethiopia; Afghanistan; the censorship of domestic and foreign journalists in South Africa and Israel.

The May and June 1989 repression in China's Tiananmen Square was given round-the-clock coverage, but not the fact that Henry Kissinger and other U.S. officials had hastened, in secret, to maintain relations with the regime. Nor did the media report the process, which took place over years, of selling the capital assets of the country – tractors and other farm machinery built by the Chinese people over four decades since the revolution – to pro-"Western" party officials and friends.

Although the Soviet invasion of Afghanistan was fully covered, not so well covered at the time was the repressive situation in Pakistan, the largest recipient in the world of U.S. military aid. Also not covered in the 1980s was the groundswell of tens of thousands of Canadians who personally visited Nicaragua and sent aid to it.

A year before Canada's 1988 federal election campaign, free trade with the United States had already been declared a tired, hopelessly complicated, and ultimately boring story with an inevitable outcome. CBC-Television's "Chief Political Correspondent" David Halton did not hide his lack of interest in the topic – then expressed surprise during the election when it became an issue, despite his pronouncements. Afterwards, the story sank into media oblivion, with an occasional item describing the "post free trade" era, although certain elements of the anti-free trade movement such as the church-sponsored GATT-Fly and some labour unions outlined and denounced the long-term disastrous effects of such a trade alliance on our economic ties with the Third World. By the close of the decade, the peace movement and the anti-free trade movement were being ignored, and the environment had become the issue of the day.

The 1990s opened with dramatic political changes in Eastern Europe, but saturation coverage of change in one country after another gave the bizarre impression that we had "seen it all before" on the previous night's TV report. The general anti-communist gloss to reporting passed for analysis, and news of a world debt crisis, not unrelated to the global militarization of economies, passed without comment. The February 1990 electoral defeat of Nicaragua's Sandinista leader Daniel Ortega was presented as part of the same "story," a lesson proving once again the failure of communist regimes (even though the governing Sandinista Party, the FSLN, was not communist and easily 60 per cent of the country's economy was in private hands). "Nicaraguans decisively slammed the book shut on the leftist revolution born here in 1979," proclaimed a Southam News correspondent, who characterized the election as a resounding defeat for Sandinista ideals and programs. [11] Yet the Sandinistas won 40 to 41 per cent of the popular vote (compared to the winning UNO party's 54 per cent) – a significantly higher percentage of the popular vote than the Progressive Conservative Party won in Canada's "landslide victory" for the Tories in 1988. [12] Meanwhile, in South Africa, the saturation press coverage of the release of Nelson Mandela neglected to mention that journalists were under censorship orders still in effect in that country.

The compartmentalization of stories results in a jumbled, disturbing but ultimately paralysing kaleidoscope of images, whether on TV, in magazines or newspapers, or at the movies. Ben Hecht says, "Trying to determine what is going on in the world by reading the newspaper is like trying to tell the time by watching the second hand of a clock." [13]

One "pocket doc" shows 15 seconds of riots in one part of the world ... another relays pictures of a hijacked airliner on a sweltering tarmack ... another brings heart-wrenching faces of starving children from somewhere in Africa ... a 45-second "live on location" report from International Monetary Fund meetings (whatever they are) suggests trouble. Ever so professionally, the media lurch from one issue to the next, carrying us in tow. Sooner or later we learn that the scope of human misery in the world today defies description, let alone comprehension, or explanation ... or action.

The vice-president of ABC programming explained how TV program decisions are made:

Program-makers are supposed to devise and produce shows that will attract mass audiences without unduly offending those audiences or too deeply moving them emotionally. Such ruffling, it is thought, will interfere with their ability to receive, recall, and respond to the commercial message. This programming reality is the unwritten, unspoken 'gemeinschaft' of all professional members of the television fraternity. [14]

The news format, with its friendly columnists and likeable anchors (CTV's "Trusted Tradition" with Lloyd Robertson), regular features or columns, a familiar signature of music and images, followed by familiar advertisements, map out the territory we pass through, steering us, defining and categorizing, reassuring and anaesthetizing. Without realizing it, we begin to share a consensus with those who give us the news.

PERSONIFICATION ... AND DISTORTION

In the mid-1980s, Penguin Books declared Winnie Mandela the "mother of the black people of South Africa ... the incarnation of the black spirit of the South African people." [15] When by 1989 the "incarnation" was suspected of complicity in a murder, the press focused on this one individual and downplayed or ignored the growing opposition to the apartheid regime, which extended to significant portions of the White population. Massive, widespread Black opposition to the apartheid regime was now characterized as "deeply divided" as a result of the Winnie Mandela incident (as it may well have been).

Downplayed in the process were the issues that Canadian institutions could do something about, to help put an end to the larger crime of apartheid – for instance, stopping loans, enforcing a trade embargo, or initiating sports, entertainment, and tourist boycotts. Instead, the media dutifully reported the shocking news that Canadian trade with South Africa had increased 60 per cent from the previous year, despite the rhetoric in the finest Canadian tradition, and then promptly relegated the story to the back pages. Upon Nelson Mandela's 1990 release from prison, commentators searched hard (but unsuccessfully) to discover fissures between the world's most famous prisoner, his African National Congress party, and other members of the South African anti-apartheid movement.

WHO CARES?

Most of the estimated 12 to 14 million refugees in the world today have fled the terror of armed conflicts, leaving behind most if not all of their possessions, their mementos, their homes, their communities, their families, even their names and identities ... only to be subjected to filth, disease, intimidation, rape (especially for the majority, women and girls), and even "disappearances" in refugee camps. Do Canadians care?

Of course we do. The active involvement of tens of thousands of Canadians in providing relief and opposing repressive immigration policies is only one measure of this concern. But according to a CBC *Journal* report of a poll conducted by the firm Environics, 50 per cent of Canadians opposed political refugees coming into the country. [16]

According to the way another poll was interpreted – this one by *Maclean's / Decima* – "The country has become more hardhearted and less virtuous." [17] In a

New Year's feature article setting the tone for the year, *Maclean's* magazine declared, "Canada's baby boom generation – the largest segment of Canadian society – is rapidly abandoning its former idealism." The people who protested against the Vietnam War, it stated, "are more likely to rally against group homes in their neighbourhood." *Maclean's* quoted a sociologist who allowed that Canadians still have concerns about "Third World poverty and so on" but are "overloaded with immediate concerns." [18]

The article's subhead "The Issues are Closer to Home" leaves the impression that opposition to war and concern about "Third World poverty" have slipped in importance in Canadians' hearts and minds. It suggests that peace and justice issues are not linked to "home" issues. This is of course what some want others to believe – or want to believe themselves (it is after all easier to live comfortably making compromises if one believes that others are doing the same). But it's not what the sociologist who was quoted meant. A second reading of the article's sentences – and qualifying phrases within the sentences – makes us wonder if the statements were taken in context:

Observers of social patterns say that the link between parenthood and a hardening of outlook among the baby boom generation is significant. "It is not that people do not have concerns about Third World poverty and so on," said Bruce O'Hara, a sociologist with Work Well, a research centre in Victoria. "But they are overloaded with immediate concerns." O'Hara noted that two-career couples face combined work schedules of at least 60 hours a week. As a result, he said, "the increased work load per family has left less time for idealistic pursuits. A lot of the fullness of life has been gutted." Clearly, many poll respondents of all ages share the perception that the country has become more hardhearted and less virtuous.

The sociologist later confirmed in a phone interview that his words were quoted correctly, but that the overall context in which they were placed led to a conclusion he did not agree with. He and his firm are concerned with the fact that employment today can easily consume up to 75 hours a week. His book, *Put Work in Its Place*, attempts to do something about it. He does not think people care less or have lost their ideals.

When people flip through *Maclean's* in doctors' offices and beauty parlours or at home – or even when they use it as a source in social studies classes at school – they do not stop to analyse every sentence. They do not track down those interviewed, phoning long-distance to find out if the quotes are accurate and in an appropriate context. They don't have personal contact with many of the able but frustrated journalists whose well researched stories are regularly reduced to shreds. Casual readers – who are the majority of readers – simply get a general impression of the news together with some new bits of information that will find their way into a worldview created in part by the very magazines they read.

How valuable is this general impression that is left in a reader's mind? You can get an idea by reading what "Canada's National Newsmagazine" has said in pitches to prospective advertisers. It's "the medium that makes your message news," says one *Maclean's* ad. [19] "The investment is paying off," says another, "for us and our advertisers": "When you advertise in Maclean's, you're investing in an environment where nothing is passive, where the relationship between writer and reader hinges on issues of importance, on a sense of urgency, a promise of *the news that matters*." [20] The news that matters is served up by "the country's most interesting columnists," who cover "the world's most fascinating people." [21] Occasionally a "fascinating person" emerges from the world's poorer nations – for example, Nicaragua's Sandinista leader Daniel Ortega ("witty, charming, even funny at times"), interviewed in a rare cover story on Central America published in 1987. [22] The inside articles, despite limitations of style and format, prove that it is possible to do independent Canadian reporting on Central America, and – what is rarely done – even mention the widespread Canadian support for Nicaragua. But this *Maclean's* issue truly was the exception that proved the rule, as a look at subsequent issues shows.

Of the 51 *Maclean's* issues that appeared in 1988, for example, only 10 had cover stories on international topics (five about Gorbachev or the Eastern block, two about the Middle East, one on global religious warfare, another on Northern Ireland, and one on the "Big Seven" economic summit in Toronto). There were cover stories on John Lennon, Crocodile Dundee, Karen Kain, Nostalgia, the Olympics (six), Ben Johnson (two), Wayne Gretzky (two), home ownership, baseball, cars, and many other topics, but not one cover story was dedicated to "Third World" countries or concerns. There was a year-later follow-up story on Canadian tastes – but no follow-up cover on Nicaragua or Central America.

Of the hundreds of potential cover stories in 1988 from the Third World that didn't rate: Panama's President General Manuel Noriega, indicted in February by a U.S. jury for international drug dealing (alternatively, *Maclean's* could have covered the ensuing political and economic upheaval in Panama); a June strike by two million Black South Africans; the August slaying in Burundi of 5,000 defenceless people by the army; Hurricane Gilbert in September which left hundreds dead and a million homeless in the Caribbean and Mexico; the flooding in the same month of three-quarters of Bangladesh, leaving at least 900 dead and 25 million homeless; the October Hurricane Joan which devastated five Central American countries, leaving Nicaragua, already staggering under a U.S.-imposed trade blockade and war, with a third of its population homeless and its hospitals, schools, and infrastructure destroyed.

"News and advertising have a lot in common," *Maclean's* says to potential advertisers. "In *Maclean's,* news and advertising have established a unique bond: readers buy us because they have an appetite for both…. You want to reach an affluent market. We've got it.... We've got the medium; you've got the message."[23] The messages are: drink Bacardi rum, Gibson's whisky, Smirnoff vodka – but do drink sensibly won't you? (Seagram's Distilleries); drive Ford cars, Toyota cars, Audis, Jaguars, Oldsmobiles. These commercial messages are not contradicted by the news stories because the news stories do not define as "news," for example, the fact that motor vehicle accidents are the leading cause of accidental death in Canada. Millions of people around the world die in excruciating pain each year in preventable automobile accidents, but this is not news. Nor is it news that tobacco kills about 2.5 million people each year, or that world-wide consumption is still increasing. Though 40,000 Canadians each year are diagnosed as having congestive heart failure, this is not "news": Why would a publication that defines itself as the "medium" for commercial messages assign reporters to a story that will follow a short path to the major contributing factors to the disease: processed foods, alcohol, tobacco, little or no exercise. The messages are: Remain a spectator; participate by consuming.[24]

A magazine with Wayne Gretzky on its cover is easier to sell than one featuring a story on Canada's economy or the world debt, the militarization of the world economy, rural and urban crises around the world, working conditions in "special economic zones" or the international exchange of expertise on torture techniques. Demographics and marketing – not some higher principle of journalistic merit – determine what you see on the newsstand. This is why if we want to hold *informed*, critical views, we have to read the entire magazine, especially the cover, as if it were an advertisement; to remember that readers are defined as consumers and spectators, not as critical, knowledgeable participants in the affairs of the day.

Writing about how uncommon it is to find journalists who dig out stories and fight for them to be published, Walter Stewart says that "investigative" journalists are seen within the business as "freaks, oddballs, misfits. Even at the *Washington Post,* they were regarded as abnormal. And so they were.... I know journalists who have operated with great success for three decades or more without ever doing a bit of work that could be called investigative with a capital I. They are the norm."[25]

FREE ENTERPRISE ALIVE AND WELL

A full-page ad jointly published by *The Globe and Mail* and CARE Canada stated that the "free enterprise system is alive and well in the Third World." The text – accompanying a picture of a smiling Peruvian – assured readers that if only generous Canadians sent drill presses or welding torches to Peru, the Latin Americans could start "contributing to the economy, not being a drain on it."

"We want your tools, not your money," the ad said. What comforting news. Business leaders and professionals alike can do their part by supporting the newspaper and charity, and everyone's personal priorities, political views, and spending habits can remain intact. The world's problems are only technical, not

285

economic or political. Given this optimistic perspective, solutions are simple too: practical, small-scale, and, best of all, quite feasible within the "free enterprise" system. Never mind that the free enterprise system of international banking and high finance created Peru's $15.4 billion foreign debt in the first place.

Photos of smiling "Third World" people would be positive in other contexts, a healthy change from the pathetic images presented by certain charities and the media. But when an ad praises the current international economic system, such images are perverse. Cutbacks in food subsidies to the poor are one of the many measures required by the International Monetary Fund (IMF), resulting in high levels of infant deaths, and mental retardation for those who survive. Between March 1988 and February 1989, prices in Peru increased by 2,933 per cent. The free enterprise system may indeed be "alive and well" there, but a lot of people aren't. In the countryside, about half the children die before age three. Since 1980, in the chaotic situation created by this "free enterprise" system, over 15,000 people have died in political violence alone, including 202 mayors, prefects, governors, peasant leaders, and other authorities.

The prejudices and preconceptions of foreign readers are what the news media supply, according to *New Internationalist* editor Vanessa Baird. Different countries come to symbolize different things:

Chile "means" torture and tear gas; Brazil, debt and dam projects; Colombia, cocaine. So it took two years for journalists in Lima to get the British press to carry a story about a civil war being fought in Peru. Human rights abuses, disappearances, mass graves – none of these things could attract the attention of Western news editors. Why? asked a Lima-based reporter. "Well, we've been running stories on mass graves in Argentina," came the reply from the foreign news desk. Argentina, evidently, had come to "mean" mass graves, while Peru, presumably, still signified Incas and llamas. [26]

One might wonder how *The Globe and Mail*, flagship newspaper of the Thomson chain, the paper that describes itself as "Canada's newspaper of record" and has published some of the country's most carefully researched articles on the Third World, could associate itself in an ad with views that appear at best naive and fuzzy-headed.

This is less puzzling given what apparently excites *Globe and Mail* publisher A. Roy Megarry about another Canadian charity with operations in Peru, among other countries: "I love it. Calmeadow cuts through the red tape."[27] Thanks to all the major Canadian banks, Peruvian peasants and the landless who participate in the country's "informal" (that is, underground, survival) economy can cut through red tape and join the cash and credit / debt economy through small-scale loans at commercial rates.

"It's the cutting edge," says John Cleghorn, president of the Royal Bank of

Canada and old friend of the charity's founder, Conwest's Martin Connell. With a 2 per cent default rate in loans, this kind of charity is hard to beat. Unlike corporations, the poor pay back their loans. Over one-third of the country's potential Gross National Product (GNP) is estimated to be generated by the informal economy.

Peruvian economist Hernando de Soto, adviser to the Canadian charity, "sees this uncharted labour force as the creative and spontaneous response of poor people to government's inability or unwillingness to respond to their basic needs. If brought into the system ... they could provide a huge source of economic energy."[28] No need for concerned Canadians to challenge the inhuman austerity demands made by the IMF and World Bank for the *big* loans to Peru – just start a new, upbeat program for the victims. Such market possibilities. An estimated *150 million* Latin Americans living below the poverty line are potential candidates.[29]

For that matter, no need for concerned Canadians to know much at all about the effects of IMF austerity measures. The optimism of a *Globe and Mail* / CARE ad might have contrasted at times with news and feature items in the same paper, but this contradictory situation may not continue much longer at *The Globe and Mail*. Early in the 1980s the newspaper's publisher articulated its editorial objectives: "By 1990, publishers of mass circulation daily newspapers will finally stop kidding themselves that they are in the newspaper business and admit that they are primarily in the business of carrying advertising messages."[30]

In any case, "concerned Canadians" are not *The Globe and Mail's* target readership. According to one of the newspaper's bids to potential advertisers:

Research has long confirmed that *Report on Business* is the most effective way of reaching the business and government elite of Canada.... What is not so commonly realized is that our managerial / professional reach exceeds the *combined* reach of *The New York Times* and *The Wall Street Journal* into the equivalent managerial / professional market in the United States.[31]

Boasting that in Canada, "We reach Canada's business elite even better," *The Globe and Mail* says that on any given day the "Report on Business" is read by "over 85 per cent of Canada's top decision-makers: the chairmen, presidents and senior officials in every major sector of Canadian business, industry and government."

If Canada's elite is the target for *The Globe and Mail*, who else does the Thomson chain serve? Here is how the chain presents the rest of us to advertisers: "If it's women you want, you can have them. Men too. On any given day, one insertion in daily newspapers will introduce you to more than 60 percent of all Canadian adults.... Newspapers are designed to let you reach a variety of specific target markets. So there's no waste."[32]

POWER AND THE PURSUIT OF PROFIT

The images Canadians have of the rest of the world (and to a large extent of ourselves) tend to come from the mass media, not from direct experience. The distortions created by this situation are multiple, the most important being those that arise naturally when the media represent the interests of a very restricted group of owners. This tiny group directly or indirectly serves its own interests, not the interests of most Canadians, and certainly not those of "Third World" peoples.

The thousands of businesses, product lines, labels, and company logos in advertising or in shopping malls give the false impression that Canada is buzzing with competition and free enterprise. In actual fact, Canada has one of the highest degrees of concentrated corporate power in the world. Various laws, regulations, royal commissions, special Senate committees and parliamentary task forces have done little if anything to stop such an accumulation of power, other than to bury some shocking figures in a mountain of reports. One technical paper, for example, contained figures showing that 0.02 per cent of Canadian companies accounted for 35 per cent of all sales in Canada.[33] In 1986 large corporations accounted for 72 per cent of all non-financial assets in the country, 53 per cent of all sales, and 65 per cent of all profits. The leading 500 companies controlled 65.5 per cent of corporate assets, 50.4 per cent of all sales, and 63.3 per cent of profits. The next largest 500 controlled a mere 4.5 per cent of corporate assets, 5.3 per cent of sales, and a mere 4.8 per cent of profits.[34]

The control of these companies is even more extensive when the kind of ownership is taken into account. Over 60 per cent of the 300 or so listings on the Toronto Stock Exchange (TSE) are closely held companies, belonging to a tiny handful of Canadians (compared to about 16 per cent similarly closely held companies in the Standard and Poor register of the top 500 U.S. companies).[35]

For the most part Canadians are unaware of this situation and its implications, not in small measure because their main information sources – the mass media – are themselves among the mostly highly concentrated industries in Canada. *Over 90 per cent* of all media are group-owned in Canada; the two chains of Thomson and Southam control most of the daily newspapers across the country.[36]

The corporate elite that controls Canada's media is linked to other power elites. According to sociologist Wallace Clement, "Not only do the media elite coincide as overlapping social circles and have common class backgrounds with the economic elite, they are in very large part identical people."[37] At least as powerful as Parliament, this unelected group makes the business and investment decisions that shape the economic, political, and cultural future of Canada, and of any other country that receives Canadian investment.

It is in the business interests of this restricted group to view information, insight, research, creativity – cultural activity of all kinds – as it views other products: as commodities. The privatization of services, including information services, along with corporate sponsorship of academic research, has all but ensured a community of thought unlikely to challenge the existing unequal distribution of wealth and power. This is no conspiracy, however. As author Peter Newman observes, those in Canada's power elite "think the same way *naturally*. They don't *need* to conspire, because their ideas mesh without their having to consult one another to weigh motives. They recognize so few conflicts of interest, in short, because their interests seldom conflict."[38]

The negative effects on the actual content of news or entertainment caused by restricted media ownership and heavy reliance on advertising for revenues, according to the Special Senate Committee on Mass Media, include "an atmosphere in which editorial initiatives are unwelcome. People who want to practise vigorous, independent journalism do not thrive in such an atmosphere."[39]

Testifying before the Senate Committee, advertising executive Jerry Goodis described the effects of this approach:

The measure of editorial acceptability becomes 'How does it fit?' or 'Will it interest the affluent?' As a consequence, the mass media increasingly reflect the attitudes and deal with the concerns of the affluent. We don't have mass media, we have class media – media for the upper and middle classes.

The poor, the young, the old, the Indian, the Eskimo, the blacks, are virtually ignored. It is as if they don't exist. More important, these minority groups are denied expression in the mass media because they cannot command attention as the affluent can.[40]

The goals and messages of the mass media – from Saturday-morning cartoons to the questions asked in opinion polls – are determined in the final analysis by advertisers and owners, not by some higher Quest for Truth or Freedom. While the giant U.S. newspaper chain Gannett sponsored ads championing Freedom of the Press, its president was quoted elsewhere. "Basically we respond to our reader studies," he said. "Whatever diet the readers want, we custom tailor the paper for that diet.... That's no great practice of journalism, but it's what the readers want."[41] While Gannett is the largest U.S.-owned chain selling newspapers in the United States, the largest chain of 116 daily newspapers belongs to the Canadian-owned Thomson group. The chain's founder, Roy Thomson, has stated his own lofty editorial objectives: "I buy newspapers to make money to buy more newspapers to make more money."[42] This cheerful corporate philosophy has taken the company far.

Thomson's bright and dynamic management did not hestitate to use layoffs, combined with other cost-cutting editorial policies, to make the company one of the top ten world media empires, publishing 23,000 trade, professional, and educational products. It is also the world's largest publisher of military information.

But Thomson's simple pursuit of profit seems positively benign in comparison with the editorial views of another Canadian press baron. The Canadian financier Conrad Black, who owns 207 newspapers, including Britain's London *Daily Telegraph,* proudly associates himself with "a renascent intellectual right, rigorous and articulate."[43] Black condemns not the military-industrial complex (as did former U.S. President Dwight Eisenhower), but an "academic-journalistic complex" of ne'er-do-wells. He says, "Journalism tends to attract the sort of person who settles whimsically on it as a calling or comes to it after disappointments elsewhere."[44] To be more precise, investigative journalists are, in his words, "swarming, grunting masses of jackals." In the words of Britain's employment secretary, the Canadian's "forcefulness and energy," particularly his "modern management techniques" (which include strike-breaking and lay-offs) reportedly won the admiration of former British prime minister Margaret Thatcher. "I like Conrad Black," the employment secretary quotes Thatcher as saying. "He makes me feel positively 'wet' in comparison."[45]

Canadians are generally aware of the "Ugly American" image of the United States at home and abroad but, thanks largely to the way our media operate, we have little sense of our own role in perpetuating poverty and exploitation throughout the world: our quiet complicity with British, French, American, German, Japanese, or other interests or in our own dealings with business and government under such repressive regimes as those of Indonesia, South Korea, Brazil, Romania, Iran, Iraq, or Chile. On the contrary, in *Saturday Night* (owned by Conrad Black), David Frum tells readers that the greatest Canadian contribution to the development of a poor country was made "not by foreign aid or young idealists" but by the Canadian founders of Brazilian Traction, Light and Power Co. Frum says the greed of the Toronto businessmen from nearly a hundred years ago "did more for a backward nation than charity ever dreamt of."[46]

Facing up to uncomfortable realities about ourselves, our history, and the rest of the world need not be a disillusioning and lonely experience. The media are powerful forces of social control, but organized, well informed people who can think for themselves are powerful forces for change. Organized people can demand better of their own media outlets. We can refuse to be portrayed (or see others portrayed) as passive "victims" or even as active "consumers." We can demand to be portrayed as *citizens,* who need not consume anything for the right to be heard. We can seek out alternative sources of information, and develop critical skills in evaluating information sources and the packaging of information and ideas.

We must re-examine institutions we take for granted as well as some of our fundamental ideas, including criteria for authority and credibility, and notions of "objectivity." There is no need and no room for critical, "media-literate" people to feel superior because of their insights, or cynical, isolated, depressed, or overwhelmed by the enormity of community and world poverty, waste, and injustice.

The media are powerful sources of social control, but organized people are powerful sources for social change. In our very act of organizing, though, we need to work towards not just a shift in power but also a profound *change* in social, economic, and other relations. Our analysis and actions must recognize something that the media continue to obscure: that the problems and struggles surrounding a myriad of issues – such as ecology, development, peace, human rights, aboriginal title, women's rights, poverty, racism, unemployment, ill-health – are both local and global, and are essentially struggles over the distribution of power and resources, and over the values and meanings we assign to them.

Such an analysis will be informed and inspired by concrete acts of solidarity that we and others make in everyday life. The decisive, historical moment in which to reflect and to act is always the present.

Notes

1. News, information, commmunications, and entertainment media are not discussed separately in this article. Such distinctions are less relevant today, given concentrated corporate power and shared communication techniques. Canadian, U.S., and other media are also discussed interchangeably, as are "domestic" and "international" issues, because that is how we experience them in everyday life.

2. Canadian Media Directors' Council, *Media Digest,* 1986 / 87, p.19.

3. Jerry Mander, *Four Arguments for the Elimination of Television* (New York: Morrow Quill Paperbacks, 1978), p.256. Don't let the title or the name of the author deter you from reading this essential work.

4. Women's Bureau, *When I Grow Up ... Career Expectations and Aspirations of Canadian Children* (Ottawa: Labour Canada, 1988). Among the responses of children: "Boys couldn't become nurses ... because they're not girls and they don't wear dresses." "Maybe a nurse is just a name for a girl ... and doctor is a name for a boy?" (p.15).

5. *Report of the Taskforce on Broadcasting Policy* (Ottawa: Minister of Supply and Services, 1986), p.691.

6. Flora MacDonald, Minister of Communications, Victoria, B.C., February 9, 1985, quoted in *Voices of Concern: The Future of Canadian Broadcasting: Report on a Series of Eleven Public Forums* (Toronto: Canadian Association for Adult Education, [1987]), p.12.

7. Winnipeg forum on public broadcasting, March 25, 1985, in *Voices of Concern,* p.41.

8. Peter O'Malley, "Media Coverage of International Affairs," *Learning,* Vol.IV, No.4 (1987), p.13.

9. Audit Bureau of Canada and Canadian Advertising Rates and Data figures cited in *The Canadian World Almanac & Book of Facts 1990* (Toronto: Global Press, 1989), p.560.

10. Donald Lazere (ed.), *American Media and Mass Culture* (Berkeley: University of California Press, 1987), p.11.

11. Les Whittington, *Vancouver Sun*, February 27, 1990, p.A3.

12. In the election the *popular* vote was won by the NDP at 36.7 per cent, the Progressive Conservatives came second with 35.2 per cent, the Liberals third with 20.3 per cent, and other parties and independents got 7.8 per cent.

13. Quoted in Robert Cirino, *Don't Blame the People* (New York: Random House, 1971), p.134.

14. Cited in Joyce Nelson, *The Perfect Machine: TV in the Nuclear Age* (Toronto: Between The Lines, 1987); original source is Bob Shanks, "Network Television: Advertising Agencies and Sponsors," in John Wright (ed.), *The Commercial Connection* (New York: Dell, 1979), p.94.

15. Cover promotion for *Winnie Mandela: Part of My Soul* (Harmondsworth, Middlesex: Penguin Books, 1984).

16. *The Journal*, CBC Television, October 26, 1988.

17. "A Retreat from Ideals," *Maclean's* (cover story), January 2, 1989.

18. Ibid., p.36.

19. *Marketing*, January 27, 1986.

20. *Maclean's* ad in *The Financial Post* (Toronto), December 2, 1978.

21. *Marketing*, January 27, 1986.

22. *Maclean's*, February 23, 1987.

23. *Maclean's* ad in *The Financial Post* (Toronto), September 1979.

24. Ads cited were sampled from the June 13, 1988, *Maclean's*. For mortality figures related to road deaths, see *Canadian World Almanac*, pp. 89-90,410.

25. Walter Stewart, "The Seven Myths of Journalism," in David Staines (ed.), *The Forty-Ninth and Other Parallels: Contemporary Canadian Perspectives* (Amherst: University of Massachusetts Press, 1986), pp.104,105.

26. *The New Internationalist*, July 1989, p.1. *The Globe and Mail* ad from July 6, 1988. The ad was frequently re-run. Inflation figures from *The Andean Report*, cited in *The New Internationalist*, p.17. Figures on political deaths from Peru's own Ministry of the Interior, quoted in *The New Internationalist*, p.16.

27. "The Patron Saint of Pragmatism," *The Financial Times of Canada*, December 4, 1989, p.20.

28. Ibid., p.20.

29. Estimate of those working in the "informal" sector in Latin America from Sue Branford and Bernardo Kucinski, *The Debt Squads: The U.S., the Banks and Latin America* (London: Zed Books, 1988), p.30.

30. *Editor and Publisher,* April 10, 1982, p.48; cited in Ben Bagdikian, *The Media Monopoly* (Boston: Beacon Press, 1982), p.197.

31. *The Globe and Mail,* January 28, 1989, p.A12.

32. Thomson newspapers ad in *Canadian Advertising Rates and Data,* March 1987.

33. See Christian Marfels, *Concentration Levels and Trends in the Canadian Economy, 1965-73,* Royal Commission on Corporate Concentration Technical Report No.31 (Ottawa: Minister of Supply and Services, 1977), p.xix.

34. The definition of a large corporation was one with $25 million or more in corporate assets. Corporations and Labour Returns Act (CALURA), Statistics Canada Cat. 61-210, Ottawa, December 1988, pp.24,30.

35. Rowland Lorimer and Jean McNulty, *Mass Communication in Canada* (Toronto: McClelland and Stewart, 1987), p.167.

36. A researcher for the Senate Committee on Mass Media said six years after its study: "We warned that concentration of media ownership was increasing, and could constitute a threat to freedom of expression. When we wrote that, 66 per cent of the nation's media outlets were owned by chains or groups; today the figure is 90 per cent." (Alexander Ross, "The Davey Report: A Case Where the Medium Really Was the Message," *The Financial Post of Canada,* May 1, 1976, p.S18.) Regarding media takeovers, the Special Senate Committee on Mass Media noted, "On no known occasion in Canada have the joint resources of the Combines and Investigation Branch and the Restrictive Trade Practices Commission prevented a newspaper sale, consolidation or merger." (*Words, Music, and Dollars: Report of the Special Senate Committee on Mass Media,* vol.2 [Ottawa: Information Canada, 1970], p.422.)

37. Wallace Clement, *The Canadian Corporate Elite* (Toronto: McClelland and Stewart, 1975), p.341.

38. Peter Newman (ed.), *Debrett's Illustrated Guide to the Canadian Establishment* (Agincourt: Methuen, 1983), p.13.

39. *The Uncertain Mirror: Report of the Special Senate Committee on Mass Media,* vol.1 (Ottawa: Information Canada, 1970), p.90.

40. Special Senate Committee on Mass Media, *Proceedings,* No.21 (February 18, 1970), p.10.

41. Gannett President Al Newharth interviewed in *Working Papers for a New Society,* July 1979; Gannett's slogan: "A world of different voices where freedom speaks." See the chapter on this important chain in Bagdikian, *Media Monopoly.*

42. Lord Thomson of Fleet, quoted in *Time,* August 15, 1977, p.47.

43. Address to the spring convocation of the faculties of business and humanities at McMaster University, reported in *The Globe and Mail,* June 7, 1979, p.8.

44. Conrad Black, "A Black View of the Press," in *Carleton Journalism Review,* Vol.2, No.4 (Winter 1979–80).

45. Jackal quote from *Maclean's,* July 17, 1989, p.28. Thatcher quote in Wallace Clement, *The Challenge of Class Analysis* (Ottawa: Carleton University Press, 1988), p.5.

46. "Gringo Business," *Saturday Night* (book review), December 1988.

TEN

Manufacturing Legitimacy: Ideology, Politics, and Third World Foreign Policy

Anton L. Allahar

CANADA'S OFFICIAL foreign policy towards the countries of Asia, Africa, and Latin America has always been consistent. Over the years it has been consistent in ideology, in the framework of choices that govern policy. It has never strayed far off a beaten ideological path. It has been consistently vague and consistently supportive of U.S. foreign policy on key political and economic issues, much to the detriment of most people living in the Third World. It has been consistently at one with the other nations of the "North" in their relations with the "South."

This is not to say that Canada's international profile is, or has been, a negative one. Quite the opposite: Canada has often been seen as a humane force in world affairs, a "peacemaker," a "middle power" that plays a conciliatory role, a bridge between rich and poor nations. It has often appeared to be "progressive" or supportive of significant change for the better. This was especially true in the 1980s when, led by its former United Nations ambassador Stephen Lewis, the country took up independent positions, to the extent that it was free to do so, on the questions of apartheid in South Africa, contra aid, and world peace in general.

Canada's profile on foreign aid has also been generally positive. In 1988 the president of the Canadian International Development Agency (CIDA) noted that Canadian aid topped U.S. $2.3 billion. Among the ventures targeted were "about 1000 Canadian-sponsored bilateral projects, 4000 projects sponsored by churches and other non-governmental organizations (NGOs), unions and universities, 400 food aid projects, 100 disaster relief projects, and hundreds of initiatives to develop links between Canadian and Third World businesses."[1] This picture of the Canadian foreign presence is beyond dispute (though open to the questions raised here and in other chapters of this book).

Nevertheless, there is a shadow side to Canada's political and economic involvement in some parts of the Third World. If you look behind the rhetoric of officialdom and assess the concrete positions and actions underlying Canadian involvement – if you compare what Canada says with what Canada does – you get quite a different picture. You find that the formulation of official Canadian policy and the Canadian approaches to the Third World are rooted in an often hidden agenda or ideology that has a distinct bearing on the political choices made. You find that often, too, the rhetoric is quite distinct from the action.

On this score the exchanges between Canadian prime minister Brian Mulroney and British prime minister Margaret Thatcher at the Commonwealth Conference in Kuala Lumpur, Malaysia, in October 1989 were highly ironic. Mulroney reportedly spearheaded a verbal attack against Thatcher who, he said, was speaking out of both sides of her mouth on the issue of apartheid in South Africa. Specifically, Mulroney criticized his British counterpart for signing a resolution supporting continued sanctions against South Africa and then for reversing herself an hour later when she issued her own public statement announcing her opposition to any form of sanctions. Stephen Lewis later joined in, calling Thatcher's actions "ideologically bizarre."

For her part, Thatcher was quick to point out that in spite of Canada's noble claims, the country's trade with South Africa had been steadily increasing over the years, up to and including the present. Figures from Statistics Canada supported Thatcher on this: Canada's imports from South Africa had a small increase from $155,389,000 in 1987 to $156,648,000 in 1988; our exports to South Africa jumped from $113,170 in 1987 to $124,457 in 1988.[2]

The point is that both Canada and Britain are capitalist countries with economies that benefit from apartheid and its associated ills, some of which are very few and very weak labour unions, low wages, high unemployment, and a generally stable investment climate. Perhaps unwittingly, then, Thatcher is implying – correctly – that the economic similarities between Canada and Britain far outweigh their political differences over apartheid. What unites these two countries is their fundamental practical commitment to the economic ideology of free enterprise capitalism, which is not necessarily incompatible with the political ideologies of liberal democracy, fascism, or dictatorship. Canada and Britain routinely do business with fascistic and dictatorial governments. In fact, over the years they have even been known to install and / or maintain them in power. For a long time – until it started finally to show signs of crumbling in the late 1980s – apartheid had simply been another political arrangement for the realization of huge corporate profits.

IDEOLOGY: A DEFINITION

What exactly is the meaning of the term ideology as it is used here? Quite simply, an ideology may be viewed as a pair of glasses through which we see the world of social reality. But unlike spectacles, of which people usually have one pair if they have them at all, ideologies are many. An individual will simultaneously hold economic, political, religious, social, racial, and gender ideologies. For example, it is common in Canada or Britain for someone to embrace the economic ideology of free trade, the political ideology of liberal democracy, the religious ideology of Christianity, the racial ideology of white supremacy, and the gender ideology of male superiority – all at the same time. These ideologies are not necessarily contradictory. On the other hand, we can consider the ideologies of socialism, black power, and feminism as rivalling those of capitalism, white power, and patriarchy. Each of these, whether individually or combined, contains elements that appeal to the *interests* of the various individuals, groups, and organizations that make up society.

People acquire ideologies as part of the normal process of living in a given society and culture. Ideologies are transmitted during the process of socialization and often have many agents: parents, teachers, religious teachers, political leaders, the media, sports and entertainment personnel, and other people who are viewed as significant either by the society as a whole or by a given individual. Ideologies, therefore, embody the beliefs, ideas, values, and preferences of groups, classes, regions, cultures, or even entire nations.

For these reasons I have argued that ideologies are effective socio-political weapons.[3] They seek to simplify certain aspects of social reality while masking other aspects of it. In the process the perception of social reality is itself distorted. For example, when describing Canada as a democratic society, we can correctly point to a variety of liberal freedoms, the electoral process, the multi-party political system, and so on. But what we do not typically point out are the undemocratic features of the society: the existence of widespread poverty in certain areas, the unfair treatment of Native peoples, institutionalized racism and sexism, or unequal educational and occupational opportunities according to class. We almost never hear of Canada's role in recognizing and supporting non-democratic governments around the world. For while there may be democracy at home, Canada also has connections with dictatorships abroad.

Then there is the relationship between ideology and social control. As a mechanism of social control, ideology can prove highly effective in the hands of the ruling class (which, for instance, controls the media and the educational system) when it is made to distract people from gaining a clear understanding of their problems and from envisaging possible solutions. Take, for example, the ideologies of racism and sexism that serve to divide workers and distract them from realizing the common source of their oppression and exploitation; or the ideology of national-ism, which can superficially unite and mobilize the majority of people in a given nation against an external enemy, while blinding them to the internal class divi-sions that characterize their own country and are at the root of their problems.

The dominant ideology in a country such as Canada, therefore, must be under-stood as the creation of a concrete set of political and economic interests linked to the dominant classes. Throughout its history the ruling class has used the ideolo-gies of race, ethnicity, nationalism, language, gender, and class, individually and in combination, to pursue its interests both locally and abroad. Especially in the Third World, Canada's position as a key member of the Western capitalist alliance has witnessed far more co-operation with countries such as Britain and the United States than conflict of the type that surfaced in Kuala Lumpur in October 1989. On matters of foreign policy in the Third World, Canada's track record has been consistently that of a developed, exploiting, imperialist nation, even if its leaders wish it to be perceived differently.

THE CANADIAN-U.S. CONNECTION

Any study of Canadian involvement in the Third World must begin by focusing on the wider context of Canadian relations with the United States. Canada, as an independent nation, maintains the principles and ideals of an independent foreign policy. Yet its policy decisions also have the same limitations that any nation among nations has. It also holds many of the same foreign-policy interests as other nations, especially the United States, and this common interest helps to determine policy. As part of the NATO and NORAD alliances, and as a leading member of the Western capitalist alliance, there is consistent pressure on Canada to help main-tain the dominant consensus, a pressure that militates against the country follow-ing a completely independent path, even if it wanted to.

The historical record of the last three decades is revealing. In the 1960s the Canadian government failed, for instance, to condemn the brutal U.S. invasion of the Dominican Republic. In the 1970s there was no official Canadian outcry against the U.S.-engineered overthrow of the democratically elected government of Chile.[4] In the 1980s Canada refused to take a stand at the United Nations on a resolution calling for the withdrawal of the U.S. troops that had invaded and occu-pied Grenada. Also, when evidence surfaced showing that the United States had killed over 4,000 Panamanians and buried them in mass graves following the December 1989 invasion of that country, the Canadian government was again silent.[5]

The issue of rhetoric versus action demands that Canadian foreign policy be understood both in terms of what Canada says and what Canada does. I am talking here about official Canadian government policy and not the feelings and actions of the Canadian public per se. For there are many private organizations and lobby groups that seek (often unsuccessfully) to influence foreign policy in directions other than those sanctioned by the U.S. government. It is precisely this "sandwiching" between external (U.S.) and internal (Canadian public) pressure that makes Canadian foreign policy appear to be so vague and so often shrouded in empty rhetoric.

At the same time Canada's foreign policy is not simply always and everywhere a faithful reflection of U.S. foreign policy. The Canadian government, unlike its U.S. counterpart, does not seek to depict all Third World conflicts as subordinate aspects of East-West tensions. The Canadian government took an independent path in refusing to go along with the U.S. embargo on Cuba from the 1960s on. Similarly, it fashioned economic and political links with the Sandinistas when they were in power in Nicaragua and it suspended aid to the U.S.-supported regime in Guatemala.

While these independent actions cannot be discounted, they have been referred to as the Canadian government's "traditional quiet deviations from U.S. policy." These deviations have also been "few and little publicized" by the government, as if it is not exactly proud of them. The deviations taken tend to only go so far and to avoid openly contradicting U.S. policy.[6] This is why there has never been an official government statement in Canada calling for the United States to get out of Cuba. It is not widely known in the first place that from 1959 to the present time U.S. marines have illegally occupied part of Cuba.[7]

On the question of Nicaragua and peace in the rest of Central America the Department of External Affairs told Canadians: "It has been the view of the government in Canada that a resolution of the difficulties in Central America requires a process of discussion, dialogue and reconciliation and that the Contadora group-sponsored meeting in Panama represented an important first step in that process."[8]

But the Canadian government has not spoken out against U.S. attempts to frustrate the peace process in Central America, and has not criticized the U.S. military and economic support for the repressive right-wing governments in El Salvador, Guatemala, and Honduras, much less broached the subject of U.S. support for regimes that give free rein to death squads. Further, in the specific case of Nicaragua, where the Sandinista government had been seeking legitimacy in the eyes of the international community, the secretary of state for external affairs, Joe Clark, announced on October 26, 1984, that "The Canadian government has decided to decline the invitation of the government of Nicaragua to send observers to the November 4th elections in that country."[9]

Clark was also quoted as saying, "Canada does not see the United States' objectives in Nicaragua as being widely different from ours."[10] This statement was wholly consistent with the remarks of Prime Minister Brian Mulroney in a speech to the Inter-American Press Association on September 15th, 1986: "In the past two years, Canada has sent observers to monitor elections in El Salvador, Honduras and Guatemala, and in each case their reports were highly positive." The governments of these three countries are firmly supported by the United States, while the government of Nicaragua is not.

It soon became clear that Canada declined to send observers to the elections in 1984 to avoid stepping on the U.S. toe. No sooner had the election results giving the Sandinistas a resounding victory been made public than the U.S. government began to denounce them as fraudulent. Playing his supportive role, Mulroney in the same speech to the Inter-American Press Association spoke about "grave civil rights violations in Nicaragua" and the regretful "extension of East-West disagreements into the area."

This confusing and contradictory stance was, again, consistent with a long line of such stances. In the same speech the prime minister went on to talk about the great job Canada had done in giving political asylum to refugees from Chile and Latin America generally. What Mulroney did not point out was that not too long after the overthrow of democracy in Chile the Canadian government (under Trudeau) recognized the dictatorship of Pinochet as the legitimate expression of the political will of the Chilean people. And that over one hundred thousand deaths and disappearances later, the Canadian government, now under Mulroney, continued to recognize and do business with the dictatorship. On the question of refugees, too, it was argued by the Latin American Working Group in Toronto that Canada had a "reluctant, slow and inadequate refugee program" when it came to Chile. [11]

Finally, and again on the matter of vague or confusing foreign policy, this time concerning Central America and the Caribbean, Secretary of State for External Affairs Mark MacGuigan stated:

I believe that the states in the region have the right to choose to follow whatever ideological path their peoples decide. I don't believe that when a people chooses a socialist or even a Marxist path it necessarily buys a "package" which automatically injects it into the Soviet orbit. This, I think, is where our views and those of the US may diverge. [12]

But not long after, in the House of Commons debates of October 27th, 1983, regarding Canada's reaction to the U.S. invasion of the tiny nation-state of Grenada, the Secretary of State for International Trade, Gerald Regan, confessed that: "The position of this government was that we were concerned about the political orientation of Grenada under the late PM Bishop since the coup of 1979 which overthrew the unpopular government of Sir Eric Gairy." [13]

In the same debate, still not willing to make a strong statement against the precipitous U.S. action, Gerald Regan took refuge in the British House of Commons debates of the previous day (October 26, 1983), citing Sir Geoffrey Howe: "The US took one view" said Howe, "the UK took another. It is no more for me to condemn them than it is for them to condemn us." Whereupon Regan added, "The Canadian position has been remarkably similar."

The inconsistency of the entire matter is to be found in the fact that Britain and Canada, two Commonwealth countries, did not come to the defence of Grenada, also a Commonwealth country, when it was invaded and occupied by the United States, a non-Commonwealth country. It was, therefore, hardly a surprise to anyone when a vote was taken at the United Nations on a resolution calling for the withdrawal of all foreign troops (which were predominantly U.S.) from Grenada, and Canada again toed the U.S. line. As its ambassador to the UN, Gérard Pelletier, explained:

We understand the concerns of our Caribbean friends over what was seen as developments in Grenada threatening the stability of the region. We understand, too, the concerns of the US over the welfare and safety of its citizens in the light of events leading to October 25th. This is a proper, indeed obligatory, concern of every government. [14]

Canada, through Pelletier, abstained on the UN vote. [15]

Actions such as this have earned Canada its reputation as an eager follower of the U.S. lead on foreign-policy issues. Indeed, it was precisely this lack of independent conviction that led writer Robert Chodos to the conclusion that Canada's Department of National Defence is so closely tied to the Pentagon that it is best understood as a minor branch of it. For to condemn Iraq's summer 1990 invasion and occupation of Kuwait as brutal and monstrous is fair and proper; but to say nothing of Israel's invasion and occupation of the West Bank, the Gaza Strip, and the Golan Heights is hypocritical, and smacks of a lack of political will and integrity. Canada has more to lose politically from alienating the Arab nations than from alienating Israel. Why then is the government so consistently supportive of U.S. interests (Israel) in the Middle East?

Chodos underlined the vacuous rhetoric that has characterized almost all External Affairs discussions of foreign policy, and raised two questions that are bound to anger both Canadian nationalists and non-nationalists alike: "After all, does Canada really need a foreign policy? And if it had a foreign policy, what would Canada do with it?" [16]

POLITICS AND INDEPENDENCE
IN FOREIGN-POLICY DEALINGS

Up to this point the argument being developed here is problematic only if one wishes to make the case that Canada's foreign policy is independent of its membership in a wider community of economic and political interests. But while this might be so for the United States, historically speaking it has not been true for

Canada. In April 1986, when the U.S. government decided to bomb Libya, it carried out the undertaking in spite of the fact that its closest allies, Canada included, had strongly opposed any such action as unwise and unwarranted.[17] Even in the case of Grenada, three years earlier, the United States did not consult key allies such as Canada before the invasion – a situation that led to grave embarrassment for the Canadian government but did not produce any open condemnation of the U.S. intervention.

U.S. foreign policy thus appears to have an independence or autonomy to a degree and in a way lacking in Canadian policy. There have been few if any instances involving major international disputes, recently or even since Confederation, in which Canada pursued a course of action that went counter to the expressed wishes of the United States. Even on such comparatively minor matters as the politics of international sport Canada has waited for the U.S. cue. Canada boycotted the 1980 Olympic Games in Moscow after the U.S. government announced it would not attend owing to the Soviet invasion of Afghanistan. But Canada did not boycott the 1984 Olympic Games in Los Angeles when many Third World countries called for a boycott due to the U.S. invasion of and military presence in Grenada.

If, on the other hand, we acknowledge the fact that Canada is not an independent actor on the stage of world politics, the argument presented thus far is unproblematic. Presiding as it does over the affairs of a capitalist economy, which is part of a larger, international capitalist system, the Canadian government understandably tends to act in the interests of that wider system. Indeed, that wider interest often complements Canada's particular interests, and so what may appear as a lack of independence in foreign policy could well be interpreted as political farsightedness. For it could be argued that the capitalist state in Canada, while having an immediate responsibility to the Canadian capitalist class, has as a prime responsibility the preservation of the international capitalist system per se.[18]

Therefore, if torn between a damaging, public condemnation of capitalist United States and a principled stand in support of socialist Cuba or revolutionary Nicaragua, Canada's political and economic well-being dictates the use of tact and diplomacy. In other words, ideological considerations come to the fore, and a condemnation turns either into a mild "exchange" between foreign ministers, or a particular handling of an incident never does become public. Compare the Canadian government's open outcry against the Soviet downing of Korean flight KAL 007 on September 1, 1983, in which 269 lives were lost, and its virtual silence over the U.S. downing of the Iranian air bus flight 655 on July 3, 1988, in which 290 lives were lost. These different responses are not mere coincidences or ironies but, rather, point to the political and ideological choices that Canada makes as a member in the alliance of Western capitalist countries.

302

IDEOLOGY AND THE LANGUAGE OF FOREIGN POLICY

When discussing the formation of policy we need to be ever mindful of the phenomenon of language, because the supposed "reality" behind political choice becomes defined through the manipulation of words.

Take, for example, the political and economic (not geographical) division of the world along East-West and North-South axes that prevailed for decades in the post-war Cold War period and still has a certain grip even in this new era of *glasnost*. Government, business, and media tend to use an East-West framework to characterize international relations, principally between the Soviet Union and the United States. But for Canada's dealings with the Third World the same institutions adopt a North-South framework. Indeed, Prime Minister Pierre Trudeau helped to popularize the notion of the North-South dialogue, according to which there was to be a free and even flow of information back and forth between the developed countries of the "North" and the developing ones to the "South." Being less concerned with political differences, the North, we are told, is keenly interested in promoting the economic development of the South.

But what is one person's dialogue easily turns into another's "monologue." In practice, as many researchers and writers have pointed out, the North-South dialogue turned out to be an elaborate guise for the continued exploitation of Third World resources and economies. A documentary film produced by the National Film Board of Canada in 1982 which was sarcastically entitled "A North-South Monologue" illustrated this guise by revealing the exploits of Canadian multinational corporations in the Caribbean. According to the NFB catalogue, in the process of making the film the director and producer "discovered that a North-South dialogue does not exist." Instead, they said, "The profit motive lurks behind the myth of foreign aid."

It is important to understand this politics of language and the fact that Canada's involvement in the countries of the periphery (South) has been fuelled just as much by East-West as by North-South considerations. For example, in an important 1982 speech on Canadian foreign policy in Central America, the secretary of state for external affairs, Mark MacGuigan, was clear on Canada's position. Referring to the Soviet Union and its links with Nicaragua he affirmed: "I don't want to convey any sort of neutrality in this regard. Along with our western allies, Canada takes Soviet expansionism in the Third World and in this hemisphere very seriously." Later in the same speech he went on to acknowledge, and even to bemoan, the fact that "East-West rivalries have now implanted themselves firmly in the region." [19]

Nowhere, however, did he say how Canada feels about the expansionism of its Northern allies in the Third World; or for that matter, Canada's own expansionism, whatever the term means, presuming that Canada could be guilty of it. For ideologically we are given to understand that while Canada's enemies have expansionist designs, Canada and its allies only have well-intentioned, North-South relations as their goal. The point is that it has not been possible to discuss North-South relations without taking the East-West issue into account.

This dichotomy is certainly not new to Canadian foreign policy makers. As far back as 1950, for example, when Lester Pearson was Canada's external affairs minister, he addressed the representatives of seven Commonwealth countries in Colombo, Ceylon, stating:

Communist expansionism may now spill over into Southeast Asia as well as into the Middle East.... If Southeast and South Asia are not to be conquered by Communism, we of the free, democratic world must demonstrate that it is we and not the Russians who stand for national liberation and economic and social progress.[20]

This position found a clear echo some seven years later in the work of two U.S. economists, Max Millikan and W.W. Rostow, who sought to explain why the United States should assist the less developed countries.[21]

According to Millikan and Rostow, communism is a "disease" that afflicts poorer countries in the early stages of development when blocked individual and social mobility clash with rising expectations and produce feelings of frustration. Because communist teachings identify class inequality and private property as sources of human misery, poor people will tend to find such teachings persuasive and convenient. For rather than blaming themselves for their miserable conditions of existence, the poor latch onto the rich capitalist class as a ready scapegoat. For Millikan and Rostow the main task of the developed capitalist countries is to assist the poor ones to pass through the early stages of development as quickly as possible before their people can be duped into embracing the misleading promises of communism.

THE POLITICAL ECONOMY OF IDEOLOGY:
DEVELOPMENT THEORIES

The Cold War notion that it was "better to be dead than red" grew out of this type of thinking, which sought to divide the world between the forces of evil (East) and the forces of good (West). As Daniel Chirot argues, by the 1950s, shortly after World War II, the major Western capitalist countries, particularly the United States, began to get even more deeply involved in the internal affairs of underdeveloped countries.[22] The main official reason given for such involvement revolved around a concern with stopping the spread of communism. But Chirot has very serious reservations about the motives behind Canadian and U.S. efforts to stem the tide of Communism:

Was it really a defensive strategy against Soviet aggression, or was it an aggressive plan to encircle the Soviet Union? Was it primarily a military strategy, or was it designed mainly to protect raw-material sources and export markets for the American economy? Was the policy idealistic and designed to help the world, or was it imperialistic and designed to help the U.S. at the expense of the poorer societies? [23]

These questions have to be understood as combatting ideologically the views of people like Lester Pearson, Max Millikan, and W. W. Rostow, along with the political and economic interests they represent. For implicit in their thinking is the idea that capitalism is the antidote for "underdevelopment." They do not consider the ways in which underdevelopment is a product of capitalism as it is operative at both the national and global levels. Nor do they make the distinction between countries that are undeveloped and those that are underdeveloped. This is a crucial distinction, which is related to politics, economic development, and the role of ideology, and which has much to do with the growth of a social theory of development.

The school of thought known as social evolutionism, for instance, seeks to describe social change in evolutionary terms, relying heavily on the biological sciences from which it borrowed the concept "development." According to Alejandro Portes, representatives of this school treat society like a living organism that passes through a series of ordered and inevitable stages that "culminate in the highest levels of societal complexity, represented by the advanced European nations" – and, I might add, North America. [24]

W. W. Rostow provided by far the clearest statement of the "stages approach" to change and development in his book *The Stages of Economic Growth*, with its ideologically provocative subtitle: *A Non-Communist Manifesto.* [25] Rostow sees underdevelopment as the original state of society, the starting point from which all change begins. From there he goes on to outline four other evolutionary stages: that in which the conditions for economic "take off" emerge; the stage of actual "take off"; the "drive to maturity"; and the stage of "high, mass consumption," as evidenced by the leading countries of Western Europe and North America. Presumably, all countries in the world could be located somewhere along this development continuum, with the overwhelming majority trying to achieve the degree of societal complexity of the mass consumer societies.

The ideological implication of Rostow's approach is clear. He opposes the word "complex" to the word "simple." Simple societies are rural, backward, and unsophisticated. They are the starting point from which the industrialized, advanced, sophisticated countries of Europe and North America "took off." The latter countries are the ones to be emulated, and an important part of such emulation entails the granting of tied aid to the backward societies so that they may conquer underdevelopment. [26] The catch is that to emulate the advanced countries the backward

305

ones have to surrender a great deal of their political and economic independence; at the ideological level this is portrayed as a "joint partnership" or as "friendly economic co-operation." Tied aid, however, is not to be used in just any way that the recipient sees fit. [27] The aid package is usually accompanied by strict instructions as to how it must be used: "By increasing aid, Canada directly bolsters trade because no less than 80% of the country's bilateral aid must be spent on Canadian goods and services. This represents one of the highest levels of tied aid among the major donor nations." [28]

The stipulated uses are generally designed to complement and enhance the political and economic interests of the donor country. In the case of Canada, for example, Dale Bisnauth argued that while "Canada's largesse has won her international respect as a rich nation committed to Third World development ... the reality is that, whatever the volume of Canadian aid, those countries remain as poor, exploited and oppressed as they were three decades ago." [29] After noting that these countries were more in need of justice than aid, Bisnauth concluded, "When the real cost of aid is computed, it can be demonstrated that it is not as costly to Canada as it is sometimes made out to be; it may even be beneficial." [30]

By way of contrast, however, Margaret Catley-Carlson, the former president of the Canadian International Development Agency (CIDA), sought to stress the fact of Canada's altruism in its dealings with the less developed countries. Her ideological message was clear as she asked rhetorically: "Why on earth – with no military aspirations in the developing parts of the world and with lamentably limited markets for our products out there so far – does Canada help the distant Third World?" [31] The answer, she said, was to be found in a 1985 joint report from the Senate and the House of Commons, which noted that because Canada's trade with the Third World is only a tiny fraction of its total trade, "Aid becomes a major element in our North-South policy. More than that, it is a Canadian vocation." [32]

Also important for our consideration of ideology is the assumption on the part of social evolutionary theorists that underdevelopment and development are unrelated stages in the universal and unilinear path to becoming modern. These are viewed as *natural* stages through which all countries must pass. The theorists make no reference to the social processes of colonialism and imperialism, or to the consequences of those processes for the making of underdevelopment. [33]

This kind of thinking informs policy makers in such key organizations as CIDA. In discussing the merits of Canada's foreign-aid program, Margaret Catley-Carlson observed, "Over the second half of the 20th century, the Third World has moved ahead faster than we ever did at comparable stages in our own development." [34] She is obviously of the opinion that the various countries of the Third World will follow the same path to development traversed by Canada.

However, the historical conditions that attended the industrial development of Canada are not, and cannot be, the same as those faced by Third World countries today. There are also differences in economic, demographic, and sheer human resources that are bound to play a major role in the development trajectory of the two areas. To expect that one will in time mirror the other makes little sense. Given that Canada itself benefits from the underdevelopment of the Third World, as many writers have pointed out, it is even less likely that Third World countries will ever come to exhibit development traits found in Canada or any of the other Northern countries.[35] As André Gunder Frank states:

Rostow's stages and thesis are incorrect primarily because they do not correspond at all to the past or present reality of the underdeveloped countries whose development they are supposed to guide.... This entire approach to development attributes a history to the developed countries but denies all history to the underdeveloped ones.[36]

There is a distinction, then, between "undeveloped" and "underdeveloped." Although the countries of Western Europe and North America were once undeveloped, they were never underdeveloped. The undeveloped is a natural state; the underdeveloped is a social product. To confuse the two is to distort and misread the history of world development.

But what this confusion does, ideologically, is to free those who were instrumental in creating the backward conditions that prevail in various parts of the world from accepting the responsibility for their actions. If underdevelopment is seen simply as a fact of nature, and when this type of explanation is accepted by those who live in the underdeveloped countries, the "developers," the multinational corporations, and the industrial magnates can continue to do profitable business in those countries, secure in the knowledge that many people around the world see their presence and their investments in a favourable light.

Another approach to change and development, modernization theory, is heavily social-psychological in focus. Briefly, modernization thinkers attribute backwardness and underdevelopment to the value and attitudinal structures common to the inhabitants of given societies. They argue that underdevelopment results in those societies where people hold traditional values and out-of-date attitudes and orientations to the world. David McClelland, for example, in talking about achievement motivation, asserts, "This is just one more piece of evidence to support the growing conviction among social scientists, that it is values, motives, or psychological forces that determine ultimately the rate of economic and social development."[37]

Another theorist, Seymour Martin Lipset, singles out the quality of "entrepreneurial behaviour" for special attention. He defines entrepreneurship as something that people learn culturally. Some cultures recognize it as important and emphasize its acquisition, while others do not: "Structural conditions make development possible; cultural factors determine whether the possibility becomes an actuality."[38] Entrepreneurial behaviour, then, is a prerequisite for economic growth and development. Where such growth and development do not occur, one can only assume that entrepreneurial behaviour does not exist.[39] Similar sentiments were expressed in a *Toronto Sun* comment: "Some races or nationalities seem to have an inclination and talent for business enterprise and hard work, others do not."[40]

Again the ideological messages are clear. The less developed countries must seek to learn from the more developed ones if they are to lift themselves out of their backwardness. To learn from them, relations between both groups of countries must remain amicable; and like any teacher-student relationship, the teacher has *control* and the student is supposed to follow the instructions issued by the teacher. This approach keeps the unequal structure intact and, more importantly, invests the teacher with a great deal of *legitimacy*.

Also, like the school of social evolutionism, modernization theory does not connect the condition of underdevelopment to the ravages or processes of colonialism and imperialism. Rather, the theory argues that underdevelopment issues from an outmoded, traditional, defective value structure that can and must be changed. Once those who live in the underdeveloped countries accept this definition of the situation, once they come to see their "small piece of the pie" as their just and fair deserve – that is, owing to their natural state or psychological make-up – they will mount programs of social, political, and economic modernization patterned along lines suggested by the developed countries. They will be firmly committed to the acquisition of those "modern" values and attitudes that promise an escape from poverty and misery. They will police and control themselves, while remaining squarely within the sphere of influence of the developed countries.

We know, however, that such modernization programs are premised upon false assumptions and an incorrect reading of history. They are ideological because they mask key aspects of social reality, relate half-truths, and propose courses of political and economic action that are tailored to preserve precisely those relationships and structures that they purport to oppose. They serve the purpose of social control by defusing potentially disruptive segments of society, while providing those segments with less accurate but more palatable explanations and understandings of their problems, and simultaneously serving to distract people from the real causes of their discontent.[41]

Reacting to the central assumptions of modernization theory, its neglect of history, and its ideologically conservative approach to change, another school of thinkers sought to account for underdevelopment in a radically different way. Known generally as dependency theorists, members of this school argue that the countries of the Third World are poor and underdeveloped because their economies are dependent on those of the leading imperialist countries.[42]

For dependency theorists, underdevelopment is not the original state or stage of all societies. They make a firm distinction between *undeveloped* and *underdeveloped* societies and argue that whereas all countries in the world were at one point undeveloped, not all of them were underdeveloped. Dependency theorists, then, see underdevelopment as the active socio-economic and political process of promoting dependence, which in turn leads to the establishment of structures and institutions that pre-empt development. Hence some countries move from undevelopment to development, while others move from undevelopment to underdevelopment.

According to the thinkers of this school, modern dependency was created by colonial expansion and imperialist penetration into Asia, Africa, Latin America, and the Caribbean. Beginning with the voyages of so-called "discovery" and the capture of colonial territories, entire countries were brought into the orbit of world capitalism and relegated to the status of satellites. In the process the economies and political structures of these colonial territories were distorted to meet the needs of the advanced capitalist countries.

Whether as mining colonies from which gold, silver, and other precious metals and minerals are extracted, or as plantation colonies that produce commodities such as sugar, coffee, cotton, tobacco, cocoa, and bananas for world markets, the countries of the Third World are not permitted to develop in an autonomous fashion. They are viewed solely as producers of raw materials destined for export in foreign-owned ships to the metropolitan centres of manufacturing and industry. Once exported, the raw materials are converted into finished products and sold back to the Third World at greatly inflated prices. In the process jobs are created for workers in the advanced countries, where most manufacturing and industrial operations are located and where capital is accumulated. As a consequence a thriving internal market develops in the centres of advanced capitalism, wages are increased, and the spread of commercial activity results in a higher demand for various other goods and services, greater economic differentiation, and higher standards of living.

Within the mining and plantation colonies the picture is quite different. There one finds less developed techniques of land cultivation, low levels of technological and scientific development, a heavy concentration on raw and unfinished agricultural and mineral exports, very few centres of industrial production, and highly labour-intensive methods of work. In the tailoring of its economies to meet the needs of the advanced countries, the Third World becomes dependent on the major centres of capitalist production and trade for supplies of credit, capital, technology, expertise, and the very market demand that makes possible continued production. Local needs and local markets tend to be neglected as the better part of all economic activity is directed towards external markets and consumers.

DEPENDENCY AND CANADA

Canada itself has sometimes been seen as a dependent and somewhat underdeveloped country. Kari Levitt, for example, describes Canada as the world's richest underdeveloped country, and Robert Chodos speaks of it as yet "another exploited colony," while Margaret Catley-Carlson sees Canada as a "middle power with some developing country characteristics."[43]

These images of Canada are less than accurate. They disguise the reality of Canada as an imperialist nation with selfish economic and political interests in the Third World. Cranford Pratt, a political scientist at the University of Toronto, states:

The most important recurrent theme in public interest group criticisms of Canadian policies towards the Third World is that it is so biased in favour of immediate, narrow economic Canadian interests that it is unable to give any weight to longer-term and more broadly defined national interests, or to moral concerns.[44]

Given the capitalist economic system of this country, we cannot reasonably expect the country's politicians and policy makers to act in ways that are antithetical to the nation's own interests. For this reason it is important to understand Canada, not just according to the rosy international image painted by commentators such as D.C. Thomson and R.F. Swanson, but also in regional and class terms.[45] There are regions and classes in Canada that are exploited for the benefit of other regions and classes in Canada and elsewhere.

In his book *Canadian Multinationals*, Jorge Niosi agrees that the Canadian economy has been subject to external control and dependence on foreign influences; but he does not go as far as Levitt and others to claim that Canada is underdeveloped.[46] He speaks of Canada's "dependent industrialization" and outlines in clear detail the processes by which U.S. corporations have "invaded" the Canadian economy and have established controlling interests in areas such as automobile manufacturing, mining and smelting, oil and gas, lumber, and electronics. Although in recent years various Canadian governments (federal and provincial) have sought to "buy back" control in several of these areas, the Canadian economy continues to exhibit traits of dependence on foreign technology, foreign markets, foreign capital, and foreign expertise. Niosi states: "Canada, after a century of pursuing a liberal policy towards foreign direct investment and the transfer of technology, now finds itself with half of its technology under outside control – one of the highest percentages of foreign control in the world."[47]

How do dependency theorists account for this situation? Their basic argument is that historically Canada's dependence on foreign powers stemmed from its status as a colony of Britain. Being politically, culturally, and economically dominated by the mother country, Canadians and Canadian society came to exhibit a pronounced European orientation as distinct from Americans and American society.[48] In economic terms the Canadian economy was geared to the production and export of raw materials that were processed and manufactured in Britain, thus creating jobs in that country and boosting its industrial development. Canada thus served as a ready market outlet for the manufactured goods produced in the metropole. Over the years, when the United States replaced Britain as Canada's foremost trading partner, Canada's external dependence increased greatly and the internal disparities between regions were accentuated.

The dependency notion of a chain of metropoles and satellites is useful for explaining the processes involved. As Wallace Clement asserts, "Regional economies are tied to national economies and national ones to international ones."[49] This is the idea of the chain. For Canada is neither developed nor underdeveloped. Some parts or regions are more developed than others. The least developed are linked to the more developed, and the more developed, in turn, are tied to even more developed international centres. As Clement says, "Canada is not unequivocally an industrial country." Only part of the country is industrialized, leaving the rest as "a resource hinterland. Most of Canada's industrial capacity is located below a line starting at Windsor, encompassing Toronto and moving to Montreal. This is industrial Canada."[50]

The economies of the Atlantic provinces are said to be underdeveloped not because they lack resources, but because they are dependent on outsiders for technology, expertise, capital, and markets. Because such "outsiders" usually present themselves in the form of multinational corporations, and because they do not necessarily have local interests at heart, it is understandable that the peripheral areas and single-industry towns will be seriously disadvantaged. Whatever economic or infrastructural development does occur is highly resource specific and does not lead to integrated development for the region as a whole. Hence *social* development is neglected; schools, hospitals, and housing are substandard; and the general life chances of the population are not as promising as those of Canadians who live, for example, in the "golden triangle" (Toronto-Montreal-Ottawa).

To explain further the dynamics of underdevelopment and dependency in Canada, theorists like Clement, Niosi, and Henry Veltmeyer have argued for a class analysis of the situation. Specifically, they direct attention to the structure of the Canadian capitalist class. That class, which is concentrated largely in the "golden triangle" area, exerts a growing dominance in matters of finance, transportation, and utilities nationally; and internationally it is able to compete effectively with the most powerful capitalist enterprises for profits and markets.

Within the underdeveloped regions of the country, the economic structures in place do not provide much opportunity for the advancement of the local populations. The jobs that are usually available tend to be of an unskilled or semi-skilled variety, and the general content of school curricula reflects the demands of that job

One of the issues often mentioned in connection with Canada's "lily white" image in the Caribbean concerns the missionary efforts of the Presbyterian Church since the early years of this century. A very different image, however, was presented by Harold "Sonny" Ladoo, a Trinidadian novelist who attended a Canadian Mission Presbyterian School as a child. His character Poonwa, going through a similar experience, feels nothing but rage and contempt for the experience and the "white school mistress, a Canadian blonde ... with her blue eyes she saw the Hindu children journeying to hell and the young Christians marching to heaven." Poonwa writes in a journal that when he grows up: "I will go into the white country with the Hindu Bible and the whip. The white Christians came with their Bibles and whips.... I will take the Bhagavad Gita with me and open a school in Canada and employ East Indian teachers. I will build a torture chamber in the school." Later Poonwa tells a friend, "My mission so help me God is to make white people good Hindus." – Harold Sonny Ladoo, *Yesterdays* (Toronto: Anansi, 1974), pp.38-39,42,77.

market. Housing conditions, health and welfare provisions, and overall lifestyles often lag behind those in the more developed parts of Ontario and Quebec. But even within Ontario and Quebec there are numerous pockets of backwardness in the so-called single industry towns and rural areas that are part of the development-underdevelopment chain. To this extent parts of Canada do resemble depressed areas in many Third World countries.

Although dependency theory can be applied to an understanding of change and development in certain regions, Canada is still far from being the underdeveloped society that Levitt and others have implied. A far more accurate view is that supplied by Niosi, who argues that today Canada is a major imperialist country whose multinational corporations have extensive control of banking, mining, transportation, and communications in many Third World countries. The Canadian capitalist class is allied internationally with other capitalist classes, and together they are responsible for much of the underdevelopment that characterizes both the Atlantic provinces and large parts of the Third World.

THE FRAMEWORK OF IDEOLOGICAL MOTIVATION

This image of Canada as an unevenly developed capitalist country with class and regional inequalities at home and imperialist concerns abroad is key to a proper understanding of its foreign policy. That policy protects the interests of both the Canadian capitalist class locally and the wider system of capitalism internationally. For the disadvantaged classes in Canada, the Third World and elsewhere, however, the government has to present a palatable image or explanation of their condition.

To avoid the possible outbreak of unrest among the disadvantaged, who may feel trapped in a situation created by, and serving the interests of, the privileged classes, the government, acting on behalf of the privileged classes, thus resorts to the creation of such ideological defences as the myth of equal opportunity, the myth of social mobility, and a whole host of other fictions concerning individual "freedoms." Whether myth, fiction, or make-believe, as ideological guises they are all tailored to cooling out or controlling a subordinate population. Edmund S. Morgan states:

Government requires make-believe. Make believe that the king is divine, make believe that he can do no wrong or make believe that the voice of the people is the voice of God. Make believe that the people *have* a voice or make believe that the representatives of the people *are* the people. Make believe that governors are the servants of the people. Make believe that all men are equal or make believe that they are not. [51]

In Canada's dealings with the Third World, the official foreign policy contains ideological elements that function as palliatives aimed at the general populations of both Canada and the Third World. For example, the role of foreign aid and the view that it is a distinctively Canadian vocation are ideological. For while it may benefit some small segment of the host society, the reality is that it opens up that society to increased capitalist penetration. And the benefits of that penetration will accrue almost exclusively to the privileged classes in Canada and their "junior partners" in the given host society.

To the extent that Canada may have a positive image in the eyes of several Third World governments and peoples, it is due in large part to the fact that this country has been able to hide behind its closest allies, Britain and the United States. In a very real sense, then, Canada "has relied on the might of England and the United States to enforce favourable investment climates and trade conditions in countries with which it does business." [52] Canada's imperialist interests, therefore, though effectively disguised, are no less direct than those of its allies. As Robert Carty and Virginia Smith illustrated, during the 1980s the United States, Great Britain, and Canada came together and agreed on a division of their Caribbean foreign-aid programs, with Canada undertaking to look after U.S. and British concerns in the area. [53] As part of that deal Canada received "responsibility for air transport, water resources, agriculture, and education programs" in the Caribbean. [54]

From this perspective, Canada's general foreign-policy dealings with the Third World are entirely intelligible. It is a foreign policy of a capitalist country and its prime responsibility is the protection of capitalism. The Trudeau government expressed this point unequivocally in its 1970 White Paper, *Foreign Policy for Canadians.* That document states that foreign policy "embraces a wide range of economic, commercial and financial objectives in the foreign field." These objectives include such things as the "promotion of exports," "trade and tariff agreements," and "loans and investments."[55] This is all subsumed under the general rubric of "fostering economic growth" *in Canada*. But as Robert Chodos points out, "Whenever there is a conflict between the dictates of fostering economic growth [in Canada] and those of promoting social justice [in the Third World] ... economic growth comes out on top."[56]

Canada's foreign-policy dealings with the Third World have to be placed, then, in this wider framework of ideological motivation. The policies are guided far less by altruistic and philanthropic considerations than by the political and economic interests of Canada's dominant classes. The pursuit of those interests is best served when accompanied by the legitimating ideologies of liberal democracy, free enterprise, and free trade, which effectively conceal or mask the true nature of capitalist exploitation. So long as workers in Canada and the Third World can be convinced that the capitalist system is their most sure guarantee of freedom and happiness, those in control – the corporate executives and their political allies – have little to fear in terms of social protest, unrest, or revolution, whether at home or abroad.

Notes

1. Margaret Catley-Carlson, "Aid: A Canadian Vocation," *Daedalus*, Vol.117, No.4 (1988).

2. Statistics Canada, *Imports by Country*, Vol.44, No.4 (1987), p.154; Vol.45, No.4 (1988), p.80; and Statistics Canada, *Exports by Country*, Vol.44, No.4 (1987), p.164; and Vol.45, No.4 (1988), p.92.

3. Anton L. Allahar, *Sociology and the Periphery: Theories and Issues* (Toronto: Garamond Press, 1989), pp.16–17.

4. Within days of the military coup of September 1973 the Canadian government saw fit to recognize the new military government of Chile, which was systematically executing tens of thousands of Chileans. Official political recognition was followed by implicit economic approval, beginning with the granting of a $5 million export credit for the sale of DeHaviland airplanes to the military junta just two weeks after the coup. Conservative estimates have placed the number of executions and "disappearances" at well over 100,000 people. That the overthrown government of President Salvador Allende was socialist also appears to have been related to private-sector economic support for the junta, for less than one year after the overthrow we were told: "Statistics Canada information on Canada-Chile trade indicates that private business is buying a great deal more of Chilean copper and selling an increased amount of mining machinery to Chile. Under Allende little such machinery was forthcoming from either the US or Canada, thereby severely affecting proper maintenance and expansion of the copper mines." *LAWG Letter*, Vol.II, No.4 (September 1974).

5. CBS News, *60 Minutes*, September 30, 1990.

6. *LAWG Letter*, Vol.IX, No.3 (February 1986).

7. The irony of this situation can be seen if you try to imagine a situation in which a foreign country would be permitted to have a military base in the United States or one of its territories. Added to this is the even less likely scenario of that foreign country being an enemy of the United States. The United States is Cuba's enemy, and since 1961 the U.S. government has made repeated attempts to assassinate Cuban leaders and reverse the revolutionary process in that country. Nevertheless, by virtue of its superior military might, the United States continues to illegally maintain its military base in Guantanamo Bay, Cuba. The idea of "might makes right" was brought home to me clearly one day when I asked the Cuban ambassador to Canada why his country tolerated a hostile, foreign power on its soil. "We ordered them to leave," he said, "and they refused. What would you have us do, declare war against the U.S.?"

8. Department of External Affairs, *Communiqué* (Ottawa, May 11, 1983).

9. Department of External Affairs, *Communiqué* (Ottawa, October 26, 1984).

10. Latin America Working Group (LAWG), *Canadians and the Crisis in Central America* (Toronto, 1986).

11. *LAWG Letter*, Vol.II, No.5 (October-November, 1974).

12. Mark MacGuigan, "Central America and Canadian Foreign Policy," speech to the University of Toronto Law Faculty, March 31, 1982.

13. Maurice Bishop, the former prime minister of Grenada, was a socialist who led a bloodless coup against the U.S.-installed dictator Eric Gairy. Bishop was a tremendously popular leader who had developed positive relations with Cuba and Nicaragua and attempted to do the same with the United States. His every move in that direction was opposed by the Reagan administration, which believed that, as President Reagan himself said, "Grenada pointed a dagger at the heart of the free world." The entire population of Grenada was around 9,000 people. The so-called free world, depending on how it is defined geographically, contained close to 2 billion people.

14. Secretary of State for External Affairs, "Statement," Ottawa, November 2, 1983.

15. In the case of Grenada there are those who would argue that the seeming harmony of interests among Canada, Britain, and the United States was fuelled more by considerations of race than anything else. Although somewhat more difficult to prove, Canada's track record on the race question has not been entirely flattering. Of particular importance here is Canadian immigration policy, which over the years has had both implicit and explicit racist provisions: see Freda Hawkins, *Canada and Immigration: Public Policy and Public Concern* (Montreal: McGill-Queen's University Press, 1972) and Alan B. Anderson and James S. Frideres, *Ethnicity in Canada* (Toronto: Butterworths, 1981). On this subject Robert Chodos comments that in their international dealings "Canadians prefer to identify with the gentle and civilized Americans, English, Germans and Dutch

who people the industrialized countries, rather than with the uncouth Blacks, Asians and Arabs of the Third World. Canada may be a raw material exporter, but it is also relatively industrialized and white." Robert Chodos, *The Caribbean Connection: The Double-Edged Canadian Presence in the West Indies* (Toronto: James Lorimer and Company, 1977), p.86.

16. Chodos, *Caribbean Connection*, p.79.

17. The bombing of Libya was said to have been carried out in specific response to the Libyan terrorist attack against a West German disco frequented by U.S. servicemen. Although evidence linking Libya with the bombing was slim, the U.S. administration nevertheless went ahead with the attack. Several weeks later the Pentagon released more firm evidence pointing to Syria and not Libya as responsible for the West German bombing. The United States government never did apologize for the unjustified attack on Libya, nor has there been any public reprimand of the United States by Canada.

18. On the responsibility of the capitalist state to the capitalist class, see Ralph Miliband, *The State in Capitalist Society* (London: Quartet Books, 1973).

19. MacGuigan, "Central America and Canadian Foreign Policy."

20. Quoted in A. Palacios Hardy and Litvinoff Martínez, *Canadian Aid: Whose Priorities?* (Toronto: LAWG, 1973), p.3.

21. Max Millikan and W.W. Rostow, *A Proposal Key to an Effective Foreign Policy* (New York: Harper and Brothers, 1957).

22. Daniel Chirot, *Social Change in the Twentieth Century* (New York: Harcourt, Brace, Jovanovich, 1957).

23. Ibid., p.2.

24. Alejandro Portes, "On the Sociology of National Development," *American Journal of Sociology*, Vol.82, No.1 (1976), p.61.

25. W.W. Rostow, *The Stages of Economic Growth: A Non-Communist Manifesto* (Cambridge: Cambridge University Press, 1962).

26. See Glyn R. Berry, "The West Indies in Canadian External Relations," in *Canada and the Commonwealth Caribbean*, ed. Brian Douglas Tennyson (New York: University Press of America, 1988), pp.358-359.

27. Ralph R. Paragg, "Canadian Aid in the Commonwealth Caribbean: Neo-colonialism or Development?" in *Canada and the Commonwealth Caribbean*, ed. Douglas.

28. Tom Barry, Beth Wood, and Deb Preusch, *The Other Side of Paradise* (New York: Grove Press, 1984), p.224.

29. Dale Bisnauth, "Canada and the Caribbean," in *Rethinking Development: Perspectives from the Caribbean and Atlantic Canada*, ed. Henry Veltmeyer (Halifax: International Education Centre, 1987), p.7.

30. Ibid, p.10.

31. Catley-Carlson, "Aid: A Canadian Vocation," p.320.

32. Ibid.

33. Allahar, *Sociology and the Periphery*, pp.82-112.

34. Catley-Carlson, "Aid: A Canadian Vocation," p.331.

35. On the question of Canada's benefit from underdevelopment, see Bisnauth, "Canada and the Caribbean"; and Cranford Pratt, "Canadian Policy Towards the Third World," *Studies in Political Economy*, No.13 (1984).

36. André Gunder Frank, *The Sociology of Development and the Underdevelopment of Sociology* (London: Pluto Press, 1971), p.19.

37. David McClelland, "Motivational Patterns in Southeast Asia," *Journal of Social Issues*, Vol.29, No.17 (1963), p.17.

38. S.M. Lipset, "Values, Education and Entrepreneurship," in *Elites in Latin America*, ed. S.M. Lipset and Aldo Solari (New York: Oxford University Press, 1967), p.3.

39. Ibid, pp.23-40.

40. Veltmeyer (ed.), *Rethinking Development*, p.8.

41. Allahar, *Sociology and the Periphery*, pp.61-62,76-81.

42. Gunder Frank, *Sociology of Development;* Theotonio Dos Santos, "The Structure of Dependence," in *The Political Economy of Development and Underdevelopment*, ed. Charles Wilber (New York: Random House, 1973); Fernando Enriqué Cardoso and Enzo Faletto, *Dependencia y Desarrollo en America Latina* (Mexico: Siglo Veintiuno, 1970); Osvaldo Sunkel and Pedro Paz, *El Subdesarrollo Latinoamericano y la Teoria del Desarrollo* (Mexico: Siglo Veintiuno, 1970).

43. Kari Levitt, *Silent Surrender: The Multinational Corporation in Canada* (Toronto: Macmillan of Canada, 1970); Chodos, *Caribbean Connection;* Catley-Carlson, "Aid: A Canadian Vocation."

44. Pratt, "Canadian Policy Towards the Third World," p.41.

45. D.C. Thomson and R.F. Swanson, *Canadian Foreign Policy: Options and Perspectives* (Toronto: McGraw-Hill Ryerson, 1971).

46. Jorge Niosi, *Canadian Multinationals* (Toronto: Garamond Press / Between The Lines, 1985), pp.33-60.

47. Ibid., p.30.

48. Seymour Martin Lipset, "Canada and the United States: The Cultural Dimension," in *Canada and the United States*, ed. Charles F. Doran and John H. Sigler (Toronto: Prentice-Hall, 1985).

49. Wallace Clement, "A Political Economy of Regionalism in Canada," in *Structured Inequality in Canada*, ed. John Harp and John R. Hofley (Toronto: Prentice-Hall, 1980), p.276.

50. Ibid.

51. Edmund S. Morgan, *Inventing the People: The Rise of Popular Sovereignty in England and America* (New York: W.W. Norton and Co., 1988), p.13.

52. Barry, Wood, and Preusch, *Other Side of Paradise,* p.222.

53. Robert Carty and Virginia Smith, *Perpetuating Poverty: The Political Economy of Canadian Foreign Aid* (Toronto: Between The Lines, 1981), pp.52–53.

54. Barry, Wood, and Preusch, *Other Side of Paradise,* p.222.

55. Department of External Affairs, *Foreign Policy for Canadians* (Ottawa: Information Canada, 1970), p.14.

56. Chodos, *Caribbean Connection,* p.85.

Bibliography

Henry Veltmeyer

1 . BOOKS ON CANADA AND THE THIRD WORLD

Adair, Dennis G. *Canada and Southern Africa*. Don Mills: Fulcrum Press, 1973.

Adams, Patricia and Solomon, Lawrence. *In the Name of Progress: The Underside of Foreign Aid*. Toronto: Energy Probe Research Foundation, 1985.

Allahar, Anton L. *Sociology and the Periphery: Theories and Issues*. Toronto: Garamond Press, 1989.

Baum, Daniel Jay. *The Banks of Canada in the Commonwealth Caribbean: Economic Nationalism and Multinational Enterprises of a Medium Power*. New York: Praeger, 1974.

Bricker, Calvin L. *Central America and Peacekeeping*. Downsview: Centre for International and Strategic Studies, York University, 1986.

Brief on Canada and Central America. Toronto: Canada-Caribbean-Central America Policy Alternatives, 1984.

Brodhead, Tim; Herbert-Copley, Brent; and Lambert, Anne-Marie. *Bridges of Hope? Canadian Voluntary Agencies and the Third World*. Ottawa: North-South Institute, 1988.

Cameron, Duncan. *Canada and the Third World Economic Order*. Ottawa: International Development Research Group, University of Ottawa, 1982.

Canada, the Caribbean and Central America. Proceedings of a Conference held November 8-9, 1985. Toronto: Canadian Institute for Strategic Studies, 1986.

Canada, the United States and Latin America: Independence and Accommodation. Washington: Woodrow Wilson International Center for Scholars, 1985.

Canada and UNESCO: A Working Partnership. Ottawa: Canadian Commission for UNESCO (Occasional Paper No. 50), 1985.

Canadian Association for Latin America. *Canada and Latin America: Partners in Development.* Toronto, 1974.

Canadian Association for Latin America. *Canada and Latin America: The Implementation of the Partnership.* Proceedings of a conference held in Caracas, Venezuela, January 30-31, 1976. Ottawa: Supply and Services, 1976.

Careau, Michel. "Canadian-Cuban Medical Collaboration Projects." In *Health, Welfare and Development in Latin America and the Caribbean.* Windsor: Ontario Cooperative Program in Latin American and Caribbean Studies, University of Windsor, 1980.

Caribbean Tourism in the Eighties: Towards Canadian / Caribbean Cooperation in Tourism Development. Proceedings of a conference held at Ryerson Polytechnical Institute, Toronto, May 1980. Toronto: Ryerson International Development Centre, 1982.

Carty, Robert and Smith, Virginia. *Perpetuating Poverty: The Political Economy of Canadian Foreign Aid.* Toronto: Between The Lines, 1981.

Chodos, Robert. *The Caribbean Connection: The Double-Edged Canadian Presence in the West Indies.* Toronto: James Lorimer, 1977.

CIDA (Canadian International Development Association). *Canada's Development Assistance to Latin America.* Ottawa, 1977.

CIDA. *Canadian International Development Assistance: To Benefit a Better World: Response of the Government of Canada to the Report of the Standing Committee on External Affairs and International Trade.* Ottawa, September 1987.

CIDA. *CIDA and the Arab World: A Profile in Development Cooperation.* Ottawa, 1983.

CIDA. *Sharing Our Future: Canadian International Development Assistance.* Ottawa, 1987.

CIDA. *Women in Development: CIDA Action Plan.* Ottawa, 1986.

Clarke, Robert and Swift, Richard, eds. *Ties That Bind: Canada and the Third World.* Toronto: Between The Lines, 1982.

Corbo, Vittorio and Havrylyshyn, Oli. *Canada's Trade Relations with Developing Countries: The Evolution of Export and Import Structures and Barriers to Trade in Canada.* Ottawa: CEC, 1980.

Deverell, John and the Latin American Working Group. *Falconbridge: Portrait of a Canadian Mining Multinational.* Toronto: James Lorimer, 1975.

Dewitt, David B. and Kirton, John J. "Canada-Middle East Relations: The End of Liberal-Internationalism." In *The Middle East at the Crossroads,* edited by Janice Ross Stein and David B. Dewitt. Oakville, Ont.: Mosaic, 1983, pp.176-199.

Di Sanza, E. "Canada's Relations with the Caribbean and Latin America: Perspectives on Canada's Role in the World System." M.A. thesis, McMaster University, 1978.

Dosman, Edgar J. and Postgate, W. Dale. *Canadian Latin American Economic Relations.* Toronto: Centre for Research on Latin American and the Caribbean, 1980.

Fairley, Bryant; Leys, Colin; and Sacouman, James, eds. *Restructuring and Resistance: Perspectives from Atlantic Canada.* Toronto: Garamond Press, 1990.

GATT-Fly. *Debt Bondage or Self-Reliance: A Popular Perspective on the Global Debt Crisis.* Toronto: GATT-Fly, 1985.

Grant, Michael and McDowall, Duncan. *The South American Experience.* Canadian Business Linkages with the Developing Countries, Vol.2. Ottawa: Conference Board of Canada, 1987.

Heron, Craig, ed. *Imperialism, Nationalism and Canada.* Toronto: New Hogtown Press / Between The Lines, 1977.

Holmes, John W. *The Changing Nature of International Organizations: The Canadian Perspective.* London: Canada House, 1980.

Holmes, John and Leys, Colin, eds. *Frontyard Backyard: The Americas in the Global Crisis.* Toronto: Between The Lines, 1987.

IDRC. *With our Own Hands: Research for Third World Development: Canada: Contribution through the International Development Research Centre, 1970-1985.* Ottawa: International Development Research Centre, 1986.

Institute for International Cooperation, ed. *Rural Development in Africa: Priorities, Problems and Prospects.* Ottawa: University of Ottawa, ICI, 1979.

Kappler, Sheila. *Canadian Government Policy, Banks, and Corporate Relations with South Africa.* New York: United Nations Center against Apartheid (Notes and documents 8 / 84), 1984.

Kirk, John and Schuyler, George. *Central America: Democracy, Development and Change.* New York: Praeger, 1988.

Laszlo, Ervin and Kurtzman, Joel. *The United States, Canada and the New International Economic Order.* New York: Pergamon for UNITAR and the Centre for Economic and Social Studies of the Third World, 1979.

Lavergne, Real. *Canadian Development Assistance to Senegal.* Ottawa: North-South Institute, 1984.

LAWG. *An Anti-Intervention Handbook: Canadians and the Crisis in Central America.* Toronto: Latin America Working Group, 1985.

Lefeber, Louis and North, Liisa, eds. *Democracy and Development in Latin America.* CERLAC-LARU Studies. Toronto: Latin American Research Unit, York University, 1980.

Lemco, Jonathan. *Canada and Central America: A Review of Current Issues.* Toronto: Behind the Headlines, Vol.XLIII, No.5 (May 1986), 19pp.

Levitt, Kari. *Silent Surrender: The Multinational Corporation in Canada.* Toronto: Macmillan of Canada, 1970.

Lyon, Peyton V. and Ismael, Tareq Y., eds. *Canada and the Third World*. Toronto: Macmillan, 1976.

MacNeill, Jim; Cox, John; and Runnalls, David. *CIDA and Sustainable Development: How Canada's Aid Policies Can Support Sustainable Development in the Third World More Effectively*. Halifax: Institute for Research on Public Policy, 1989.

MacDonald, David. *The African Famine and Canada's Response: A Report*. Hull: ACDI, 1985.

Matthews, Robert O. and Pratt, Cranford, eds. *Church and State: Christian Churches and Canadian Foreign Policy*. Proceedings of a Canadian Institute of International Affairs Consultation, Toronto, September 28, 1982. Toronto: ICAI, 1983.

Matthews, Roy A. *Canada and the Little Dragons: An Analysis of Canadian Economic Relations with Hong Kong, Taiwan and South Korea*. Montreal: Institute for Research on Public Policy, 1983.

Matthews, Roy A. *Canadian Industry and the Developing Countries*. Ottawa: CEC, Conference on Industrial Adaptation, 1978.

McFarlane, Peter. *Northern Shadows: Canadians and Central America*. Toronto: Between The Lines, 1989.

McGee, Terry G. *Canada and the Changing Economy of the Pacific Basin: An Introductory Overview*. Canada and the Changing Economy of the Pacific Basin, working paper 1. Vancouver: Institute of Asian Research, University of British Columbia, 1983.

McLean, Eleanor. *Between The Lines: How to Detect Bias and Propaganda in the News and Everyday Life*. Montreal: Black Rose Books, 1981.

Molot, Maureen and Tomlin, Brian W., eds. *The Tory Record 1988*. Canada Among Nations series. Toronto: James Lorimer and Company, 1988.

Morrison, David R. *Canadian Enterprise in Latin America and the Caribbean: A Study in the Political Economy of Government-Business Relations*. (In Preparation.)

Naiman, Joanne et al. *Relations Between Canada and South Africa*. New York: United Nations Center Against Apartheid (Notes and documents 10 / 84), 1984.

Nef, Jorge. *Canada and the Latin American Challenge*. University of Guelph, CCPLAC, 1978.

Niosi, Jorge. *Canadian Multinationals*. Toronto: Garamond Press / Between The Lines, 1985.

North, Liisa, ed. *Between War and Peace in Central America: Choices for Canada*. Toronto: Between The Lines, 1990.

North-South Institute. *North-South Relations 1980-85: Priorities for Canadian Policy*. Ottawa, 1980.

North-South Institute. *A New International Order and Canadian Realities.* Discussion paper for the seminar "A New International Order, Canadian Roles and Priorities," Ottawa, November 1977.

Paragg, Ralph R. *Canada and the Commonwealth Caribbean: The Political Economy of a Relationship in Transition.* Ph.D. thesis, Queen's University (Canadian theses on microfiche 39542), 1978.

Pratt, Cranford. *Canadian Policy Towards the Third World: The Search For a Paradigm.* University of Toronto Development Studies Programme (Working Paper A-2). Toronto, 1983.

Rahman, Syed Sajjadur and Balcome, David. *The Asian Experience.* Canadian Business Linkages with the Developing Countries, Vol.1. Ottawa: Conference Board of Canada, 1987.

Regehr, Ernie. *Arms Canada: The Deadly Business of Military Exports.* Toronto: James Lorimer and Company, 1987.

Reuber, Grant L. *Canada's Economic Policies Toward the Less Developed Countries.* Cambridge, Ont.: Collier-Macmillan Canada, 1972.

Ritter, A.R.M. *Conflict and Coincidence of Canadian and Less Developed Country Interests in International Trade in Primary Commodities.* CEC Discussion paper 109. Ottawa, 1978.

Ritter, A.R.M., ed. *Latin America and the Caribbean: Geopolitics, Development and Culture.* Conference Proceedings, October 1983. Ottawa: ACELAC, 1984.

Rugman, Alan M. *Canadian Multinational Enterprises and Developing Countries.* Montreal: Ecole des Hautes Etudes Commerciales (Cahiers du CETAI 81-18), 1981.

Sanger, Clyde. *Half a Loaf: Canada's Semi-Role Among Developing Countries.* Toronto: Ryerson, 1969.

Schuyler, George and Veltmeyer, Henry, eds. *Rethinking Caribbean Development.* Halifax: IEC, 1987.

Stevenson, Garth, ed. *A Foremost Nation: Canadian Foreign Policy and a Changing World.* Toronto: McClelland and Stewart, 1977.

Swift, Jamie and DEC. *The Big Nickel: Inco at Home and Abroad.* Kitchener: Between The Lines, 1977.

Taskforce on the Churches and Corporate Responsibility. *Canadian Economic Relations with Countries That Violate Human Rights: A Brief to the Sub-Committee on Latin America and the Caribbean of the Standing Committee on External Affairs and National Defence.* Toronto, 1982.

Taskforce on the Churches and Corporate Responsibility. *Investment in Oppression: Canadian Response to Apartheid.* Toronto, 1979.

Thompson, Suteera. *Food for the Poor: The Role of CIDA in Agricultural, Fisheries and Rural Development.* Discussion paper D 80 / 1. Ottawa: Science Council of Canada, 1980.

Tomlinson, J.W.C. *A Study of Canadian Joint Ventures in Brazil*. Ottawa: Technology Branch, Department of Industry, Trade and Commerce, 1979.

Torrie, Jill, ed. *Banking on Poverty: The Global Impact of the IMF and the World Bank*. Toronto: Between The Lines, 1983.

Veltmeyer, Henry, ed. *Rethinking Development: Perspectives from the Caribbean and Atlantic Canada*. Halifax: IEC, 1987.

Weaver, Clyde and Richards, Peter. *East-West, North-South: Planning Canada's Role in the New Global Economy*. Vancouver: School of Community and Regional Planning, University of British Columbia, 1984.

Williams, Douglas and Young, Roger. *Taking Stock: World Food Security in the Eighties*. Ottawa: North-South Institute, 1981.

2. OTHER BOOKS

Acker, Alison. *Children of the Volcano*. Toronto: Between The Lines, 1986.

Acker, Alison. *Honduras: The Making of a Banana Republic*. Toronto: Between The Lines, 1988.

Agarwal, Bina, ed. *Structures of Patriarchy: The State, the Community and the Household*. London: Zed Books, 1988.

Altvater, Elmar, ed. *The Poverty of Nations: A Guide to the Debt Crisis from Argentina to Zaire*. London: Zed Books, 1990.

Ambursley, Fitzroy and Cohen, Robert, eds. *Crisis in the Caribbean*. London: Heinemann, 1983.

Amin, Samir. *Delinking Towards a Polycentric World*. London: Zed Books, 1990.

Amin, Samir. *Imperialism and Unequal Development*. New York: Monthly Review Press, and Hassocks, Sussex: Harvester, 1977.

Amin, Samir. *Unequal Development: An Essay on the Social Formations of Peripheral Capitalism*. New York: Monthly Review Press and Hassocks, Sussex: Harvester, 1976.

Andrae, Gunilla and Beckman, Bjorn. *The Wheat Trap: Bread and Underdevelopment in Nigeria*. London: Zed Books, 1985.

Andreas, Carol. *When Women Rebel: The Rise of Popular Feminism in Peru*. Westport, Conn.: Lawrence Hill, 1985.

Annis, Sheldon and Hakim, Peter, eds. *Direct to the Poor: Grassroots Development in Latin America*. Boulder, Col.: Lynne Rienner Publishers, 1991.

Anyang'Nyong'o, Peter, ed. *Popular Struggles for Democracy in Africa*. London: Zed Books, 1987.

Archetti, Eduardo P.; Cammack, Paul; and Roberts, Bryan, eds. *Latin America*. New York: Monthly Review Press, 1987.

Armstong, Robert and Shenk, Janet. *El Salvador: The Face of Revolution*. Boston: South End, 1982.

Armstrong, W. and McGee, T.G. *Theatres of Accumulation: Studies in Asian and Latin American Urbanization.* London / New York: Methuen, 1985.

Banería, Lourdes, ed. *Women and Development: The Sexual Role in Rural Societies.* New York: Praeger, 1985.

Banería, Lourdes and Roldan, Martha. *The Crossroads of Class and Gender.* Chicago: University of Chicago Press, 1987.

Baran, Paul. *The Political Economy of Growth.* Harmondsworth, Middlesex: Penguin Books, 1973.

Barker, Jonathan, ed. *The Politics of Agriculture in Tropical Africa.* Beverly Hills: Sage, 1984.

Barndt, Deborah. *To Change This House: Popular Education Under the Sandinistas.* Toronto: Between The Lines, 1991.

Barnet, R. and Müller, R. *Global Reach: The Power of the Multinational Corporations.* New York: Simon & Shuster, 1974.

Barraclough, Solon and Scott, Michael. *The Rich Have Already Eaten: Roots of Catastrophe in Central America.* Amsterdam: Transnational Institute, 1987.

Barry, Tom. *Roots of Rebellion: Land and Hunger in Central America.* Boston: South End Press, 1987.

Bennett, D. and Sharpe, K. *Transnational Corporations Versus the State: The Political Economy of the Mexican Auto Industry.* Princeton, N.J.: Princeton University Press, 1985.

Berryman, Phillip. *Liberation Theology.* New York: Pantheon, 1987.

Bhagavan, M.R. *Technological Advance in the Third World: Strategies and Prospects.* London: Zed Books, 1990.

Biersteker, T. *Distortion or Development? Contending Perspectives on the Multinational Corporation.* Boston: MIT Press, 1978.

Bird, Richard and Horton, Susan, eds. *Government Policy and the Poor in Developing Countries.* Toronto: University of Toronto Press, 1989.

Bissio, Remo et al, eds. *Third World Guide 91 / 92.* Toronto: Garamond Press, 1991.

Black, George. *Garrison Guatemala.* New York: Monthly Review Press, 1984.

Blomström, M. and Hettne, B. *Development Theory in Transition: The Dependency Debate and Beyond: Third World Responses.* London: Zed Books, 1984.

Blussé, L.; Wesseling, H.L.; and Winius, G.D., eds. *History and Underdevelopment.* Leiden: Leiden University Press, 1980.

Bodley, John. *Tribal Peoples and Development Issues.* Mountain View, Cal.: Mayfield Publishing Company, 1988.

Bonpane, Blase. *Guerrillas of Peace: Liberation Theology and the Central American Revolution.* Boston: South End Press, 1985.

Boserup, Ester. *Woman's Role in Economic Development*. New York: St. Martin's Press, 1970.

Brandt, Willy et al. *North-South: A Program for Survival: The Report of the Independent Commission on International Development Issues under the Chairmanship of Willy Brandt*. London: Pan, 1980.

Branford, S. and Glock, O. *The Last Frontier: Fighting over Land in the Amazon*. London: Zed Books, 1985.

Brenner, Philip et al., eds. *The Cuba Reader: The Making of a Revolutionary Society*. New York: Grove, 1989.

Brewer, A. *Marxist Theories of Imperialism: A Critical Survey*. London: Routledge & Kegan Paul, 1980.

Bromley, Rosemary D.F. and Bromley, R. *South American Development: A Geographical Introduction*. New York: Cambridge University Press, 1982, 1988.

Bromley, R., ed. *Planning for Small Enterprises in Third World Cities*. New York: Pergamon, 1985.

Brown, Lester et al. *State of the World 1990*. New York and London: W.W. Norton and Co., 1990.

Brown, Lester et al. *State of the World 1989: A World Watch Institute Report on Progress Toward a Sustainable Society*. New York: W.W. Norton and Co., 1989.

Burbach, Roger and Nunez, Orlando. *Fire in the Americas: Forging a Revolutionary Agenda*. London: Verso, 1987.

Burback, Roger and Flynn, Patricia. *Agribusiness in the Americas*. New York: Monthly Review Press, 1980.

Campbell, Bonnie K. and Loxley, John, eds. *Structural Adjustment in Africa*. London: Macmillan, 1989.

Carlsson, Jerker and Shaw, Timothy, M., eds. *Newly Industrializing Countries and the Political Economy of South-South Relations*. London: Macmillan, 1988.

Cassen, Robert, ed. *Rich Country Interests and Third World Development*. New York: St. Martin's Press, 1982.

Castro, Fidel. *The World Economic and Social Crisis*. Havana: Council of State, 1983.

Chambers, Robert. *Rural Development: Putting the Last First*. London: Longman, 1983.

Chen, Edward K.Y. *Multinational Corporations, Technology, and Employment*. London: Macmillan, 1983.

Cheru, Fantu. *The Silent Revolution in Africa: Debt, Development and Democracy*. London: Zed Books, 1989.

Chomsky, Noam. *Turning the Tide: The U.S. and Latin America*. Montreal: Black Rose Books, 1986.

Christodoulou, Demetrios. *The Unpromised Land: Agrarian Conflict and Reform Worldwide.* London: Zed Books, 1989.

Clapham, Christopher S. *Third World Politics: An Introduction.* London: Croom Helm, 1985.

Cockcroft, James D. *Mexico: Class Formation, Capital Accumulation, and the State.* New York: Monthly Review Press, 1983.

Collins, Joseph et al. *Nicaragua: What Difference Could a Revolution Make? Food and Farming in the New Nicaragua.* 3rd ed. New York: Grove Press, 1986.

Cornia, Giovanni Andrea et al., eds. *Adjustment with a Human Face: Protecting the Vulnerable and Promoting Growth.* Oxford: Oxford University Press, 1987.

Creevey, Lucy E., ed. *Women Farmers in Africa: Rural Development in Mali and Sahel.* Syracuse, N.Y.: Syracuse University Press, 1986.

Davies, Miranda, ed. *Third World-Second Sex: Women's Struggles and National Liberation: Third World Women Speak Out.* London: Zed Books, 1983.

Davies, Miranda, ed. *Third World – Second Sex 2.* London: Zed Books, 1987.

Devlin, Robert. *Debt and Crisis in Latin America: The Supply Side of the Story.* Princeton, N.J.: Princeton University Press, 1989.

Dietz, James L. and Street, James H., eds. *Latin America's Economic Development: Institutionalist and Structuralist Perspectives.* Boulder, Col.: Lynne Rienner Publishers, 1991.

Dube, S.C. *Modernization and Development: The Search for Alternative Paradigms.* London: Zed Books, 1988.

Dunkerley, James. *Rebellion in the Veins: Political Struggle in Bolivia, 1952-82.* London: Verso, 1984.

Dunning, J. *International Production and the Multinational Enterprise.* London: George Allen & Unwin, 1981.

Dupriez, Hughes, et al. *Land and Life: Agriculture in African Rural Communities Crops and Soils.* New York: Collier / Macmillan, 1988.

Ellis, Pat, ed. *Women of the Caribbean.* London: Zed Books, 1986.

Evans, P. *Dependent Development: The Alliance of Multinational, State, and Local Capital in Brazil.* Princeton, N.J.: Princeton University Press, 1979.

Fagen, Richard et al., eds. *Transition and Development: Problems of Third World Socialism.* New York: Monthly Review Press, 1986.

Fanon, Frantz. *The Wretched of the Earth.* New York: Grove Press, 1968.

Fenton, P. and Heffron, Mary, eds. *Africa: A Directory of Resources.* New York: Orbis Books, 1987.

Fenton, P. and Heffron, Mary, eds. *Asia and Pacific: A Directory of Resources.* New York: Orbis Books, 1986.

Fenton, P. and Heffron, Mary, eds. *Food, Hunger, Agribusiness: A Directory of Resources.* New York: Orbis Books, 1987.

Fenton, P. and Heffron, Mary, eds. *Latin America and Caribbean: A Directory of Resources*. New York: Orbis Books, 1986.

Fenton, P. and Heffron, Mary, eds. *Third World Resource Directory: A Guide to Organizations and Publications*. New York: Orbis Books, 1984.

Fenton, P. and Heffron, Mary, eds. *Women in the Third World: A Directory of Resources*. New York: Orbis Books, 1987.

Frank, André Gunder. *Crisis in the Third World*. New York: Holmes & Meir, 1981.

Frank, André Gunder. *Latin America: Underdevelopment or Revolution: Essays on the Development of Underdevelopment and the Immediate Enemy*. New York: Monthly Review Press, 1969.

Fransman, Martin and King, Kenneth, eds. *Technological Capability in the Third World*. London: Macmillan, 1984.

Galeano, Eduardo. *Open Veins of Latin America: Five Centuries of the Pillage of a Continent*. New York: Monthly Review Press, 1973.

George, Susan. *A Fate Worse than Debt*. Harmondsworth, Middlesex: Penguin Books, 1988.

Ghai, Dharam, ed. *The IMF and the South: The Social Impact of Crisis and Adjustment*. London: Zed Books, 1991.

Girvan, Norman. *Foreign Capital and Economic Underdevelopment in Jamaica*. Kingston, Jamaica: Institute of Social and Economic Research, 1971.

Girvan, Norman. *Corporate Imperialism: Conflict and Expropriation*. New York: Monthly Review Press, 1976.

Glover, David and Kusterer, Ken. *Small Farmers, Big Business*. London: Macmillan, 1990.

Griffin, Keith. *World Hunger and the World Economy and Other Essays in Development Politics*. London: Macmillan, 1987.

Griffin, Keith. *International Inequality and National Poverty*. London: Macmillan, 1978.

Guevara, Che. *Che Guevara and the Cuban Revolution*. New York: Pathfinder, 1987.

Gupta, Avijit. *Ecology and Development in the Third World*. London: Routledge Chapman and Hall, 1988.

Handy, Jim. *Gift of the Devil: A History of Guatemala*. Toronto: Between The Lines, 1984.

Harnecker, Marta. *Cuba: Dictatorship or Democracy?* Westport, Conn.: Lawrence Hill, 1980.

Harnecker, Marta. *Fidel Castro's Political Strategy: From Moncada to Victory*. New York: Pathfinder, 1987.

Harris, Nigel. *The End of the Third World: Newly Industrialized Countries and the Decline of an Ideology*. Harmondsworth, Middlesex: Penguin Books, 1987.

Harris, Nigel. *Of Bread and Guns: The World Economy in Crisis.* Harmondsworth, Middlesex: Penguin Books, 1983.

Harrison, Paul. *Inside the Third World: The Anatomy of Poverty.* 2nd ed. Harmondsworth, Middlesex: Penguin Books, 1981.

Harrison, Paul. *The Greening of Africa.* London: Paladin Grafton Books, 1989.

Hayashi, Takeshi. *The Japanese Experience in Technology: From Transfer to Self-Reliance.* New York: United Nations Publications, 1990.

Hayter, Teresa. *The Creation of World Poverty: An Alternative View to the Brandt Report.* London: Pluto Press, 1981.

Helleiner, G.K., ed. *For Good or Evil: Economic Theory and North-South Negotiations.* Toronto: University of Toronto Press, 1982.

Hinrichsen, Don. *Our Common Future: A Reader's Guide: The Brundtland Report Explained.* London: Earthscan, 1987.

Hodges, Donald and Gandy, Ross. *Mexico, 1910-1982: Reform or Revolution?* London: Zed Books, 1983.

Hoogvelt, Ankie M.M. *The Sociology of Developing Societies.* 2nd ed. London: Macmillan, 1978.

Hoogvelt, Ankie M.M. *The Third World in Global Development.* London: Macmillan, 1982.

Hutchful, Eboe, ed. *The IMF and Ghana: The Confidential Record.* London: Zed Books, 1987.

Hyden, G. *Beyond Ujamaa in Tanzania: Underdevelopment and an Uncaptured Peasantry.* London: Heinemann, 1980.

IMF, *Foreign Private Investment in Developing Countries.* Washington: International Monetary Fund, 1985.

Independent Commission on International Humanitarian Issues. *Indigenous Peoples: A Global Quest for Justice.* London: Zed Books, 1987.

ISIS. *Women in Development: A Resource Guide for Organization and Action.* Philadelphia: New Society Publishers, 1984.

Jayawardena, Kumari. *Feminism and Nationalism in the Third World.* London: Zed Books, 1986.

Jelin, Elizabeth, ed. *Women and Social Change in Latin America.* London: Zed Books, 1990.

Jenkins, R.O. *Transnational Corporations, Competition and Monopoly.* London: Macmillan, 1984.

Jenkins, Rhys. *Transnational Corporations and Uneven Development.* London and New York: Methuen, 1987.

Johnson, Hazel and Bernstein, Hazel, eds. *Third World Lives of Struggle.* London: Heinemann, 1982.

Kaufman, Michael. *Jamaica Under Manley: Dilemmas of Socialism and Democrary.* Toronto: Between The Lines, 1985.

Kay, Cristobal. *Latin American Theories of Development*. London and New York: Routledge Chapman and Hall, 1989.

Kemp, Tom. *Industrialization in the Non-Western World*. London: Longman, 1983.

Kidron, Michael and Segal, Ronald. *New State of the World Atlas*. London: Pan, 1984.

Kirkpatrick, C.; Lee, N.; and Mixson, F. *Industrial Structure and Policy in Less Developed Countries*. London: Allen & Unwin, 1984.

Kitching, G.N., ed. *Development and Underdevelopment in Historical Perspective: Populism, Nationalism and Industrialization*. London: Routledge Chapman and Hall, 1989.

Kneen, Brewster. *From Land to Mouth: Understanding the Food System*. Toronto: NC Press, 1989.

Kolko, Gabriel. *Confronting the Third World: United States Foreign Policy 1945-1980*. New York: Random House, 1989.

Kolko, Joyce. *Restructuring the World Economy*. New York: Pantheon / Random House, 1988.

Korner, Peter et al. *The IMF and the Debt Crisis: A Guide to the Third World's Dilemmas*. London: Zed Books, 1987.

Korsmeyer, Pamela and Ropes, George, eds. *The Development Directory 1990: A Guide to the International Development Community in the United States and Canada*. Detroit: Omnigraphics Inc., 1990.

Kruijer, Gerald J. *Development Through Liberation: Third World Problems and Solutions*. University of Amsterdam: Humanities Press, 1987.

Lal, Victor. *Fiji: Coups in Paradise: Race, Politics and Military Intervention*. London: Zed Books, 1990.

Langdon, S. *Multinational Corporations in the Political Economy of Kenya*. London: Macmillan, 1981.

Latin America Bureau, *Guyana: Fradulent Revolution*. London: LAB, 1984.

Leeson, P.F. and Musgove, M.M., eds. *Perspectives on Development: Cross-Disciplinary Themes in Development*. Manchester and New York: Manchester University Press, 1988.

Leys, Colin, ed. *Politics and Change in Developing Countries: Studies in the Theory and Practice of Development*. London: Cambridge University Press, 1969.

Lipton, M. *Why Poor People Stay Poor: A Study of Urban Bias in World Development*. London: Temple Smith, 1977.

Loxley, John. *Debt and Disorder: External Financing for Development*. Boulder, Col., and London: Westview Press / North-South Institute, 1986.

Macdonald, Theodore. *Making a New People: Education in Revolutionary Cuba*. Vancouver: New Star Books, 1985.

Mackintosh, Maureen. *Gender, Class and Rural Transition: Agribusiness and the Food Crisis in Senegal.* London: Zed Books, 1989.

MacPherson, Stewart. *Social Policy in the Third World: The Social Dilemma of Underdevelopment.* Sussex: Wheatsheaf Books, 1985.

Maguire, Andrew and Brown, Janet Welsh, eds. *Bordering on Trouble: Resources and Politics in Latin America.* Bethesda, Md.: Adler & Adler Publishers, 1986.

Manley, Michael. *Up the Down Escalator: Development and the International Economy-A Jamaican Case Study.* London: André Deutsch, 1989.

Mansour, Fawzy. *The Arab World: Nation, State and Democracy.* London: Zed Books, 1990.

Marcussen, H. and Torp, J. *The Internationalization of Capital: The Prospects for the Third World.* London: Zed Books, 1982.

Mattelart, Armand. *Transnationals and the Third World: The Struggle for Culture.* S. Hadley, Mass.: Bergin & Garvey, 1983.

McDougall, A., ed. *Sustainable Agriculture in Africa.* Trenton, N.J.: Africa World Press, 1990 (includes 48 pp. annotated bibliography on agriculture in Africa).

Miles, Maria. *Patriarchy and Accumulation on a World Scale: Women in the International Division of Labour.* London: Zed Press, 1988.

Mittelman, James. *Out from Underdevelopment: Prospects for the Third World.* London: Macmillan, 1988.

Munck, Ronaldo. *Politics and Dependency in the Third World: The Case of Latin America.* London: Zed Books, 1984.

Murray, R., ed. *Multinationals Beyond the Market: Intra-Firm Trade and the Control of Transfer Pricing.* Brighton, Sussex: Harvester, 1981.

Naylor, R.T. *Hot Money and the Politics of Debt.* Toronto: McClelland and Stewart, 1987.

Nelson, Joan M., ed. *Economic Crisis and Policy Choice: The Politics of Adjustment in the Third World.* Princeton, N.J.: Princeton University Press, 1990.

New Internationalist, *Women: A World Report.* London: Methuen, 1985.

Newfarmer, R., ed. *Profits, Progress, Poverty: Studies of International Industries in Latin America.* Notre Dame, Ind.: Notre Dame University Press, 1985.

Niosi, Jorge and Bellan, Bertrand. *The Decline of the American Economy.* Montreal: Black Rose Books, 1988.

Nore, Petter and Turner, Terisa, eds. *Oil and Class Struggle.* London: Zed Books, 1980.

North, Liisa. *Bitter Grounds: Roots of Revolt in El Salvador.* 2nd ed. Toronto: Between The Lines, 1985.

Nyong'o, Peter Anyang', ed. *Popular Struggles for Democracy in Africa.* London: Zed Books, 1987.

Perlman, Janice E. *The Myth of Marginality: Urban Poverty and Politics in Rio de Janeiro.* Berkeley: University of California Press, 1976.

Petras, James. *Latin America: Bankers, Generals, and the Struggle for Social Justice.* Totawa, N.J.: Rowman and Littlefield, 1986.

Pirages, Dennis C. and Sylvester, Christine, eds. *Transformations in the Global Political Economy.* London: Macmillan, 1990.

Raghavan, Chakravarti. *GATT: The Uruguay Round and a New Global Economy: A Third World Perspective.* London: Zed Books, 1990.

Randall, Margaret. *Sandino's Daughters: Testimonies of Nicaraguan Women in Struggle.* Vancouver: New Star Books, 1981.

Redclift, Michael. *Development and the Environmental Crisis: Red or Green Alternatives?* London: Methuen, 1984.

Redclift, Michael. *Sustainable Development: Exploring the Contradictions.* London: Methuen, 1987.

Richardson, Boyce. *Time to Change: Canada's Place in a World in Crisis.* Toronto: Summerhill Press, 1990.

Rigby, Peter. *Persistent Pastoralists: Nomadic Societies in Transition.* London: Zed Books, 1985.

Riuchwarger, Gary. *People in Power: Forging a Grassroots Democracy in Nicaragua.* S. Hadley, Mass.: Bergin and Garvey, 1987.

Roddick, Jackie. *The Dance of the Millions: Latin America and the Debt Crisis.* London: Latin America Bureau, 1988.

Rodney, Walter. *How Europe Underdeveloped Africa.* London: Bogle-L'Ouverture Publications and Dar es Salaam: Tanzania Publishing House, 1972.

Rodriques, Mario Menendez, ed. *Voices from El Salvador.* San Francisco: Solidarity Publications, 1983.

Rogers, Barbara. *The Domestication of Women: Discrimination in Developing Societies.* London: Routledge Chapman and Hall, 1988.

Saul, John S. *Socialist Ideology and the Struggle for Southern Africa.* Trenton, N.J.: Africa World Press, 1989.

Sen, Gita, and Grown, Caren. *Development, Crises and Alternative Visions: Third World Women's Perspectives.* New York: Monthly Review Press, 1987.

Shiva, Vandana. *Staying Alive: Women, Ecology and Development.* London: Zed Books, 1988.

Shiva, Vandana. *The Violence of the Green Revolution: Ecological Degradation and Political Conflict.* London: Zed Books, 1990.

Sivard, Ruth Leger. *World Military and Social Expenditures 1989.* Washington: World Priorities, 1989.

Slater, David. *Territory and State Power in Latin America: The Peruvian Case.* New York: St. Martin's Press, 1989.

The South Commission. *The Challenge to the South.* New York: Oxford University Press, 1990.

Stubbs, Jean. *Cuba: The Test of Time.* London: Latin America Bureau, 1989.

Szentes, Tamás. *The Transformation of the World Economy: New Directions and New Interests*. London: Zed Books, 1988.

Tanzer, Michael. *The Race for Resources: Continuing Struggles over Minerals and Fuels*. New York: Monthly Review Press, 1980.

Thomas, Clive Y. *The Poor and the Powerless: Economic Policy and Change in the Caribbean*. New York: Monthly Review Press, 1988.

Thompson, Marilyn. *Women of El Salvador: The Price of Freedom*. London: Zed Books, 1986.

Toye, John. *Dilemmas of Development: Reflections on the Counter-Revolution in Development Theory and Policy*. Oxford: Blackwell, 1987.

Trainer, F.E. *Abandon Affluence!* London: Zed Books, 1985.

Truong, Thanh-Dam. *Sex, Money and Morality: Prostitution and Tourism in Southeast Asia*. London: Zed Books, 1990.

UNICEF. *The State of the World's Children 1990*. Oxford: Oxford University Press, 1990.

United Nations. *Global Outlook 2000*. New York: UN Publications, 1990.

United Nations. *Multinational Corporations in World Development*. New York: UN Department of Economic and Social Affairs, 1987.

United Nations. *The World Economic Survey*. New York: UN Publications, 1990.

United Nations Economic Commission for Africa. *African Alternative Framework to Structural Adjustment Programmes for Socio-Economic Recovery and Transformation*. New York: UN Publications, 1989.

Verhelst, Thierry. *No Life Without Roots: Culture and Development*. London: Zed Books, 1990.

Vilas, Carlos M. *The Sandinista Revolution: National Liberation and Social Transformation in Central America*. New York: Monthly Review Press, 1986.

Villamil, J., ed. *Transnational Capitalism and National Development: New Perspectives on Dependence*. Hassocks, Sussex: Harvester, 1979.

Wallerstein, Immanuel. *Historical Capitalism*. London: Verso, 1984.

Wallerstein, Immanuel. *The Modern World System*. New York: Academic Press, 1989.

Warnock, John W. *The Politics of Hunger: The Global Food System*. Toronto and New York: Methuen, 1987.

Warren, Bill. *Imperialism: Pioneer of Capitalism*. London: Verso, 1980.

Weir, David. *The Bhopal Syndrome: Pesticides, Environment and Health*. San Francisco: Sierra Club Books, 1987.

Welsh, Brian W.W. and Butorin, Pavel, eds. *Dictionary of Development: Third World Economy, Environment, Society*. New York: Garland Publishing, 1990.

Whitaker, Cathy Seitz, ed. *Alternative Publications: A Guide to Directories, Indexes, Bibliographies and Other Sources*. Jefferson, N.C.: McFarland & Co., 1990.

Williams, Raymond. *Keywords: A Vocabulary of Culture and Society.* Revised and
Expanded. London: Fontana Paperbacks, 1983.

Winn, Peter. *Weavers of Revolution: The Yarur Workers and Chile's Road to
Socialism.* Oxford: Oxford University Press, 1986.

Winson, Anthony. *Coffee and Democracy in Modern Costa Rica.* Toronto: Between
The Lines, 1989.

World Commission on Environment and Development. *Our Common Future.*
Oxford: Oxford University Press, 1987.

Worsley, Peter. *The Three Worlds: Culture and World Development.* Chicago:
University of Chicago Press, 1984.

Yoffe, D.B. *Power and Protectionism: Strategies of the Newly Industrialized
Countries.* New York: Columbia University Press, 1983.

Zwerling, Philip, and Martin, Connie, eds. *Nicaragua: A New Kind of
Revolution.* Westport, Conn.: Lawrence Hill, 1985.

3. SELECTED PERIODICALS

Canadian Journal of Development Studies (Ottawa)
CEPAL Review (Santiago, Chile)
Development and Change (The Hague)
Development Dialogue (Uppsala)
Development Policy Review (London)
Economic and Political Weekly (India)
Economic Development and Cultural Change
GATT-Fly Reports (Toronto)
IDS Bulletin (Sussex, U.K.)
Journal of Developing Areas (Illinois)
Journal of Development Studies (London)
Labour, Capital and Society (Montreal)
Latin American Monitor (London)
Latin America Research Review
LAWG Letter (Toronto)
Manushi (India)
Monthly Review (New York)
NACLA Report on the Americas (New York)
MERIP Reports (on the Middle East) (New York)
The New Internationalist (Oxford, U.K., and Toronto)
Ploughshares Monitor (Waterloo, Ont.)
Race and Class (London)
Review of African Political Economy (Sheffield, U.K.)
South (London)

Southern Africa Reports (Toronto)
Studies in Comparative International Development (New Brunswick)
Third World Quarterly (London)
Third World Review (London)
Women In Action (ISIS, Rome)
World Development Report (Oxford, U.K.)

Contributors

Anton L. Allahar is in the Department of Sociology at the University of Western Ontario, where he specializes in the economics and political sociology of Latin America and the Caribbean. He is the author of *Sociology and the Periphery: Theories and Issues* and, more recently, *Class, Politics and Sugar in Colonial Cuba*. He is currently working on a study of Marxism and Caribbean society.

Pam Colorado teaches in the Faculty of Social Welfare, University of Calgary. For the preparation of this chapter she acknowledges her teachers – Xilonem, Mazatl, S. Kounosu, Findhorn Foundation, Willis Harmon, David Peat, Amethyst First Rider – and the sites – Rock Cairns at Forres, Petroglyphs on Prince of Wales Island, Teotihuacan, Bighorn Medicine Wheel, TLOLOC – "And to trees whose body went into these pages, fire, air, a cut into paper, minerals into ink."

The Ecumenical Coalition for Economic Justice (formerly GATT-Fly) is a project of Canadian churches mandated to do research, education, and action in solidarity with peoples' organizations both in Canada and globally.

Esther Epp-Tiessen is administrative co-ordinator for Olive Branch (Mennonite) Church in Waterloo, Ontario. From 1982 to 1986 she and her husband served as country representatives for the Mennonite Central Committee program in the Philippines. The chapter in this book has its origins in a paper she wrote while working as a researcher with Project Ploughshares in 1986-87.

Charles Lane is a British development worker who first went to Tanzania as a volunteer (VSO) agricultural extension worker in 1975. His field research for a D.Phil. at the Institute of Development Studies, University of Sussex, was spent with the Barabaig pastoralists in Tanzania. He now works as a consultant with the International Institute for Environment and Development (IIED) in London, England.

Brian K. Murphy works at INTER PARES, a non-governmental development agency in Ottawa, where he focuses on issues related to Central America and anti-poverty work in Canada. He has written widely for Canadian periodicals and has co-authored a series of booklets on environment and development issues, published by Fitzhenry and Whiteside.

Eleanor O'Donnell is author of (as Eleanor MacLean) *Between The Lines: How to Detect Bias and Propaganda in the News and Everyday Life* and *Leading the Way: An Unauthorized Guide to the Sobey Empire*. Both books, and many subsequent lectures and workshops, grew out of her work with Oxfam-Canada and other international solidarity groups, and her work as an educator, journalist, and active member of her own community. She is now working and studying in Vancouver.

Betty Plewes has worked with CUSO for ten years and now holds the position of manager of program operations. From 1986 to 1988 she was the chair of the Board of Partnership Africa Canada, a coalition of about 80 Canadian agencies working in development co-operation in Africa. During a leave of absence in 1988 she travelled to a number of African and Asian countries, looking at how government and non-governmental agencies incorporate gender issues into their work.

Rieky Stuart works at the Coady International Institute, a training centre for development workers located at St. Francis Xavier University in Antigonish, Nova Scotia. She teaches gender relations and organizational development and has worked in this field with Canadian non-governmental organizations for over 20 years.

Jamie Swift is a freelance writer living in Kingston, Ontario. He is the author of several books, including *The Big Nickel: Inco at Home and Abroad, Cut and Run: The Assault on Canada's Forests, Getting Started on Social Analysis in Canada* (co-authored with Michael Czerny, S.J.), and *Odd Man Out: The Life and Times of Eric Kierans*.

Richard Swift is a Toronto-based researcher and writer who has worked with the Development Education Centre, Toronto, has served on the board of Oxfam-Canada, and is now the Canadian co-editor of *The New Internationalist* magazine.

Brian Tomlinson worked during the 1980s with CUSO in Ottawa as Co-ordinator of its Latin America Program. From 1974 to 1980 he worked with Oxfam-Canada as a policy analyst, focusing on current development issues and advocacy programs. He is the author of the chapter "Reaching An Impasse: The North-South Debate" in *Ties That Bind: Canada and the Third World.*

Henry Veltmeyer is co-ordinator of the International Development Studies program and professor of sociology at Saint Mary's University, Halifax. He is the author of *Canadian Class Structure, Canadian Corporate Power,* and *Rethinking Development: Perspectives from the Caribbean and Atlantic Canada.*

Index

Mauritania, 218
McClelland, David, 307
McDougall, Barbara, 22
McNamara, Robert, 16, 25, 109
McPhail, Margaret, 110-111
Megarry, Roy A., 286
Mendes, Chico, 63, 235
Mennonite Central Committee, 202
Mexico,
    agriculture and environment in, 219-220
    and Brady Plan, 96-97
    and debt crisis, 16, 46, 90-91
    move to free trade with U.S., 68
Michael Mascall and Associates, 150-151
Mies, Maria, 111, 115
Militarization, 17
    alternative approaches, 261
    Canada's role in, 257-260
    economic motives for, 253-254
    effects of in Third World, 242
    as factor in debt crisis, 46
    of governments, 242
    and health care, 241
    and human rights, 256-257
    of Latin American societies, 35
    link to environment, 219
    links to underdevelopment, 242-243,
        254-256, 257
    rationales for, 252-254
    and Third World armed forces, 66
    see also: Arms production; Arms trade; Arms
        transfer; Military bases; Military exports;
        Military spending; Military training;
        Third World military spending
Military bases in Third World, 246
Military exports, 247-248, 250, 251, 253-254
Military spending, 241-242
    see also: Third World military spending
Military training, 245-246
Millikan, Max, 304, 305
Mobutu Sese Seko, 88
Modernization theory, 307-308
Moffitt, Michael, 81
Mohammed, Mahathir, 214
Montes, Manuel, 95
Montezuma, 272
Morgan, Edmund S., 313
Morgan Guaranty Trust, 46, 90
Moser, Caroline, 115
Movement for an Independent and Nuclear-
    Free Pacific, 236
Mulholland, William, 86
Mulroney, Brian,
    role at Commonwealth Conference (1989),
        296

speech on Central America, 299-300
Muntemba, Shimwaayi, 95
Musumali, Cosmas, 14-15

National Agriculture and Food Corporation
    (NAFCO) of Tanzania, 134, 135
    sets up Tanzania-Canada Wheat Program, 136
    attempts to outmanoeuvre the Barabaig, 149
    see also: Tanzania-Canada Wheat Program
National Council for Peoples' Development,
    183
National Federation of Sugarworkers (NFSW),
    182-183
Native people, 21, 141
    and environment, 267-268
    policy of pacifism, 273-274
    and science, 270-273
Naylor, Tom, 98
Nepal, 220
New International Economic Order (NIEO),
    and women, 109
Newly Industrialized Countries (NICs), 37
    industrial production of, 38
Newman, Peter, 289
Nicaragua,
    election (1990), 281
    women's movement, 123
Niosi, Jorge, 310, 312
Nixon, Richard,
    abandons gold standard, 85
Non-Governmental Organizations (NGOs), 21
    as charities, 164
    child and family sponsorship, 175
    and churches, 171
    and CIDA, 181-182
    and commitment, 193-195
    critiques of, 176-179
    development assistance programs, 174, 175
    development education work, 176
    and El Salvador, 185-186, 199-200
    and Ethiopian crisis, 201
    and Guatemala, 161, 162, 185-186, 201-202
    history of in Canada, 169-172, 179-184
    impact of programs, 188-191
    and limits of pluralism, 196-198
    and local church-based organizations,
        186-187
    material assistance, 175
    and network of community centres, 171
    origin of term, 163
    as part of Canadian society, 163-165, 166
    placement of personnel overseas, 174,
        175-176
    and Philippines, 183, 200-201

Walker, Martin, 218
Warioba, Joseph, 149
Weapons transfers: see Arms transfers
Weir, David, 222
White, H.D., 82
Williams, Raymond, 9-10, 29
Wolpin, Miles, 245
Women, 21, 64, 107-128
  affirmation of feminism, 122
  in Canadian NGOs, 124-126
  declining position of internationally, 107-108
  divisions in international movement, 114
  and a Gender and Development Approach, 126-128
  and military bases in Third World, 256
  organizing in the Third World, 111-112, 123
  reproductive and productive labour, 110
  role of women's movement, 110-111
  and World Bank programs, 119
Women in Development (WID), 21, 108-109, 113
  and CIDA action plan, 116
  as critiqued by feminists, 118-122, 128
  and development strategies, 116-117
  and growth in "experts,", 117-118
  historical roots, 109
  introduction of gender analysis, 117-118, 128
  shift in strategies, 115
  weaknesses in approach, 120-121
Wood, Bernard, 69

World Bank,
  approach to development financing, 29
  belief in economic growth, 33
  comments on structure of trade, 38
  and emphasis on private sector, 226
  and environmental concerns, 225-226
  founding of, 82
  impact of programs on women, 119
  and Narmada Dam project, 234
  as part of development strategy, 190
  shift in role, 94
  and structural adjustment, 97
  and Three Gorges Dam project, 230
World Commission on Environment and Development: see Brundtland Commission
World economy,
  Canada's role, 67
  declining position of U.S., 67
  internationalization of, 19-20
  recession of 1980s, 26
World Neighbors, 237

Young, Kate, 114

Zaire,
  corruption in, 88
  and debt crisis, 97
Zambia,
  and debt crisis, 95
  and foreign aid, 15
  impact of Persian Gulf War, 18
  and IMF austerity programs, 14-15

Printed in Canada